TRANSFORMERS WAR WITHIN

THE DARK AGES

TRANSFORMERS™
WAR WITHIN
THE DARK AGES

Written by
SIMON FURMAN

Art by
ANDREW WILDMAN

Inks by
ERIK SANDER

Colors by
ESPEN GRUNDETJERN
ALAN WANG

Additional Inks by
ROB ARMSTRONG

Letters by
BENJAMIN LEE

Additional Colors by
RAMIL SUNGA
ROB RUFFOLO

Design by
SHAUN LINSAO

President
Pat Lee

Vice President/Editor-in-Chief
Roger Lee

Director of New Business Development
Rich Young

Production Manager
Derek Choo-wing

Project Manager
Graham Cruz

Pre-Press/I.T.
Ted Pun

Post-Production Manager
Matt Moylan

Public Relations Manager
Candice Chan

TRANSFORMERS WAR WITHIN (Vol. 2), Trade Paperback, 2004. First Printing. Published by Dreamwave Productions, 11 Allstate Parkway, Suite 200, Markham, Ontario L3R 9T8, Canada.

TRANSFORMERS
WAR WITHIN
The Dark Ages

"What do you consider to be your favorite work in comics?"

A question often asked by fans at *Transformers* conventions. As they look expectantly at me wearing their assorted Autobot and Decepticon T-shirts I know that they want me to be on their side. To say that the best fun I ever had in the whole world ever ever ever was when I drew *Transformers* the first time round. Thing is it wasn't like that. Let me take you back...

1988 and I had finally become a freelance comic book artist. A childhood dream. I had been drawing comics from the age of seven when I had seen my first Marvel comic while on holiday. Here in England they were not that easy to come by in the late '60s and therefore became treasured items. "One day I am gonna draw these," was what went around in my head as a child. Twenty or so years later and I had done it. I was 'a comic book artist' and proud of it. One thing led to another and after drawing *Thundercats*, *Ghostbusters* and *Galaxy Rangers,* amongst others, I was asked by the then editor of the UK *Transformers* comic if I would like to draw some robots. "Yeah" was the reply, "Wot?" was the Woody Allen style subtitle that was silently going on in my head. I had no clue what *Transformers* were. So there we were. I was an official *Transformers* comic artist. I penciled my first job lovingly, with all the care and attention a fresh faced professional comic book artist could muster and sent in my pages. Next day. Phone call. It was the editor. "Hello Andrew. It's Simon". (Yes, that one). Onslaught ensued. He liked practically nothing about what I had done (or that's how it felt). After asking for a number of changes to the penciled artwork he said, "I guess we can rely on the inker (Stephen Baskerville) to save some of it". Roll on a couple of years and that editor had become the writer on the US *Transformers* comic. Geoff Senior was the artist and needed a break to work on the now legendary *Death's Head* Graphic Novel. I was given the opportunity of working on the US *Transformers* book and was asked to submit some penciled samples. Guess what? They rejected me, saying that I didn't make them look enough like robots. One issue later they gave me the book anyway. Maybe they just couldn't find anyone else. Reaction was good and (other than the legendary issue 75 by Geoff) I finished the run. That was it. That was my introduction to the world of American comics and I was up and running! Work on *G.I. Joe*, *X-Men*, *Spider-Man* and many others followed. Finally I could draw 'real' people rather than robots. Finally I was achieving what had I always wanted. I was drawing super heroes!

So. The question. They all look at me expectantly in their Autobot and Decepticon T-shirts. Imagery that is so, so familiar to me now. A world of robots that, back then, I knew nothing about and wanted only to move on from. An introduction to drawing American comics that served to simply act as a springboard onto greater things. What is the most fun I have had in comics? Hindsight is a great thing. That pedantic editor became one of the best writers I have had the privilege to work with and his comments served simply to improve my work. Those fans have unparalleled dedication. Those robots? Love 'em to bits and after all the work that I have done over the years it was the story of those robots that I was desperate to have the opportunity to contribute to again. Their world continues to expand and evolve and the story is never over. I didn't know it then but working on *Transformers* was the best fun I had in comics and I was lucky enough to have a second bite. Read on and enjoy.

Andrew Wildman
June 2004

Cybertron, long before the Transformers came to Earth... civil war rages across the planet, the inhabitants divided into two distinct factions, Autobots and Decepticons. But behind the overt show of force by the Decepticons lies the guile and strategy of Megatron, his long-term plan to reboot the long-defunct engines within Cybertron, and turn the planet into a star-going Warworld. When Autobot leader Sentinel Prime is killed, the Matrix - the sacred lifeforce of the Transformers - is passed to

Optimus Prime, who - believing Cybertron is not worth the cost in lives lost - promptly orders a planet-wide evacuation. His decision finds little favor with the Autobot forces, least of all with the volatile commander, Grimlock, who sees Prime's logic as weakness.

As he covets the Matrix for himself, Megatron acts to prevent the exodus. The power contained within the Matrix casing will, he believes, fire the vast planetary turbines. Prime is lured into subterranean Cybertron, whereupon surface Decepticon forces led by Shockwave attack Iacon, the Autobots' Capital city, cutting off any hope of aid or assistance for their leader. But the treachery of Megatron's first lieutenant, Starscream, result in both Prime and Megatron falling toward the planetary core, and to their apparent deaths.

They survive, and begin their conflict anew, in the course of which the Matrix casing is cracked, granting both an illuminating glimpse of the future. Determined now that the Decepticons must be stopped at all costs, Prime vows to kill Megatron. Meanwhile, Grimlock leads a rescue mission into the heart of Cybertron,

discovering the true scale of the threat they face. Starscream, having assumed command, is preparing to activate a Mechaforming Substructure under the surface of Cybertron, which will destroy Iacon and the Autobot command hub once and for all.

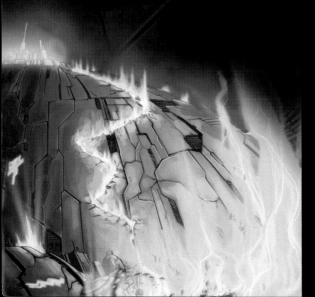

As Prime faces Megatron in final battle, Grimlock's forces attempt to stop Starscream, but - despite their efforts - he triggers the Mechaforming machinery. Above ground, chaos reigns in Iacon, and Shockwave is forced to retreat. Prime defeats Megatron, but leaves him alive, reining in the beast within. His subsequent reappearance turns the tide of the battle against Starscream, and the planetary turbines are destroyed. Iacon, though, is in ruins. Prime vows to fight on, to regroup under Iacon. Cybertron, he now knows, is too important to abandon, their destiny more far-reaching than he ever imagined. Megatron's memories of events within Cybertron are elusive, but he remains more committed than ever to spreading his evil far, far beyond Cybertron itself...

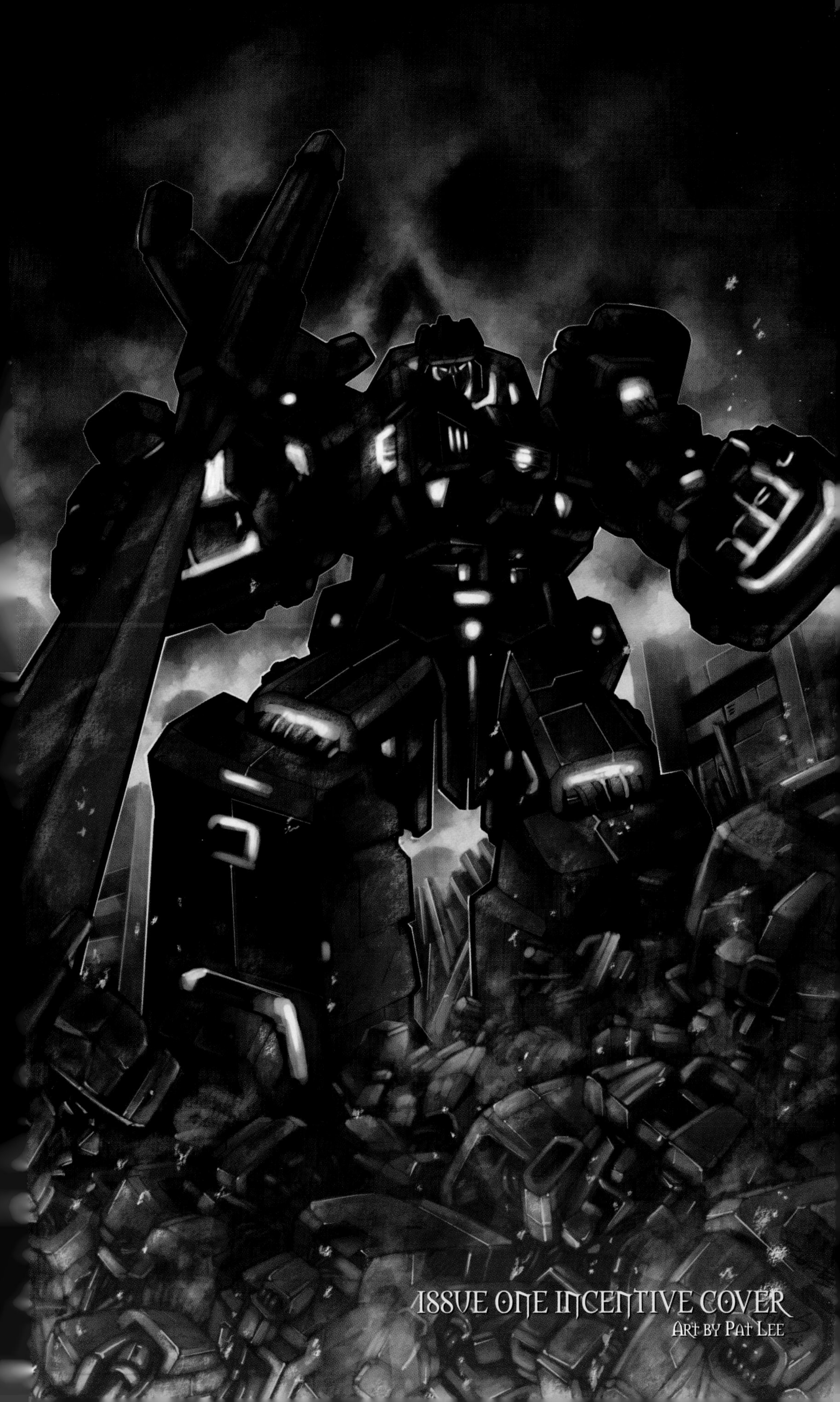

ISSUE ONE INCENTIVE COVER
Art by Pat Lee

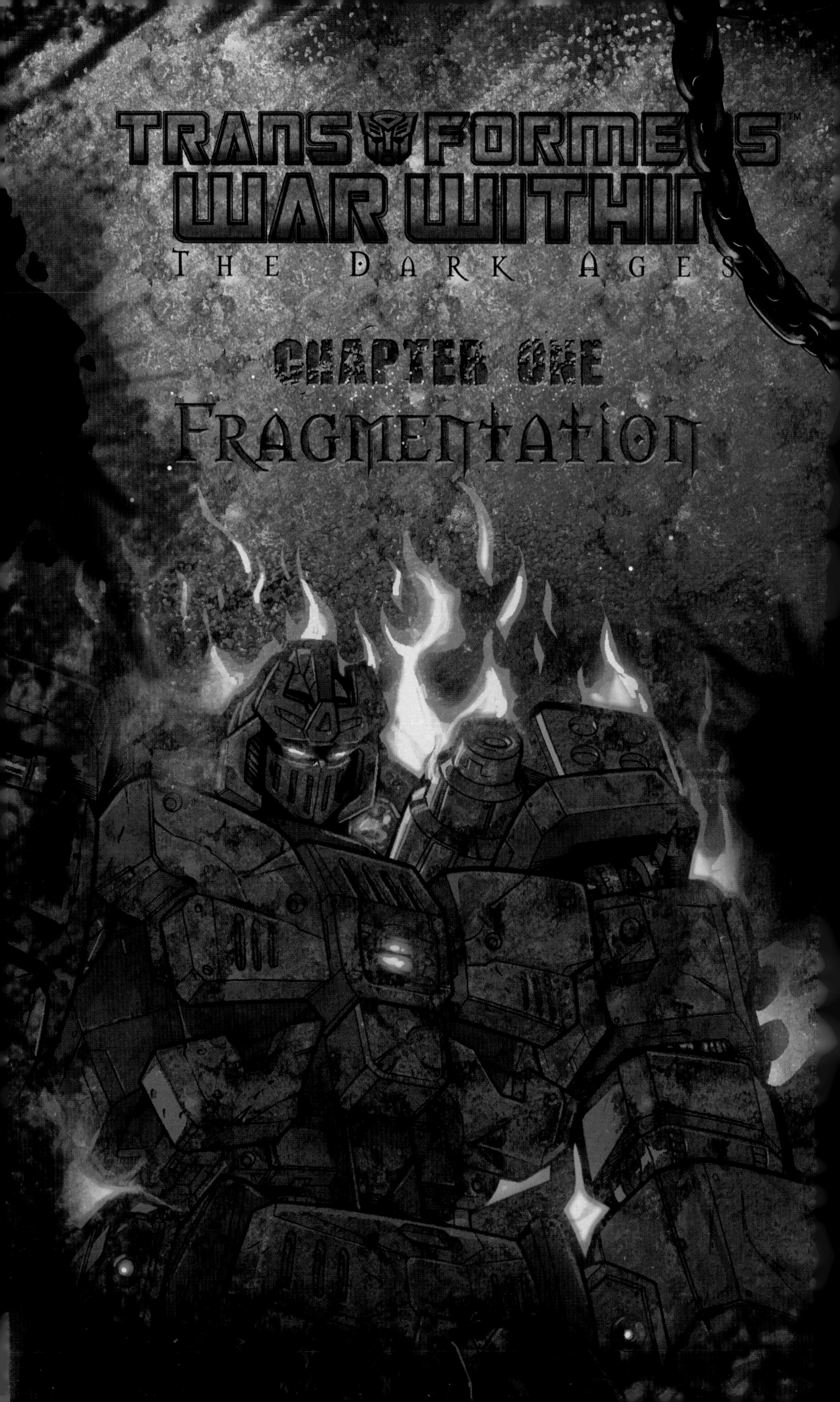
TRANSFORMERS™
WAR WITHIN
THE DARK AGES
CHAPTER ONE
FRAGMENTATION

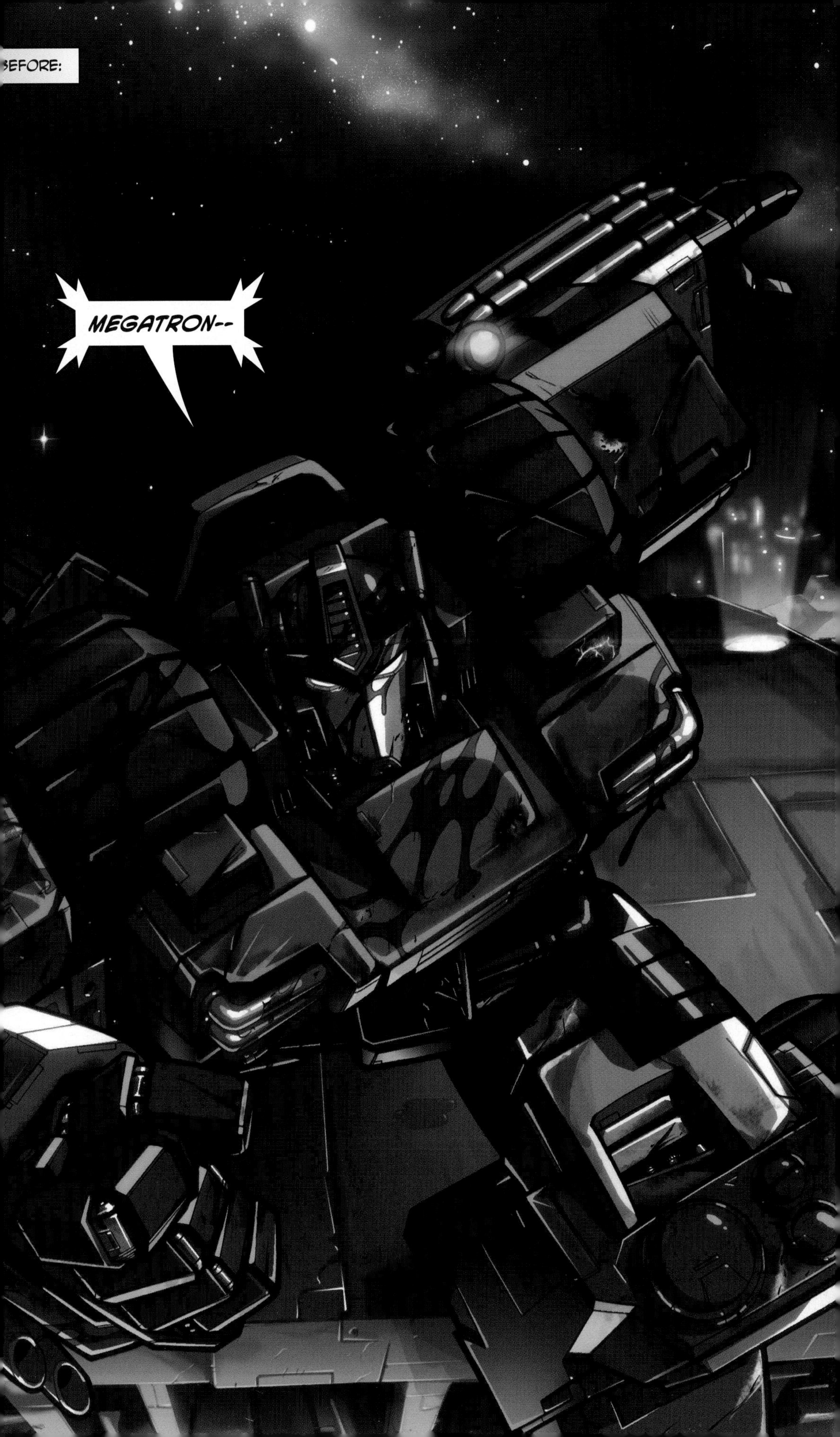

BEFORE:
MEGATRON--

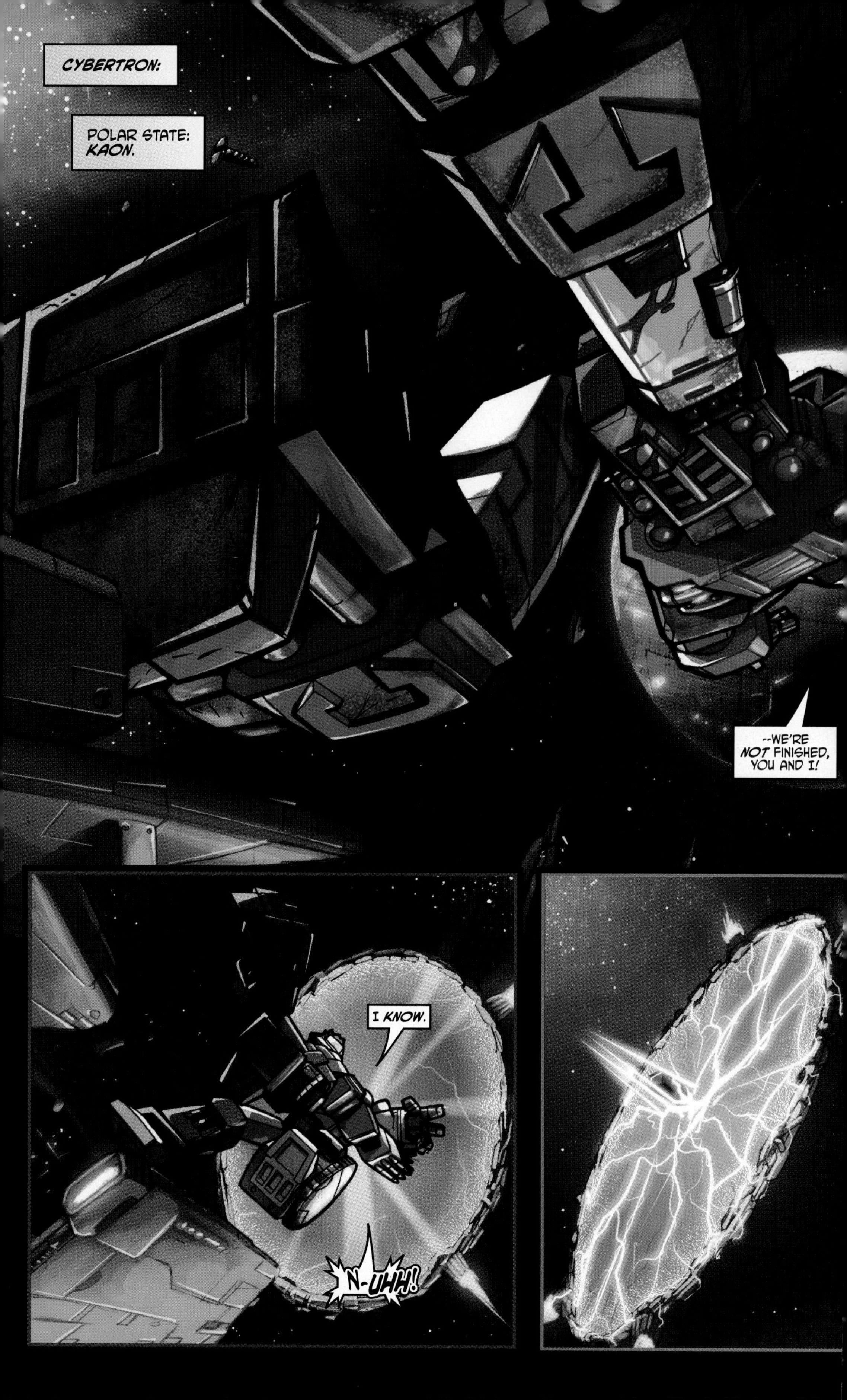
CYBERTRON:
POLAR STATE: KAON.
--WE'RE NOT FINISHED, YOU AND I!
I KNOW.
N-UHH!

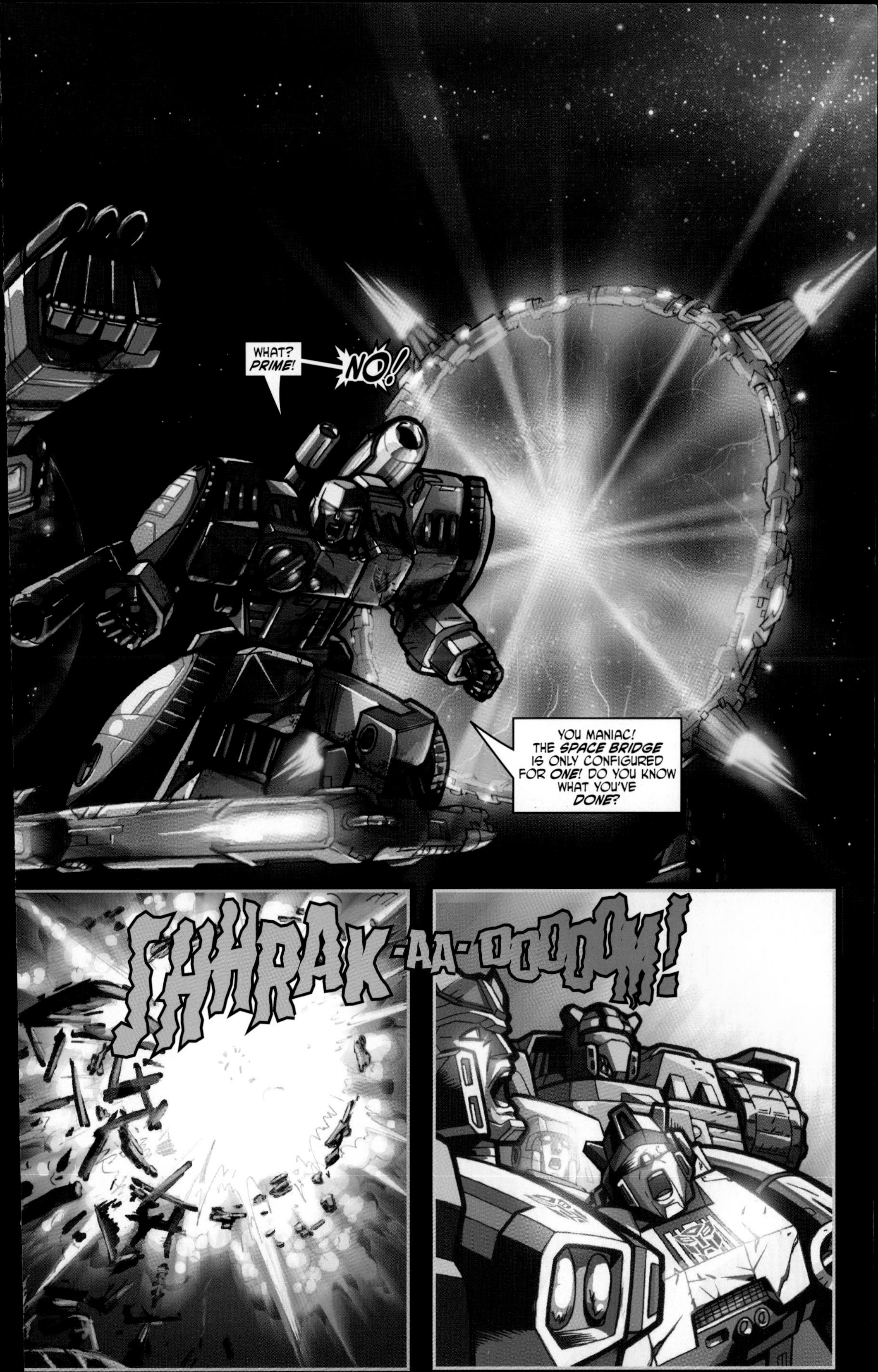
WHAT? PRIME!
NO!
YOU MANIAC! THE SPACE BRIDGE IS ONLY CONFIGURED FOR ONE! DO YOU KNOW WHAT YOU'VE DONE?
SHHRAK-AA-OOOOOM!

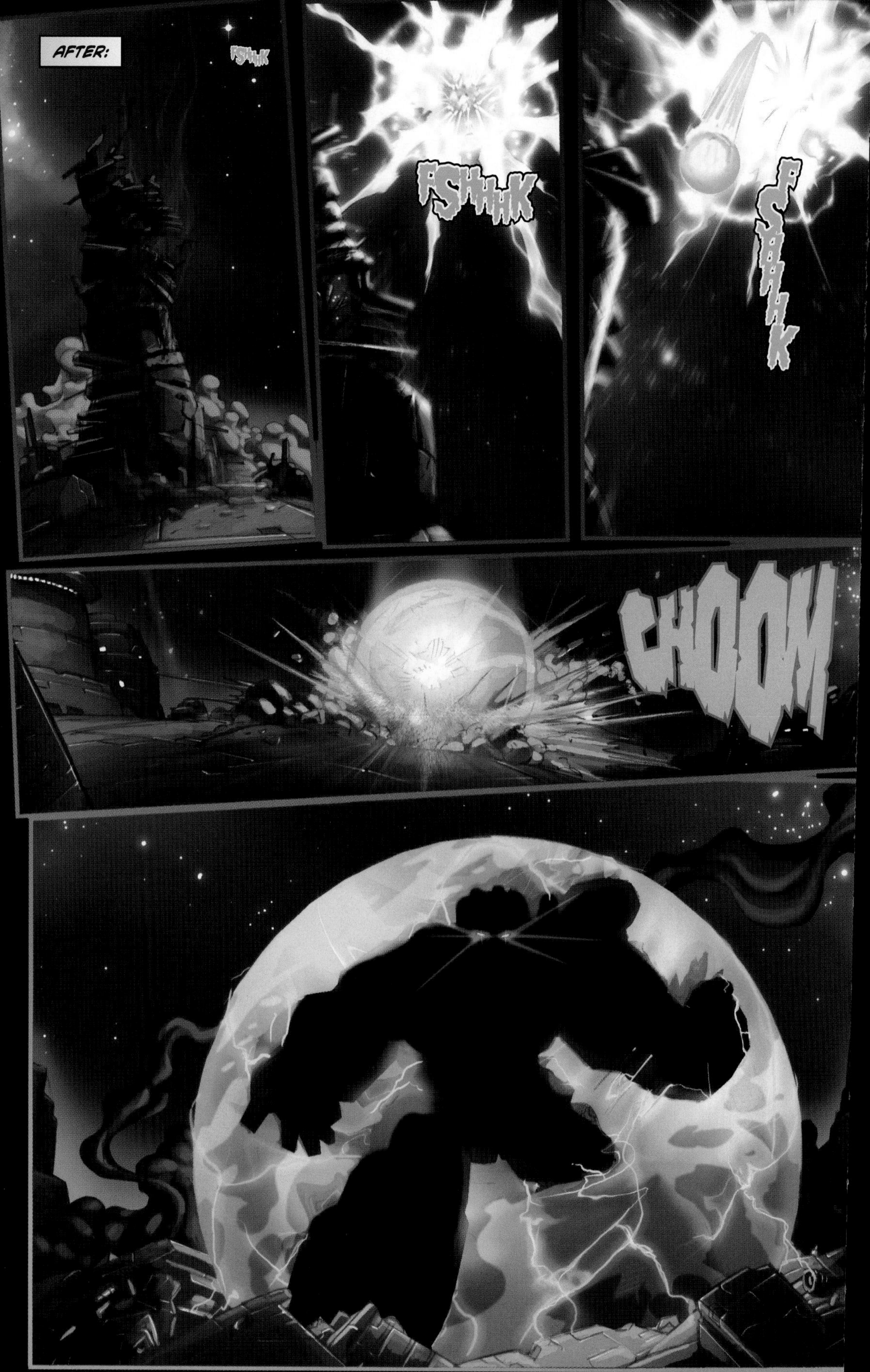

AFTER:
FSHHHK
FSHHHK
FSHHHK
CHOOM

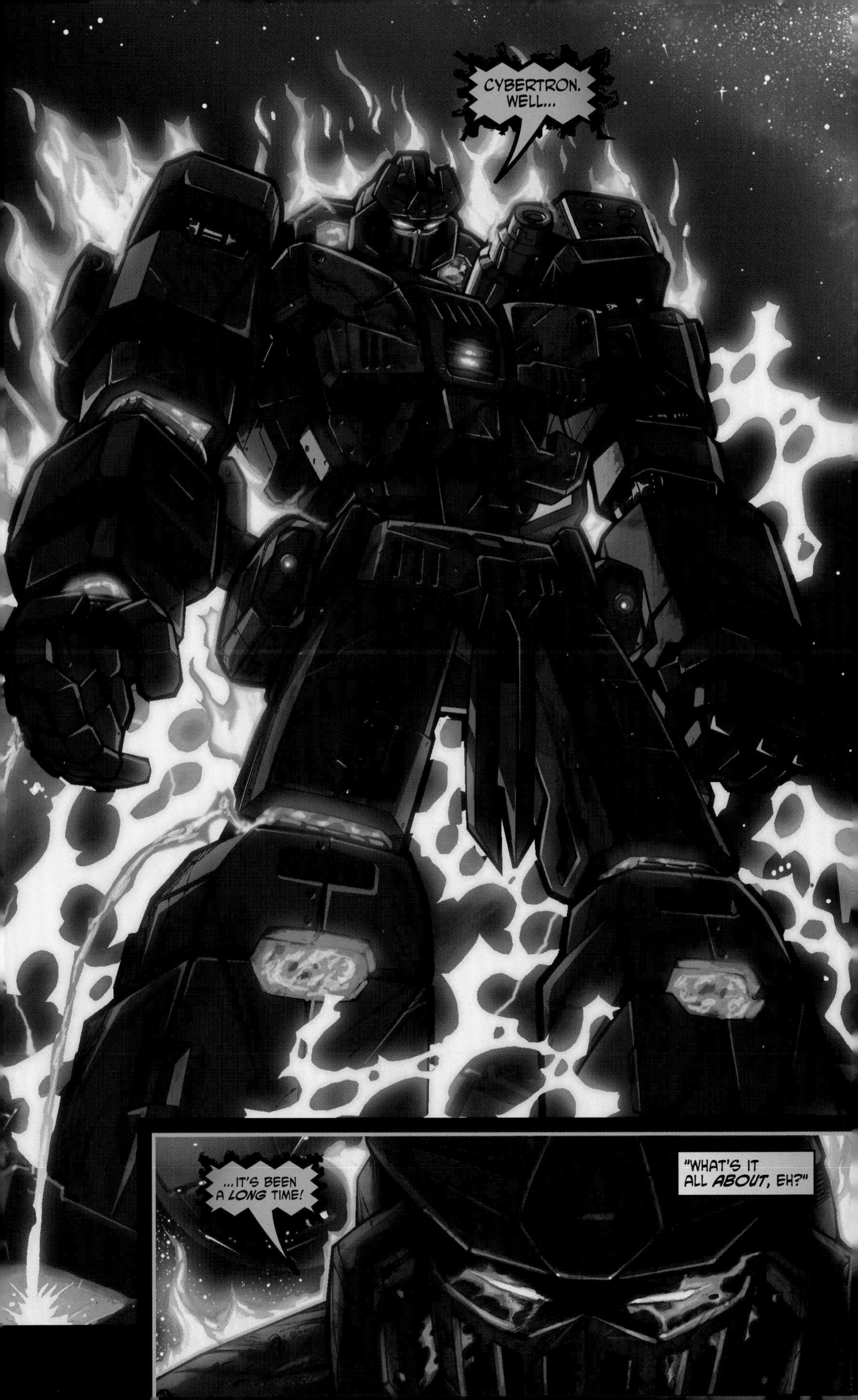
CYBERTRON. WELL...
...IT'S BEEN A *LONG* TIME!
"WHAT'S IT ALL *ABOUT*, EH?"

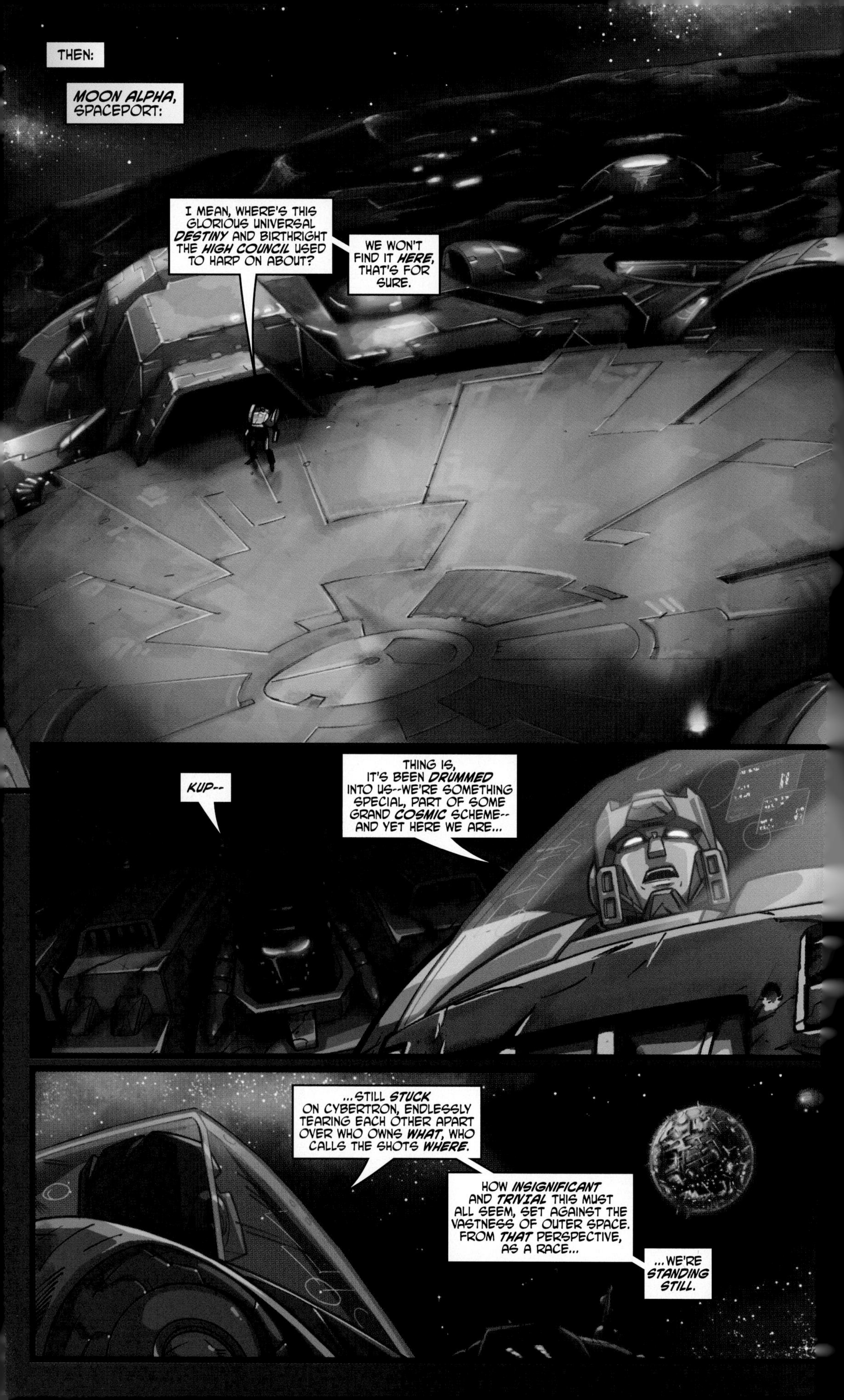
THEN:
MOON ALPHA, SPACEPORT:
I MEAN, WHERE'S THIS GLORIOUS UNIVERSAL DESTINY AND BIRTHRIGHT THE HIGH COUNCIL USED TO HARP ON ABOUT?
WE WON'T FIND IT HERE, THAT'S FOR SURE.
KUP--
THING IS, IT'S BEEN DRUMMED INTO US--WE'RE SOMETHING SPECIAL, PART OF SOME GRAND COSMIC SCHEME--AND YET HERE WE ARE...
...STILL STUCK ON CYBERTRON, ENDLESSLY TEARING EACH OTHER APART OVER WHO OWNS WHAT, WHO CALLS THE SHOTS WHERE.
HOW INSIGNIFICANT AND TRIVIAL THIS MUST ALL SEEM, SET AGAINST THE VASTNESS OF OUTER SPACE. FROM THAT PERSPECTIVE, AS A RACE...
...WE'RE STANDING STILL.

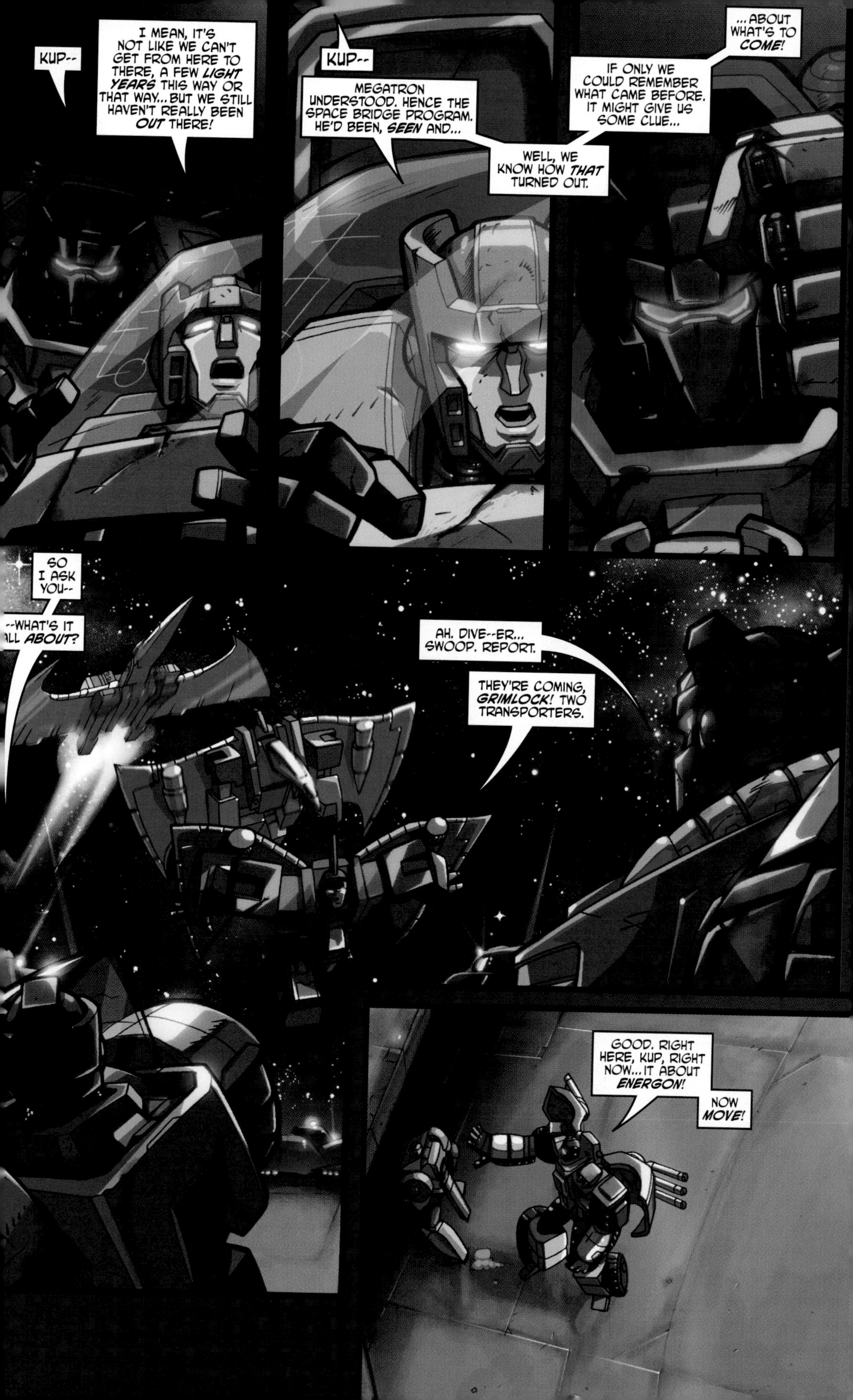
KUP--
I MEAN, IT'S NOT LIKE WE CAN'T GET FROM HERE TO THERE, A FEW *LIGHT YEARS* THIS WAY OR THAT WAY...BUT WE STILL HAVEN'T REALLY BEEN *OUT* THERE!
KUP--
MEGATRON UNDERSTOOD. HENCE THE SPACE BRIDGE PROGRAM. HE'D BEEN, *SEEN* AND...
WELL, WE KNOW HOW *THAT* TURNED OUT.
IF ONLY WE COULD REMEMBER WHAT CAME BEFORE. IT MIGHT GIVE US SOME CLUE...
...ABOUT WHAT'S TO *COME!*
SO I ASK YOU--
--WHAT'S IT ALL *ABOUT?*
AH. DIVE--ER... SWOOP. REPORT.
THEY'RE COMING, *GRIMLOCK!* TWO TRANSPORTERS.
GOOD. RIGHT HERE, KUP, RIGHT NOW...IT ABOUT *ENERGON!*
NOW *MOVE!*

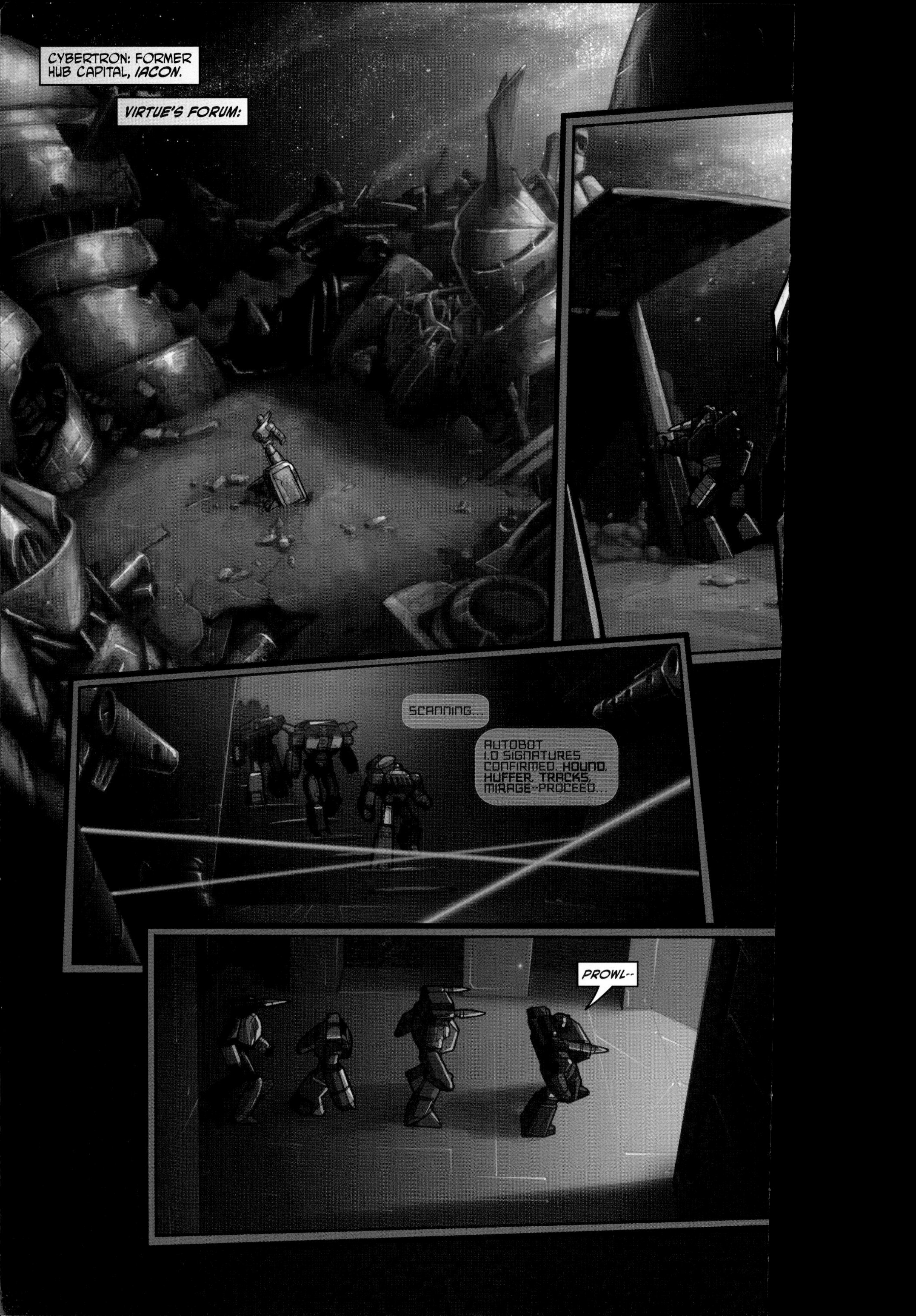
CYBERTRON: FORMER HUB CAPITAL, IACON.
VIRTUE'S FORUM:
SCANNING...
AUTOBOT I.D SIGNATURES CONFIRMED. HOUND, HUFFER, TRACKS, MIRAGE--PROCEED...
PROWL--

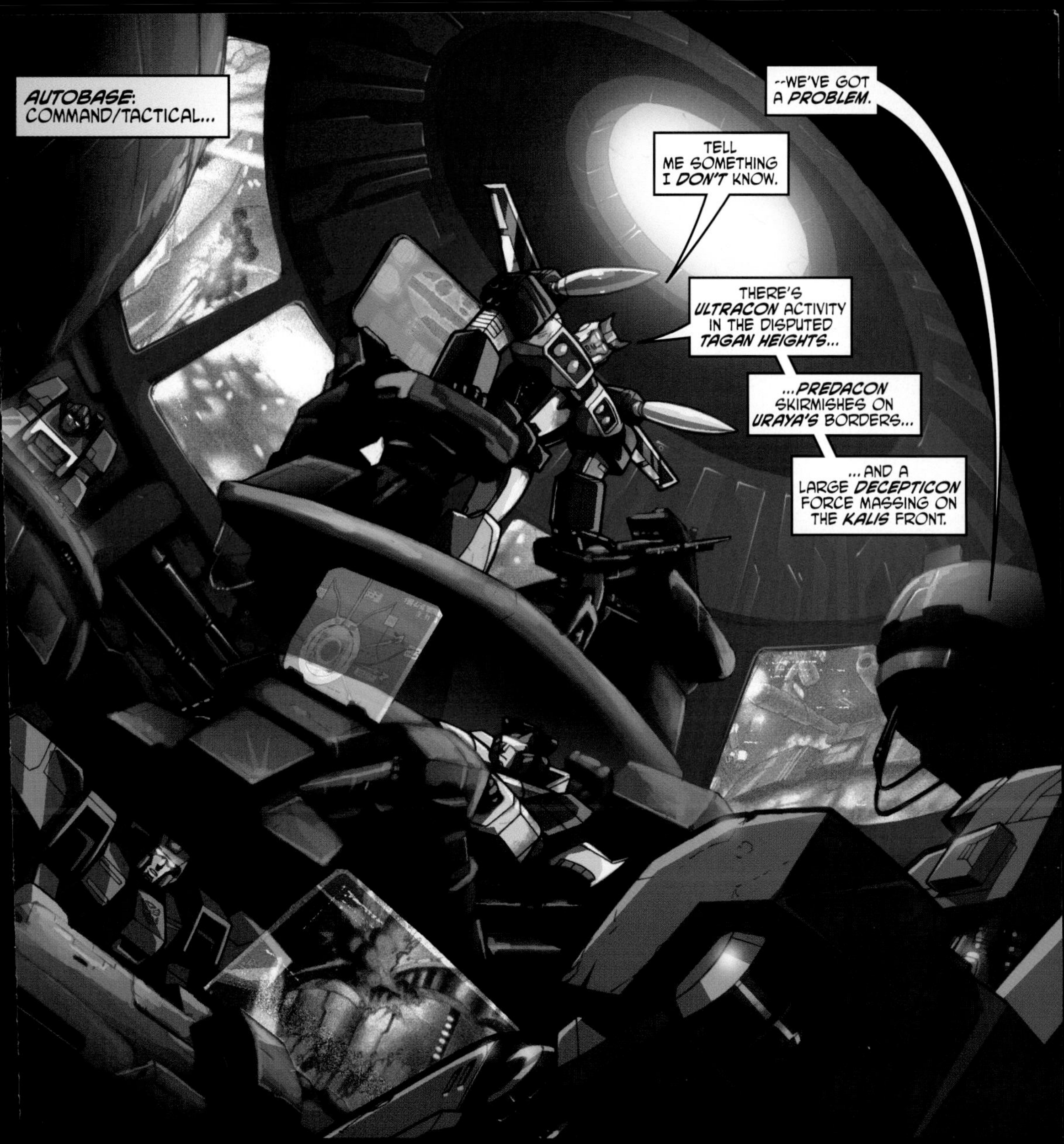
AUTOBASE: COMMAND/TACTICAL...
--WE'VE GOT A PROBLEM.
TELL ME SOMETHING I DON'T KNOW.
THERE'S ULTRACON ACTIVITY IN THE DISPUTED TAGAN HEIGHTS...
...PREDACON SKIRMISHES ON URAYA'S BORDERS...
...AND A LARGE DECEPTICON FORCE MASSING ON THE KALIS FRONT.

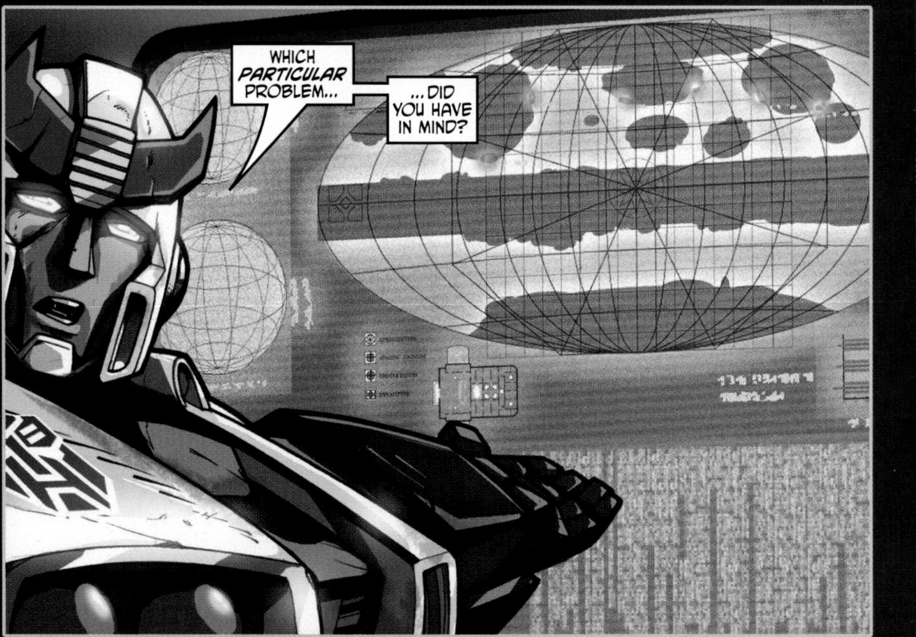
WHICH PARTICULAR PROBLEM...
...DID YOU HAVE IN MIND?

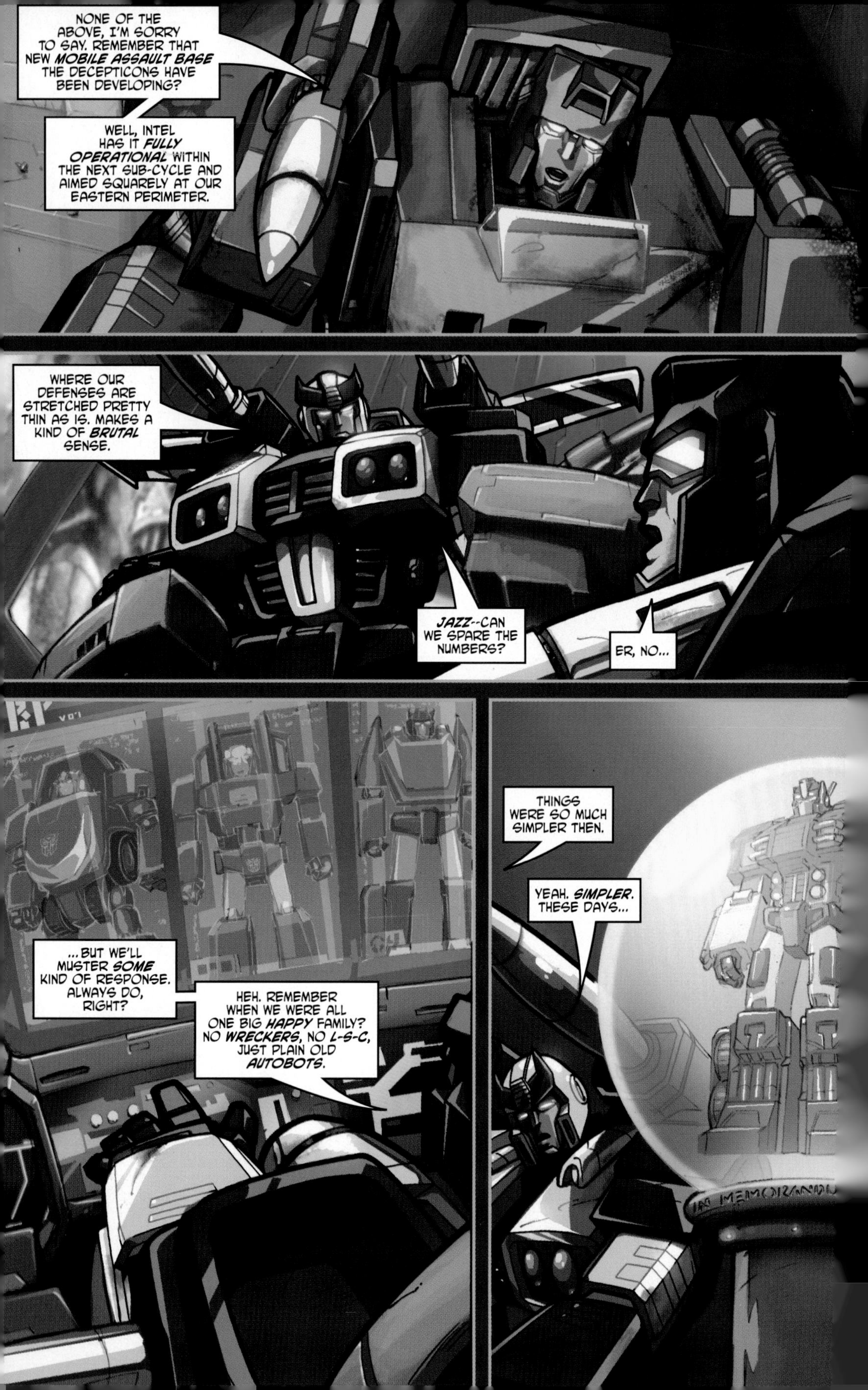
NONE OF THE ABOVE, I'M SORRY TO SAY. REMEMBER THAT NEW *MOBILE ASSAULT BASE* THE DECEPTICONS HAVE BEEN DEVELOPING?
WELL, INTEL HAS IT *FULLY OPERATIONAL* WITHIN THE NEXT SUB-CYCLE AND AIMED SQUARELY AT OUR EASTERN PERIMETER.
WHERE OUR DEFENSES ARE STRETCHED PRETTY THIN AS IS. MAKES A KIND OF *BRUTAL* SENSE.
JAZZ--CAN WE SPARE THE NUMBERS?
ER, NO...
...BUT WE'LL MUSTER *SOME* KIND OF RESPONSE. ALWAYS DO, RIGHT?
HEH. REMEMBER WHEN WE WERE ALL ONE BIG *HAPPY* FAMILY? NO *WRECKERS*, NO *L-S-C*, JUST PLAIN OLD *AUTOBOTS*.
THINGS WERE SO MUCH SIMPLER THEN.
YEAH. *SIMPLER*. THESE DAYS...

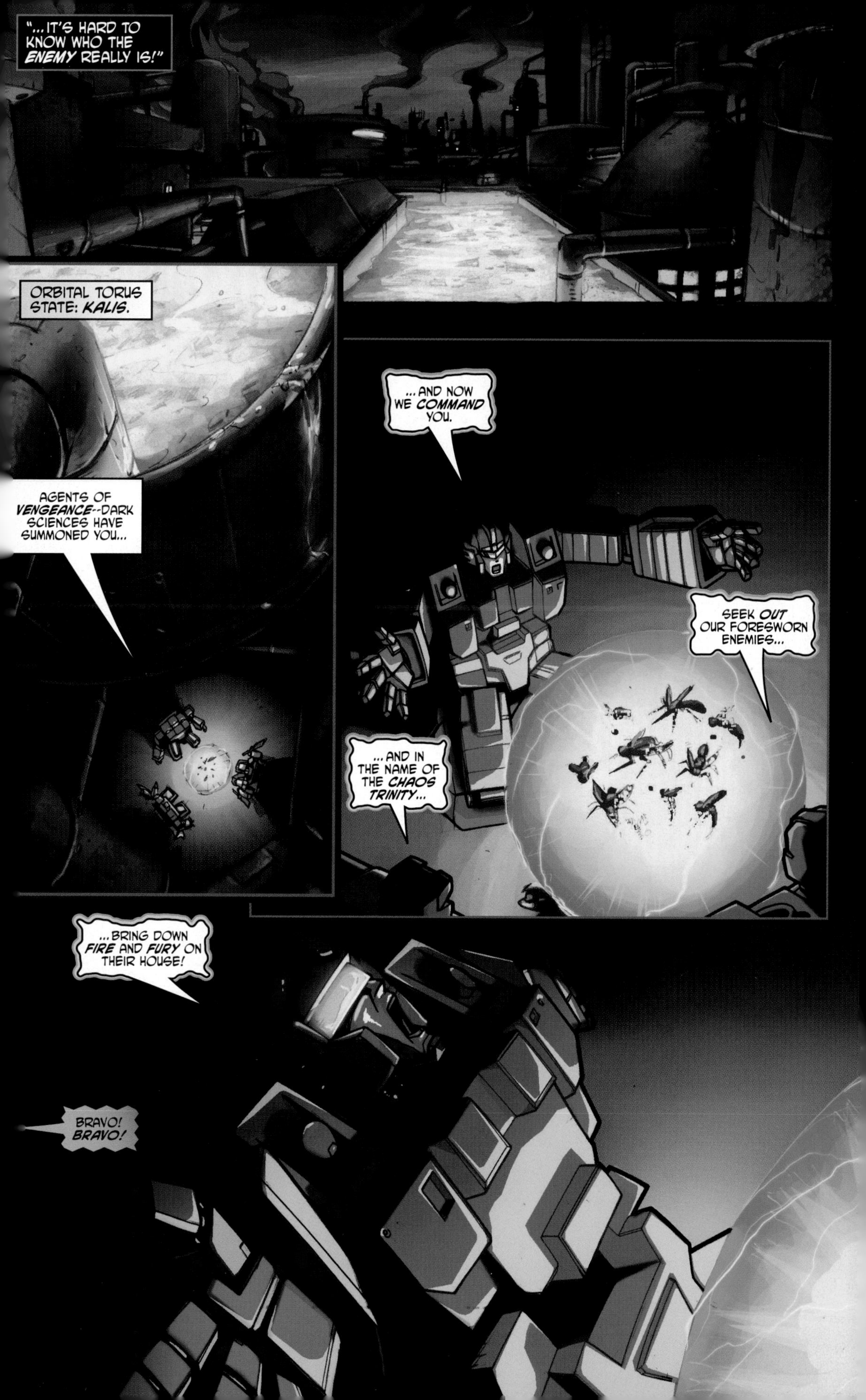
"...IT'S HARD TO KNOW WHO THE ENEMY REALLY IS!"
ORBITAL TORUS STATE: KALIS.
AGENTS OF VENGEANCE--DARK SCIENCES HAVE SUMMONED YOU...
...AND NOW WE COMMAND YOU.
SEEK OUT OUR FORESWORN ENEMIES...
...AND IN THE NAME OF THE CHAOS TRINITY...
...BRING DOWN FIRE AND FURY ON THEIR HOUSE!
BRAVO! BRAVO!

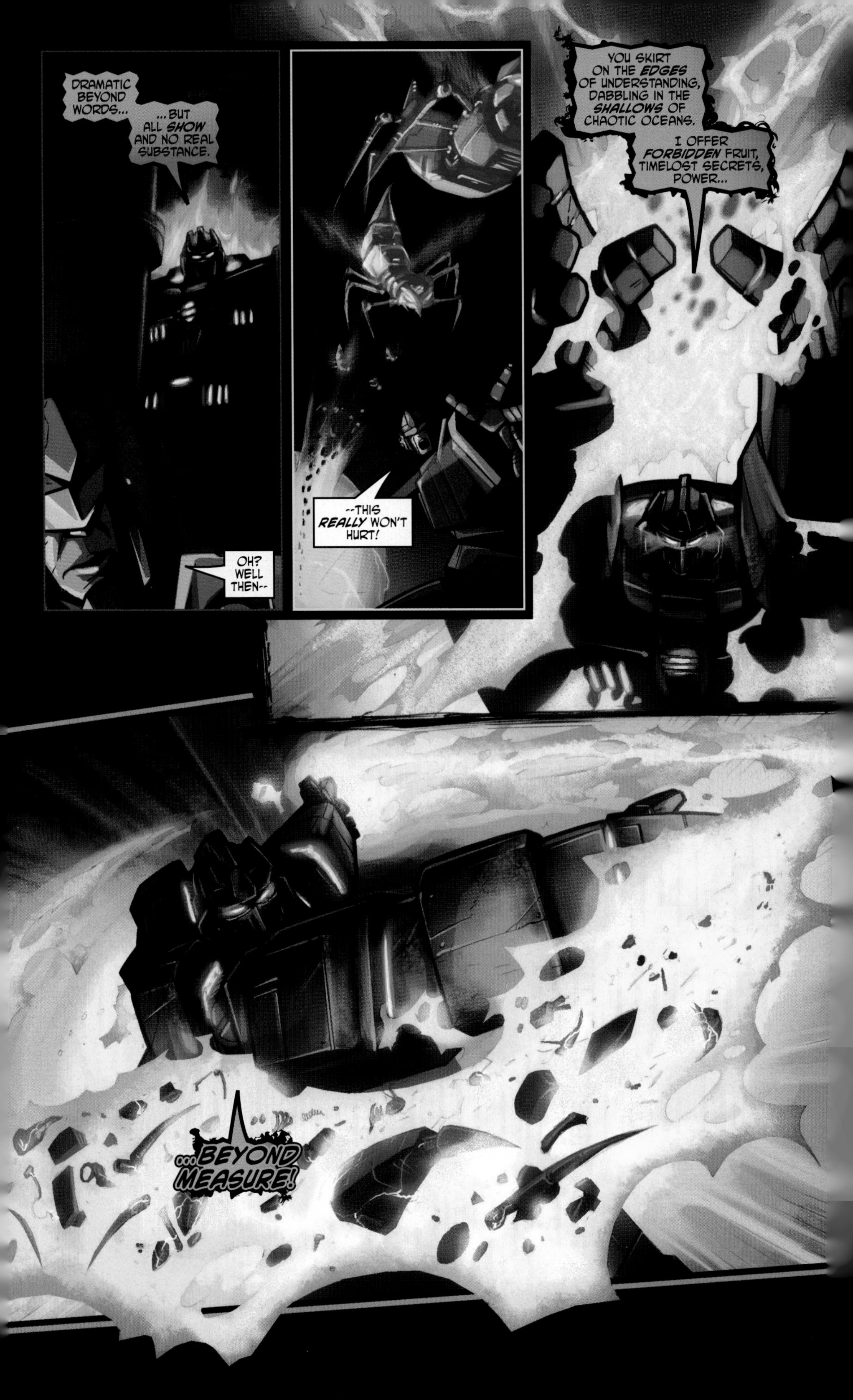
DRAMATIC BEYOND WORDS...
...BUT ALL SHOW AND NO REAL SUBSTANCE.
OH? WELL THEN--
--THIS REALLY WON'T HURT!
YOU SKIRT ON THE EDGES OF UNDERSTANDING, DABBLING IN THE SHALLOWS OF CHAOTIC OCEANS.
I OFFER FORBIDDEN FRUIT, TIMELOST SECRETS, POWER...
...BEYOND MEASURE!

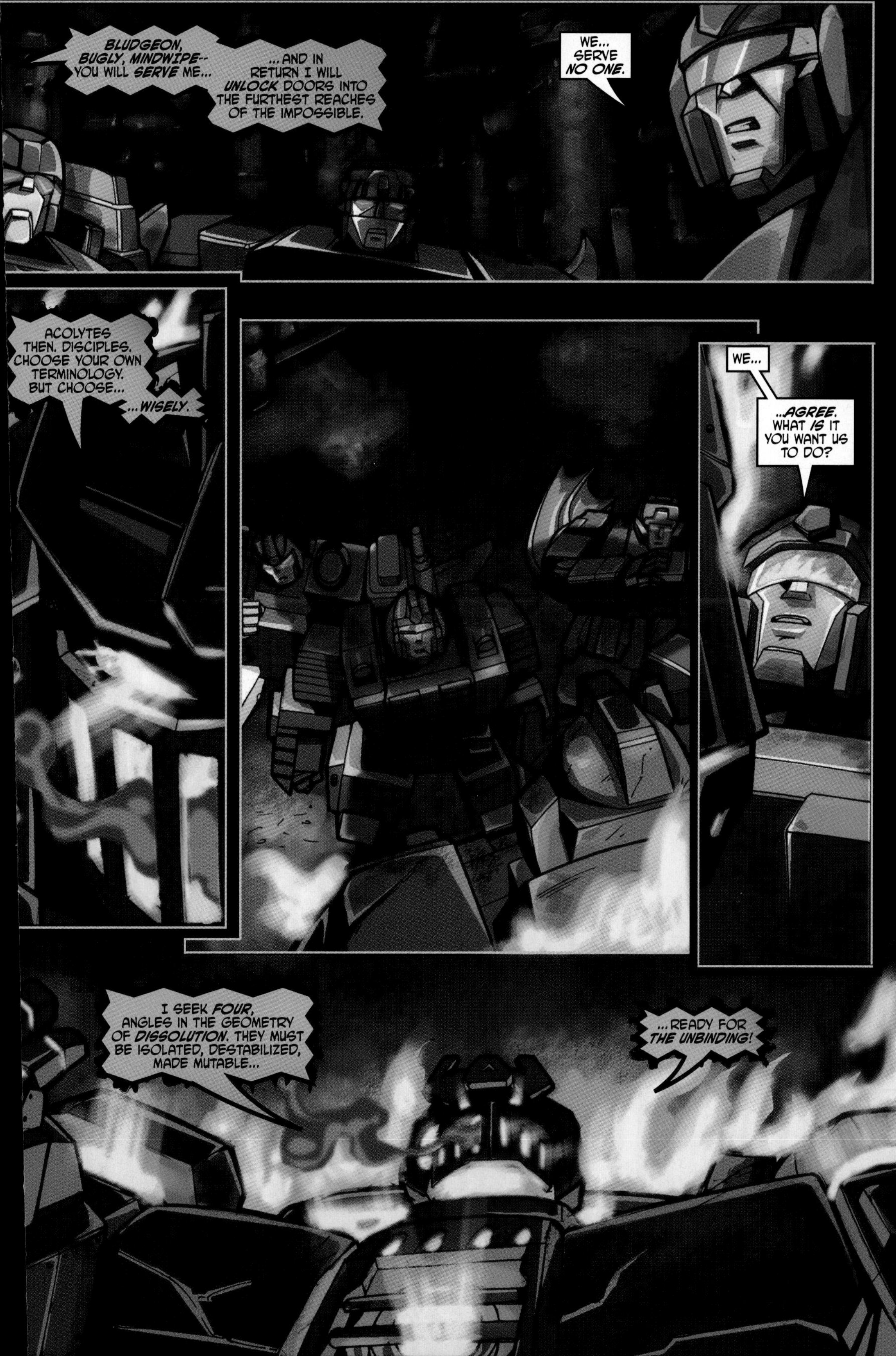
BLUDGEON, BUGLY, MINDWIPE-- YOU WILL SERVE ME...
...AND IN RETURN I WILL UNLOCK DOORS INTO THE FURTHEST REACHES OF THE IMPOSSIBLE.
WE... SERVE NO ONE.
ACOLYTES THEN. DISCIPLES. CHOOSE YOUR OWN TERMINOLOGY. BUT CHOOSE...
...WISELY.
WE...
...AGREE. WHAT IS IT YOU WANT US TO DO?
I SEEK FOUR, ANGLES IN THE GEOMETRY OF DISSOLUTION. THEY MUST BE ISOLATED, DESTABILIZED, MADE MUTABLE...
...READY FOR THE UNBINDING!

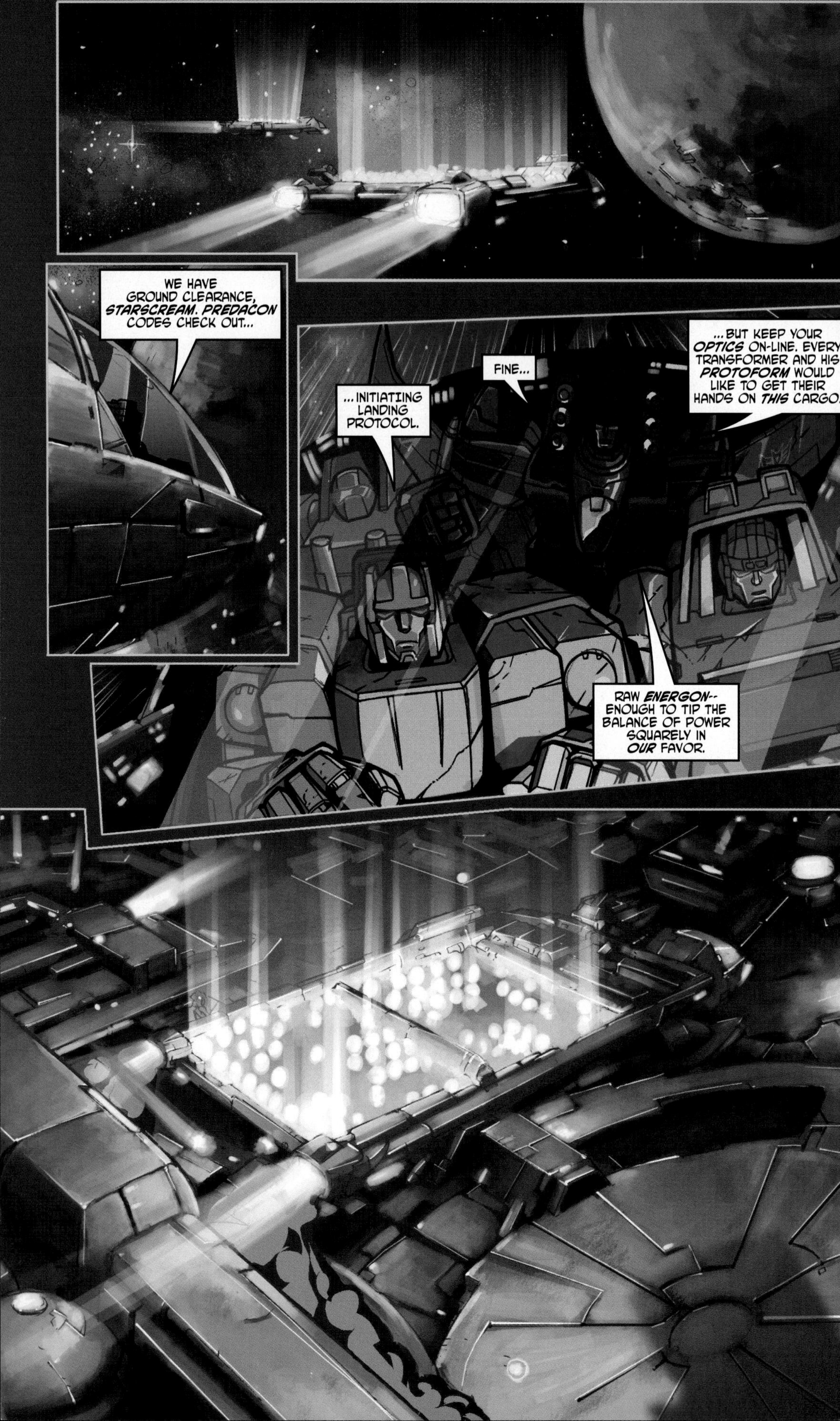
WE HAVE GROUND CLEARANCE, STARSCREAM. PREDACON CODES CHECK OUT...
...INITIATING LANDING PROTOCOL.
FINE...
...BUT KEEP YOUR OPTICS ON-LINE. EVERY TRANSFORMER AND HIS PROTOFORM WOULD LIKE TO GET THEIR HANDS ON THIS CARGO.
RAW ENERGON--ENOUGH TO TIP THE BALANCE OF POWER SQUARELY IN OUR FAVOR.

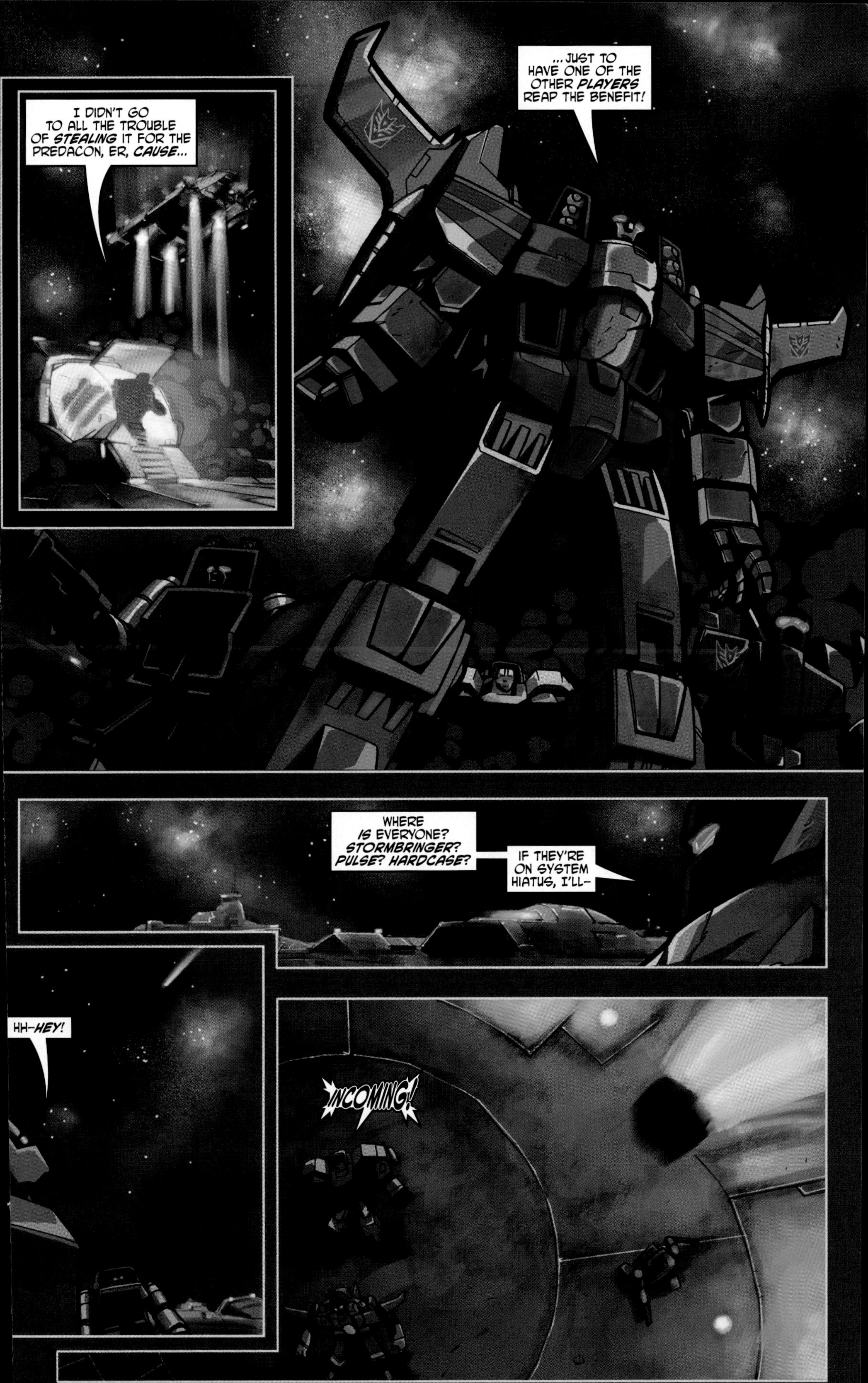
I DIDN'T GO TO ALL THE TROUBLE OF STEALING IT FOR THE PREDACON, ER, CAUSE...
... JUST TO HAVE ONE OF THE OTHER PLAYERS REAP THE BENEFIT!
WHERE IS EVERYONE? STORMBRINGER? PULSE? HARDCASE?
IF THEY'RE ON SYSTEM HIATUS, I'LL–
HH–HEY!
INCOMING!

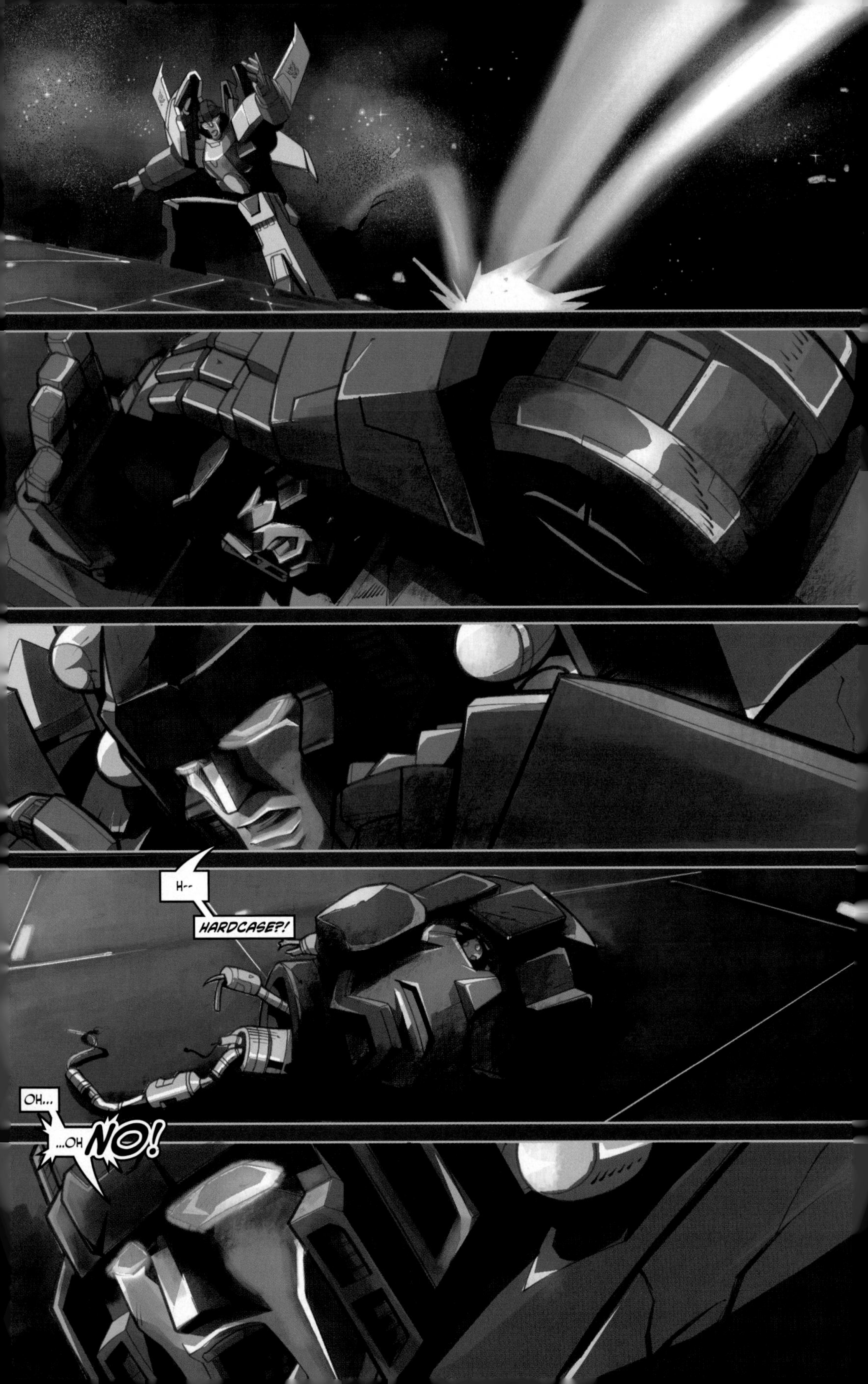
H--
HARDCASE?!
OH...
...OH NO!

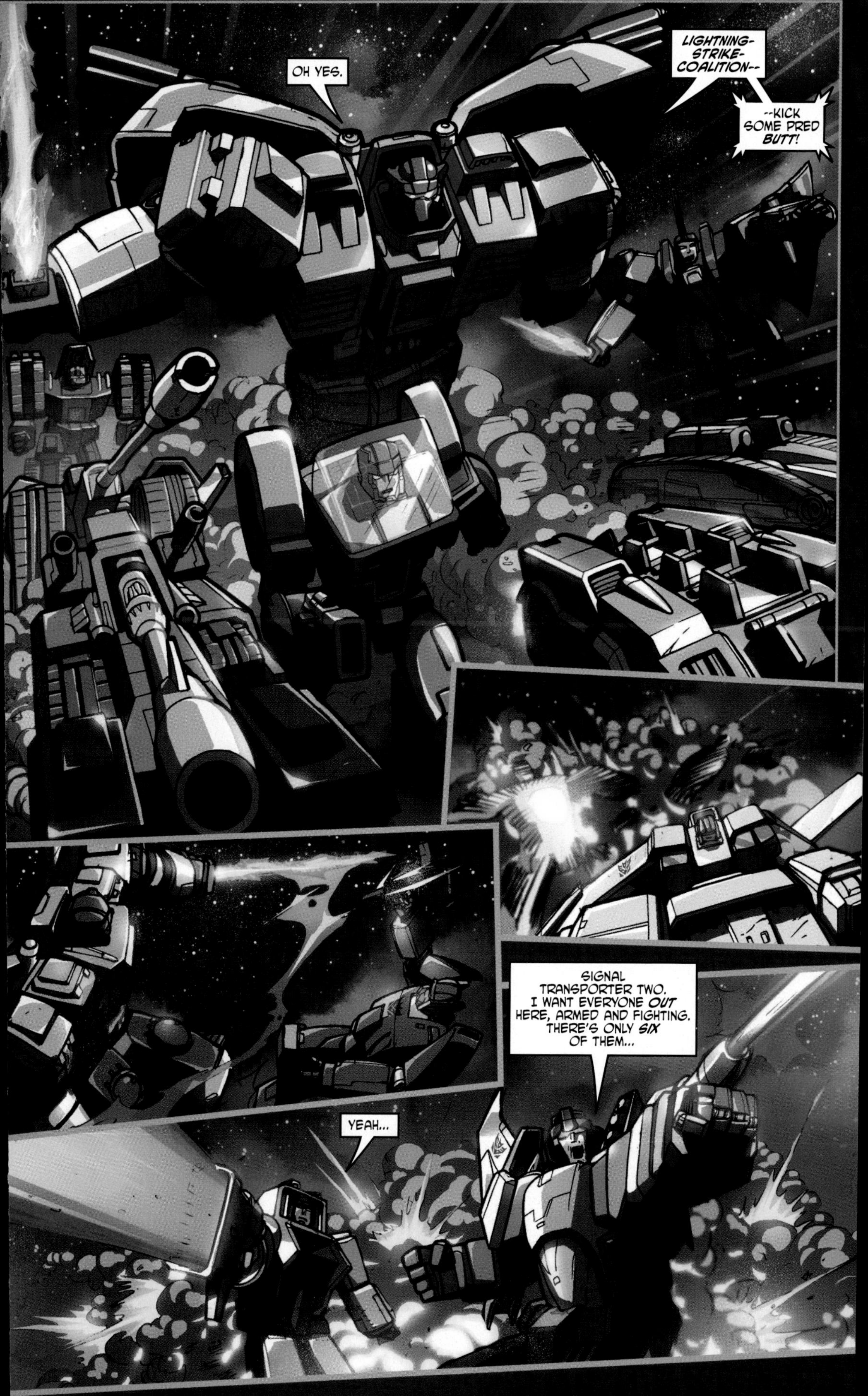

OH YES.
LIGHTNING-STRIKE-COALITION--
--KICK SOME PRED BUTT!
SIGNAL TRANSPORTER TWO. I WANT EVERYONE OUT HERE, ARMED AND FIGHTING. THERE'S ONLY SIX OF THEM...
YEAH...

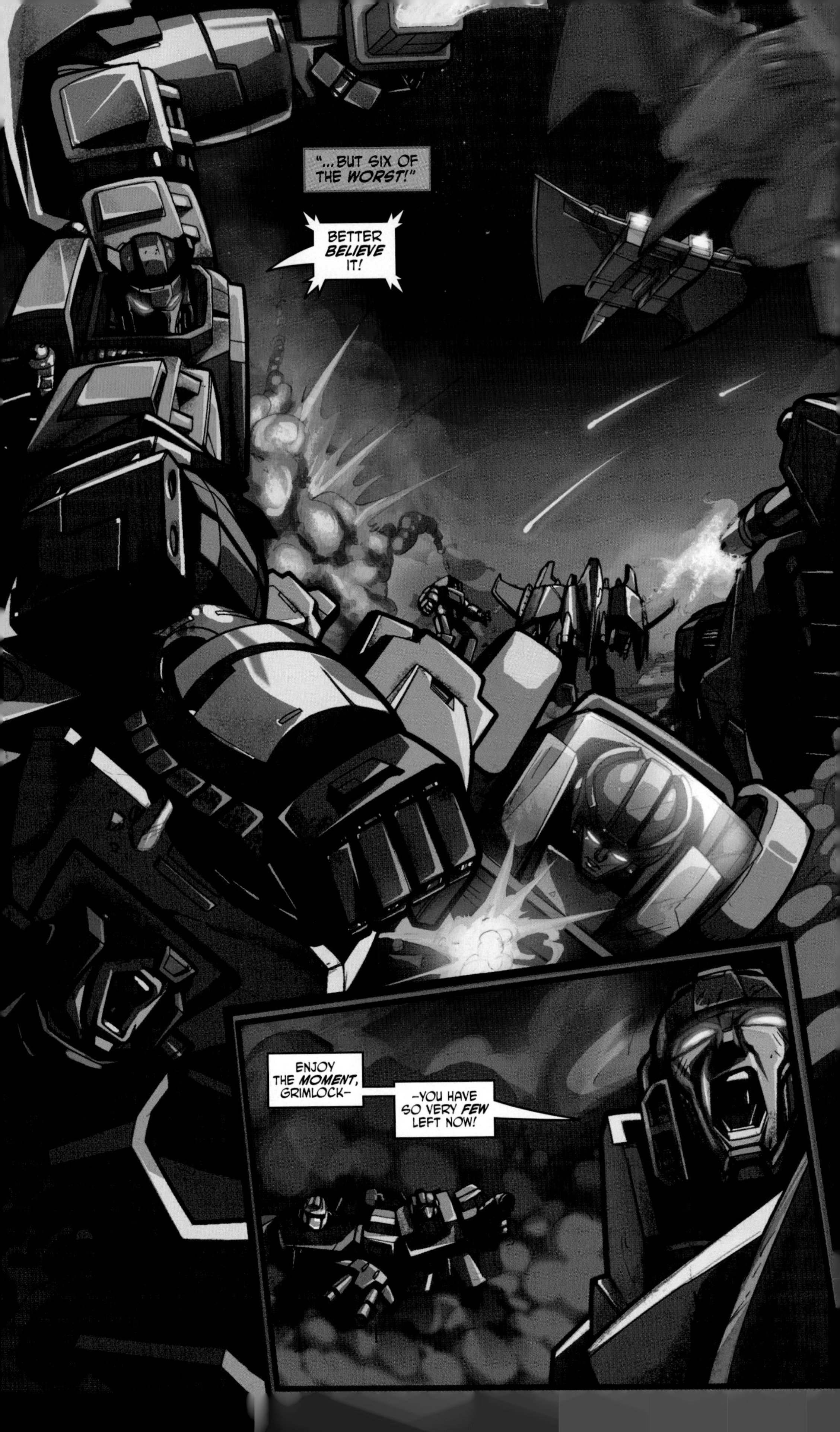
"...BUT SIX OF THE WORST!"
BETTER BELIEVE IT!
ENJOY THE MOMENT, GRIMLOCK-
-YOU HAVE SO VERY FEW LEFT NOW!

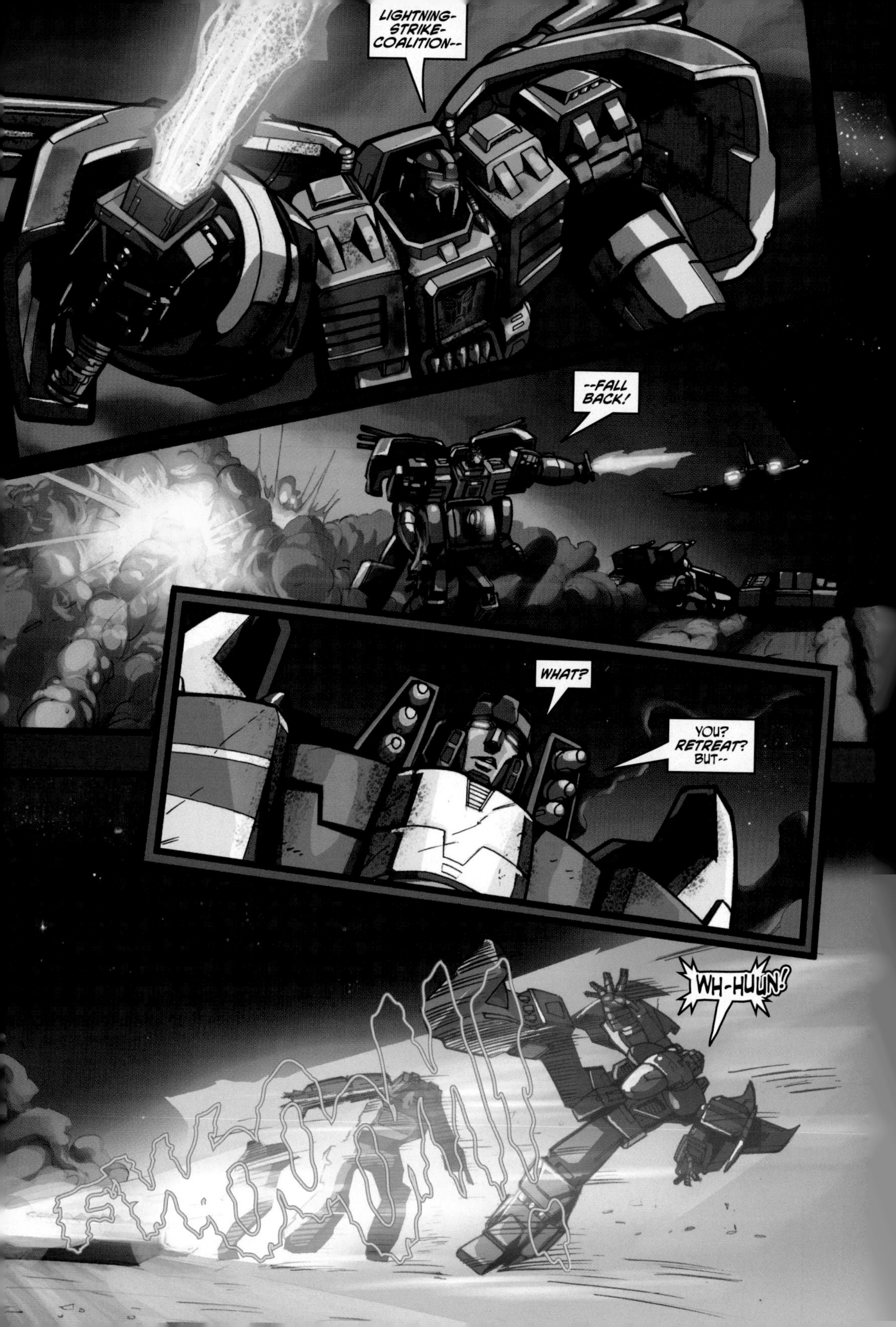
LIGHTNING-STRIKE-COALITION--
--FALL BACK!
WHAT?
YOU? RETREAT? BUT--
WH-HUUN!
FWOOOM

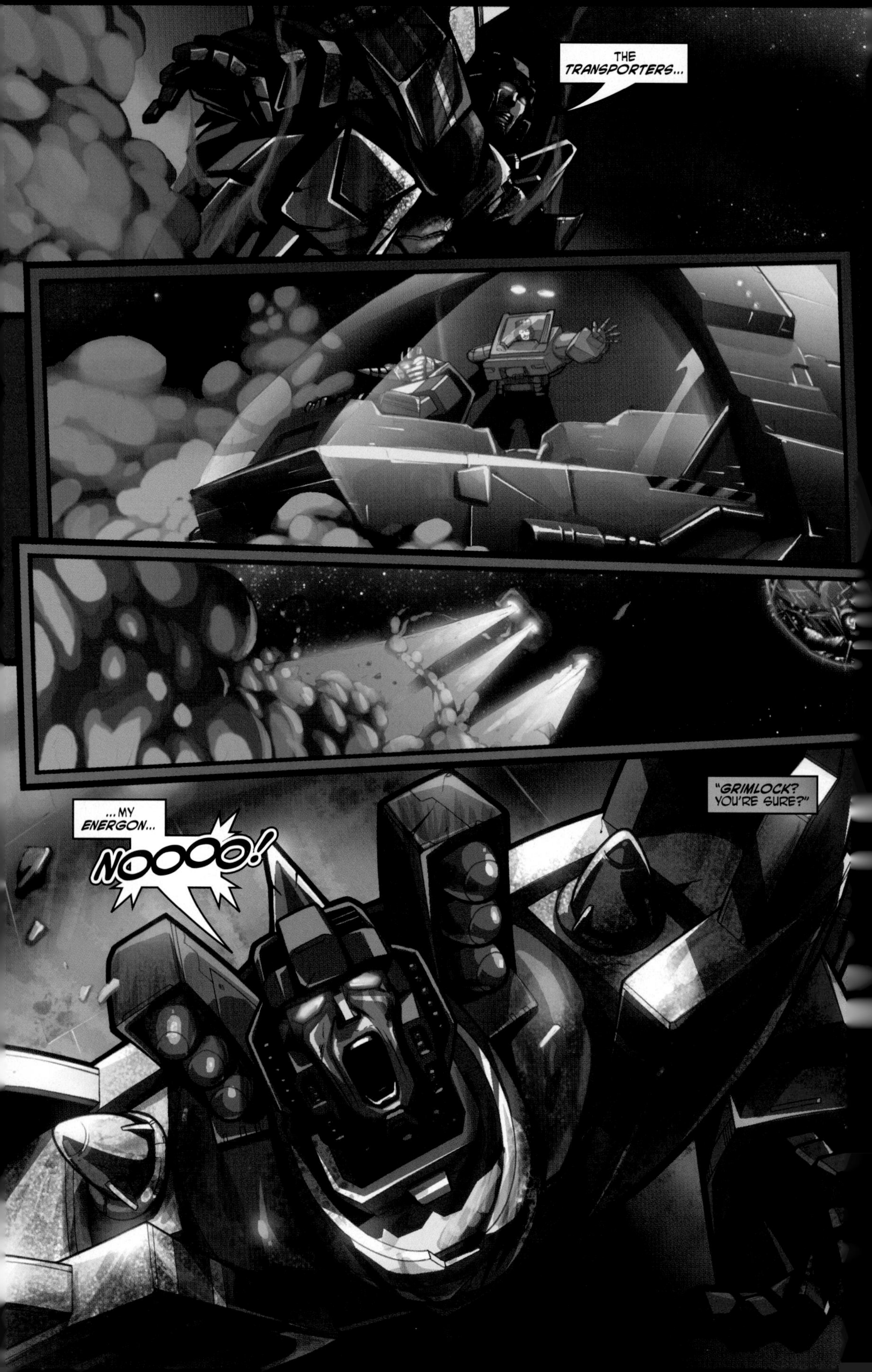
THE TRANSPORTERS...
...MY ENERGON...
NOOOO!
"GRIMLOCK? YOU'RE SURE?"

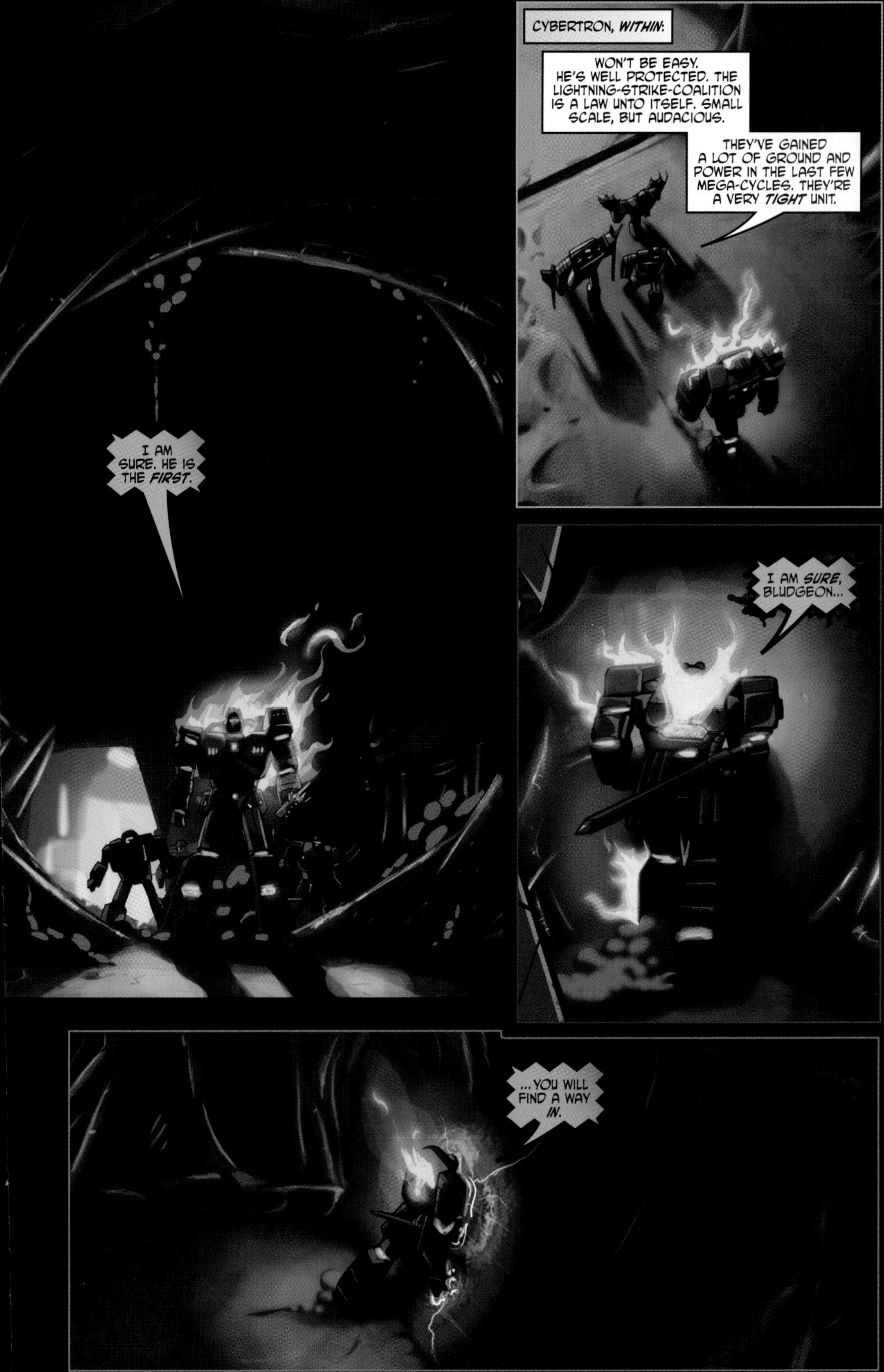

CYBERTRON, *WITHIN*:
WON'T BE EASY. HE'S WELL PROTECTED. THE LIGHTNING-STRIKE-COALITION IS A LAW UNTO ITSELF. SMALL SCALE, BUT AUDACIOUS.
THEY'VE GAINED A LOT OF GROUND AND POWER IN THE LAST FEW MEGA-CYCLES. THEY'RE A VERY *TIGHT* UNIT.
I AM SURE. HE IS THE *FIRST*.
I AM *SURE*, BLUDGEON...
...YOU WILL FIND A WAY *IN*.

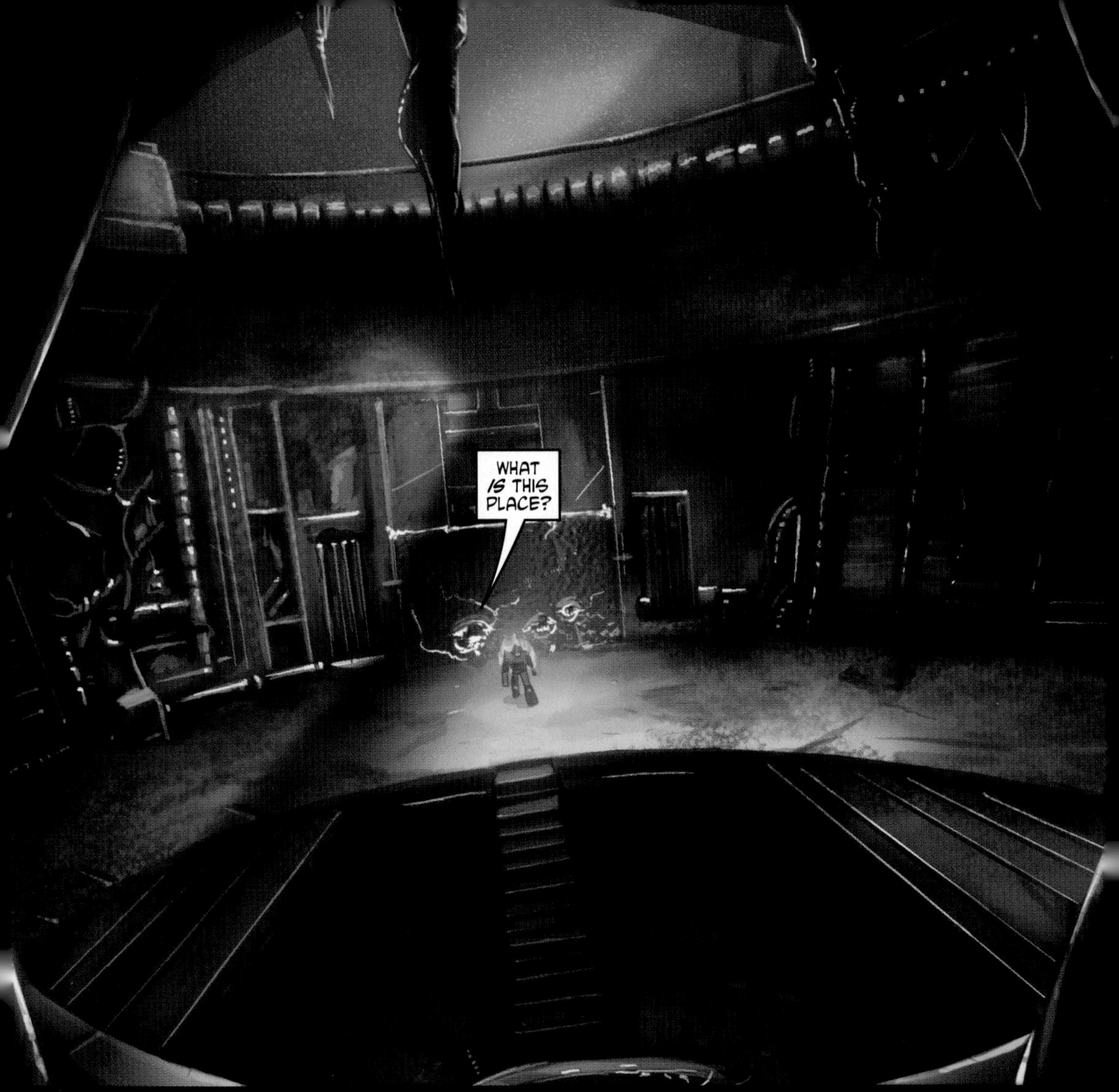
WHAT *IS* THIS PLACE?

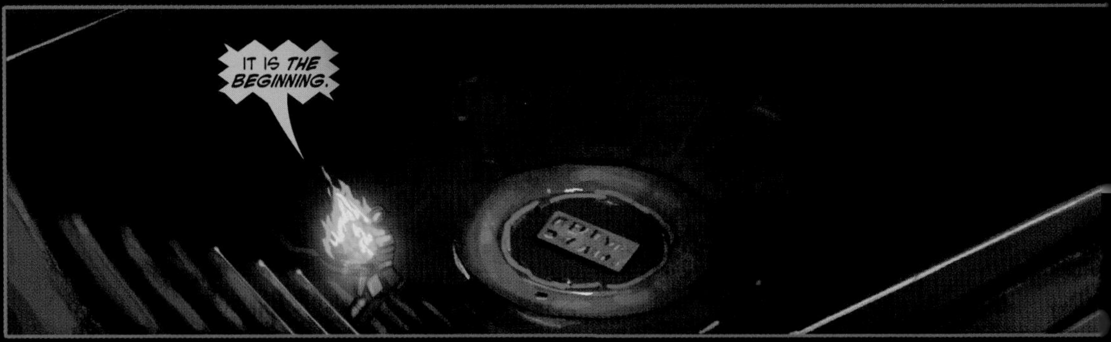
IT IS *THE BEGINNING.*

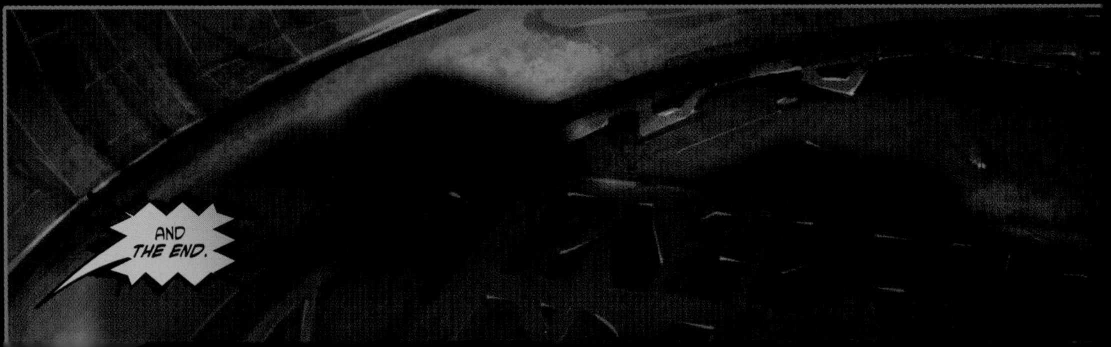
AND *THE END.*

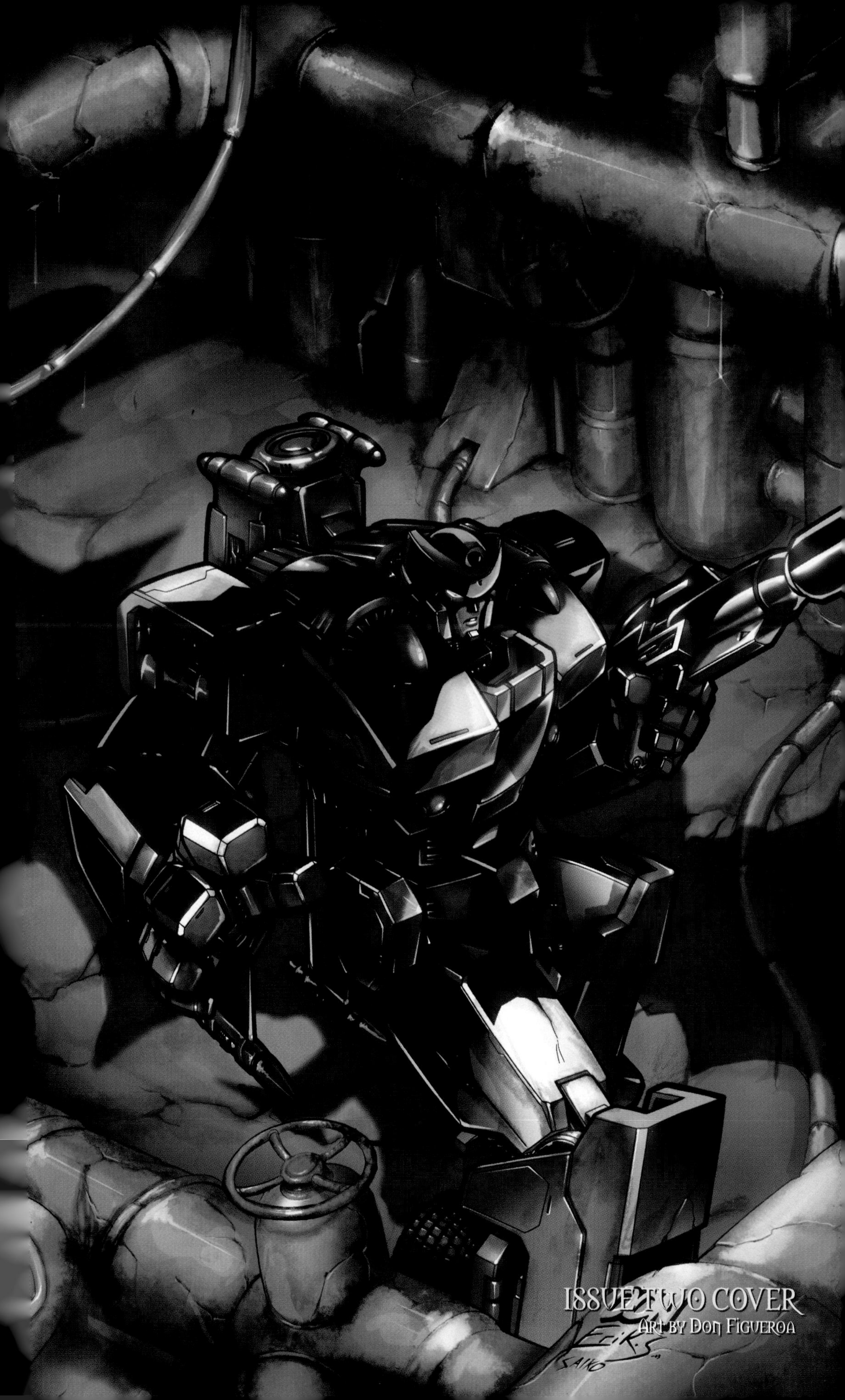

ISSUE TWO COVER
Art by Don Figueroa

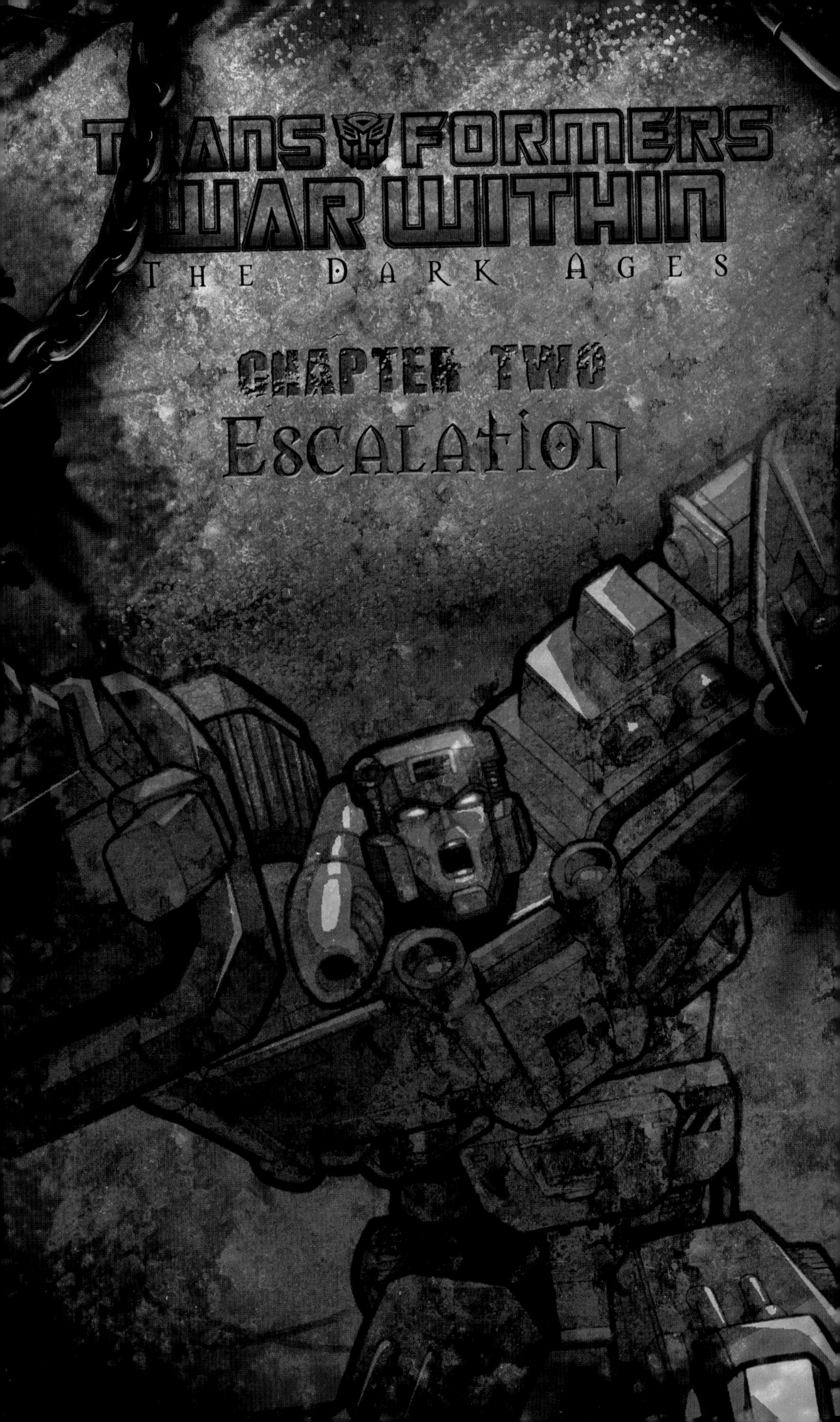
TRANSFORMERS
WAR WITHIN
THE DARK AGES
CHAPTER TWO
Escalation

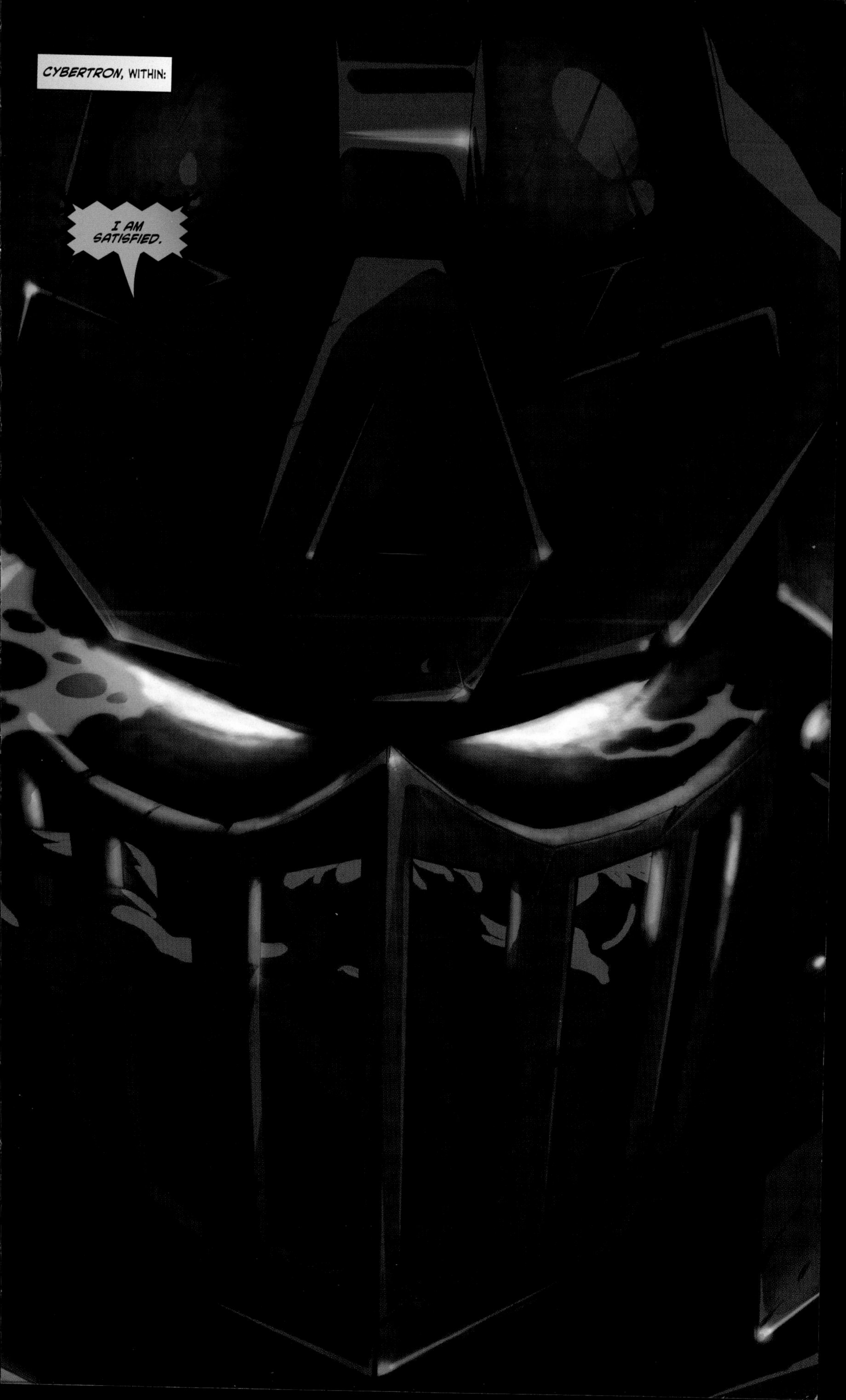
CYBERTRON, WITHIN:
I AM SATISFIED.

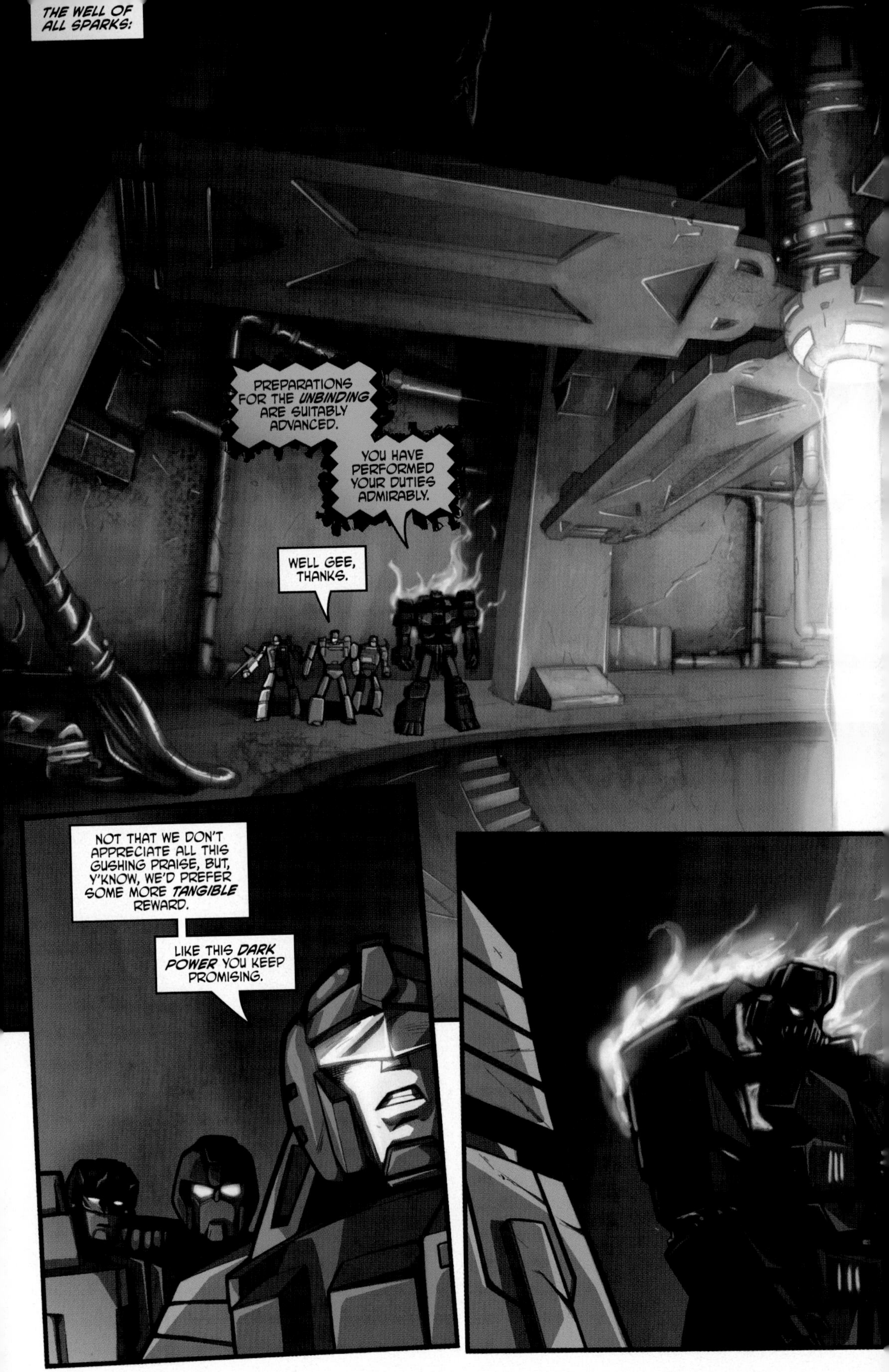
THE WELL OF ALL SPARKS:
PREPARATIONS FOR THE UNBINDING ARE SUITABLY ADVANCED.
YOU HAVE PERFORMED YOUR DUTIES ADMIRABLY.
WELL GEE, THANKS.
NOT THAT WE DON'T APPRECIATE ALL THIS GUSHING PRAISE, BUT, Y'KNOW, WE'D PREFER SOME MORE TANGIBLE REWARD.
LIKE THIS DARK POWER YOU KEEP PROMISING.

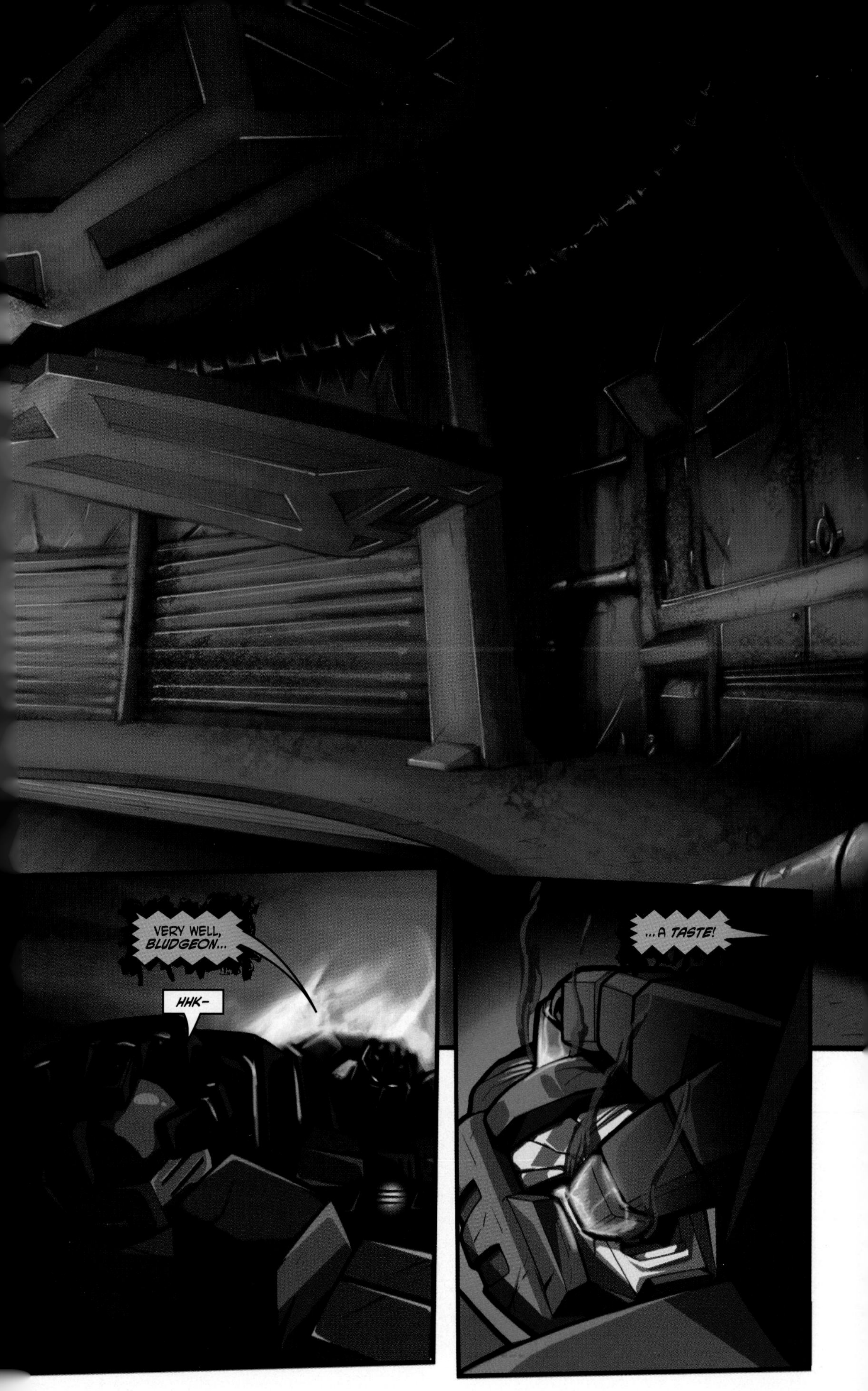
VERY WELL, BLUDGEON...
HHK-
...A TASTE!

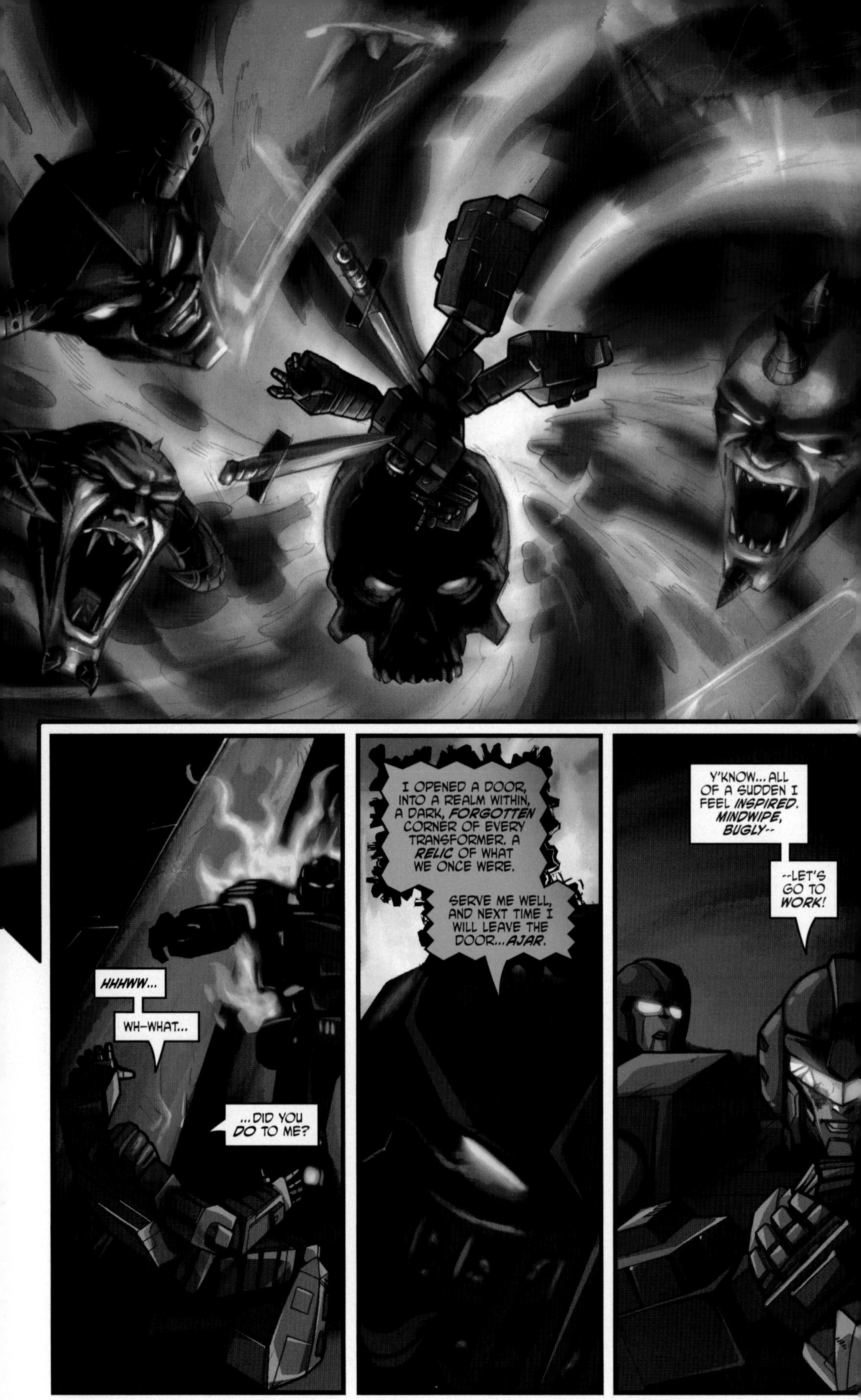

HHHWW...
WH-WHAT...
...DID YOU DO TO ME?
I OPENED A DOOR, INTO A REALM WITHIN, A DARK, FORGOTTEN CORNER OF EVERY TRANSFORMER. A RELIC OF WHAT WE ONCE WERE.
SERVE ME WELL, AND NEXT TIME I WILL LEAVE THE DOOR...AJAR.
Y'KNOW... ALL OF A SUDDEN I FEEL INSPIRED. MINDWIPE, BUGLY--
--LET'S GO TO WORK!

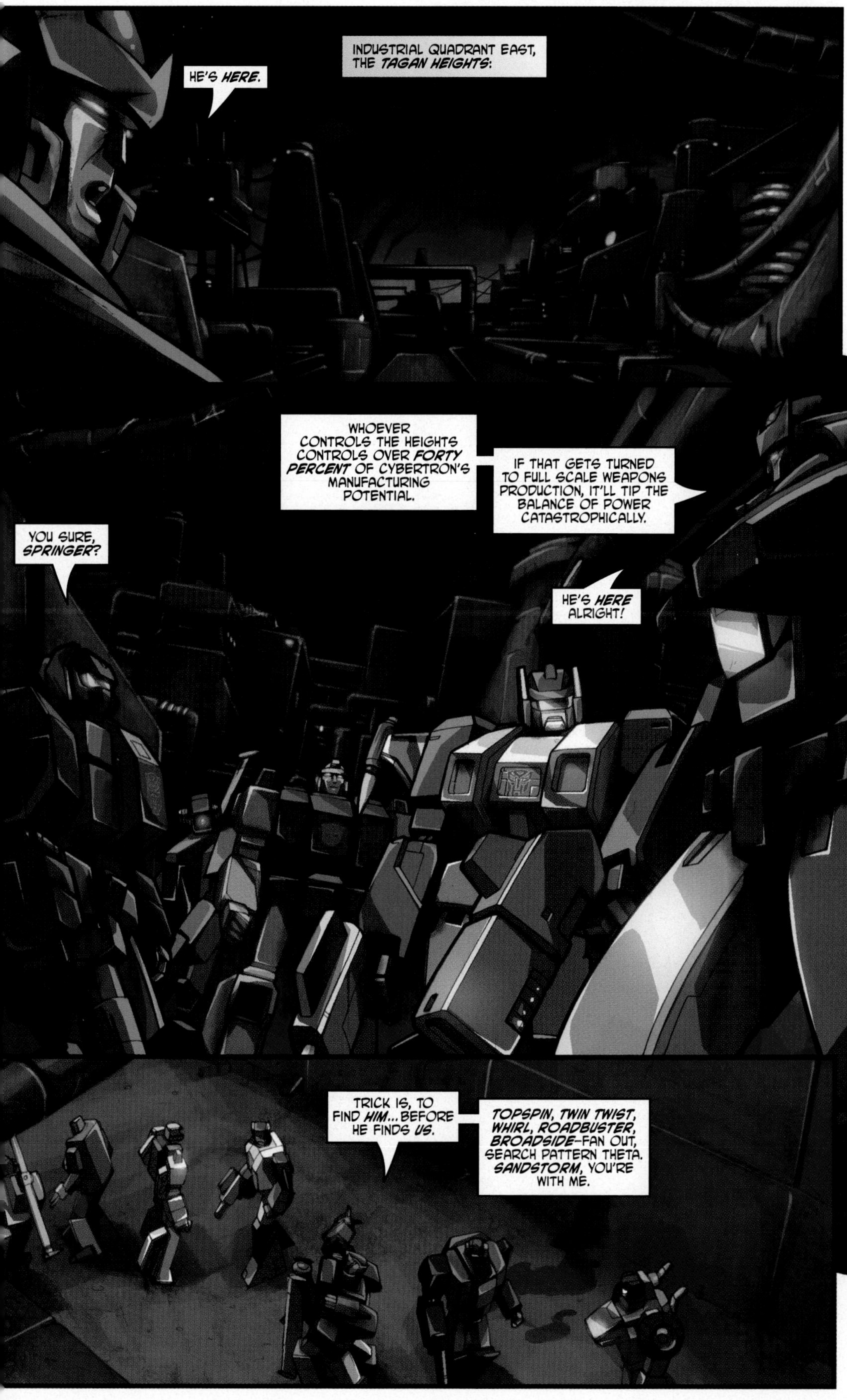
INDUSTRIAL QUADRANT EAST, THE TAGAN HEIGHTS:
HE'S HERE.
WHOEVER CONTROLS THE HEIGHTS CONTROLS OVER FORTY PERCENT OF CYBERTRON'S MANUFACTURING POTENTIAL.
IF THAT GETS TURNED TO FULL SCALE WEAPONS PRODUCTION, IT'LL TIP THE BALANCE OF POWER CATASTROPHICALLY.
YOU SURE, SPRINGER?
HE'S HERE ALRIGHT!
TRICK IS, TO FIND HIM... BEFORE HE FINDS US.
TOPSPIN, TWIN TWIST, WHIRL, ROADBUSTER, BROADSIDE–FAN OUT, SEARCH PATTERN THETA. SANDSTORM, YOU'RE WITH ME.

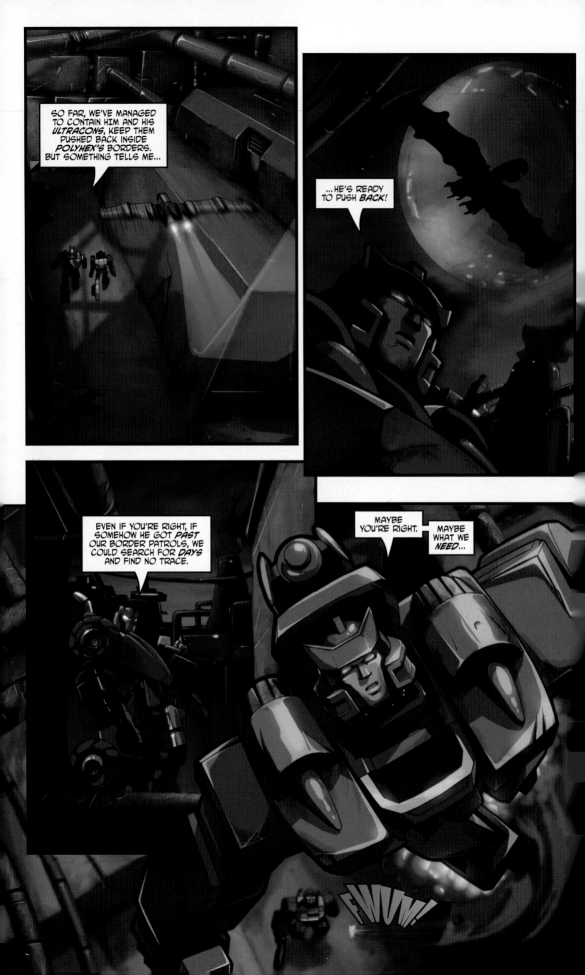

SO FAR, WE'VE MANAGED TO CONTAIN HIM AND HIS *ULTRACONS*, KEEP THEM PUSHED BACK INSIDE *POLYHEX'S* BORDERS. BUT SOMETHING TELLS ME...

...HE'S READY TO PUSH *BACK!*

EVEN IF YOU'RE RIGHT, IF SOMEHOW HE GOT *PAST* OUR BORDER PATROLS, WE COULD SEARCH FOR *DAYS* AND FIND NO TRACE.

MAYBE YOU'RE RIGHT. MAYBE WHAT WE *NEED*...

FWUM!

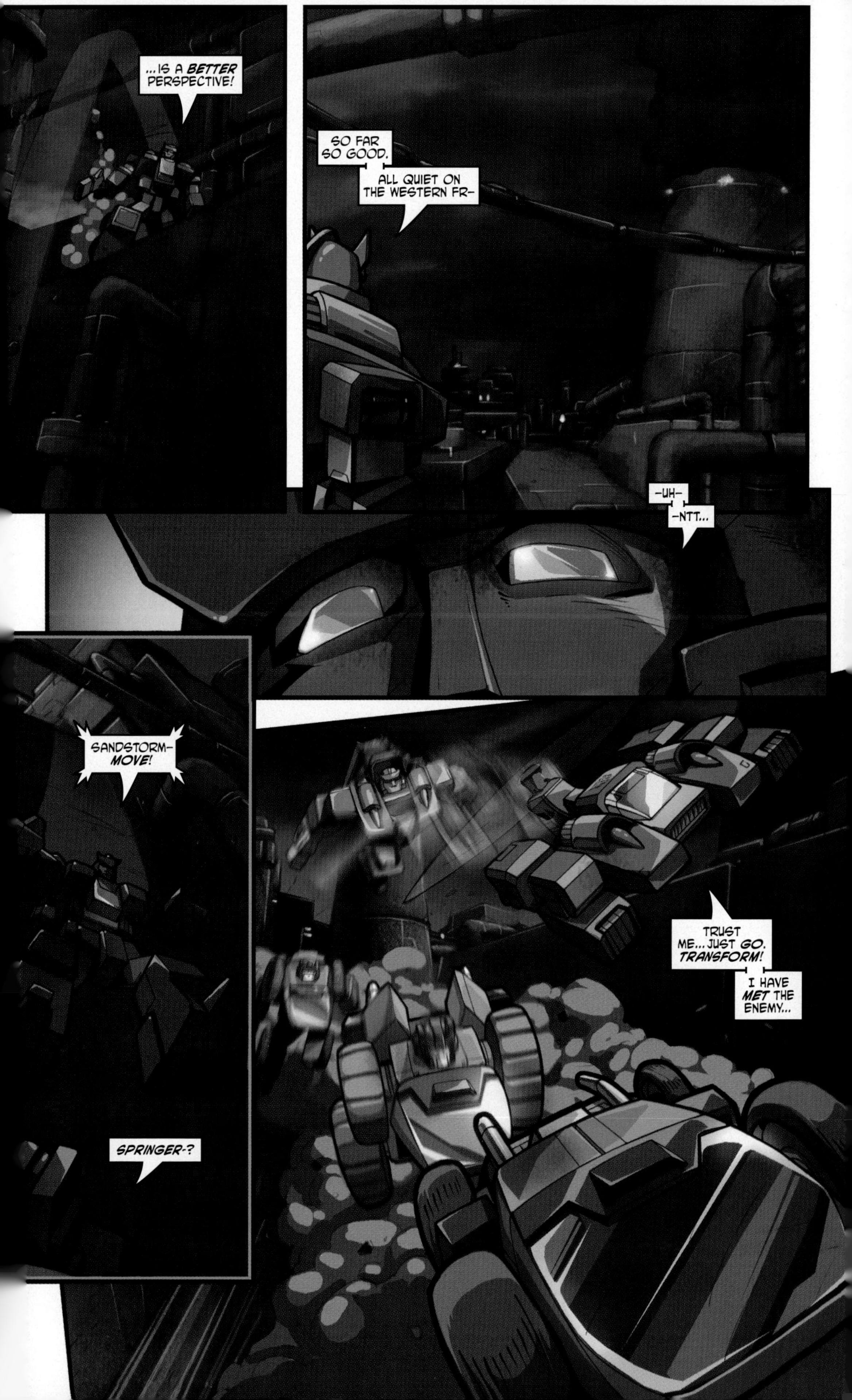
...IS A *BETTER* PERSPECTIVE!
SO FAR SO GOOD.
ALL QUIET ON THE WESTERN FR–
–UH–
–NTT...
SANDSTORM– *MOVE!*
SPRINGER–?
TRUST ME... JUST *GO*. *TRANSFORM!*
I HAVE *MET* THE ENEMY...

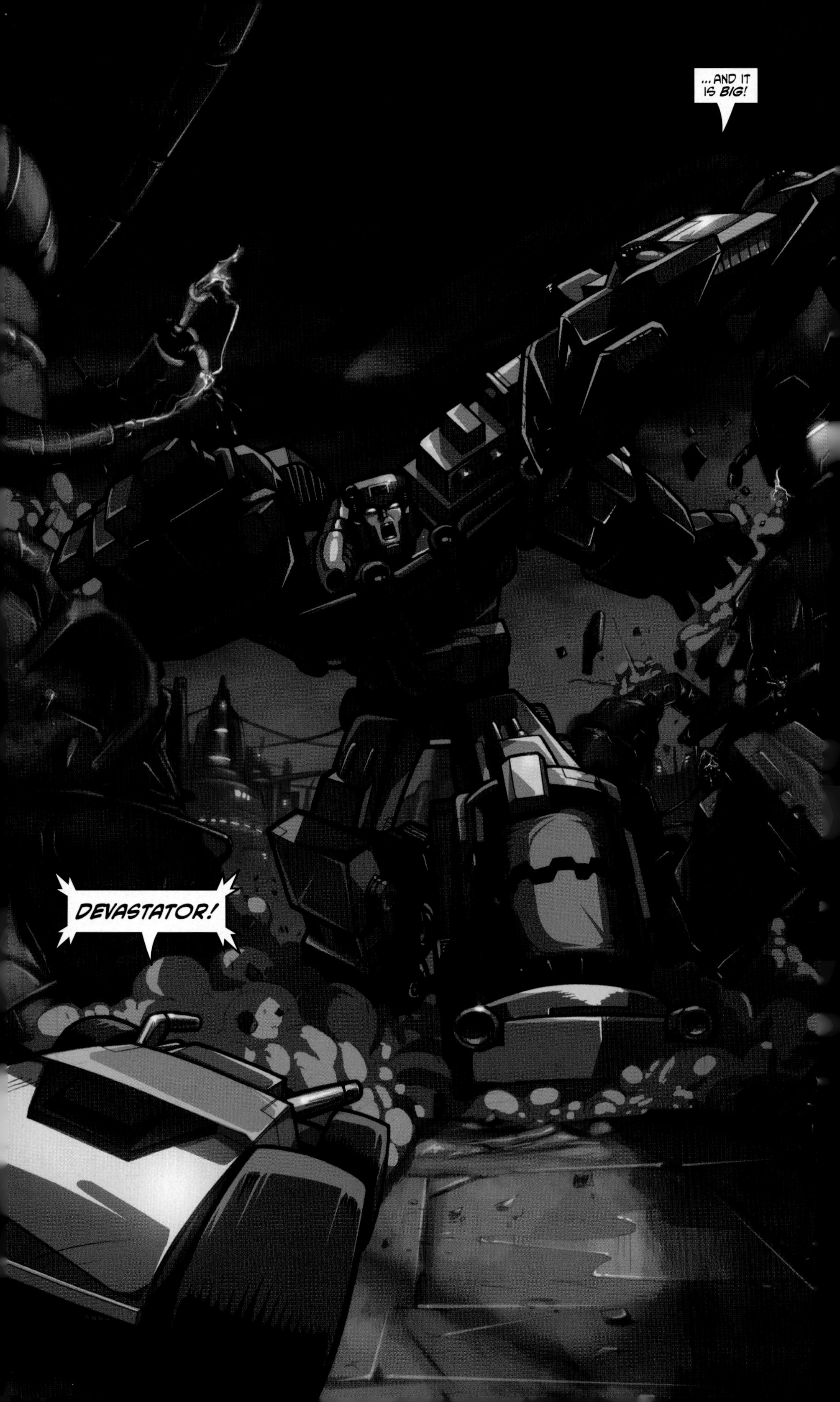
...AND IT IS BIG!
DEVASTATOR!

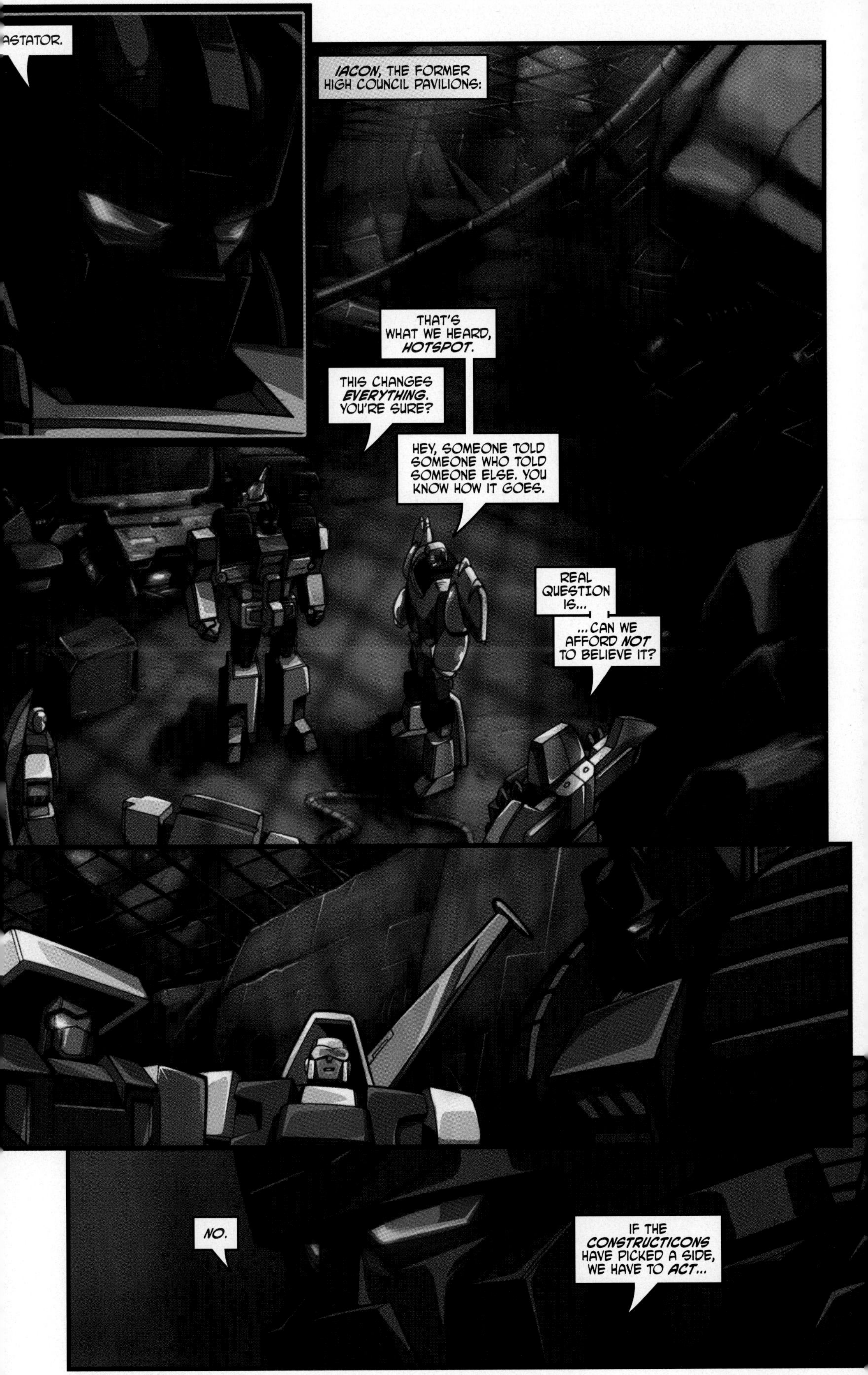
ASTATOR.
IACON, THE FORMER HIGH COUNCIL PAVILIONS:
THIS CHANGES *EVERYTHING*. YOU'RE SURE?
THAT'S WHAT WE HEARD, *HOTSPOT*.
HEY, SOMEONE TOLD SOMEONE WHO TOLD SOMEONE ELSE. YOU KNOW HOW IT GOES.
REAL QUESTION IS...
...CAN WE AFFORD *NOT* TO BELIEVE IT?
NO.
IF THE *CONSTRUCTICONS* HAVE PICKED A SIDE, WE HAVE TO *ACT*...

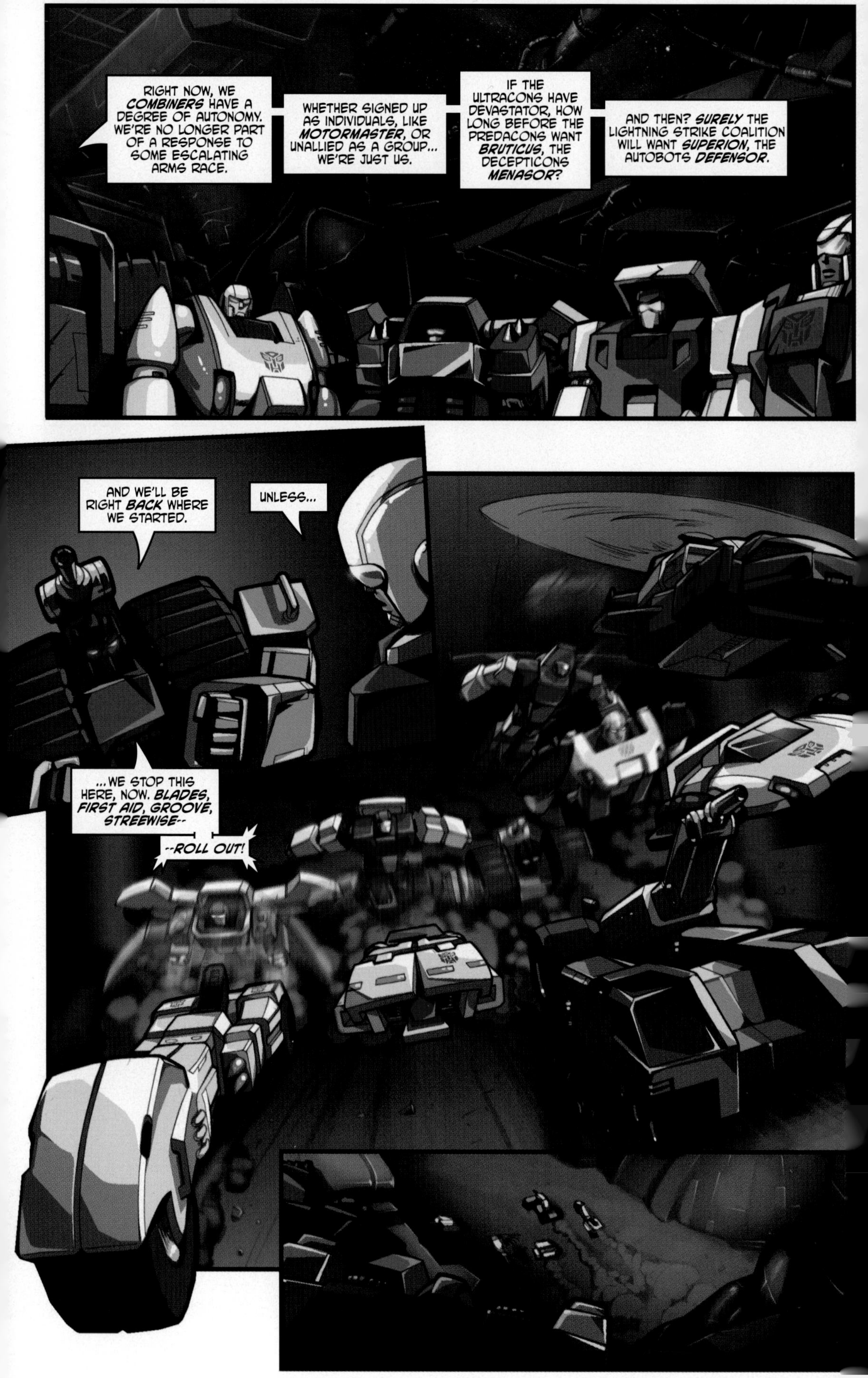
RIGHT NOW, WE COMBINERS HAVE A DEGREE OF AUTONOMY. WE'RE NO LONGER PART OF A RESPONSE TO SOME ESCALATING ARMS RACE.
WHETHER SIGNED UP AS INDIVIDUALS, LIKE MOTORMASTER, OR UNALLIED AS A GROUP... WE'RE JUST US.
IF THE ULTRACONS HAVE DEVASTATOR, HOW LONG BEFORE THE PREDACONS WANT BRUTICUS, THE DECEPTICONS MENASOR?
AND THEN? SURELY THE LIGHTNING STRIKE COALITION WILL WANT SUPERION, THE AUTOBOTS DEFENSOR.
AND WE'LL BE RIGHT BACK WHERE WE STARTED.
UNLESS...
...WE STOP THIS HERE, NOW. BLADES, FIRST AID, GROOVE, STREEWISE--
--ROLL OUT!

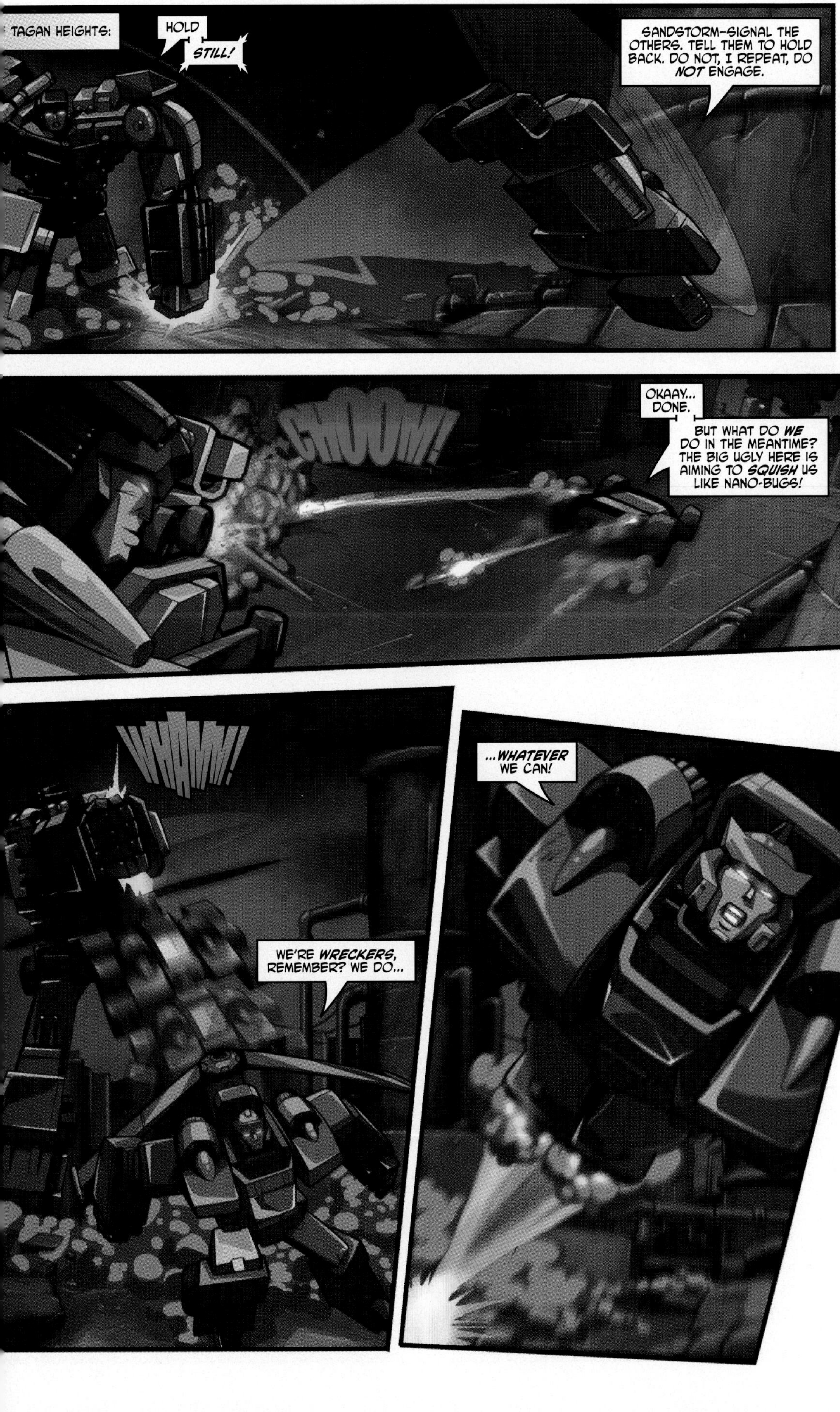
TAGAN HEIGHTS:
HOLD
STILL!
SANDSTORM–SIGNAL THE OTHERS. TELL THEM TO HOLD BACK. DO NOT, I REPEAT, DO NOT ENGAGE.
CHOOOM!
OKAAY... DONE.
BUT WHAT DO WE DO IN THE MEANTIME? THE BIG UGLY HERE IS AIMING TO SQUISH US LIKE NANO-BUGS!
WHAMM!
WE'RE WRECKERS, REMEMBER? WE DO...
...WHATEVER WE CAN!

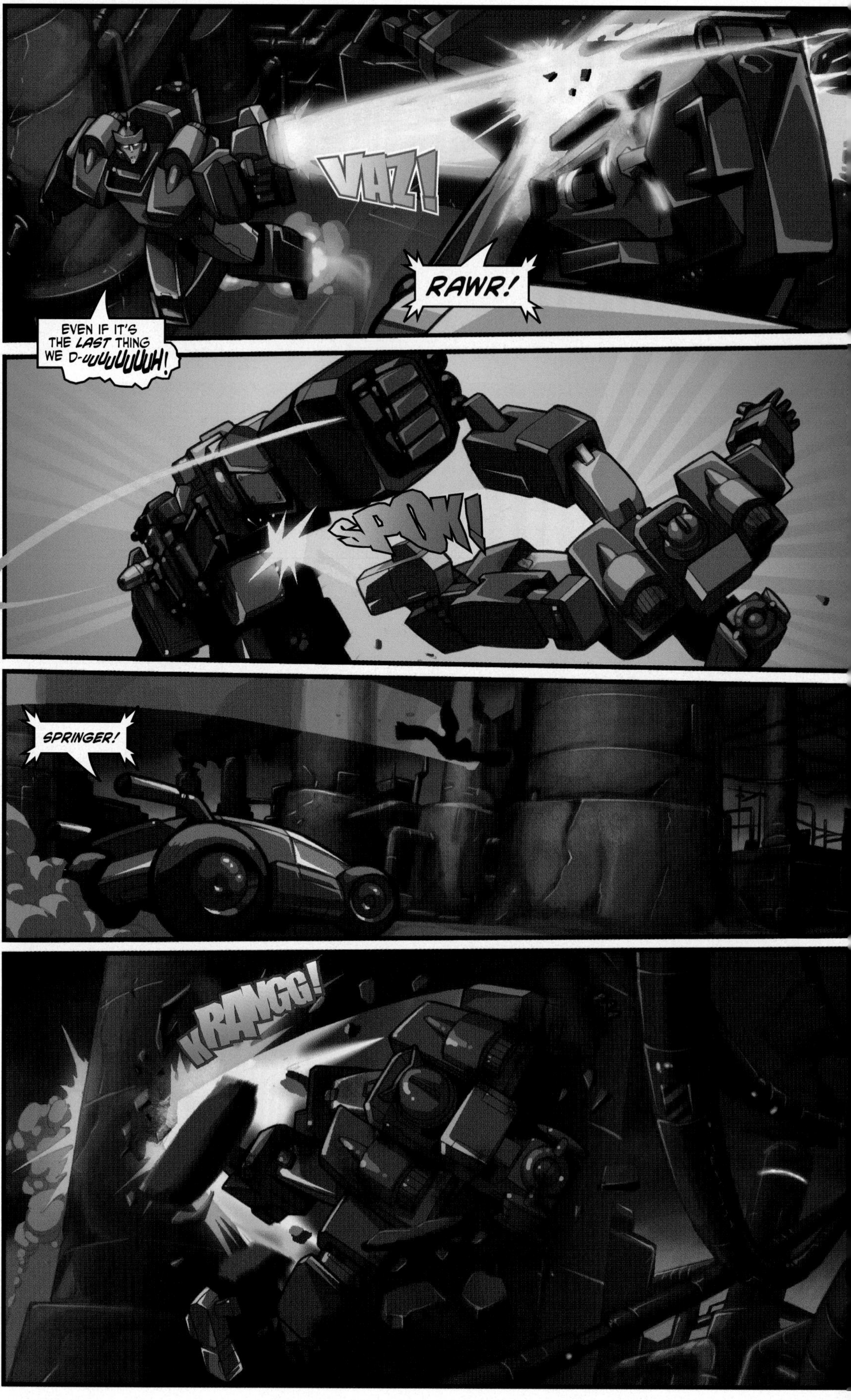
VAZ!
RAWR!
EVEN IF IT'S THE LAST THING WE D-UUUUUUUUH!
SPOK!
SPRINGER!
KRANGG!

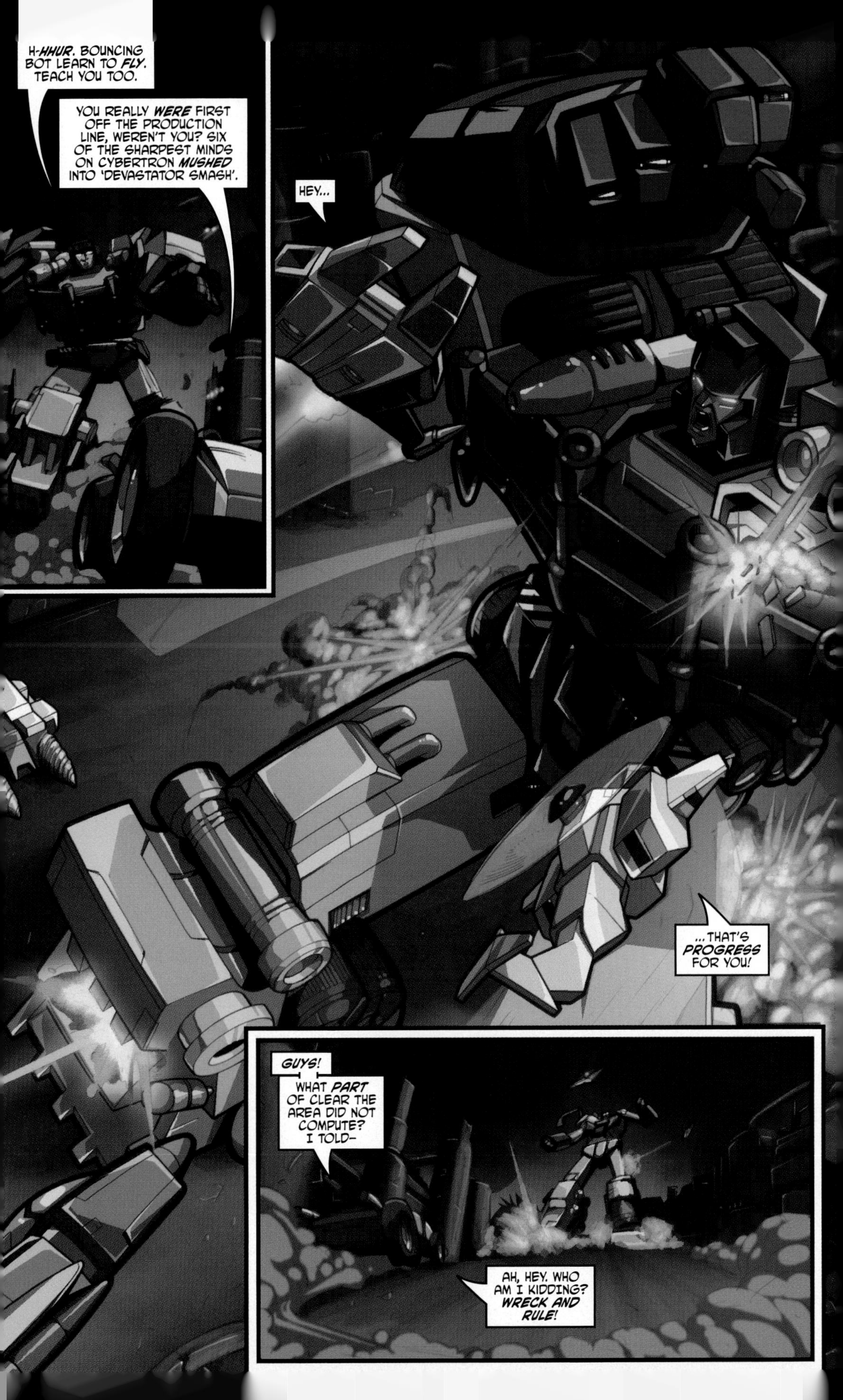
H-*HHUR*. BOUNCING BOT LEARN TO *FLY*. TEACH YOU TOO.
YOU REALLY *WERE* FIRST OFF THE PRODUCTION LINE, WEREN'T YOU? SIX OF THE SHARPEST MINDS ON CYBERTRON *MUSHED* INTO 'DEVASTATOR SMASH'.
HEY...
...THAT'S *PROGRESS* FOR YOU!
GUYS!
WHAT *PART* OF CLEAR THE AREA DID NOT COMPUTE? I TOLD–
AH, HEY. WHO AM I KIDDING? *WRECK AND RULE!*

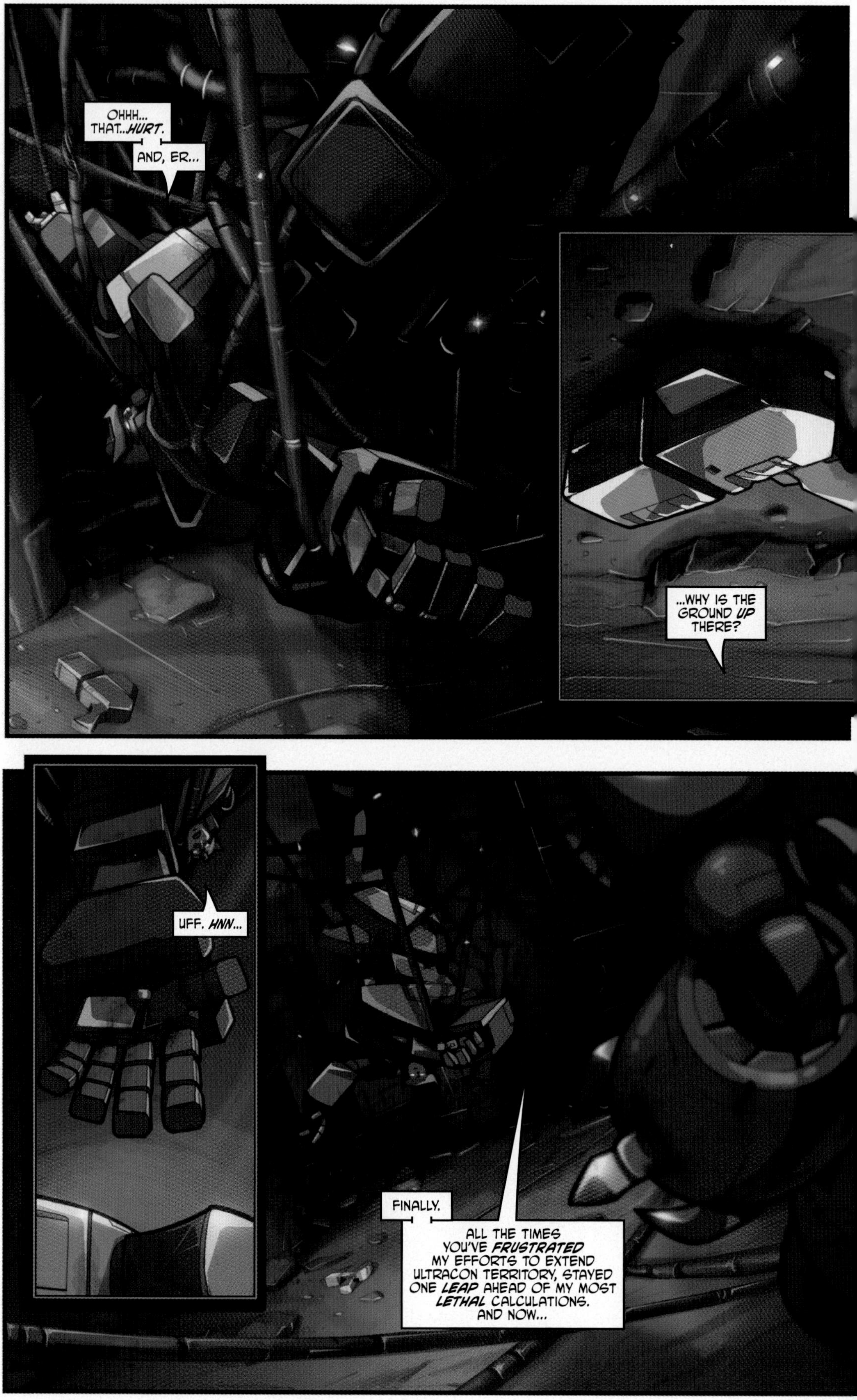
OHHH... THAT...*HURT*.
AND, ER...
...WHY IS THE GROUND *UP* THERE?
UFF. *HNN*...
FINALLY.
ALL THE TIMES YOU'VE *FRUSTRATED* MY EFFORTS TO EXTEND ULTRACON TERRITORY, STAYED ONE *LEAP* AHEAD OF MY MOST *LETHAL* CALCULATIONS. AND NOW...

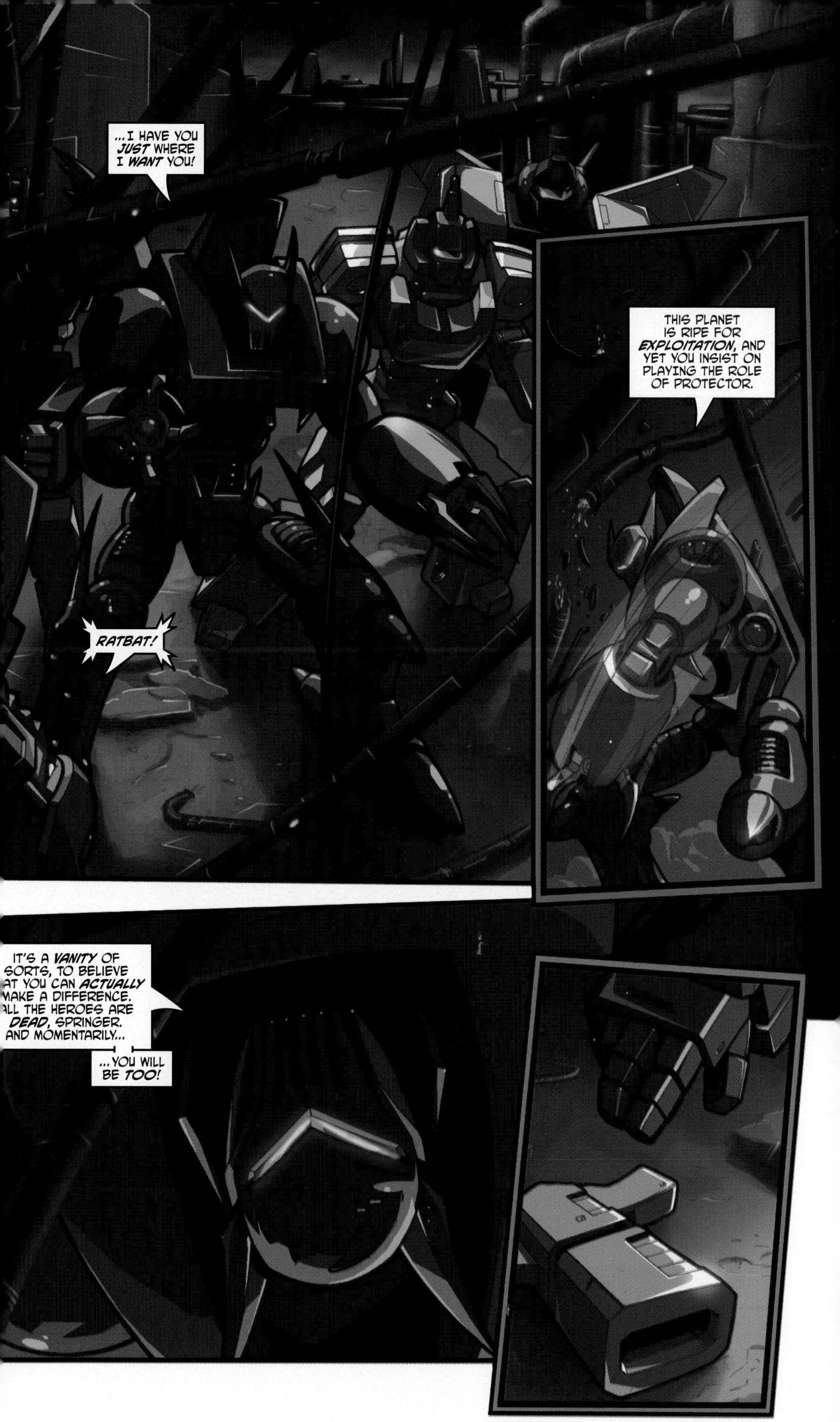
...I HAVE YOU *JUST* WHERE I *WANT* YOU!
THIS PLANET IS RIPE FOR *EXPLOITATION*, AND YET YOU INSIST ON PLAYING THE ROLE OF PROTECTOR.
RATBAT!
IT'S A *VANITY* OF SORTS, TO BELIEVE AT YOU CAN *ACTUALLY* MAKE A DIFFERENCE. LL THE HEROES ARE *DEAD*, SPRINGER. AND MOMENTARILY...
...YOU WILL BE *TOO!*

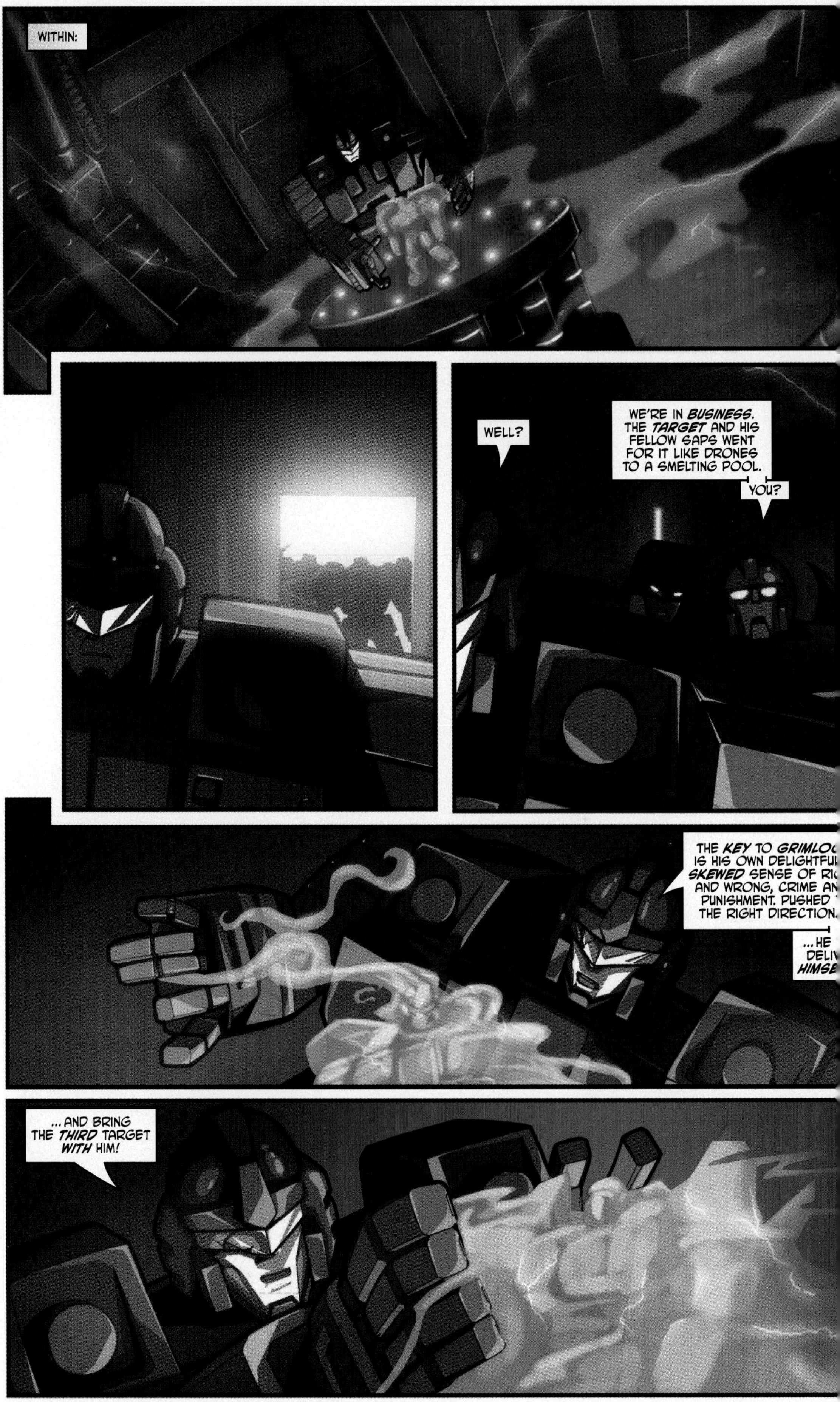
WITHIN:
WELL?
WE'RE IN *BUSINESS*. THE *TARGET* AND HIS FELLOW SAPS WENT FOR IT LIKE DRONES TO A SMELTING POOL.
YOU?
THE *KEY* TO *GRIMLO*
IS HIS OWN DELIGHTFU
SKEWED SENSE OF RI
AND WRONG, CRIME AN
PUNISHMENT. PUSHED
THE RIGHT DIRECTION.
...HE
DELI
HIMSE
...AND BRING THE *THIRD* TARGET *WITH* HIM!

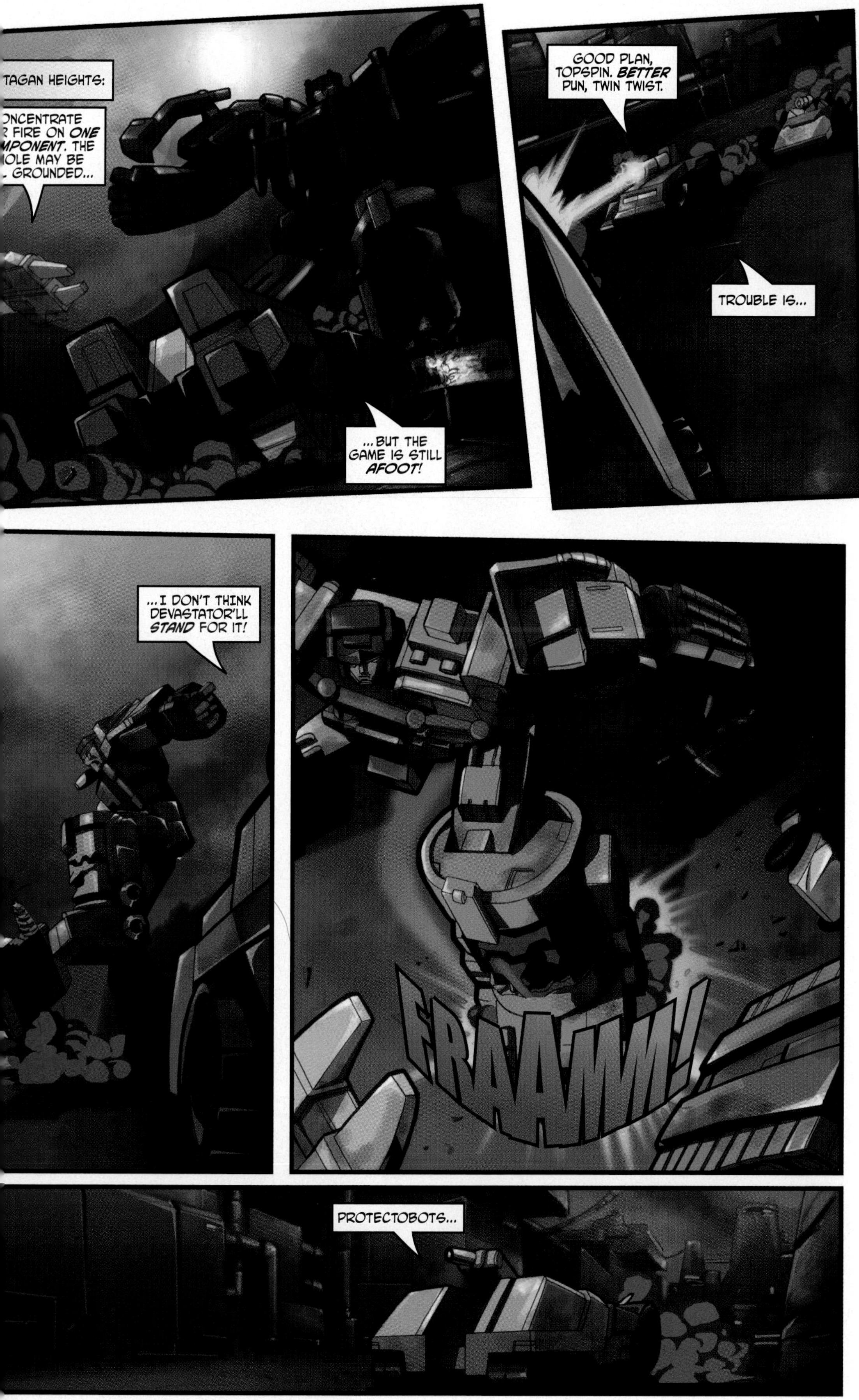

TAGAN HEIGHTS:
ONCENTRATE R FIRE ON *ONE* MPONENT. THE HOLE MAY BE GROUNDED...
...BUT THE GAME IS STILL *AFOOT!*
GOOD PLAN, TOPSPIN. *BETTER* PUN, TWIN TWIST.
TROUBLE IS...
...I DON'T THINK DEVASTATOR'LL *STAND* FOR IT!
FRAAMM!
PROTECTOBOTS...

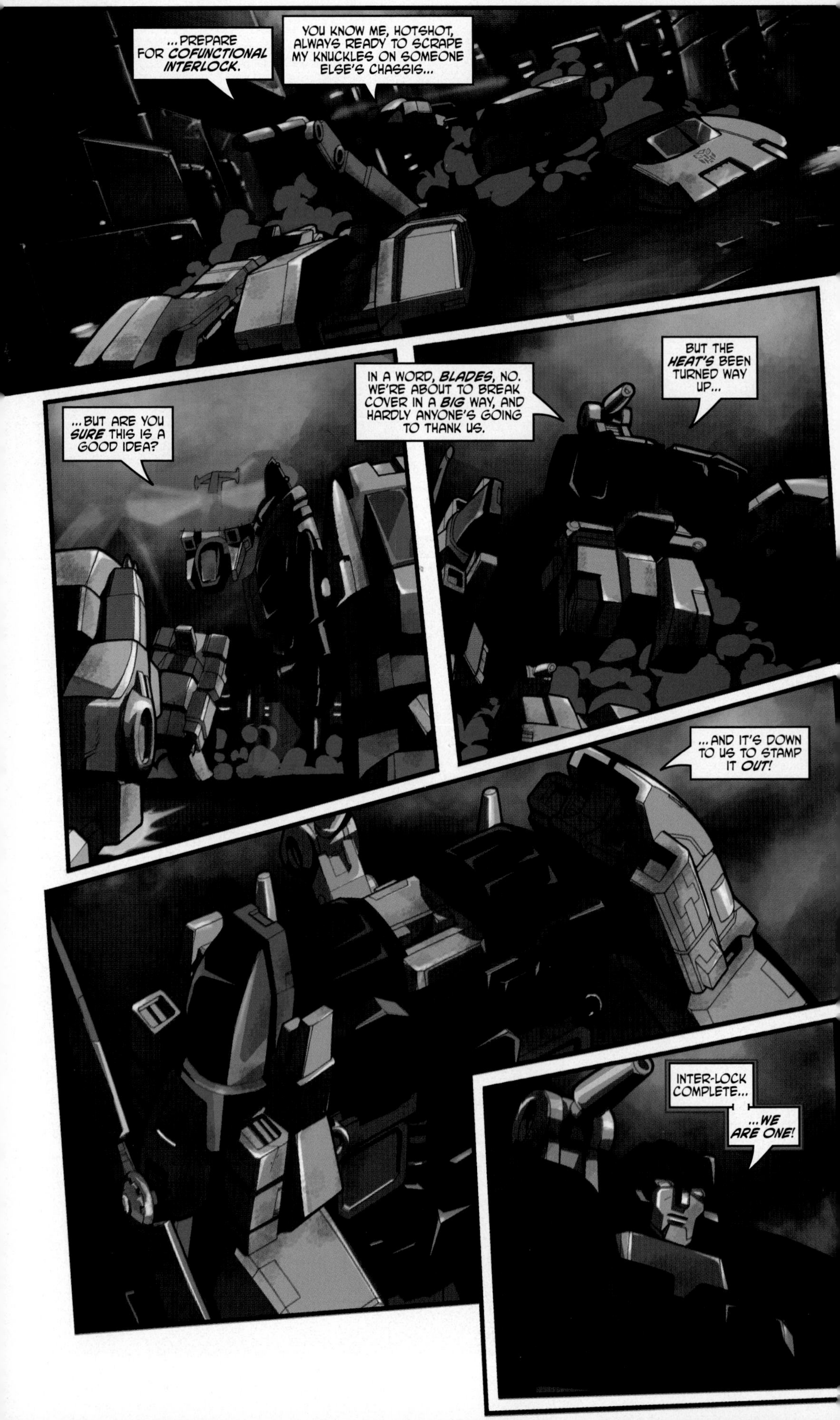
...PREPARE FOR COFUNCTIONAL INTERLOCK.
YOU KNOW ME, HOTSHOT, ALWAYS READY TO SCRAPE MY KNUCKLES ON SOMEONE ELSE'S CHASSIS...
...BUT ARE YOU SURE THIS IS A GOOD IDEA?
IN A WORD, BLADES, NO. WE'RE ABOUT TO BREAK COVER IN A BIG WAY, AND HARDLY ANYONE'S GOING TO THANK US.
BUT THE HEAT'S BEEN TURNED WAY UP...
...AND IT'S DOWN TO US TO STAMP IT OUT!
INTER-LOCK COMPLETE...
...WE ARE ONE!

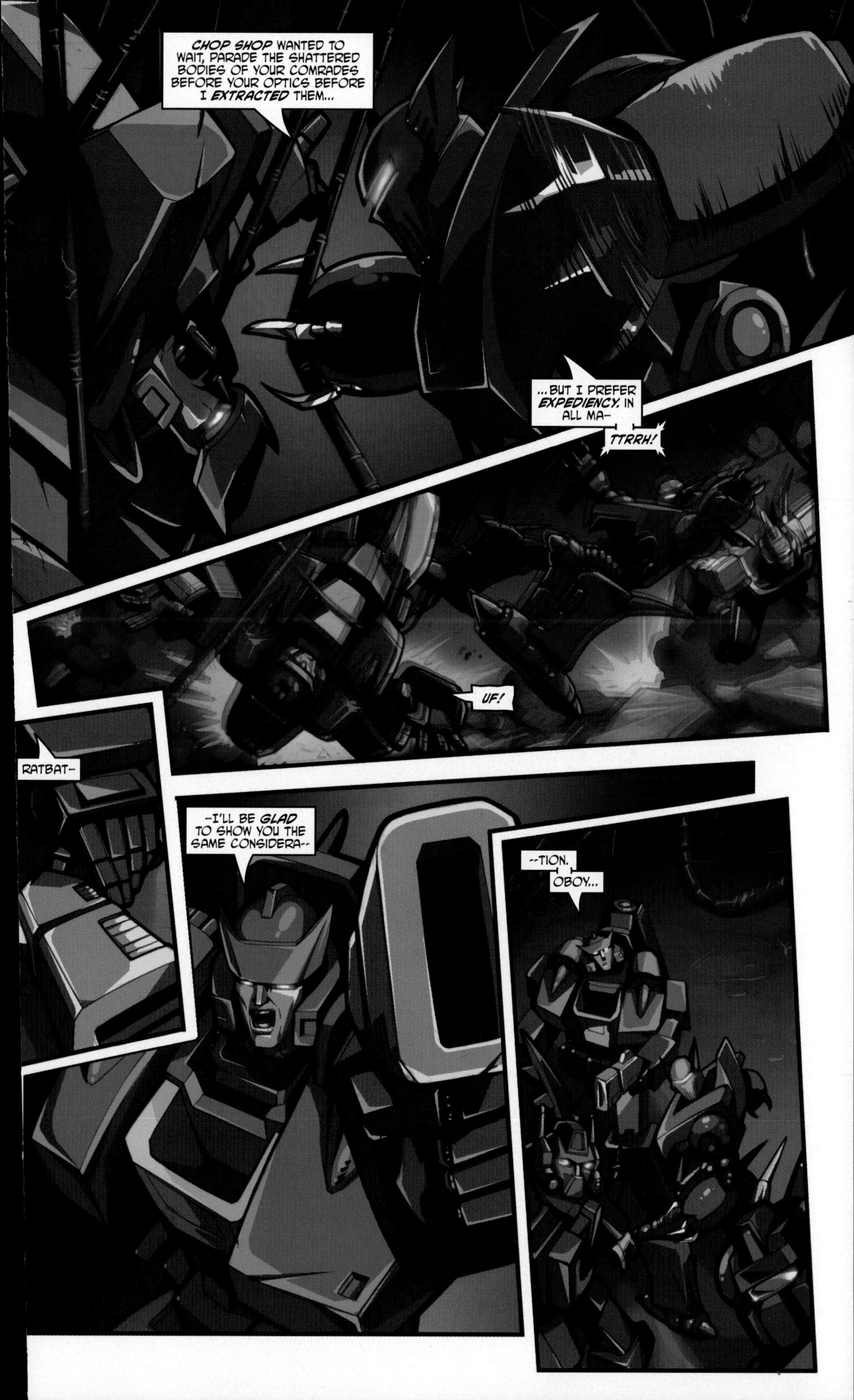

CHOP SHOP WANTED TO WAIT, PARADE THE SHATTERED BODIES OF YOUR COMRADES BEFORE YOUR OPTICS BEFORE I EXTRACTED THEM...
...BUT I PREFER EXPEDIENCY. IN ALL MA–
TTRRH!
UF!
RATBAT–
–I'LL BE GLAD TO SHOW YOU THE SAME CONSIDERA--
--TION.
OBOY...

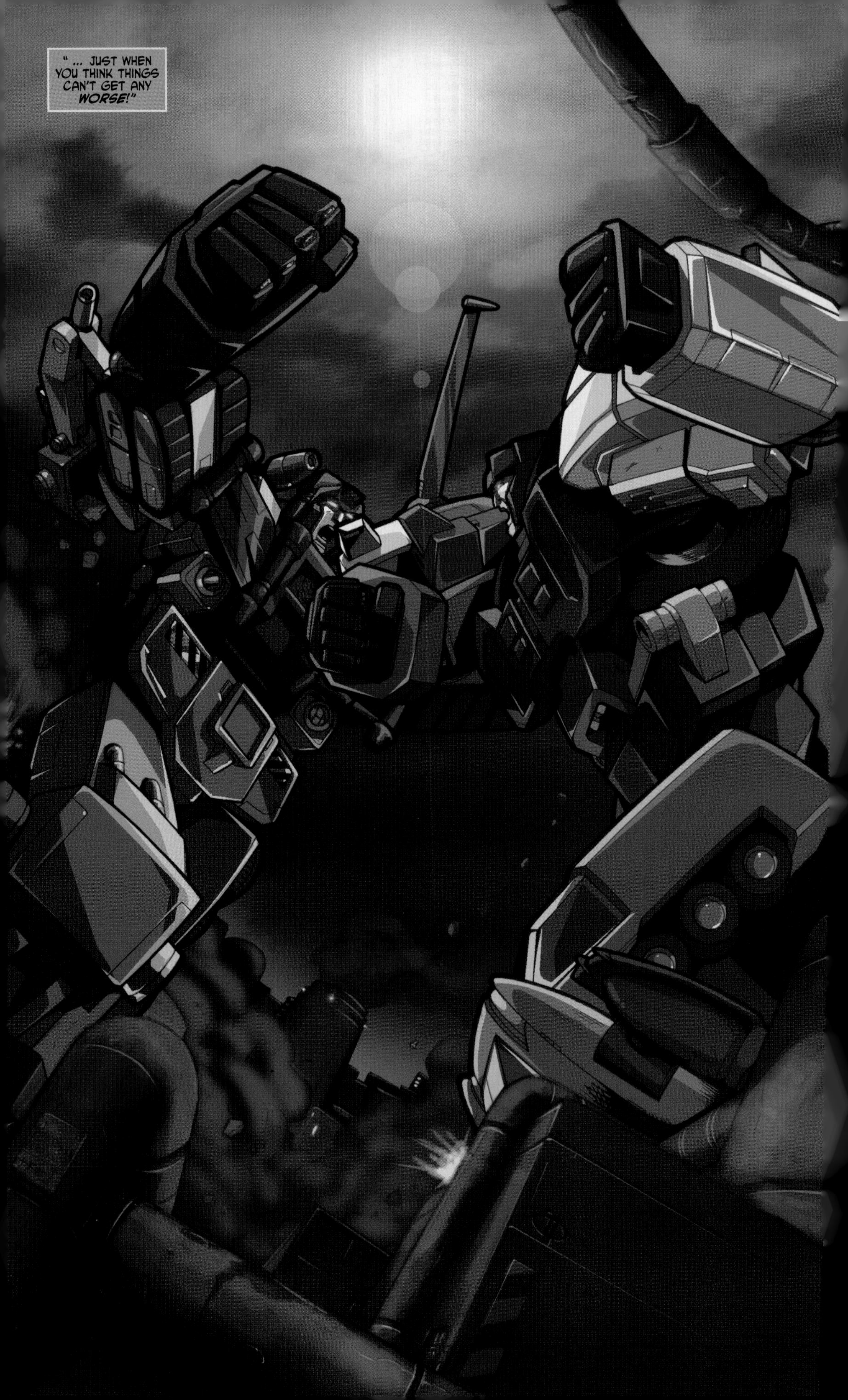
"... JUST WHEN YOU THINK THINGS CAN'T GET ANY *WORSE!*"

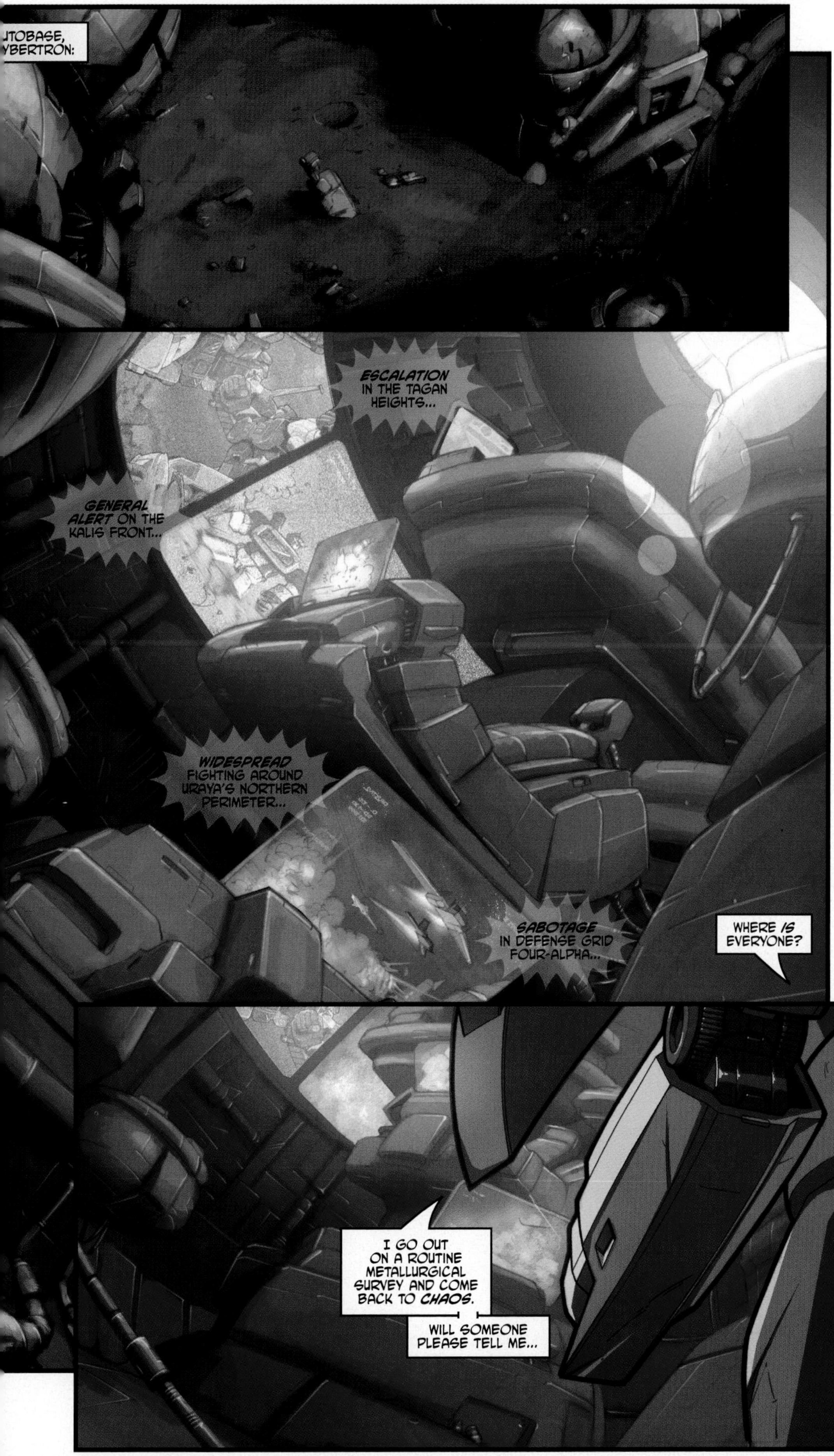

UTOBASE,
YBERTRON:
ESCALATION IN THE TAGAN HEIGHTS...
GENERAL ALERT ON THE KALIS FRONT...
WIDESPREAD FIGHTING AROUND URAYA'S NORTHERN PERIMETER...
SABOTAGE IN DEFENSE GRID FOUR-ALPHA...
WHERE IS EVERYONE?
I GO OUT ON A ROUTINE METALLURGICAL SURVEY AND COME BACK TO CHAOS.
WILL SOMEONE PLEASE TELL ME...

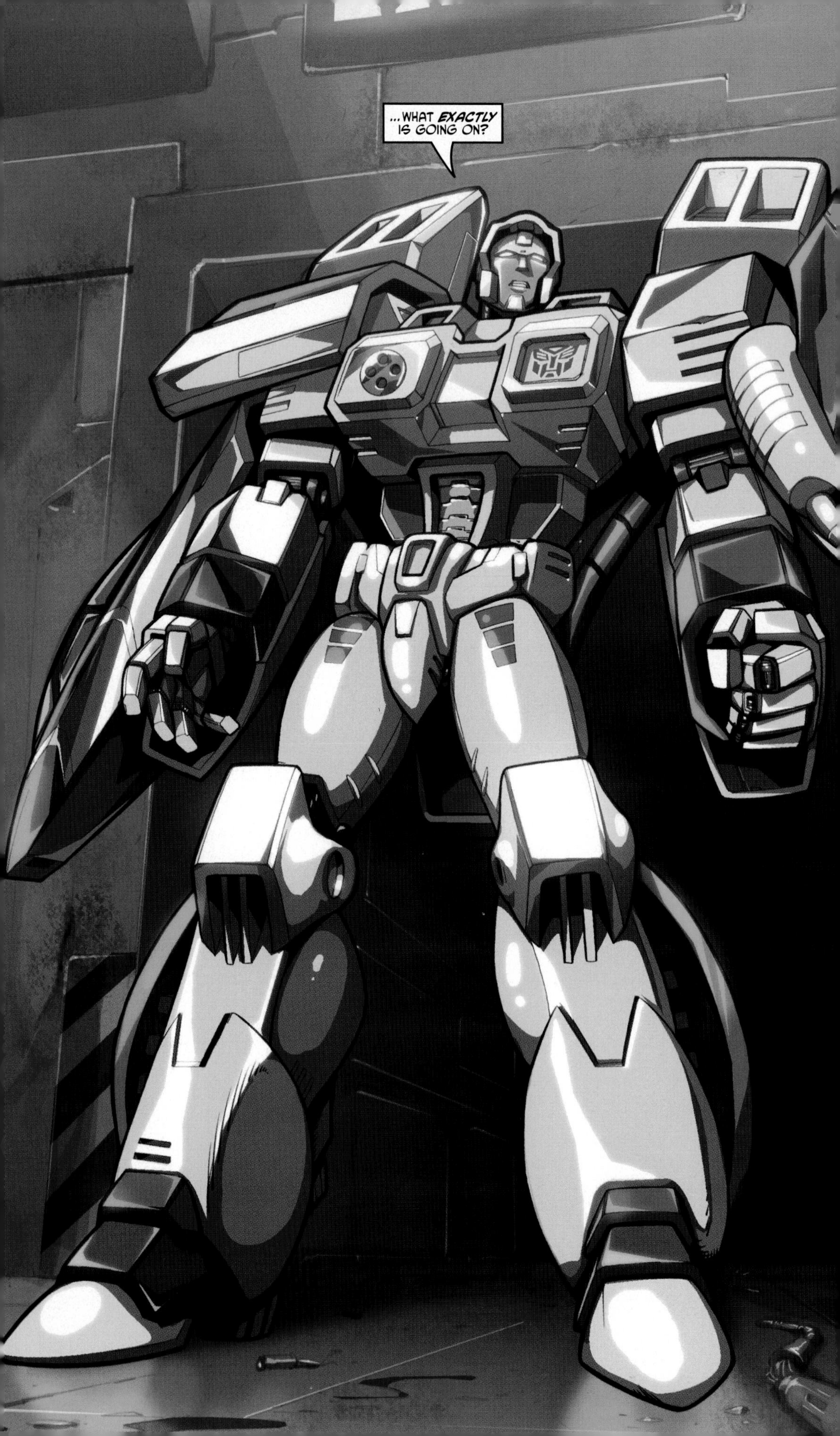
...WHAT *EXACTLY* IS GOING ON?

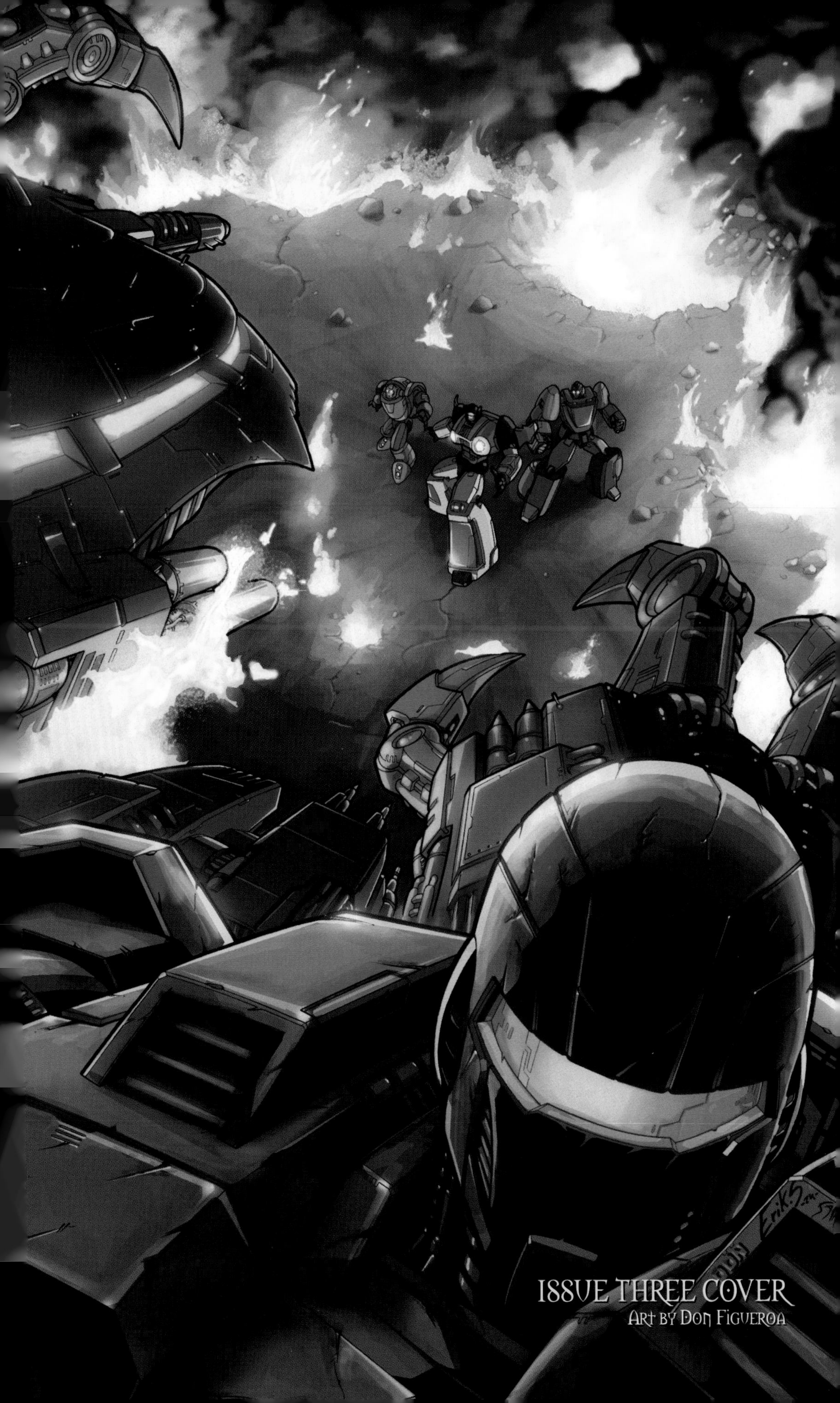

ISSUE THREE COVER
Art by Don Figueroa

TRANSFORMERS™ WAR WITHIN
THE DARK AGES

CHAPTER THREE
Devastation

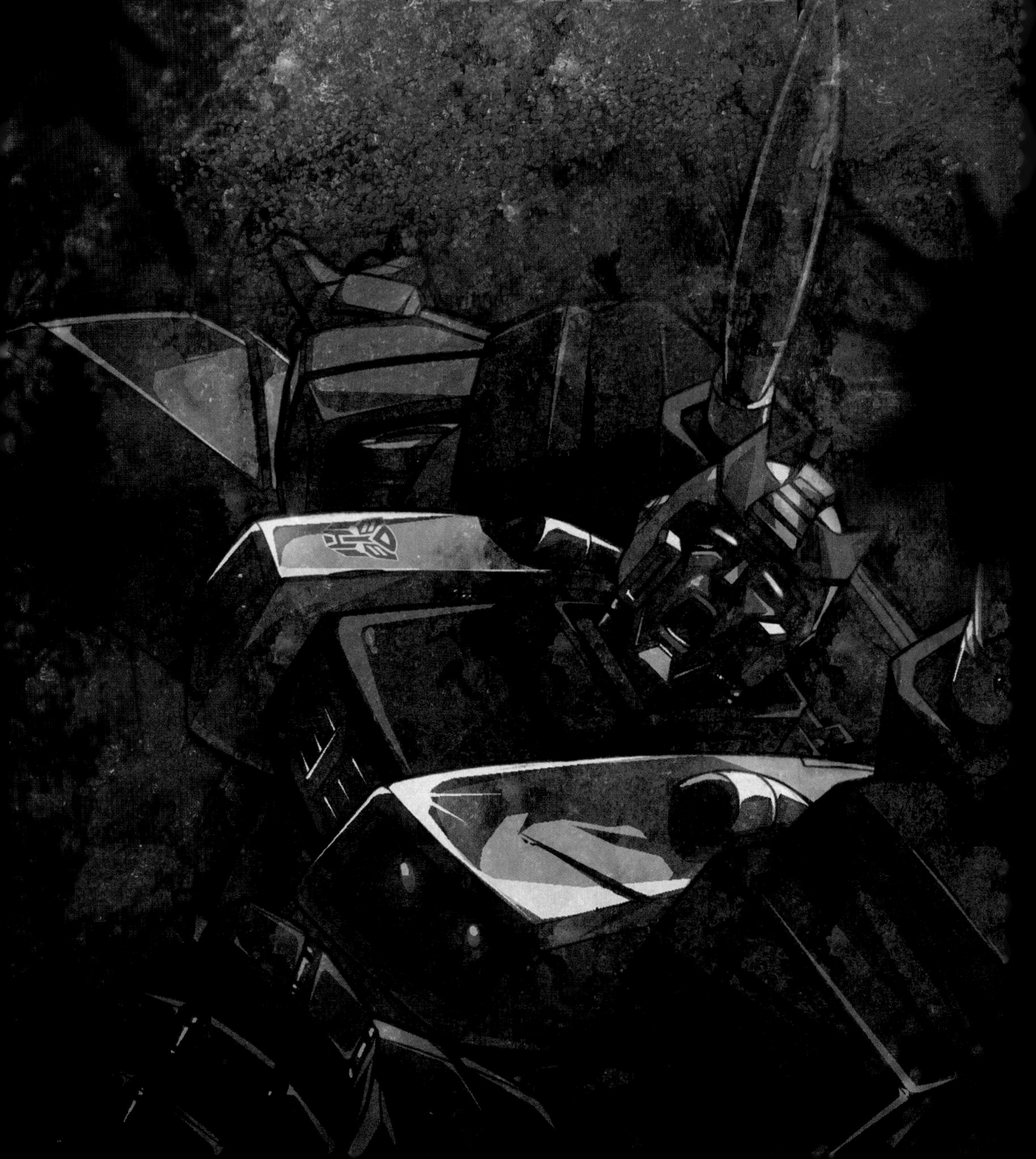

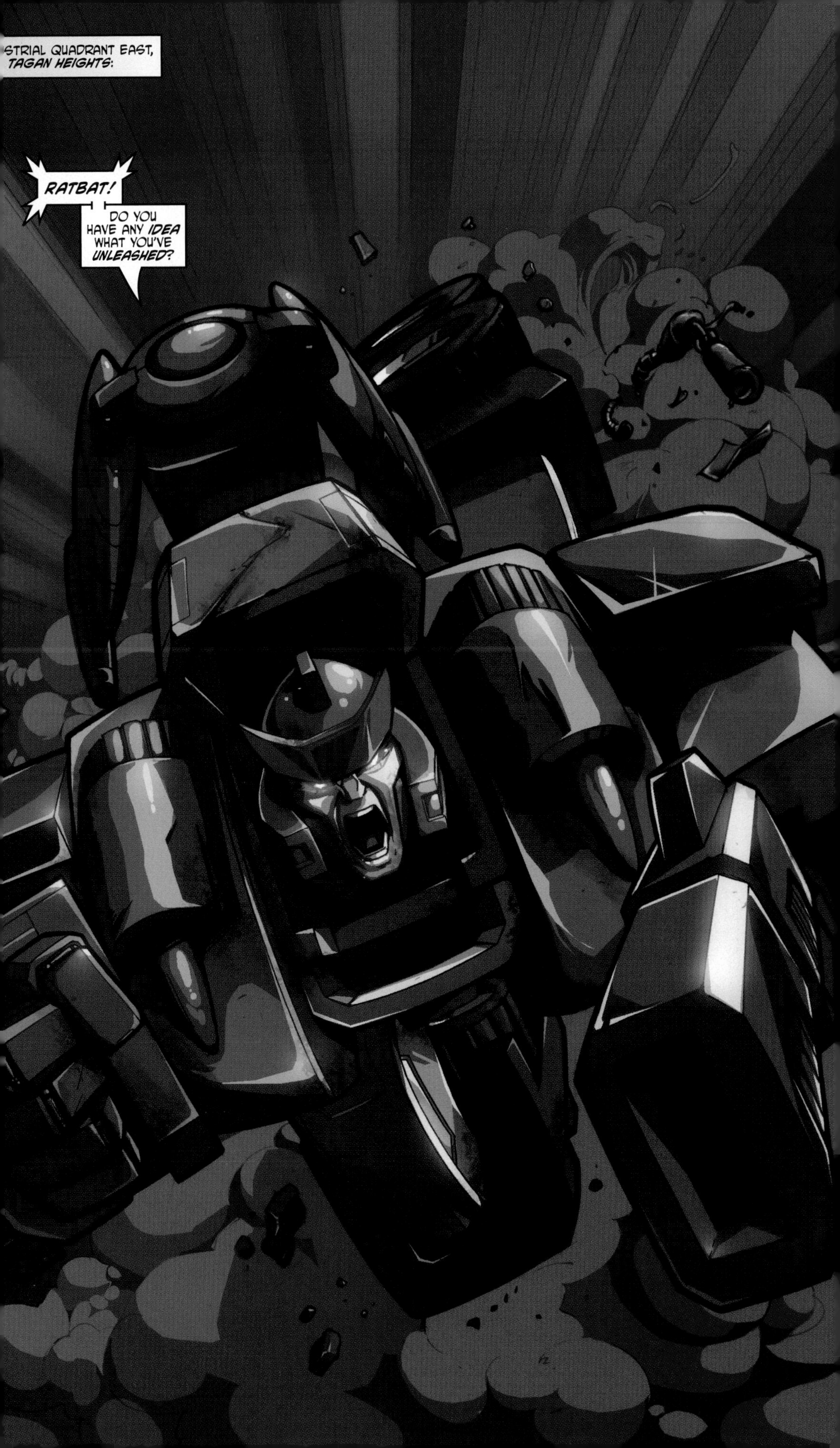
STRIAL QUADRANT EAST, TAGAN HEIGHTS:
RATBAT!
DO YOU HAVE ANY IDEA WHAT YOU'VE UNLEASHED?

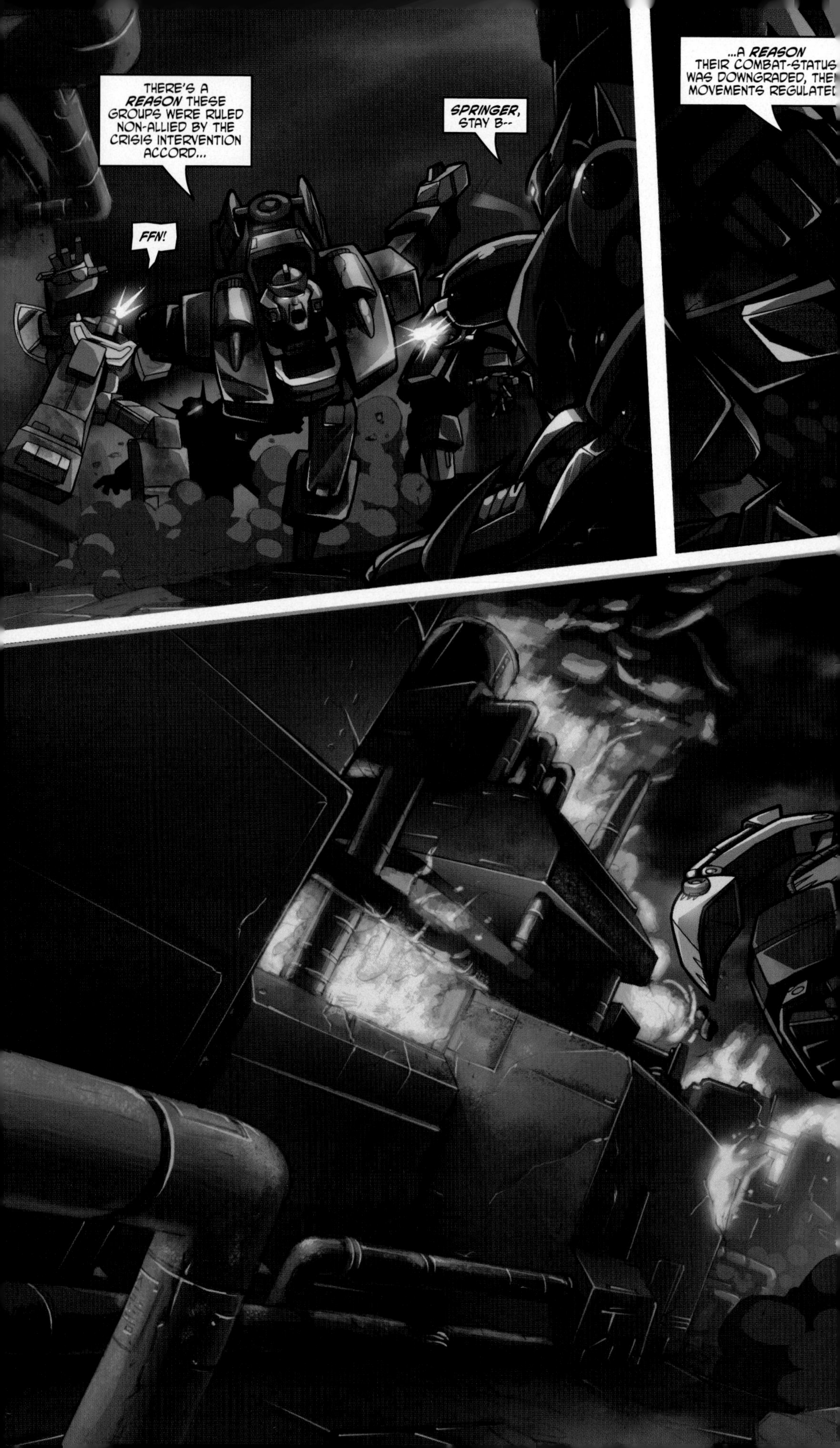
THERE'S A REASON THESE GROUPS WERE RULED NON-ALLIED BY THE CRISIS INTERVENTION ACCORD...
FFN!
SPRINGER, STAY B--
...A REASON THEIR COMBAT-STATUS WAS DOWNGRADED, THEI MOVEMENTS REGULATED

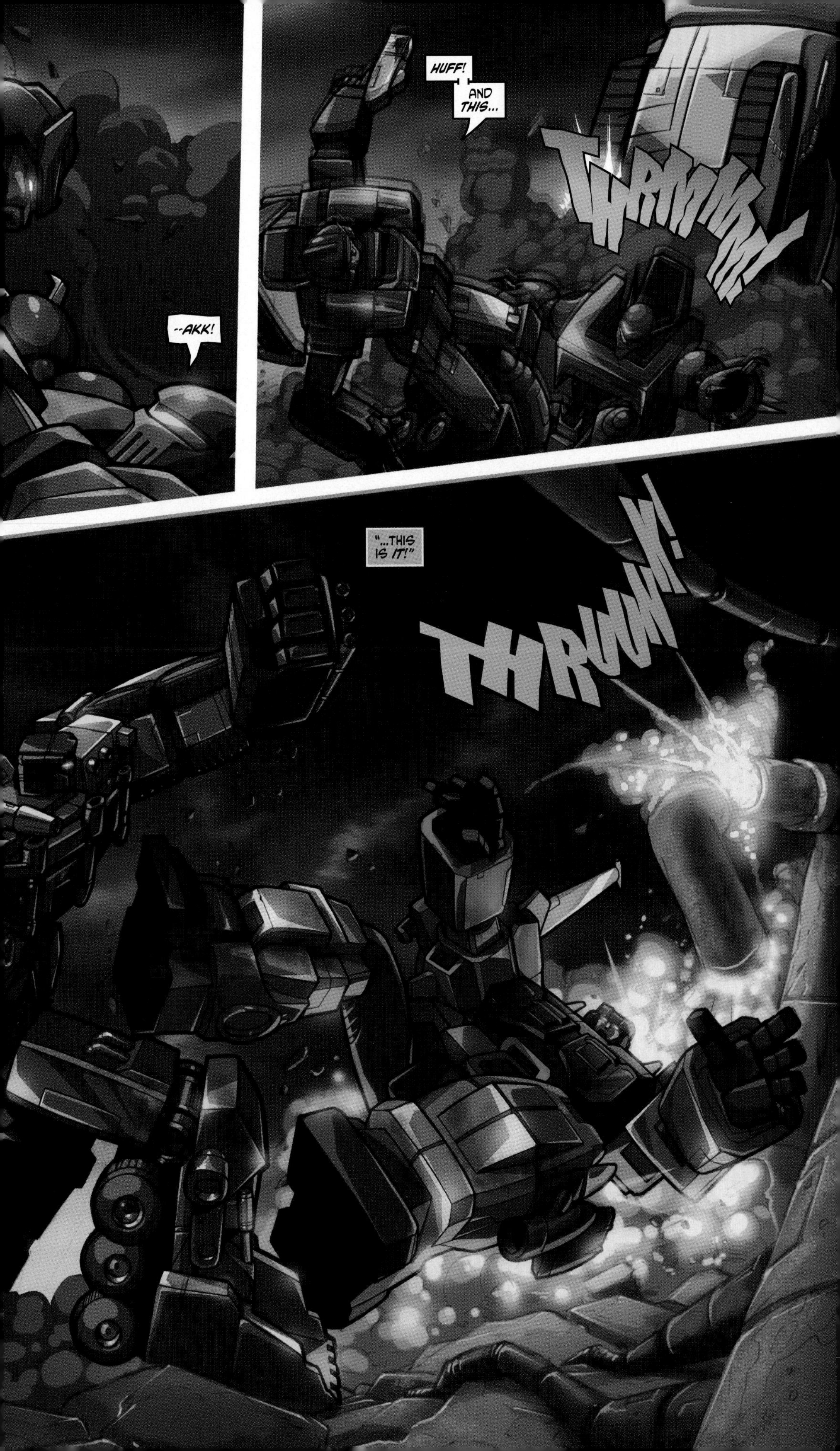
--AKK!
HUFF!
AND THIS...
THRMMM!
"...THIS IS IT!"
THRUUNK!

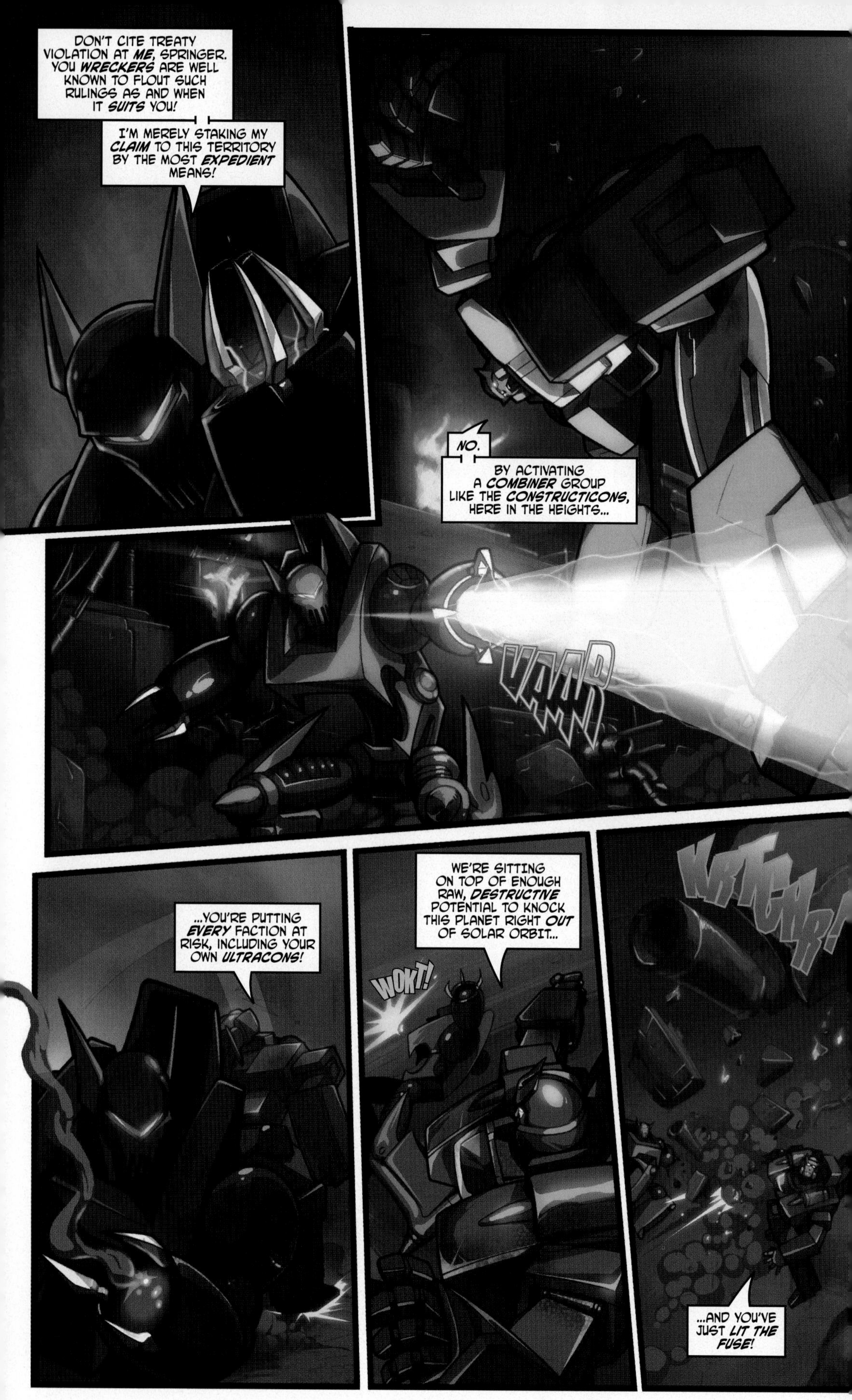
DON'T CITE TREATY VIOLATION AT *ME*, SPRINGER. YOU *WRECKERS* ARE WELL KNOWN TO FLOUT SUCH RULINGS AS AND WHEN IT *SUITS* YOU!
I'M MERELY STAKING MY *CLAIM* TO THIS TERRITORY BY THE MOST *EXPEDIENT* MEANS!
NO.
BY ACTIVATING A *COMBINER* GROUP LIKE THE *CONSTRUCTICONS*, HERE IN THE HEIGHTS...
VAAR
...YOU'RE PUTTING *EVERY* FACTION AT RISK, INCLUDING YOUR OWN *ULTRACONS*!
WE'RE SITTING ON TOP OF ENOUGH RAW, *DESTRUCTIVE* POTENTIAL TO KNOCK THIS PLANET RIGHT *OUT* OF SOLAR ORBIT...
WOKT!
KRTCHR!
...AND YOU'VE JUST *LIT THE FUSE*!

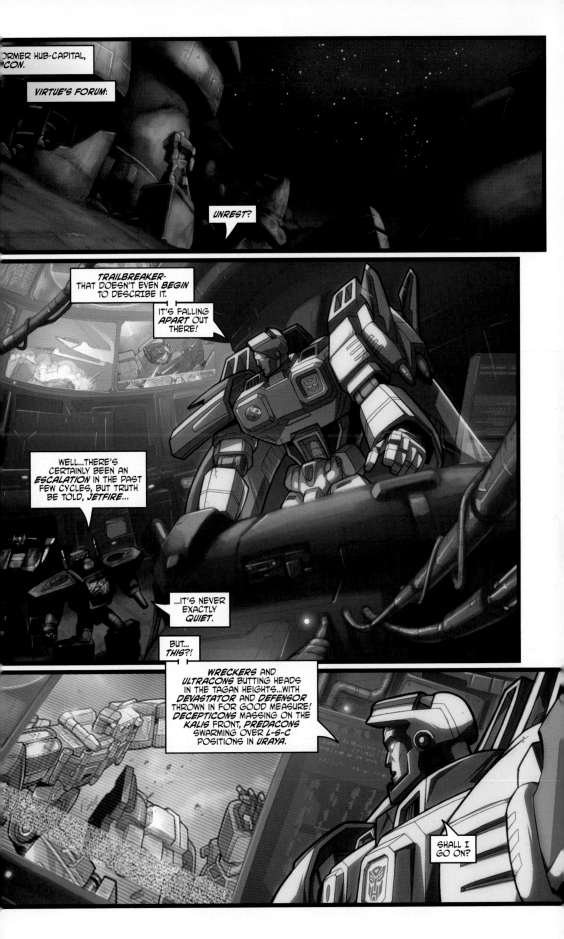

ORMER HUB-CAPITAL,
ICON.

VIRTUE'S FORUM:

UNREST?

TRAILBREAKER-
THAT DOESN'T EVEN *BEGIN*
TO DESCRIBE IT.

IT'S FALLING
APART OUT
THERE!

WELL...THERE'S
CERTAINLY BEEN AN
ESCALATION IN THE PAST
FEW CYCLES, BUT TRUTH
BE TOLD, *JETFIRE*...

...IT'S NEVER
EXACTLY
QUIET.

BUT...
THIS?!

WRECKERS AND
ULTRACONS BUTTING HEADS
IN THE TAGAN HEIGHTS...WITH
DEVASTATOR AND *DEFENSOR*
THROWN IN FOR GOOD MEASURE!
DECEPTICONS MASSING ON THE
KALIS FRONT, *PREDACONS*
SWARMING OVER *L-S-C*
POSITIONS IN *URAYA.*

SHALL I
GO ON?

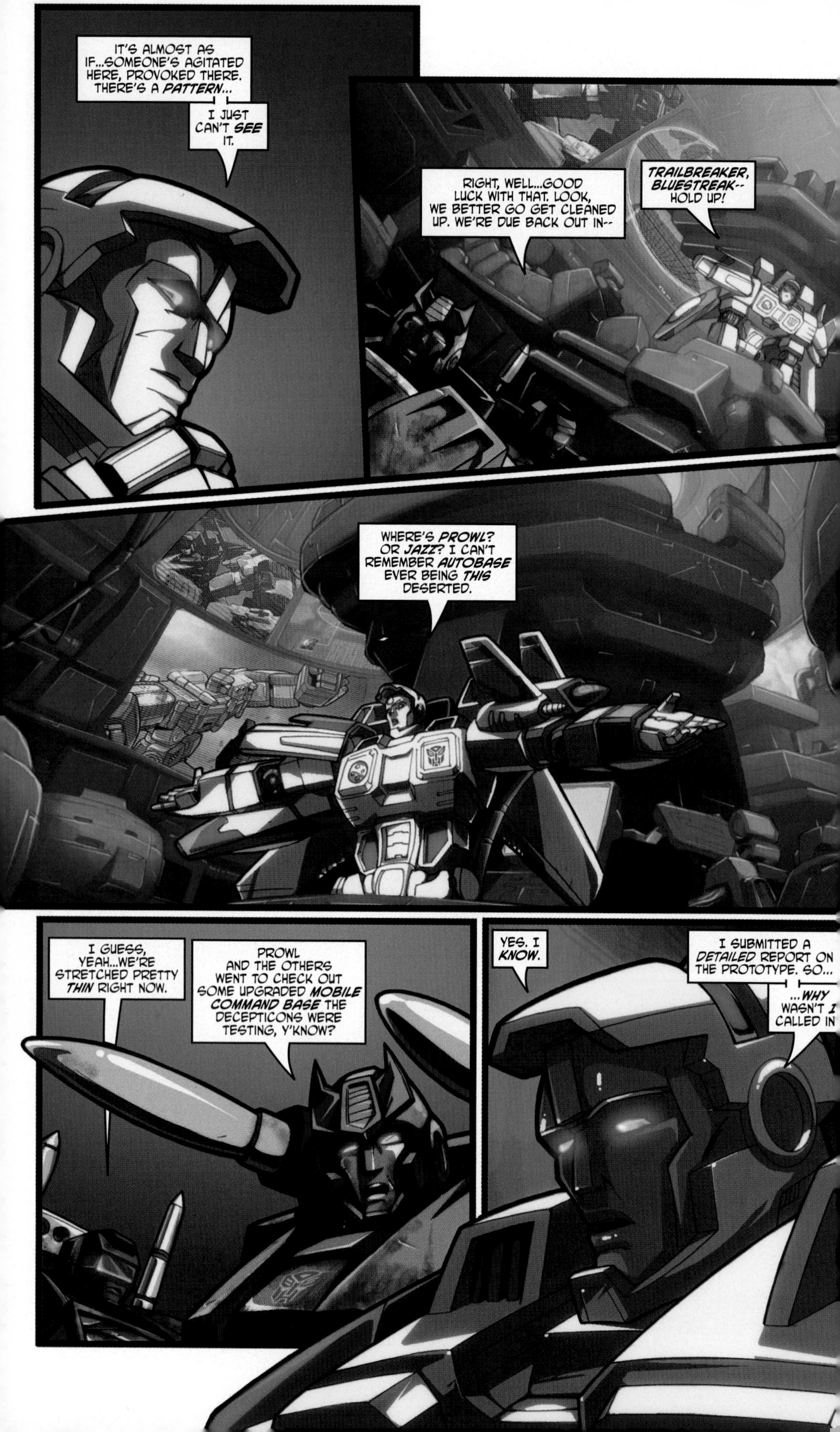
IT'S ALMOST AS IF...SOMEONE'S AGITATED HERE, PROVOKED THERE. THERE'S A *PATTERN*...
I JUST CAN'T *SEE* IT.
RIGHT, WELL...GOOD LUCK WITH THAT. LOOK, WE BETTER GO GET CLEANED UP. WE'RE DUE BACK OUT IN--
TRAILBREAKER, BLUESTREAK-- HOLD UP!
WHERE'S *PROWL*? OR *JAZZ*? I CAN'T REMEMBER *AUTOBASE* EVER BEING *THIS* DESERTED.
I GUESS, YEAH...WE'RE STRETCHED PRETTY *THIN* RIGHT NOW.
PROWL AND THE OTHERS WENT TO CHECK OUT SOME UPGRADED *MOBILE COMMAND BASE* THE DECEPTICONS WERE TESTING, Y'KNOW?
YES. I *KNOW*.
I SUBMITTED A *DETAILED* REPORT ON THE PROTOTYPE. SO...
...*WHY* WASN'T *I* CALLED IN

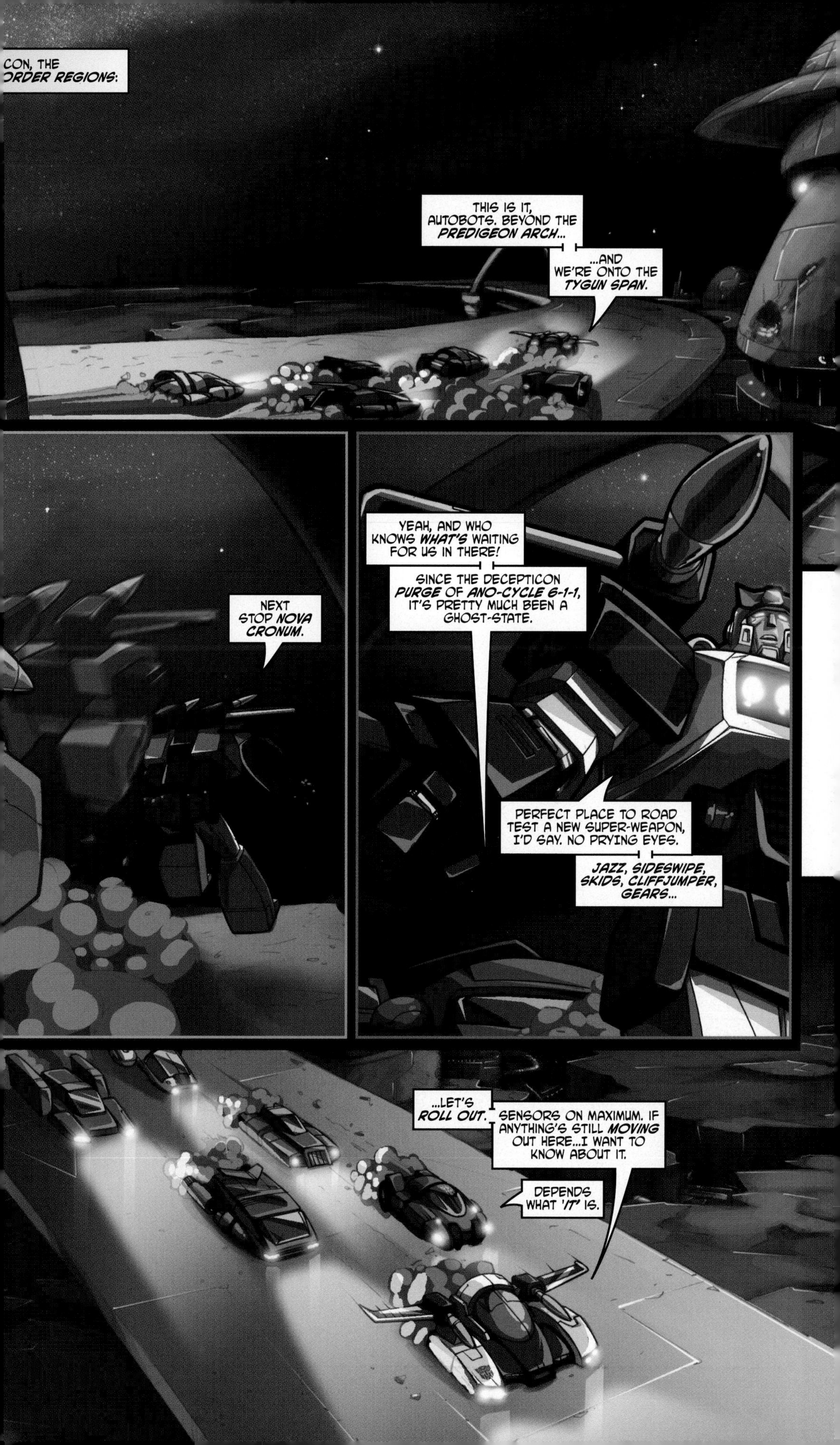
CON, THE
ORDER REGIONS:
THIS IS IT, AUTOBOTS. BEYOND THE PREDIGEON ARCH...
...AND WE'RE ONTO THE TYGUN SPAN.
NEXT STOP NOVA CRONUM.
YEAH, AND WHO KNOWS WHAT'S WAITING FOR US IN THERE!
SINCE THE DECEPTICON PURGE OF ANO-CYCLE 6-1-1, IT'S PRETTY MUCH BEEN A GHOST-STATE.
PERFECT PLACE TO ROAD TEST A NEW SUPER-WEAPON, I'D SAY. NO PRYING EYES.
JAZZ, SIDESWIPE, SKIDS, CLIFFJUMPER, GEARS...
...LET'S ROLL OUT.
SENSORS ON MAXIMUM. IF ANYTHING'S STILL MOVING OUT HERE...I WANT TO KNOW ABOUT IT.
DEPENDS WHAT 'IT' IS.

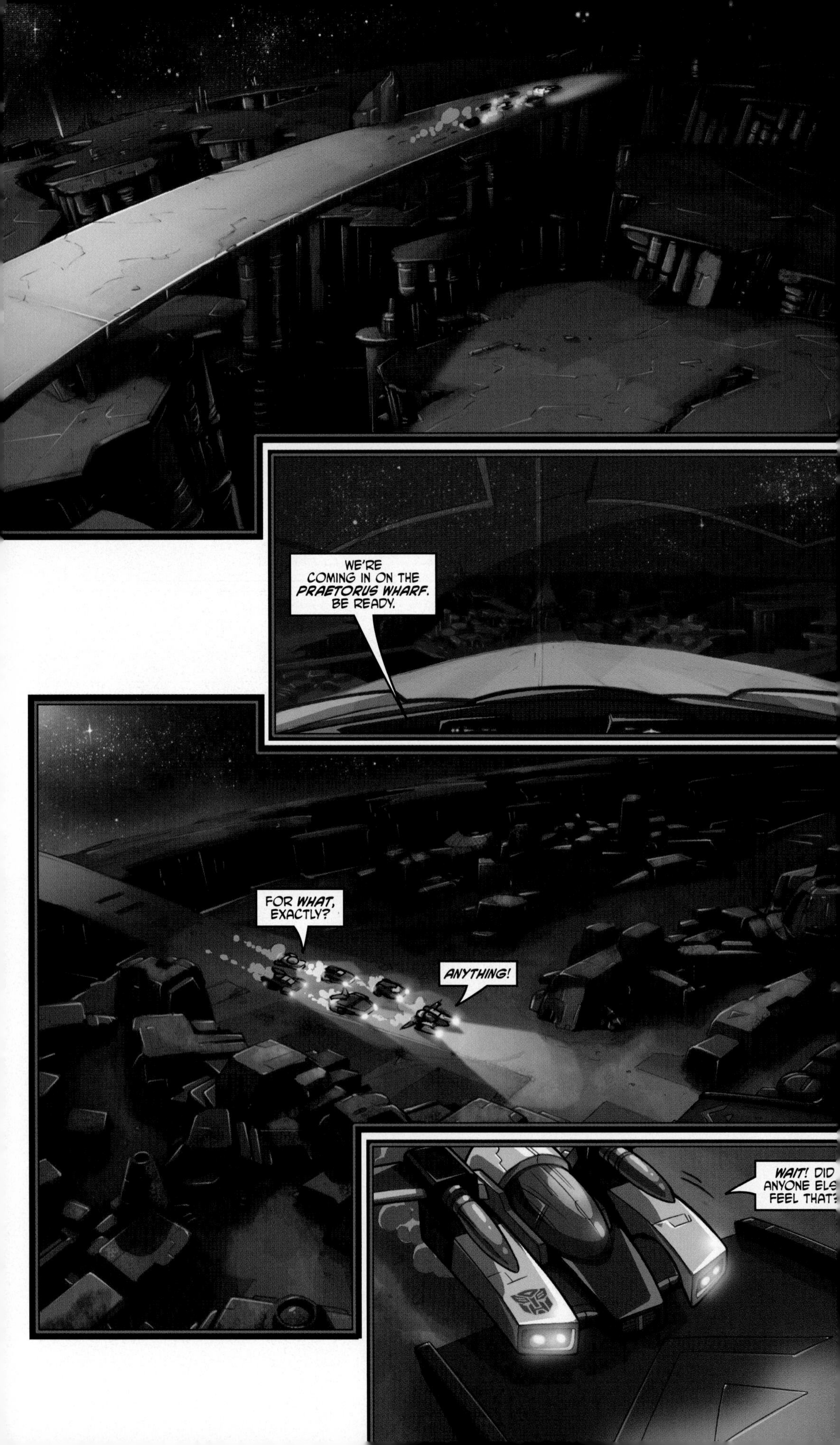
WE'RE COMING IN ON THE PRAETORUS WHARF. BE READY.
FOR WHAT, EXACTLY?
ANYTHING!
WAIT! DID ANYONE ELS FEEL THAT?

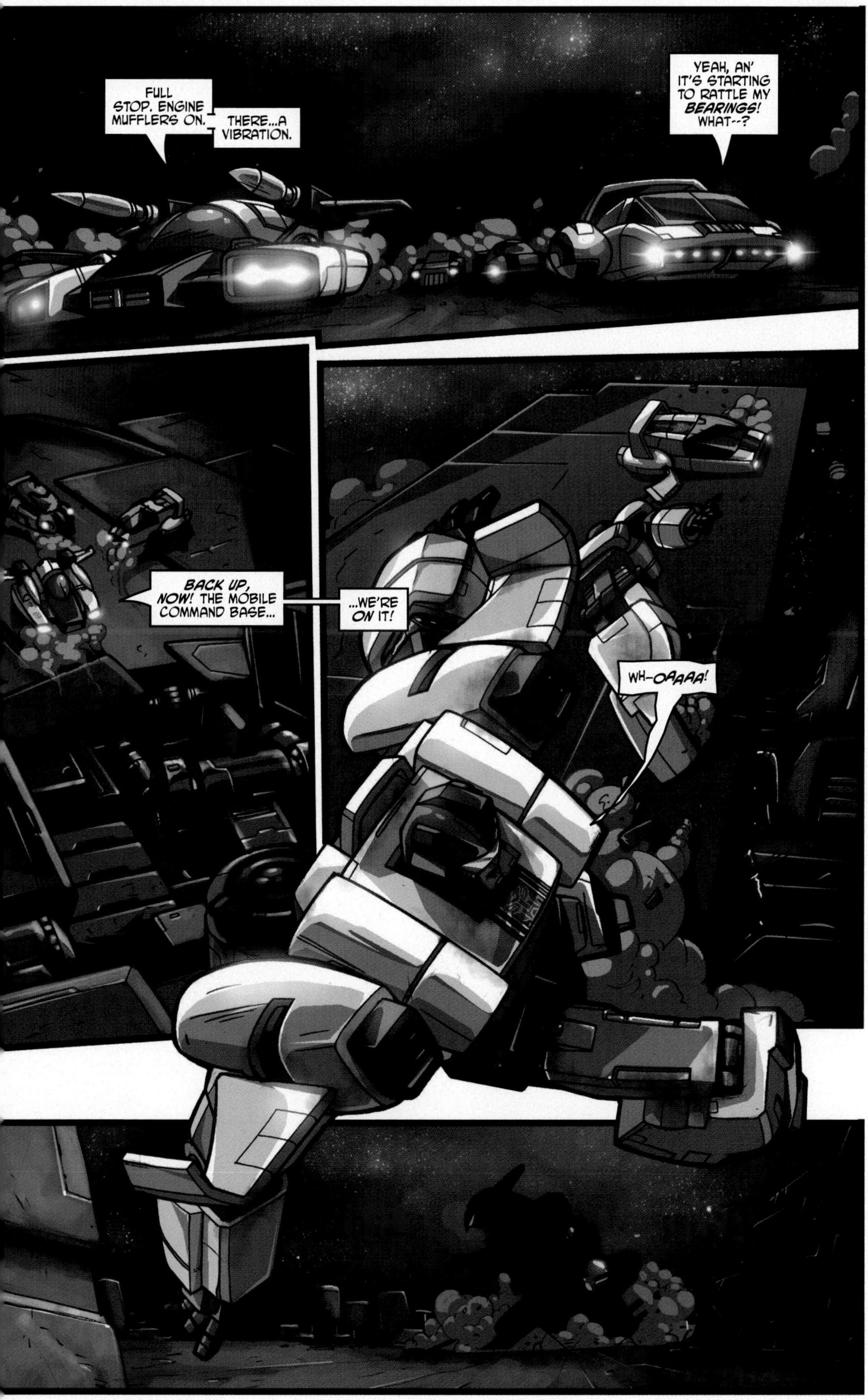
FULL STOP. ENGINE MUFFLERS ON.
THERE...A VIBRATION.
YEAH, AN' IT'S STARTING TO RATTLE MY *BEARINGS!* WHAT--?
BACK UP, NOW! THE MOBILE COMMAND BASE...
...WE'RE *ON* IT!
WH-*OAAAA!*

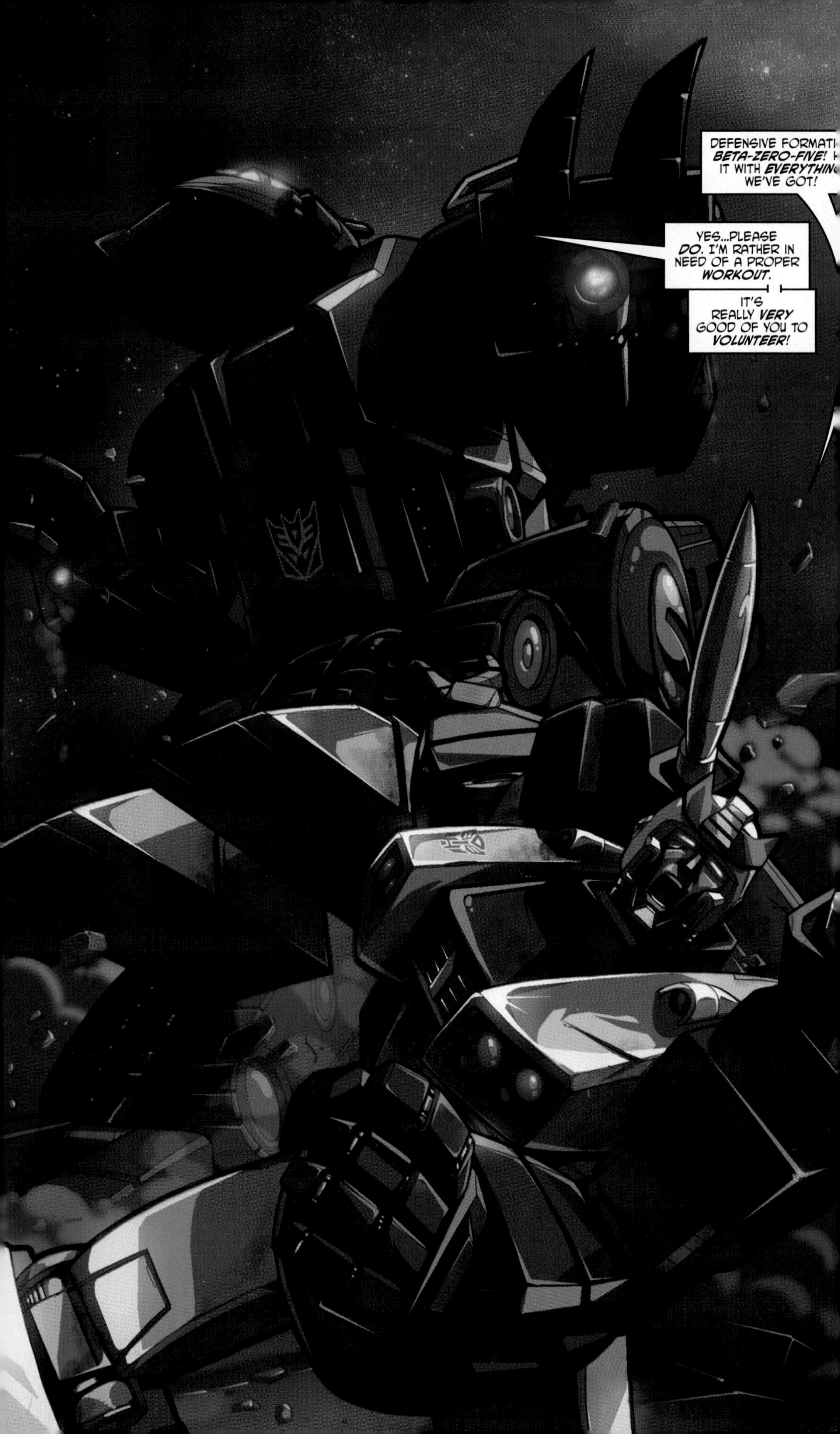
DEFENSIVE FORMATI BETA-ZERO-FIVE! H IT WITH EVERYTHIN WE'VE GOT!
YES...PLEASE DO. I'M RATHER IN NEED OF A PROPER WORKOUT.
IT'S REALLY VERY GOOD OF YOU TO VOLUNTEER!

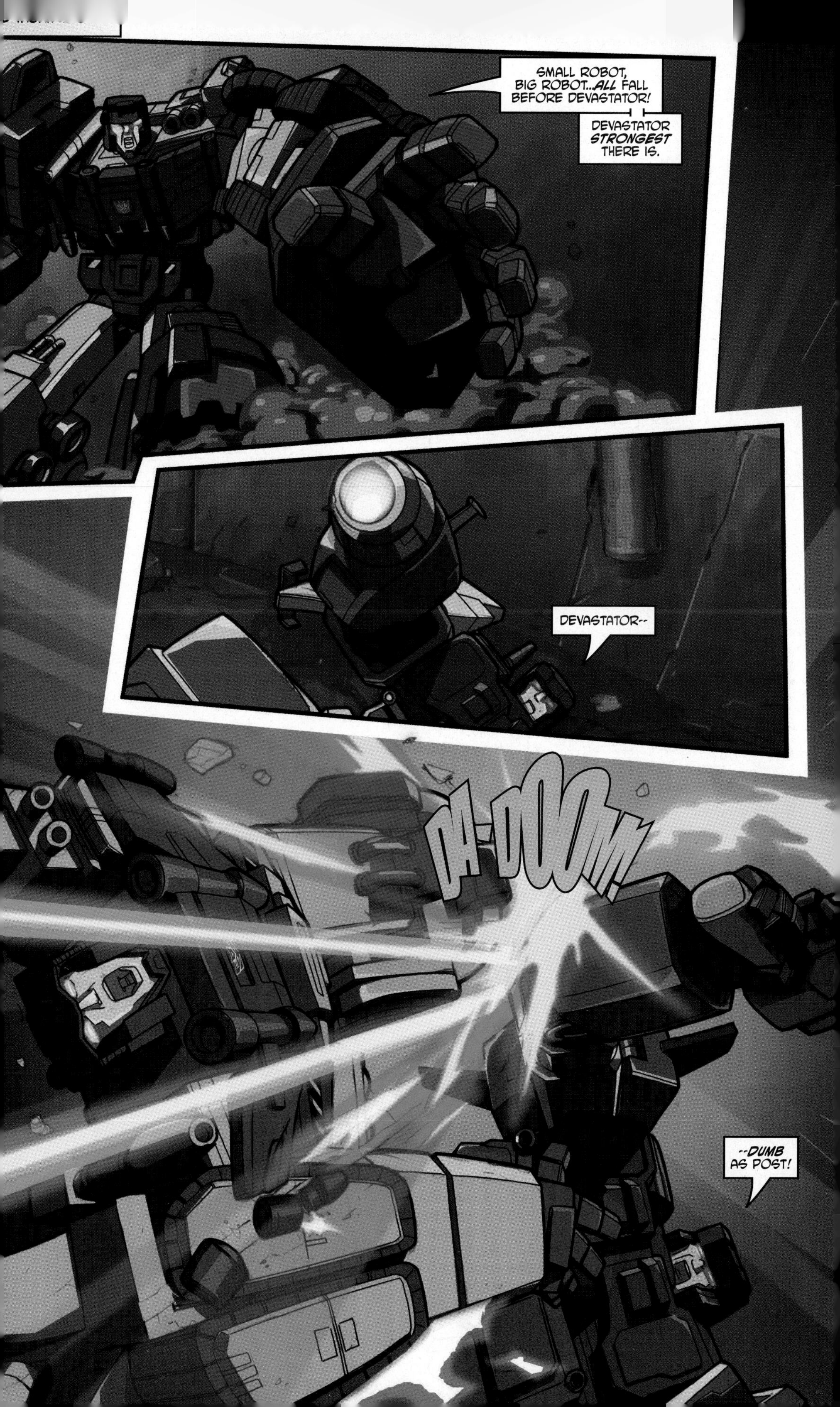

SMALL ROBOT, BIG ROBOT...ALL FALL BEFORE DEVASTATOR!
DEVASTATOR STRONGEST THERE IS.
DEVASTATOR--
DA-DOOM!
--DUMB AS POST!

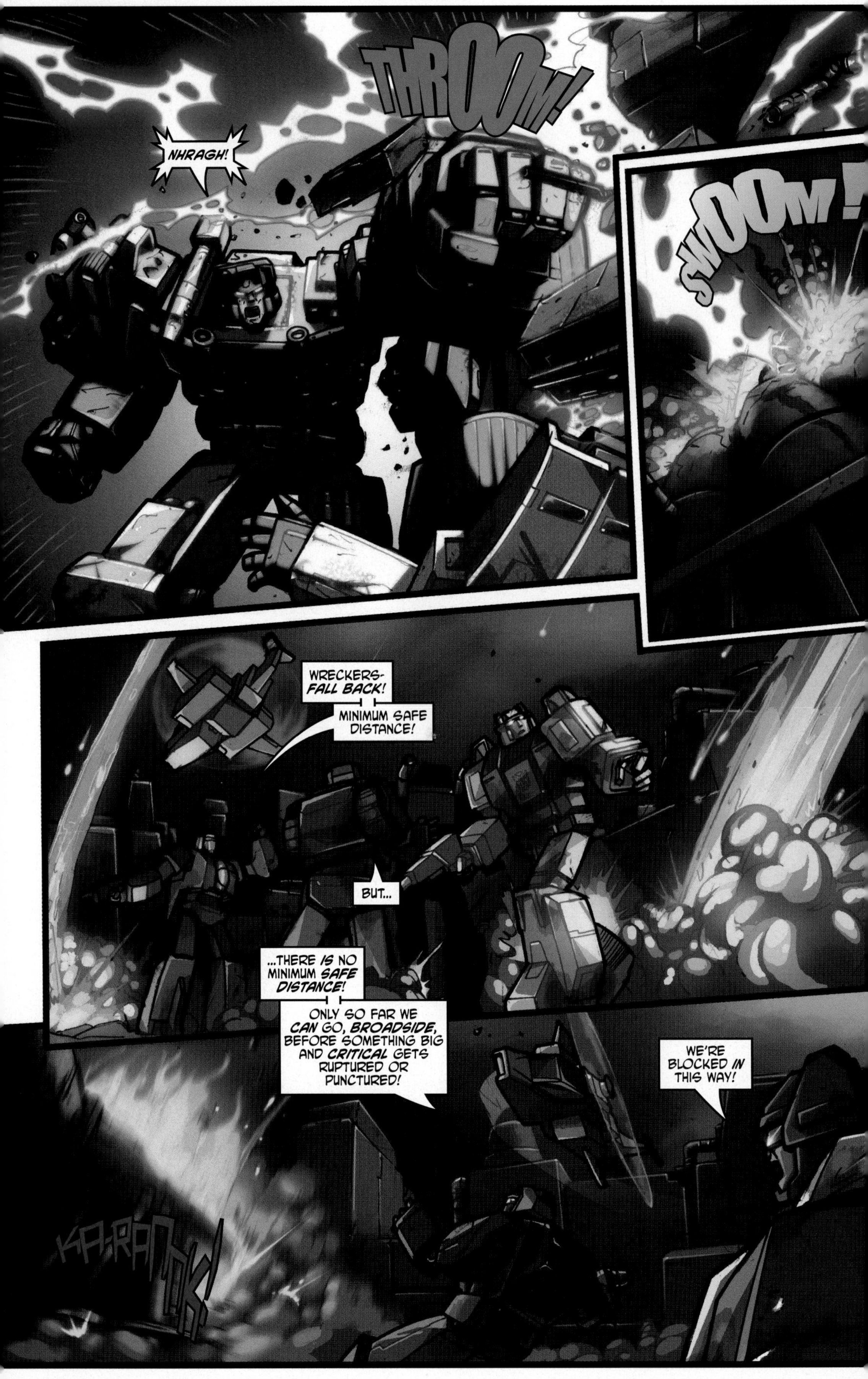
THROOM!
NHRAGH!
SWOOM!
WRECKERS-
FALL BACK!
MINIMUM SAFE DISTANCE!
BUT...
...THERE IS NO MINIMUM SAFE DISTANCE!
ONLY SO FAR WE CAN GO, BROADSIDE, BEFORE SOMETHING BIG AND CRITICAL GETS RUPTURED OR PUNCTURED!
WE'RE BLOCKED IN THIS WAY!
KA-RANK!

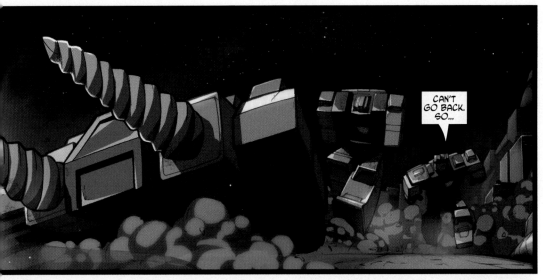

CAN'T GO BACK. SO...

...I GUESS WE GO UNDER!

I HATE THIS, ROADBUSTER-- I HATE RUNNING OUT ON A FIGHT!

UH-HUH. BUT THIS IS OUT OF OUR HANDS NOW...

"...OUT OF OUR LEAGUE!"

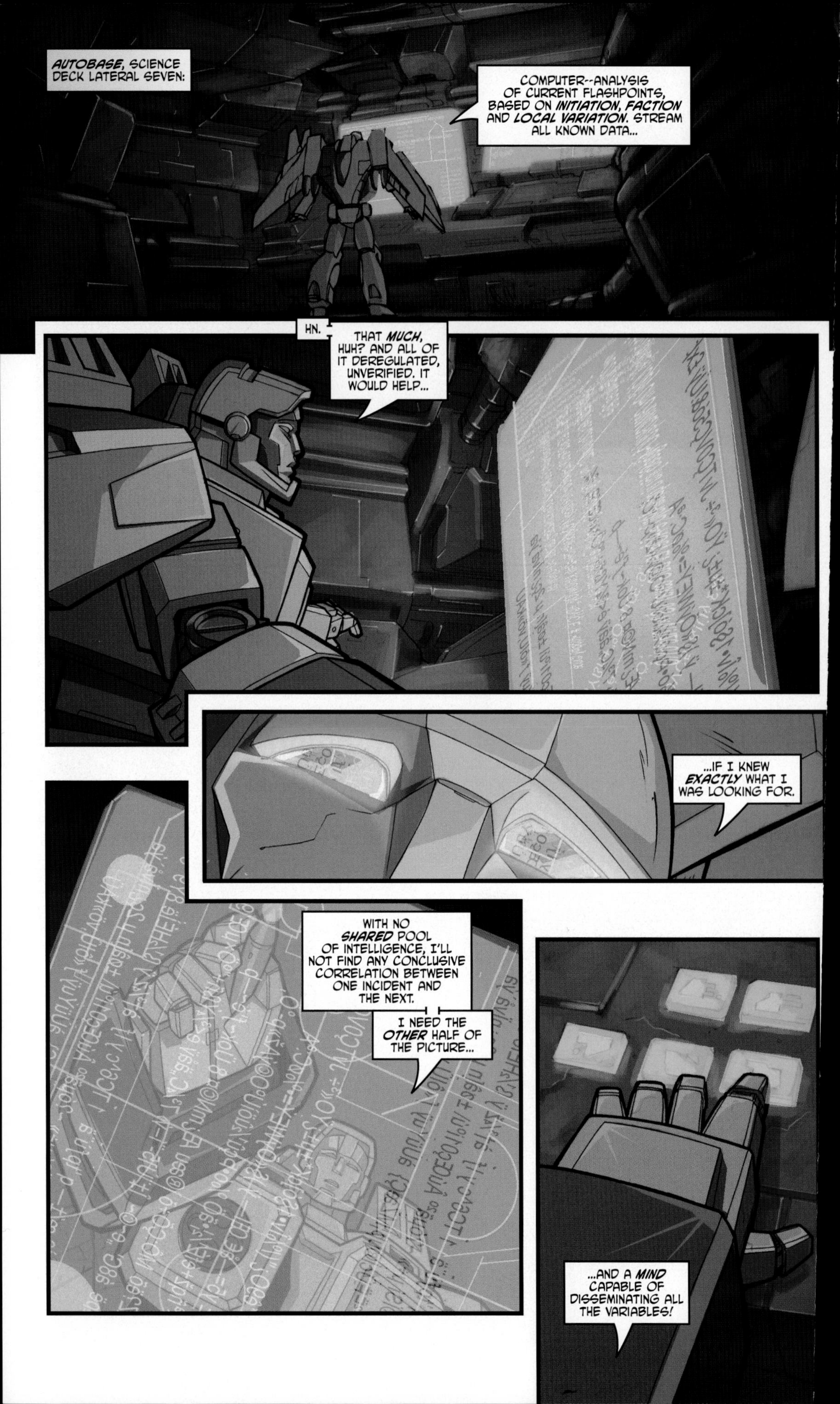
AUTOBASE, SCIENCE DECK LATERAL SEVEN:
COMPUTER--ANALYSIS OF CURRENT FLASHPOINTS, BASED ON INITIATION, FACTION AND LOCAL VARIATION. STREAM ALL KNOWN DATA...
HN.
THAT MUCH, HUH? AND ALL OF IT DEREGULATED, UNVERIFIED. IT WOULD HELP...
...IF I KNEW EXACTLY WHAT I WAS LOOKING FOR.
WITH NO SHARED POOL OF INTELLIGENCE, I'LL NOT FIND ANY CONCLUSIVE CORRELATION BETWEEN ONE INCIDENT AND THE NEXT.
I NEED THE OTHER HALF OF THE PICTURE...
...AND A MIND CAPABLE OF DISSEMINATING ALL THE VARIABLES!

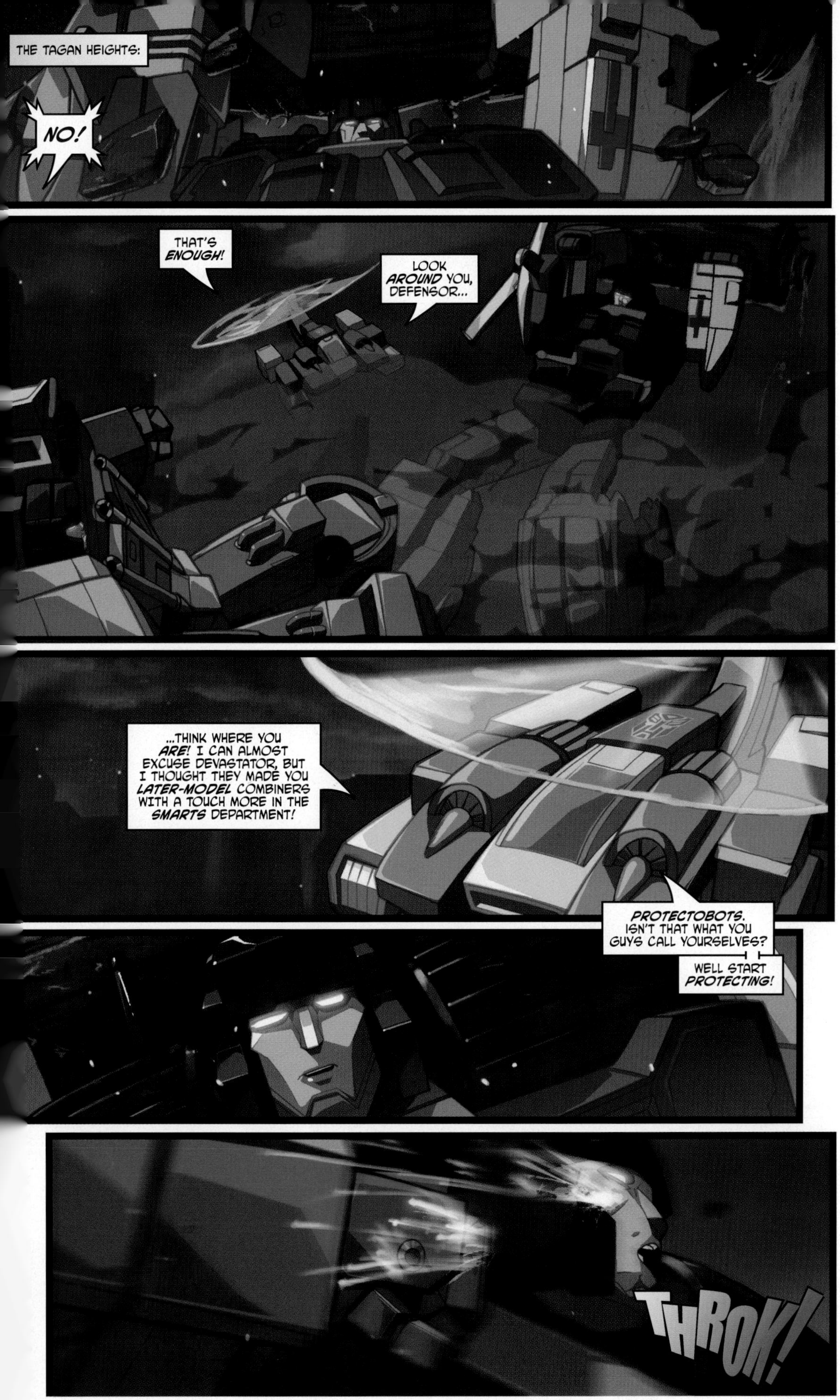
THE TAGAN HEIGHTS:
NO!
THAT'S ENOUGH!
LOOK AROUND YOU, DEFENSOR...
...THINK WHERE YOU ARE! I CAN ALMOST EXCUSE DEVASTATOR, BUT I THOUGHT THEY MADE YOU LATER-MODEL COMBINERS WITH A TOUCH MORE IN THE SMARTS DEPARTMENT!
PROTECTOBOTS. ISN'T THAT WHAT YOU GUYS CALL YOURSELVES?
WELL START PROTECTING!
THROK!

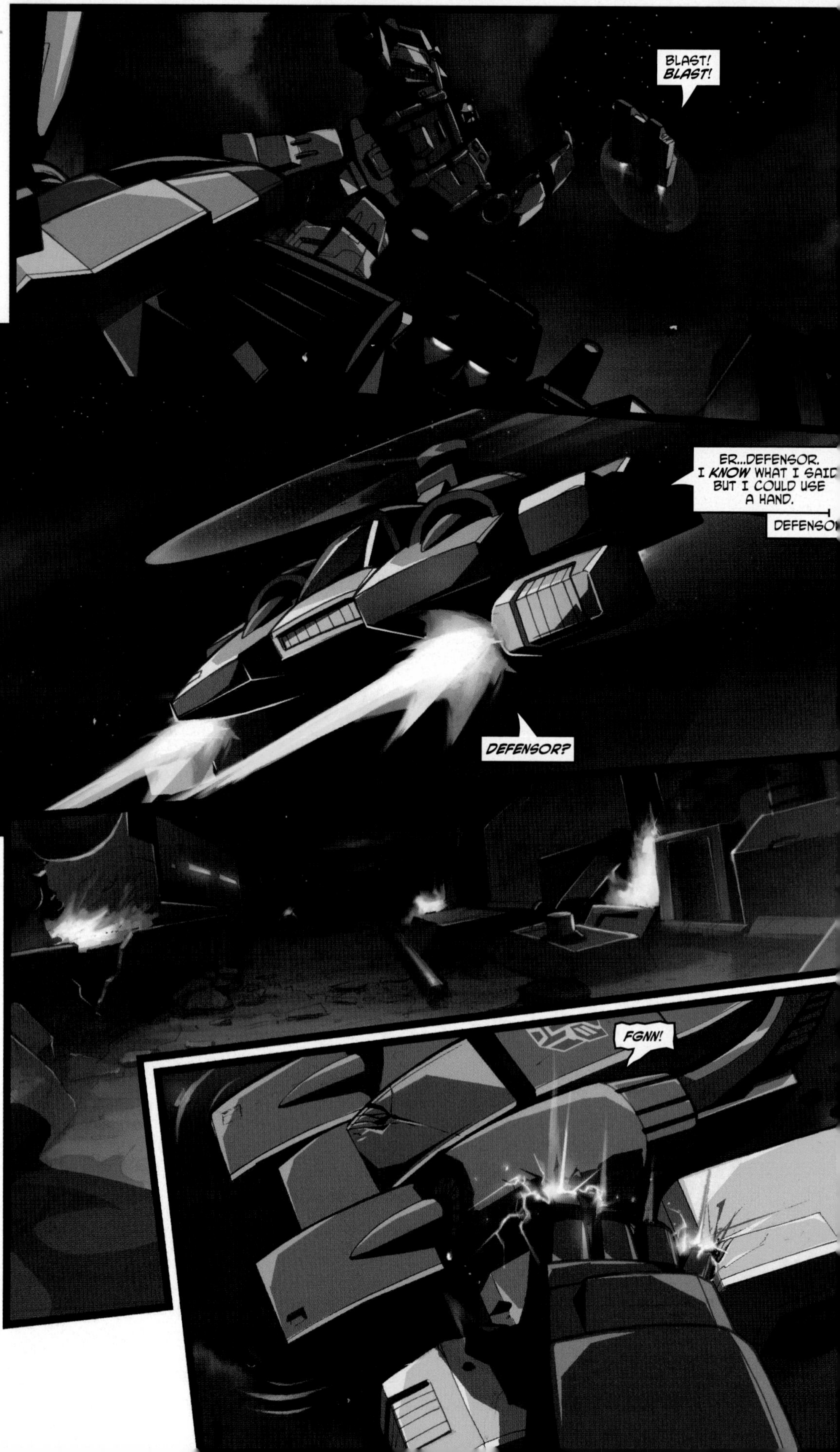
BLAST! BLAST!
ER...DEFENSOR. I KNOW WHAT I SAID BUT I COULD USE A HAND.
DEFENSOR?
FGNN!

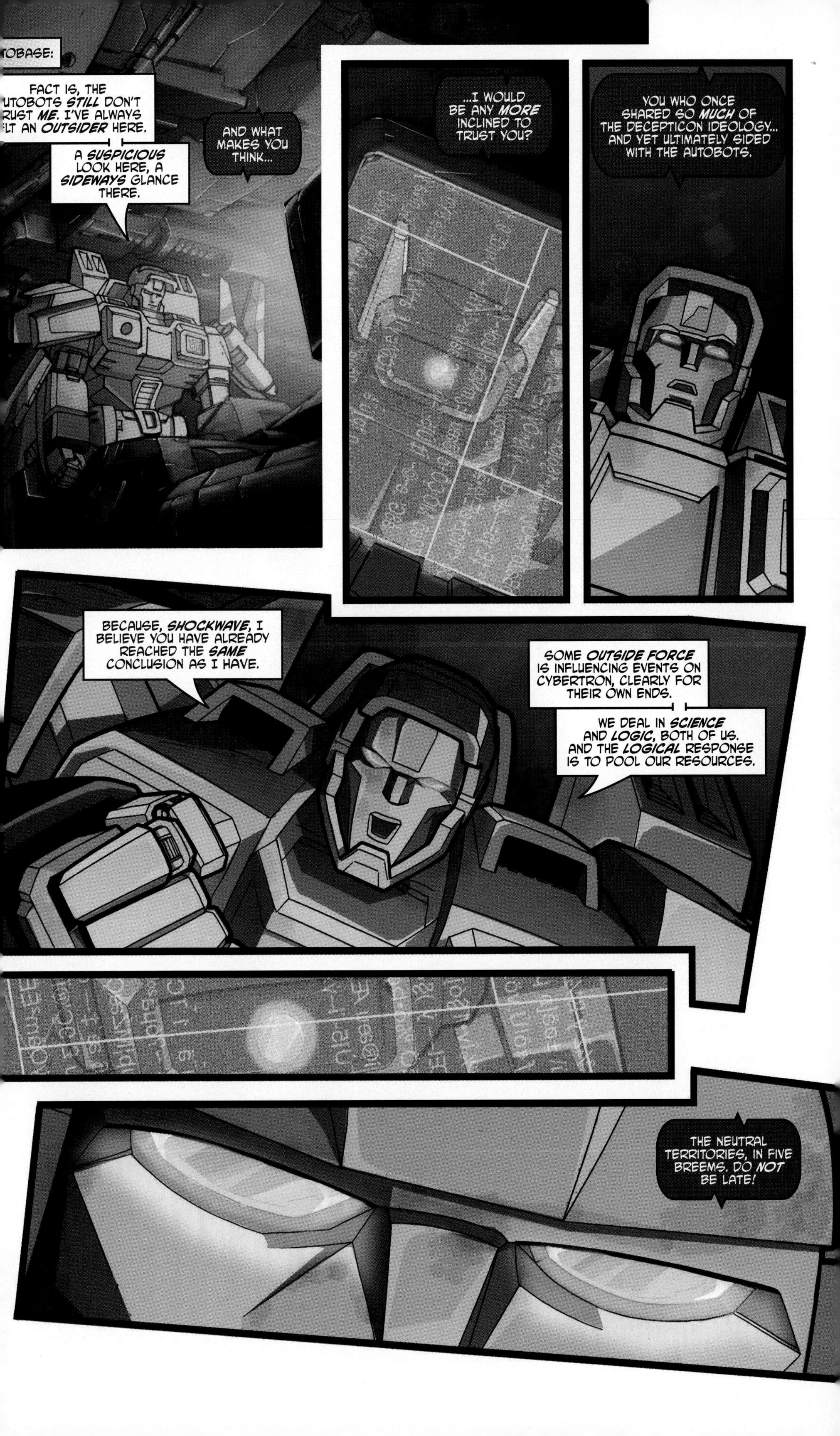

TOBASE:
FACT IS, THE UTOBOTS STILL DON'T RUST ME. I'VE ALWAYS ELT AN OUTSIDER HERE.
A SUSPICIOUS LOOK HERE, A SIDEWAYS GLANCE THERE.
AND WHAT MAKES YOU THINK...
...I WOULD BE ANY MORE INCLINED TO TRUST YOU?
YOU WHO ONCE SHARED SO MUCH OF THE DECEPTICON IDEOLOGY... AND YET ULTIMATELY SIDED WITH THE AUTOBOTS.
BECAUSE, SHOCKWAVE, I BELIEVE YOU HAVE ALREADY REACHED THE SAME CONCLUSION AS I HAVE.
SOME OUTSIDE FORCE IS INFLUENCING EVENTS ON CYBERTRON, CLEARLY FOR THEIR OWN ENDS.
WE DEAL IN SCIENCE AND LOGIC, BOTH OF US. AND THE LOGICAL RESPONSE IS TO POOL OUR RESOURCES.
THE NEUTRAL TERRITORIES, IN FIVE BREEMS. DO NOT BE LATE!

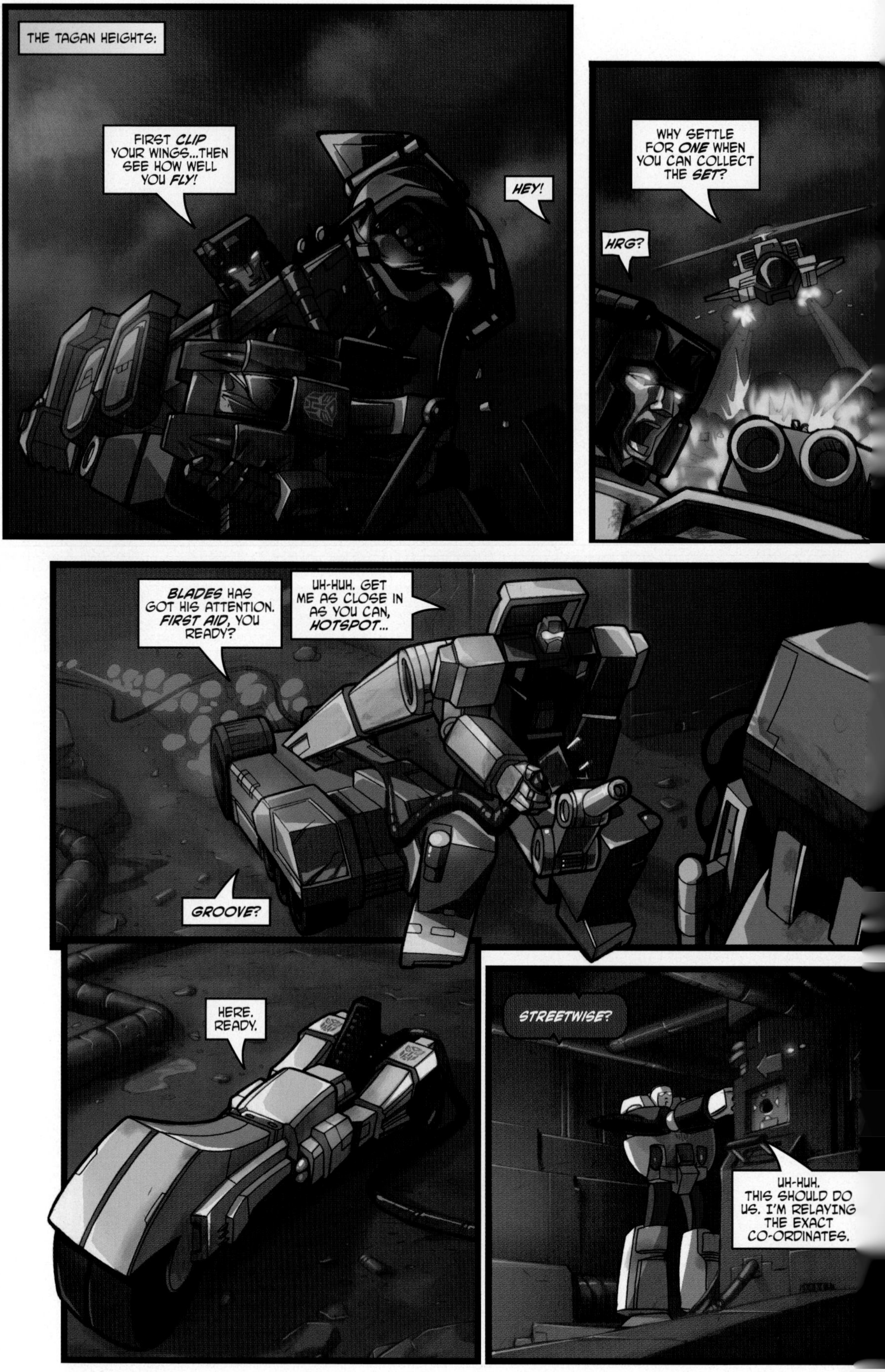
THE TAGAN HEIGHTS:
FIRST CLIP YOUR WINGS...THEN SEE HOW WELL YOU FLY!
HEY!
WHY SETTLE FOR ONE WHEN YOU CAN COLLECT THE SET?
HRG?
BLADES HAS GOT HIS ATTENTION. FIRST AID, YOU READY?
UH-HUH. GET ME AS CLOSE IN AS YOU CAN, HOTSPOT...
GROOVE?
HERE. READY.
STREETWISE?
UH-HUH. THIS SHOULD DO US. I'M RELAYING THE EXACT CO-ORDINATES.

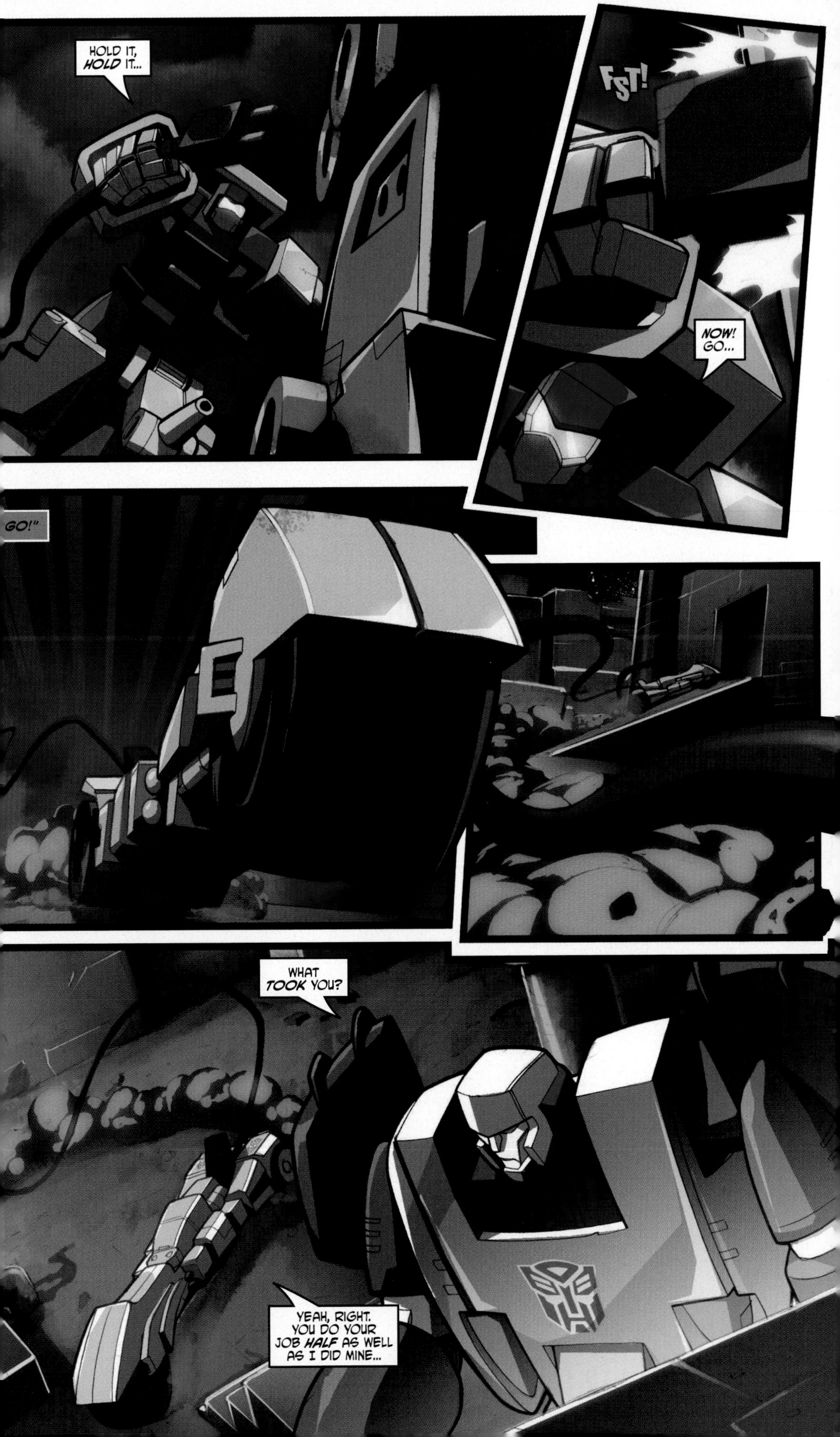
HOLD IT, *HOLD* IT...
FST!
NOW! GO...
GO!"
WHAT *TOOK* YOU?
YEAH, RIGHT. YOU DO YOUR JOB *HALF* AS WELL AS I DID MINE...

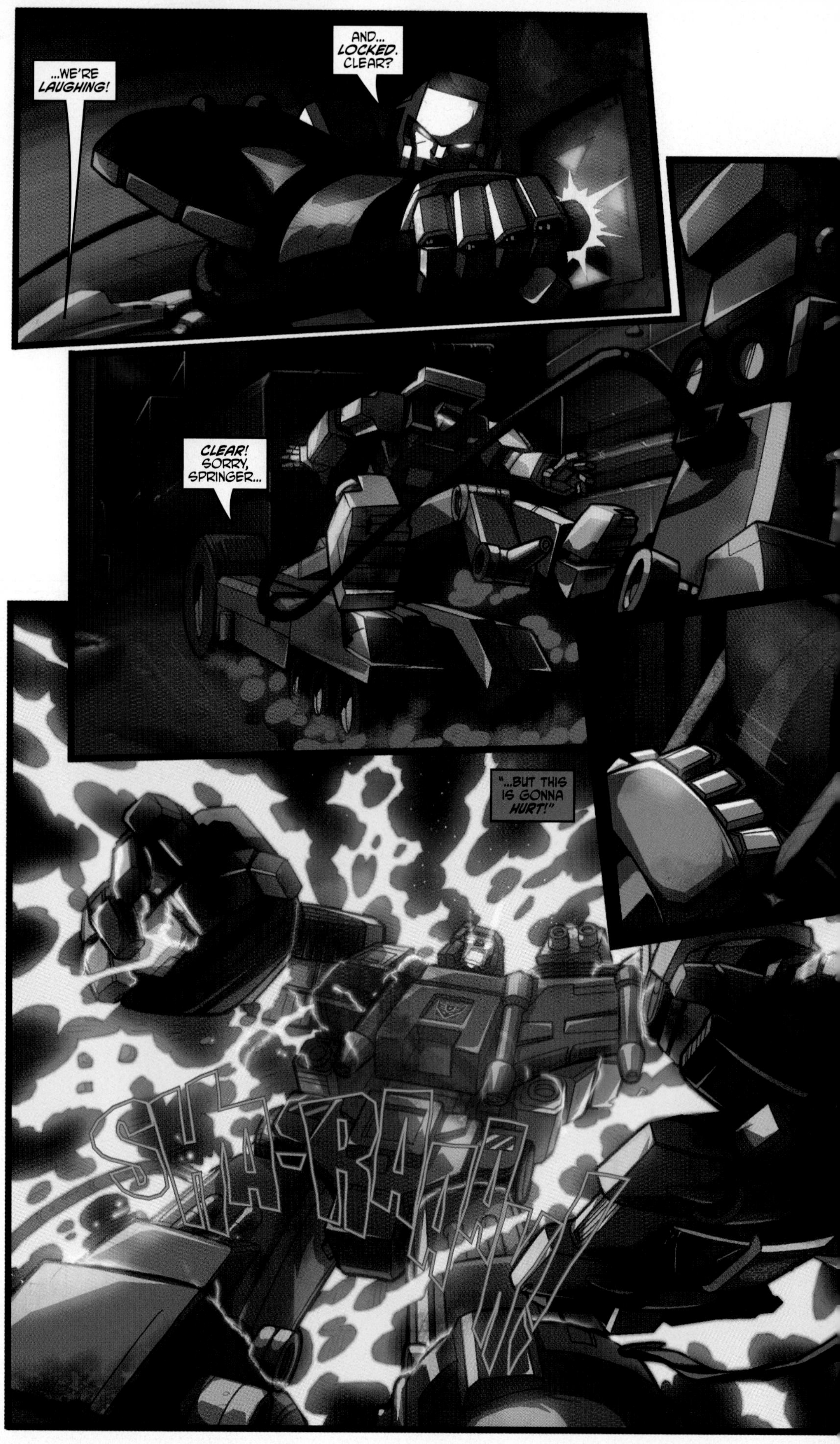
...WE'RE LAUGHING!
AND... LOCKED. CLEAR?
CLEAR! SORRY, SPRINGER...
"...BUT THIS IS GONNA HURT!"
SHA-RAKOOM

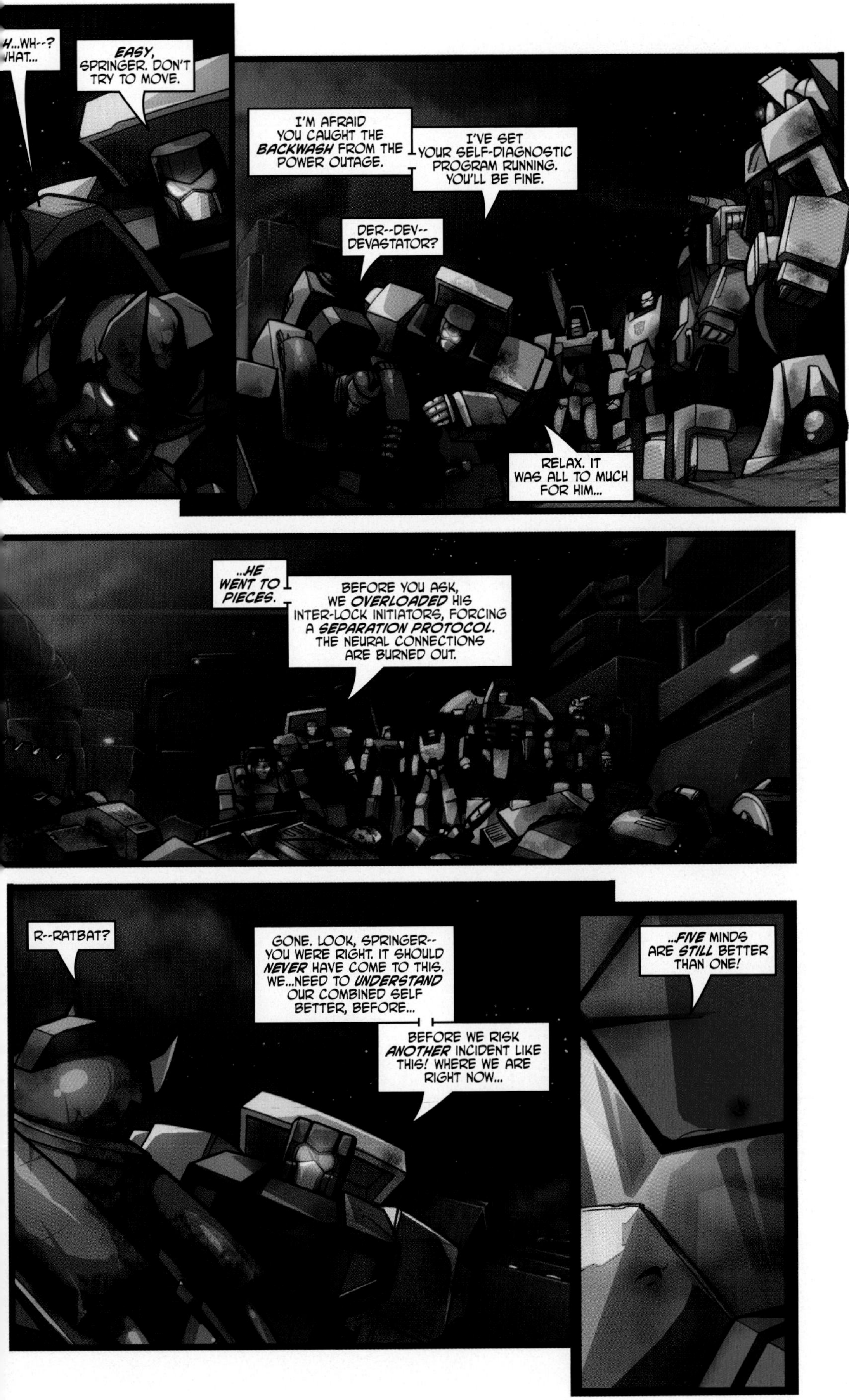

H...WH--? WHAT...
EASY, SPRINGER. DON'T TRY TO MOVE.
I'M AFRAID YOU CAUGHT THE BACKWASH FROM THE POWER OUTAGE.
I'VE SET YOUR SELF-DIAGNOSTIC PROGRAM RUNNING. YOU'LL BE FINE.
DER--DEV--DEVASTATOR?
RELAX. IT WAS ALL TO MUCH FOR HIM...
...HE WENT TO PIECES.
BEFORE YOU ASK, WE OVERLOADED HIS INTER-LOCK INITIATORS, FORCING A SEPARATION PROTOCOL. THE NEURAL CONNECTIONS ARE BURNED OUT.
R--RATBAT?
GONE. LOOK, SPRINGER--YOU WERE RIGHT. IT SHOULD NEVER HAVE COME TO THIS. WE...NEED TO UNDERSTAND OUR COMBINED SELF BETTER, BEFORE...
BEFORE WE RISK ANOTHER INCIDENT LIKE THIS! WHERE WE ARE RIGHT NOW...
...FIVE MINDS ARE STILL BETTER THAN ONE!

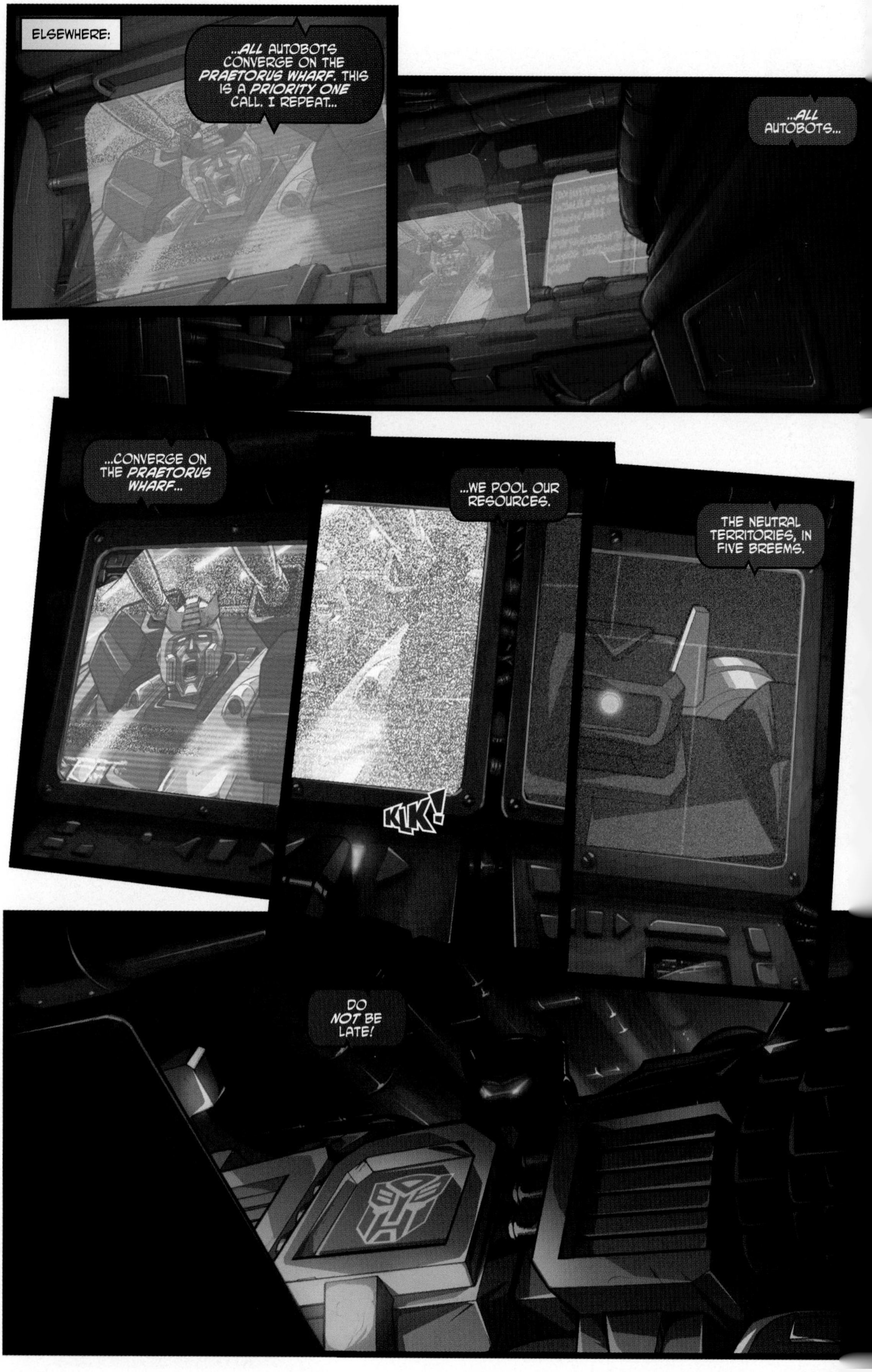

ELSEWHERE:
...ALL AUTOBOTS CONVERGE ON THE PRAETORUS WHARF. THIS IS A PRIORITY ONE CALL. I REPEAT...
...ALL AUTOBOTS...
...CONVERGE ON THE PRAETORUS WHARF...
...WE POOL OUR RESOURCES.
THE NEUTRAL TERRITORIES, IN FIVE BREEMS.
KLIK!
DO NOT BE LATE!

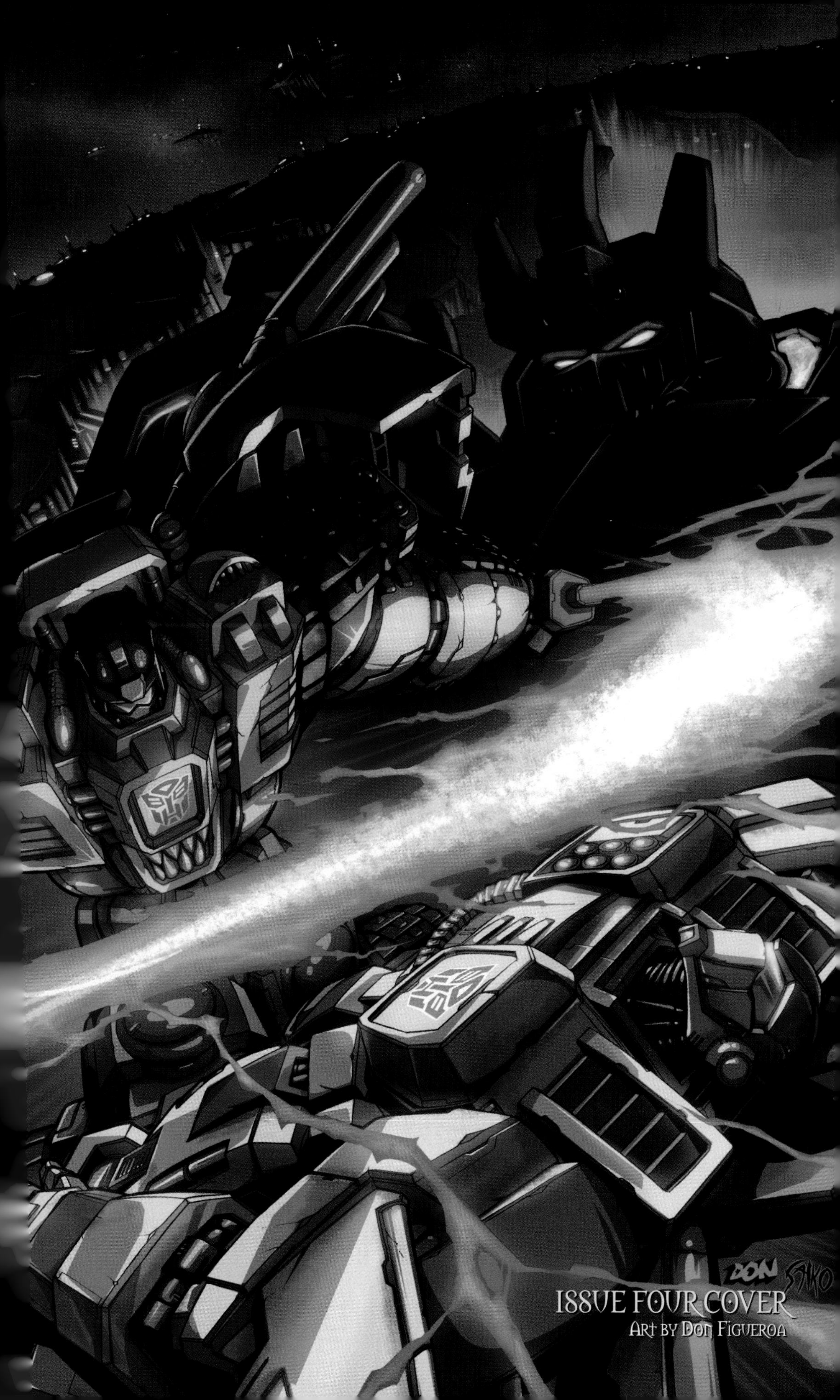

ISSUE FOUR COVER
Art by Don Figueroa

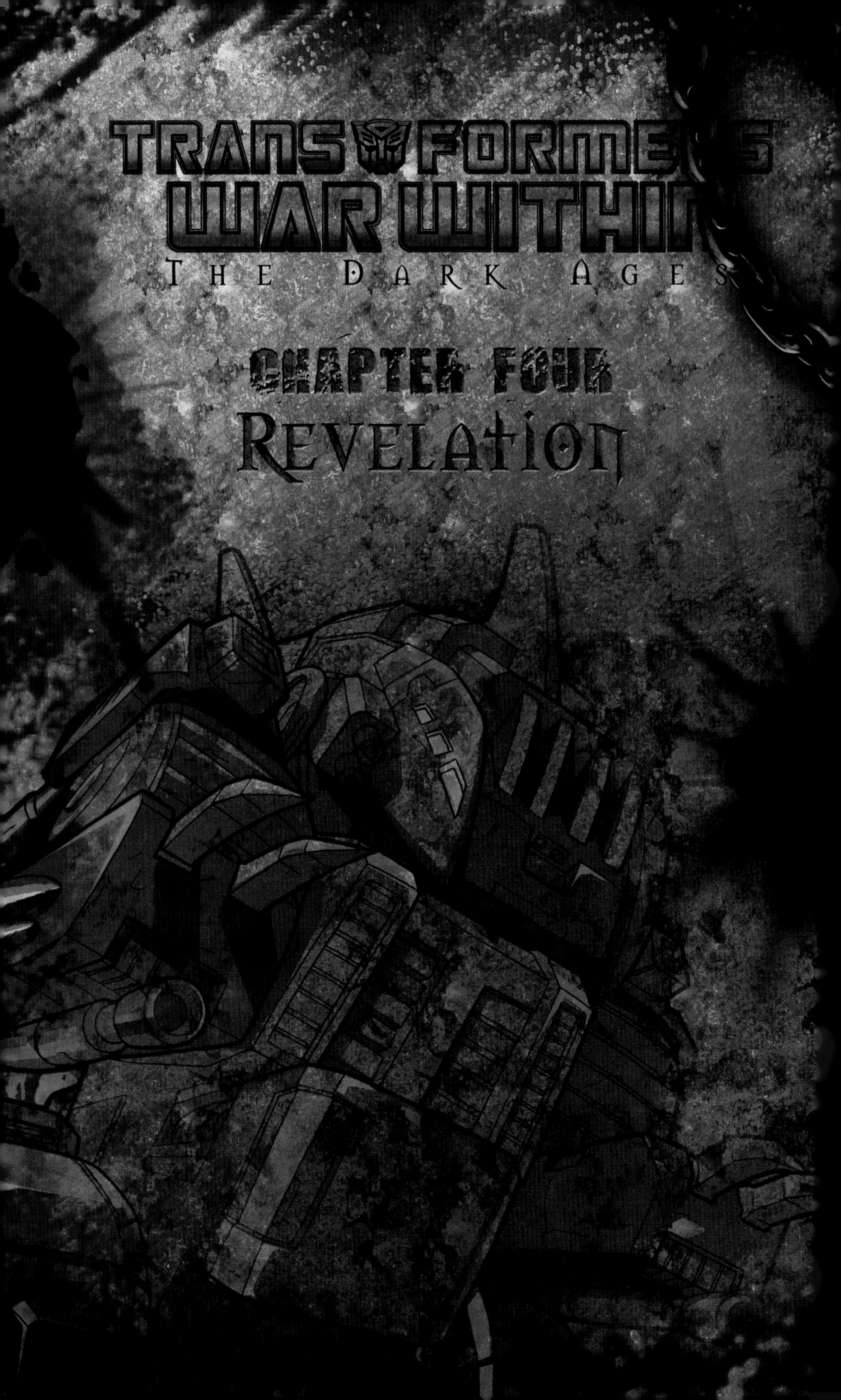
TRANSFORMERS
WAR WITHIN
THE DARK AGES
CHAPTER FOUR
Revelation

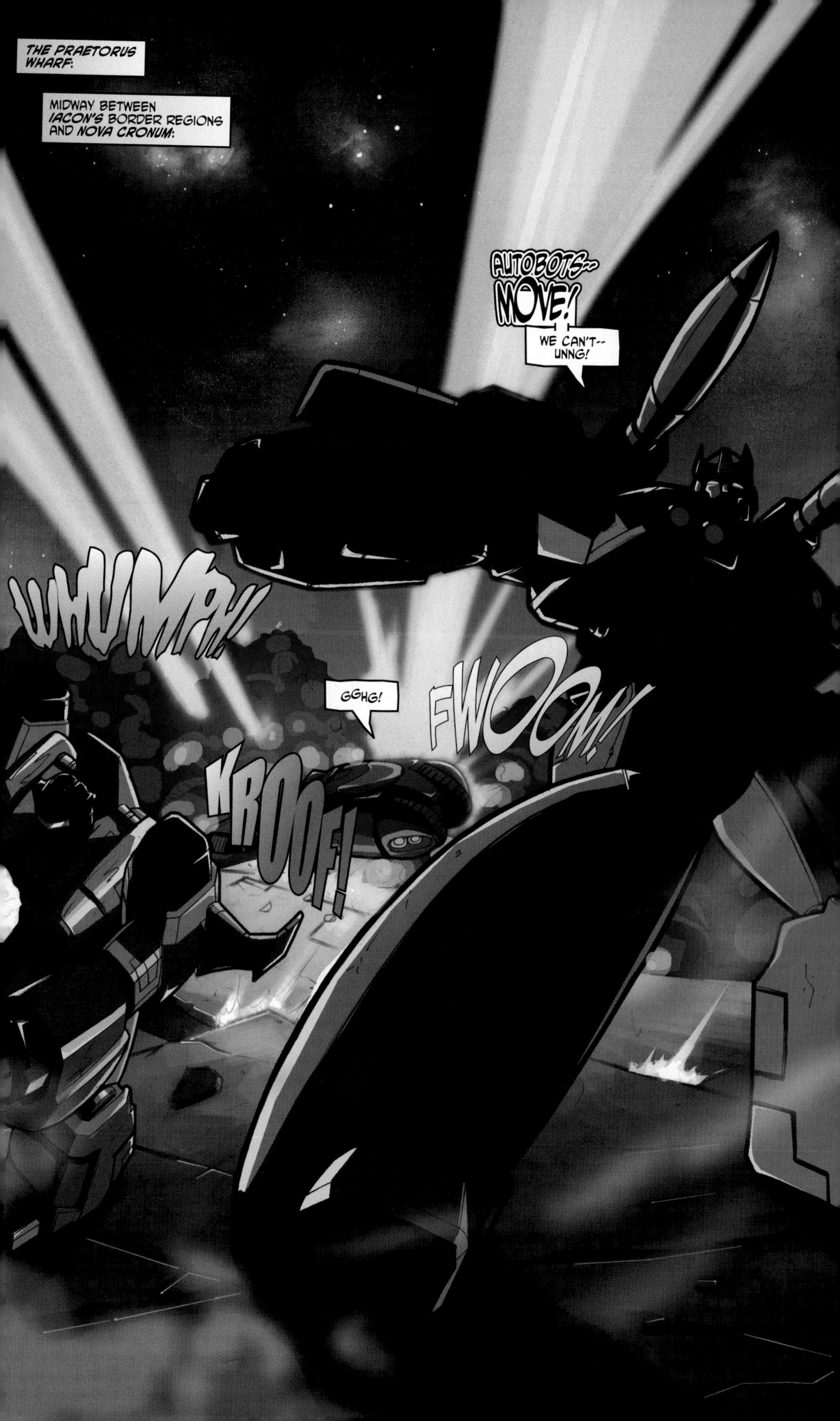
THE PRAETORUS WHARF:
MIDWAY BETWEEN IACON'S BORDER REGIONS AND NOVA CRONUM:
AUTOBOTS-- MOVE!
WE CAN'T-- UNNG!
WHUMPH!
GGHG!
FWOOM!
KROOF!

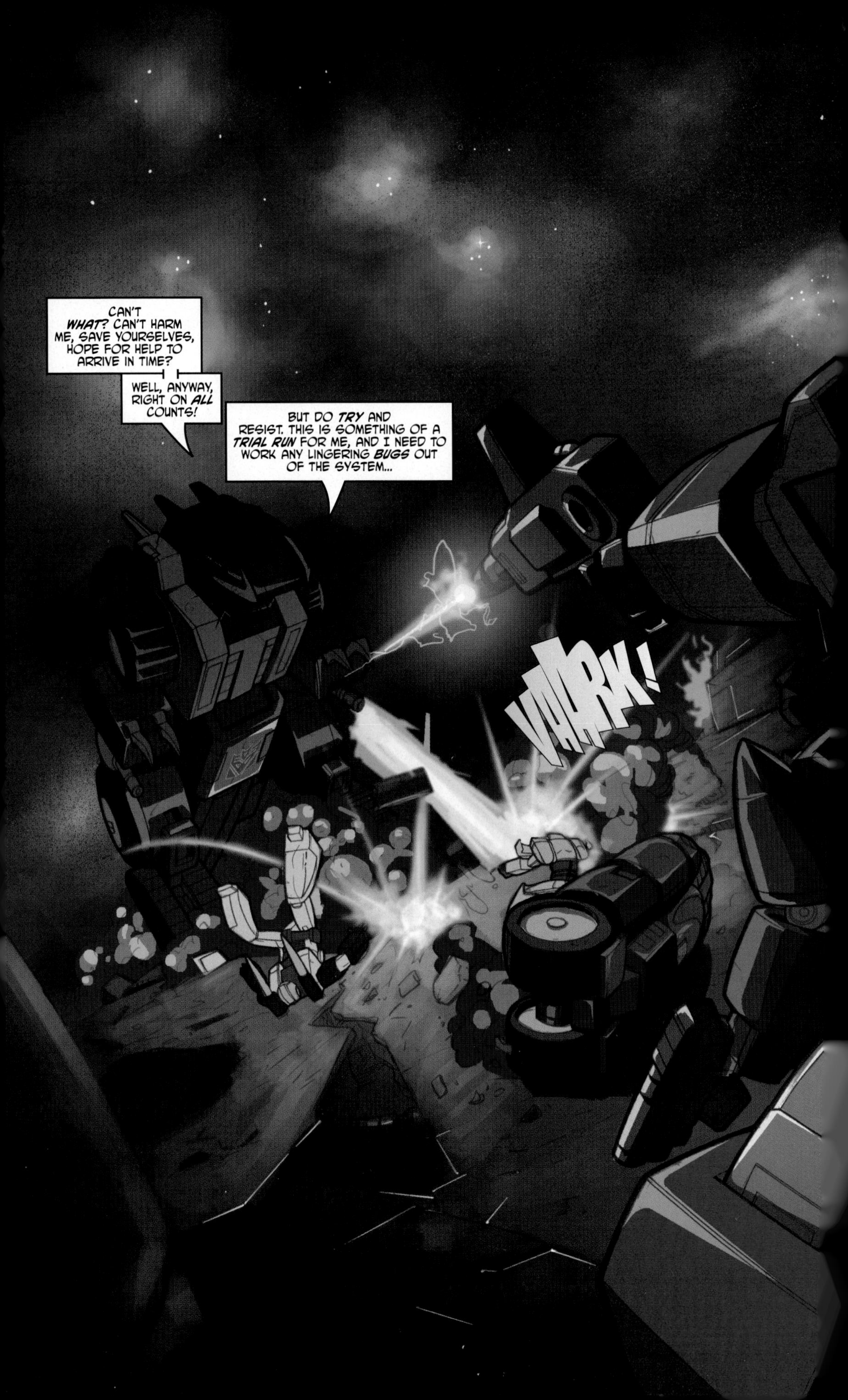

CAN'T WHAT? CAN'T HARM ME, SAVE YOURSELVES, HOPE FOR HELP TO ARRIVE IN TIME?
WELL, ANYWAY, RIGHT ON ALL COUNTS!
BUT DO TRY AND RESIST. THIS IS SOMETHING OF A TRIAL RUN FOR ME, AND I NEED TO WORK ANY LINGERING BUGS OUT OF THE SYSTEM...
VVARK!

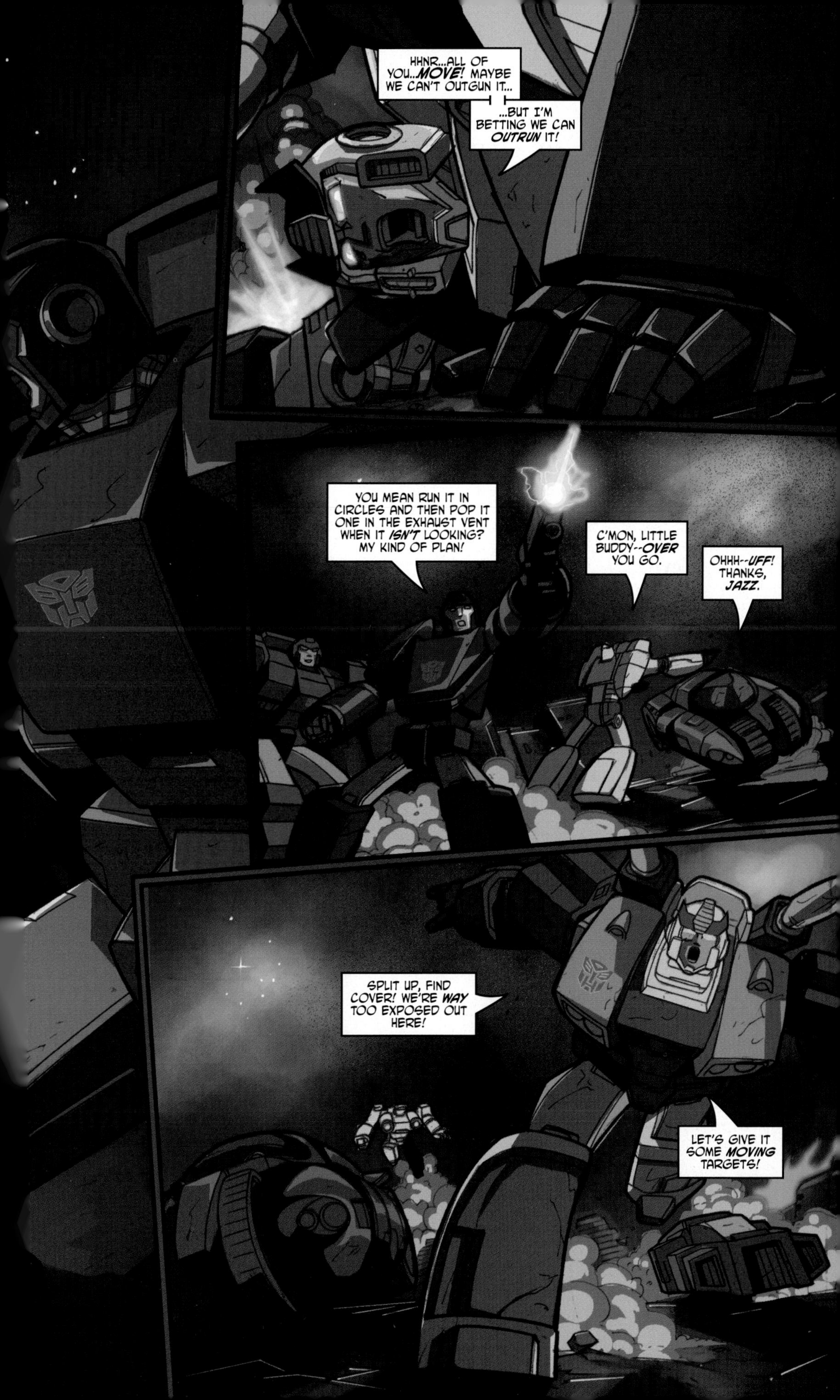

HHNR...ALL OF YOU...MOVE! MAYBE WE CAN'T OUTGUN IT...
...BUT I'M BETTING WE CAN OUTRUN IT!
YOU MEAN RUN IT IN CIRCLES AND THEN POP IT ONE IN THE EXHAUST VENT WHEN IT ISN'T LOOKING? MY KIND OF PLAN!
C'MON, LITTLE BUDDY--OVER YOU GO.
OHHH--UFF! THANKS, JAZZ.
SPLIT UP, FIND COVER! WE'RE WAY TOO EXPOSED OUT HERE!
LET'S GIVE IT SOME MOVING TARGETS!

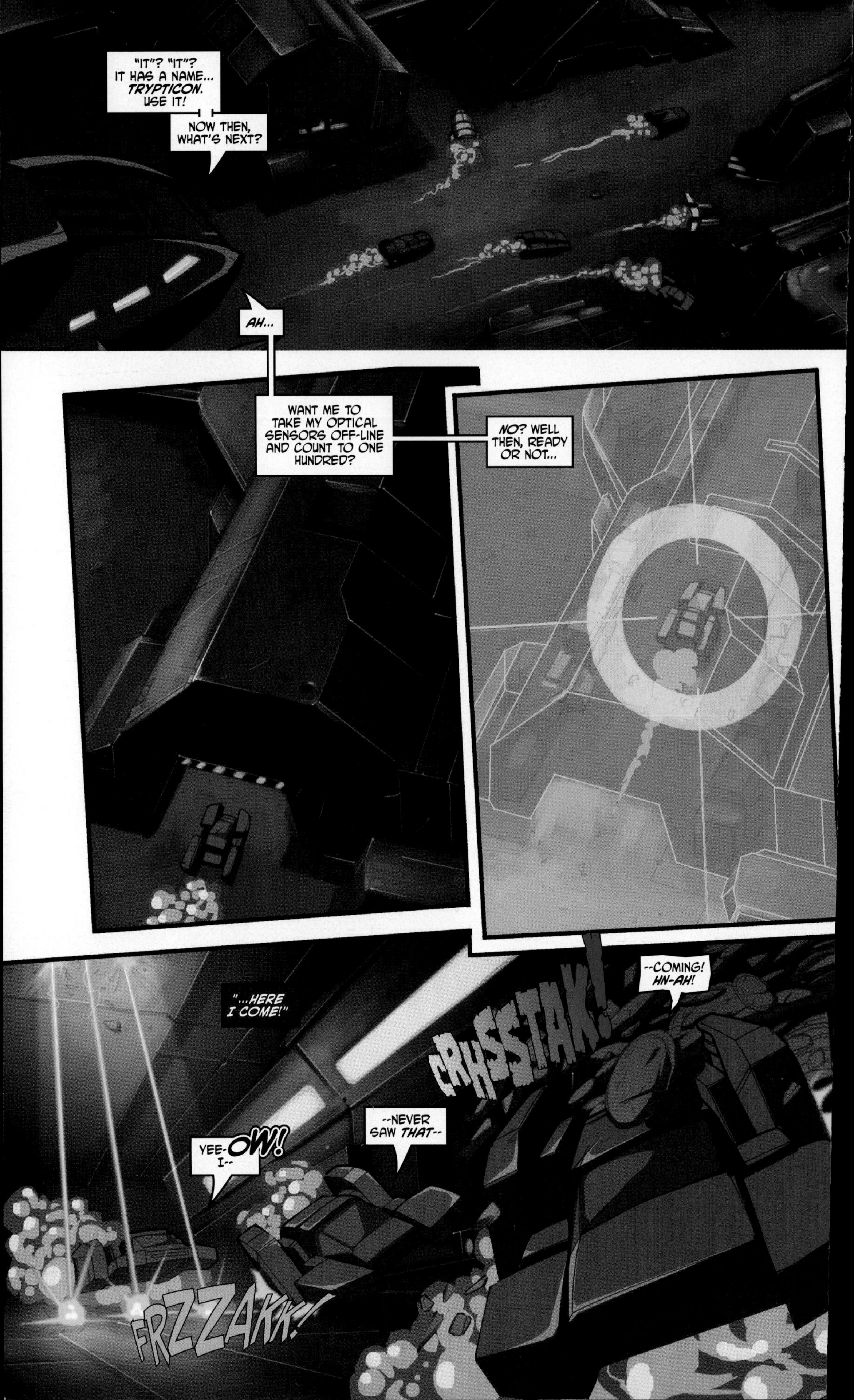
"IT"? "IT"? IT HAS A NAME... TRYPTICON. USE IT!
NOW THEN, WHAT'S NEXT?
AH...
WANT ME TO TAKE MY OPTICAL SENSORS OFF-LINE AND COUNT TO ONE HUNDRED?
NO? WELL THEN, READY OR NOT...
"...HERE I COME!"
CRHSSTAK!
--COMING! HN-AH!
--NEVER SAW THAT--
YEE-OW! I--
FRZZAKK!

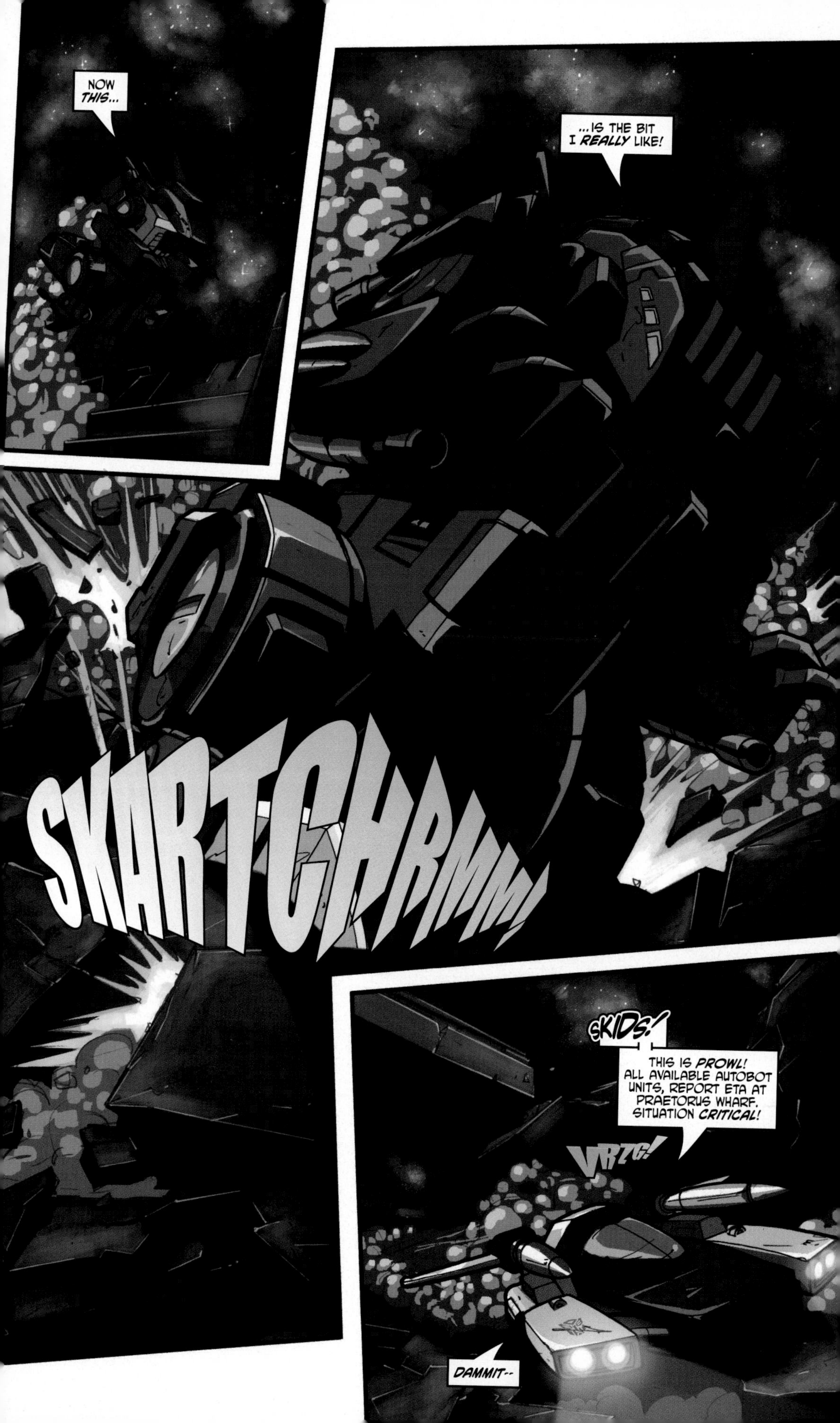
NOW THIS...
...IS THE BIT I REALLY LIKE!
SKARTCHRMM!
SKIDS!
THIS IS PROWL! ALL AVAILABLE AUTOBOT UNITS, REPORT ETA AT PRAETORUS WHARF. SITUATION CRITICAL!
VRZG!
DAMMIT--

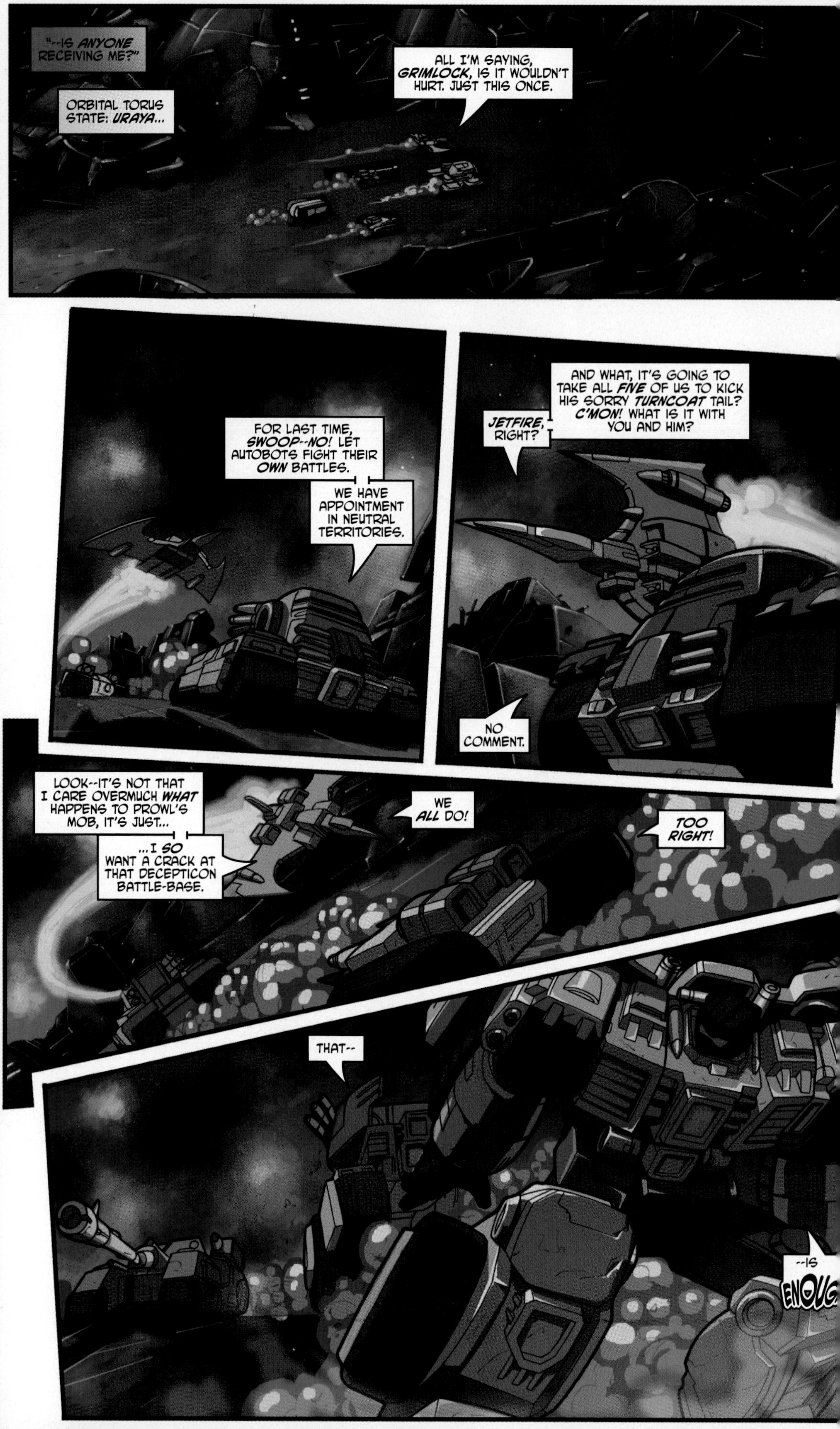
"--IS ANYONE RECEIVING ME?"
ORBITAL TORUS STATE: URAYA...
ALL I'M SAYING, GRIMLOCK, IS IT WOULDN'T HURT. JUST THIS ONCE.
FOR LAST TIME, SWOOP--NO! LET AUTOBOTS FIGHT THEIR OWN BATTLES.
WE HAVE APPOINTMENT IN NEUTRAL TERRITORIES.
AND WHAT, IT'S GOING TO TAKE ALL FIVE OF US TO KICK HIS SORRY TURNCOAT TAIL? C'MON! WHAT IS IT WITH YOU AND HIM?
JETFIRE, RIGHT?
NO COMMENT.
LOOK--IT'S NOT THAT I CARE OVERMUCH WHAT HAPPENS TO PROWL'S MOB, IT'S JUST...
...I SO WANT A CRACK AT THAT DECEPTICON BATTLE-BASE.
WE ALL DO!
TOO RIGHT!
THAT--
--IS
ENOUG

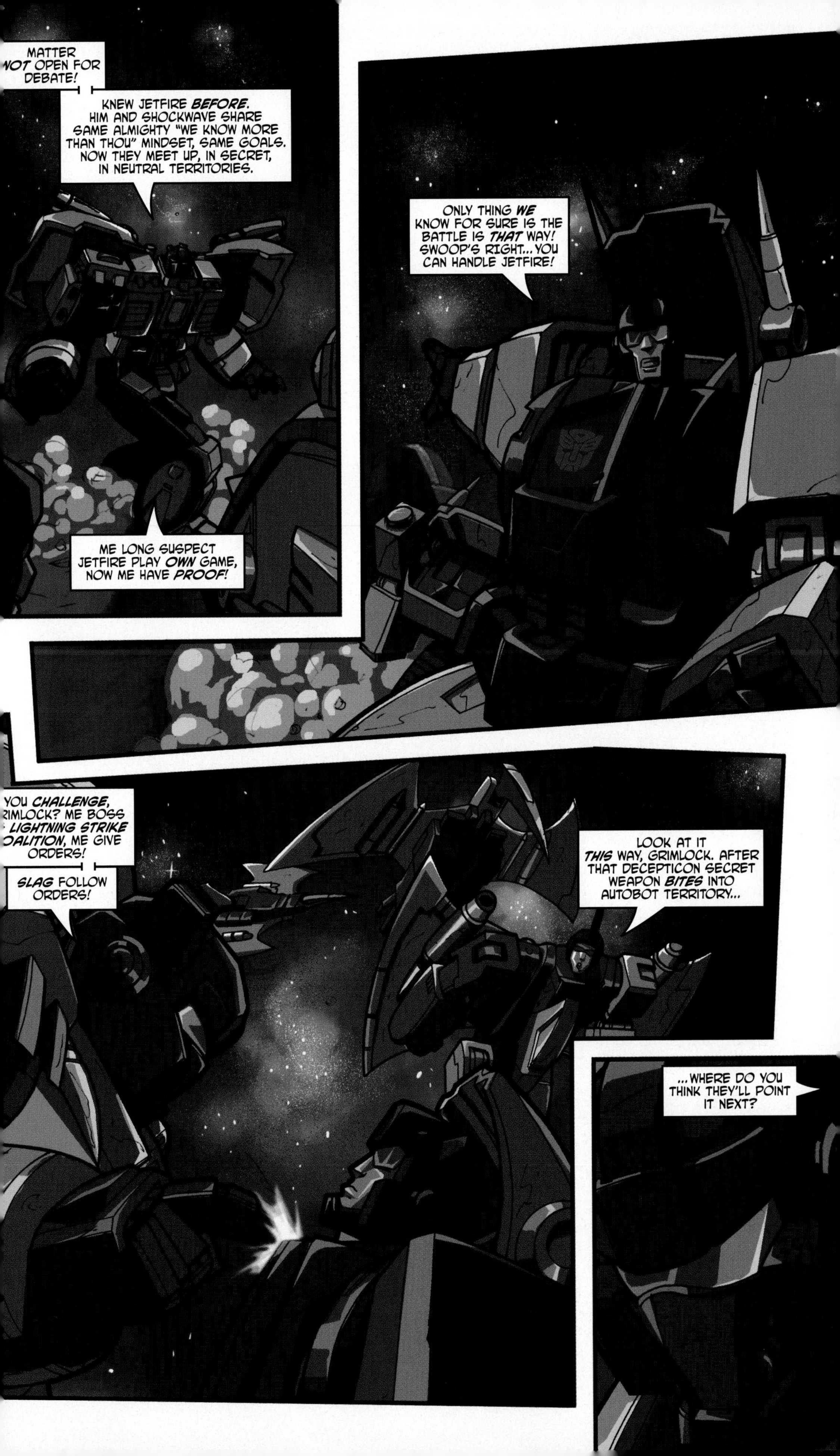
MATTER NOT OPEN FOR DEBATE!
KNEW JETFIRE BEFORE. HIM AND SHOCKWAVE SHARE SAME ALMIGHTY "WE KNOW MORE THAN THOU" MINDSET, SAME GOALS. NOW THEY MEET UP, IN SECRET, IN NEUTRAL TERRITORIES.
ME LONG SUSPECT JETFIRE PLAY OWN GAME, NOW ME HAVE PROOF!
ONLY THING WE KNOW FOR SURE IS THE BATTLE IS THAT WAY! SWOOP'S RIGHT... YOU CAN HANDLE JETFIRE!
YOU CHALLENGE, RIMLOCK? ME BOSS LIGHTNING STRIKE OALITION, ME GIVE ORDERS!
SLAG FOLLOW ORDERS!
LOOK AT IT THIS WAY, GRIMLOCK. AFTER THAT DECEPTICON SECRET WEAPON BITES INTO AUTOBOT TERRITORY...
...WHERE DO YOU THINK THEY'LL POINT IT NEXT?

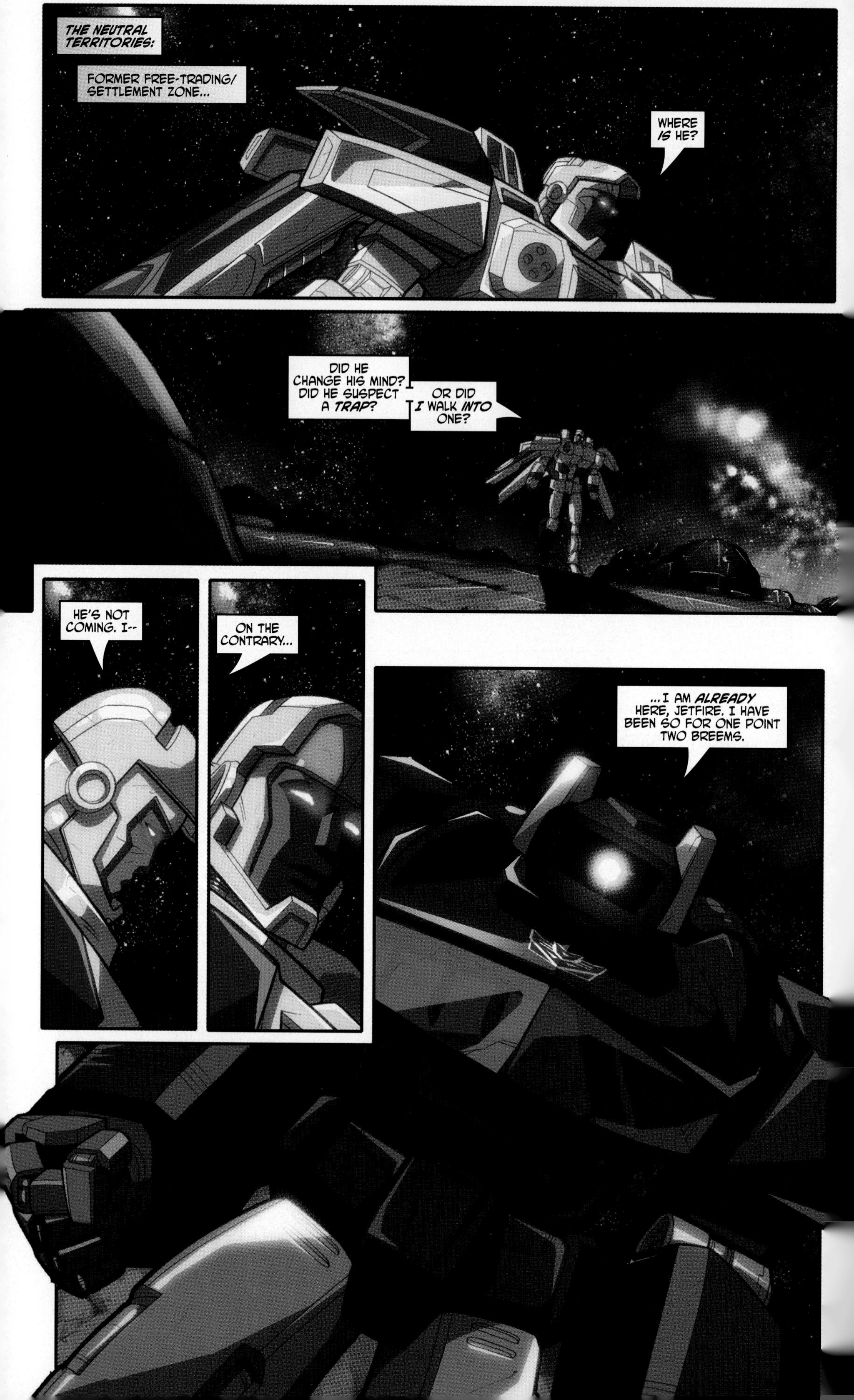
THE NEUTRAL TERRITORIES:
FORMER FREE-TRADING/ SETTLEMENT ZONE...
WHERE IS HE?
DID HE CHANGE HIS MIND? DID HE SUSPECT A TRAP?
OR DID I WALK INTO ONE?
HE'S NOT COMING. I--
ON THE CONTRARY...
...I AM ALREADY HERE, JETFIRE. I HAVE BEEN SO FOR ONE POINT TWO BREEMS.

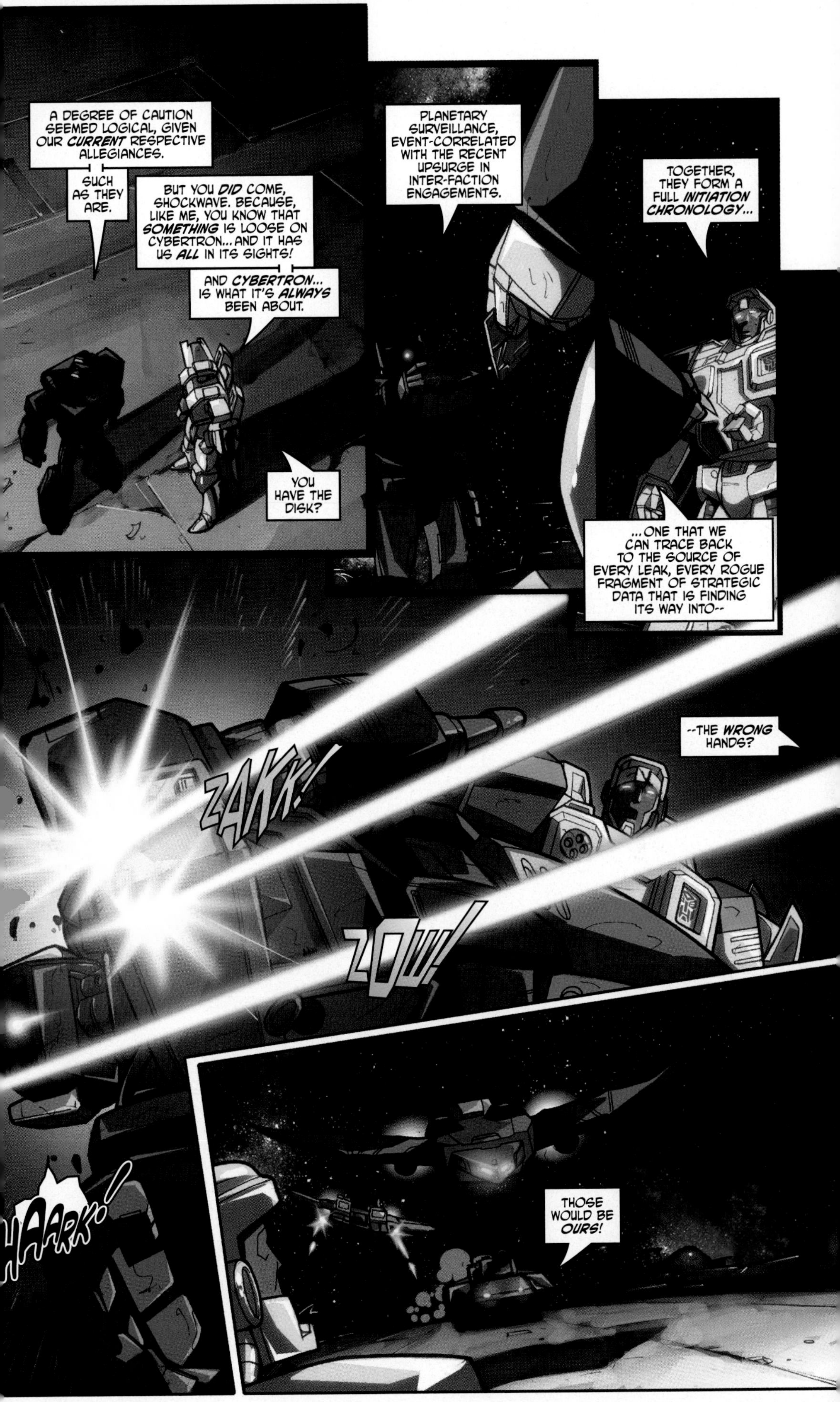
A DEGREE OF CAUTION SEEMED LOGICAL, GIVEN OUR *CURRENT* RESPECTIVE ALLEGIANCES.
SUCH AS THEY ARE.
BUT YOU *DID* COME, SHOCKWAVE. BECAUSE, LIKE ME, YOU KNOW THAT *SOMETHING* IS LOOSE ON CYBERTRON... AND IT HAS US *ALL* IN ITS SIGHTS!
AND *CYBERTRON*... IS WHAT IT'S *ALWAYS* BEEN ABOUT.
YOU HAVE THE DISK?
PLANETARY SURVEILLANCE, EVENT-CORRELATED WITH THE RECENT UPSURGE IN INTER-FACTION ENGAGEMENTS.
TOGETHER, THEY FORM A FULL *INITIATION CHRONOLOGY*...
...ONE THAT WE CAN TRACE BACK TO THE SOURCE OF EVERY LEAK, EVERY ROGUE FRAGMENT OF STRATEGIC DATA THAT IS FINDING ITS WAY INTO--
--THE *WRONG* HANDS?
ZAKK!
ZOW!
HAARK!
THOSE WOULD BE *OURS*!

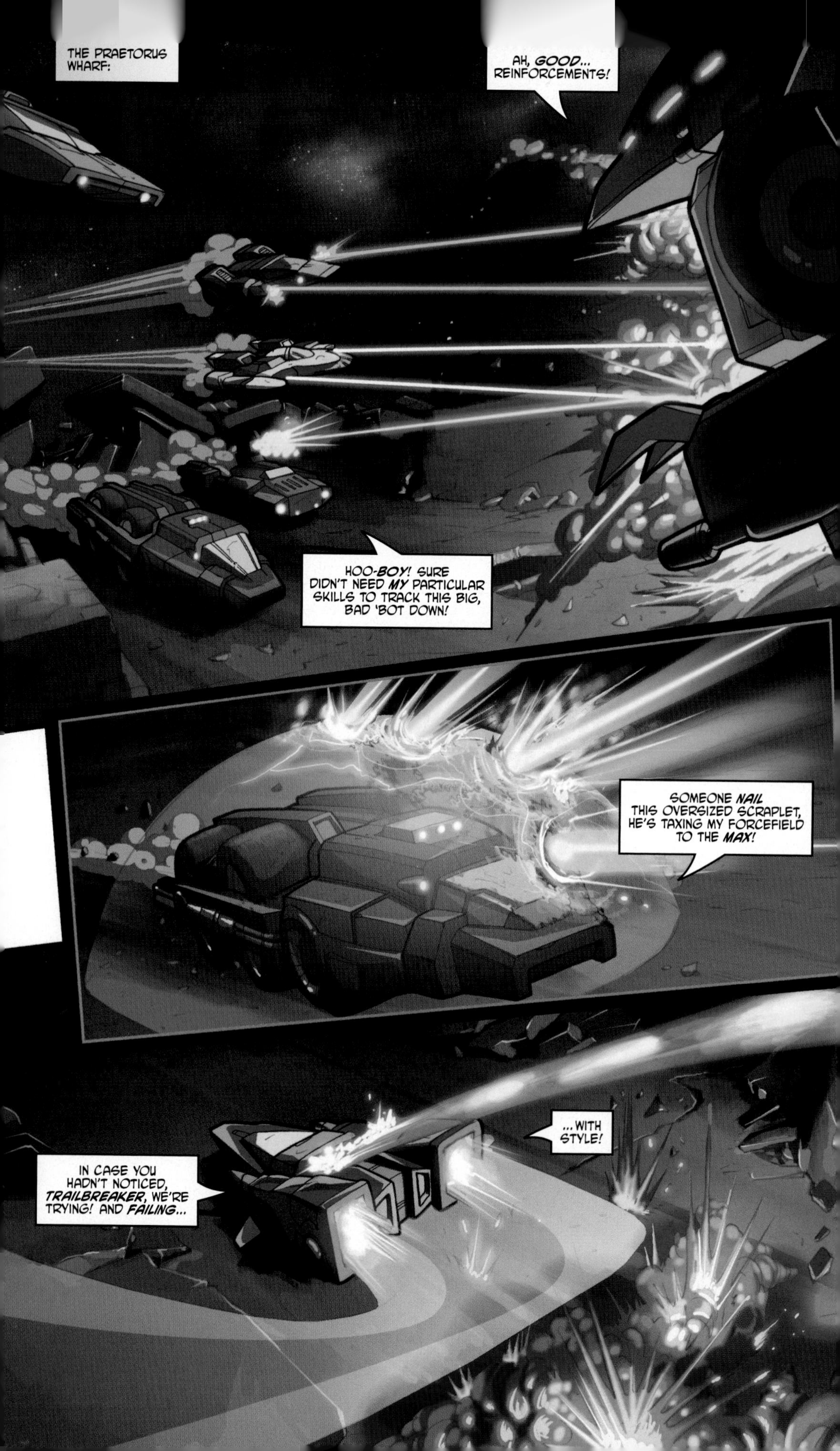
THE PRAETORUS WHARF:
AH, GOOD... REINFORCEMENTS!
HOO-BOY! SURE DIDN'T NEED MY PARTICULAR SKILLS TO TRACK THIS BIG, BAD 'BOT DOWN!
SOMEONE NAIL THIS OVERSIZED SCRAPLET, HE'S TAXING MY FORCEFIELD TO THE MAX!
IN CASE YOU HADN'T NOTICED, TRAILBREAKER, WE'RE TRYING! AND FAILING...
...WITH STYLE!

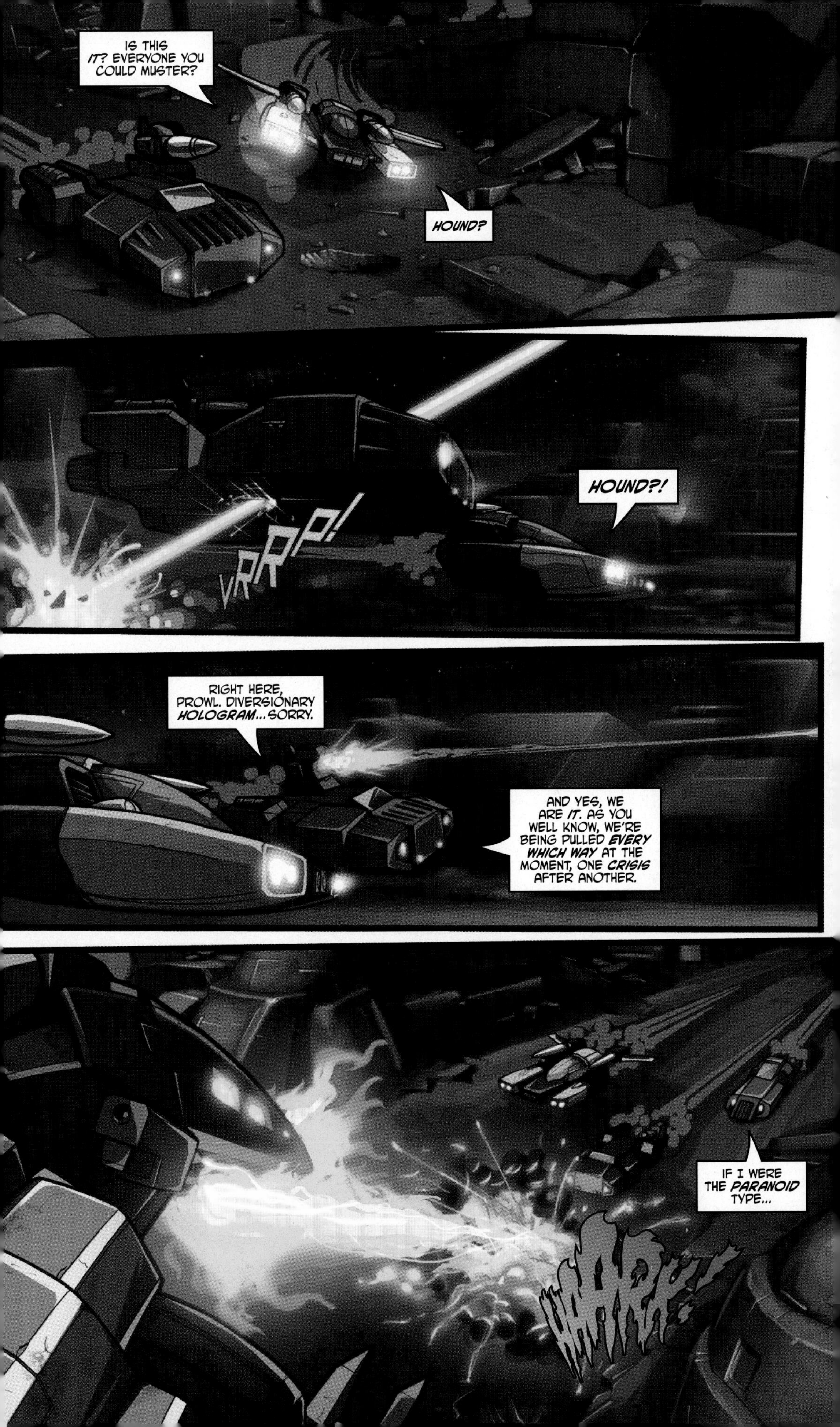
IS THIS *IT*? EVERYONE YOU COULD MUSTER?
HOUND?
HOUND?!
VRRP!
RIGHT HERE, PROWL. DIVERSIONARY *HOLOGRAM*... SORRY.
AND YES, WE ARE *IT*. AS YOU WELL KNOW, WE'RE BEING PULLED *EVERY WHICH WAY* AT THE MOMENT, ONE *CRISIS* AFTER ANOTHER.
IF I WERE THE *PARANOID* TYPE...

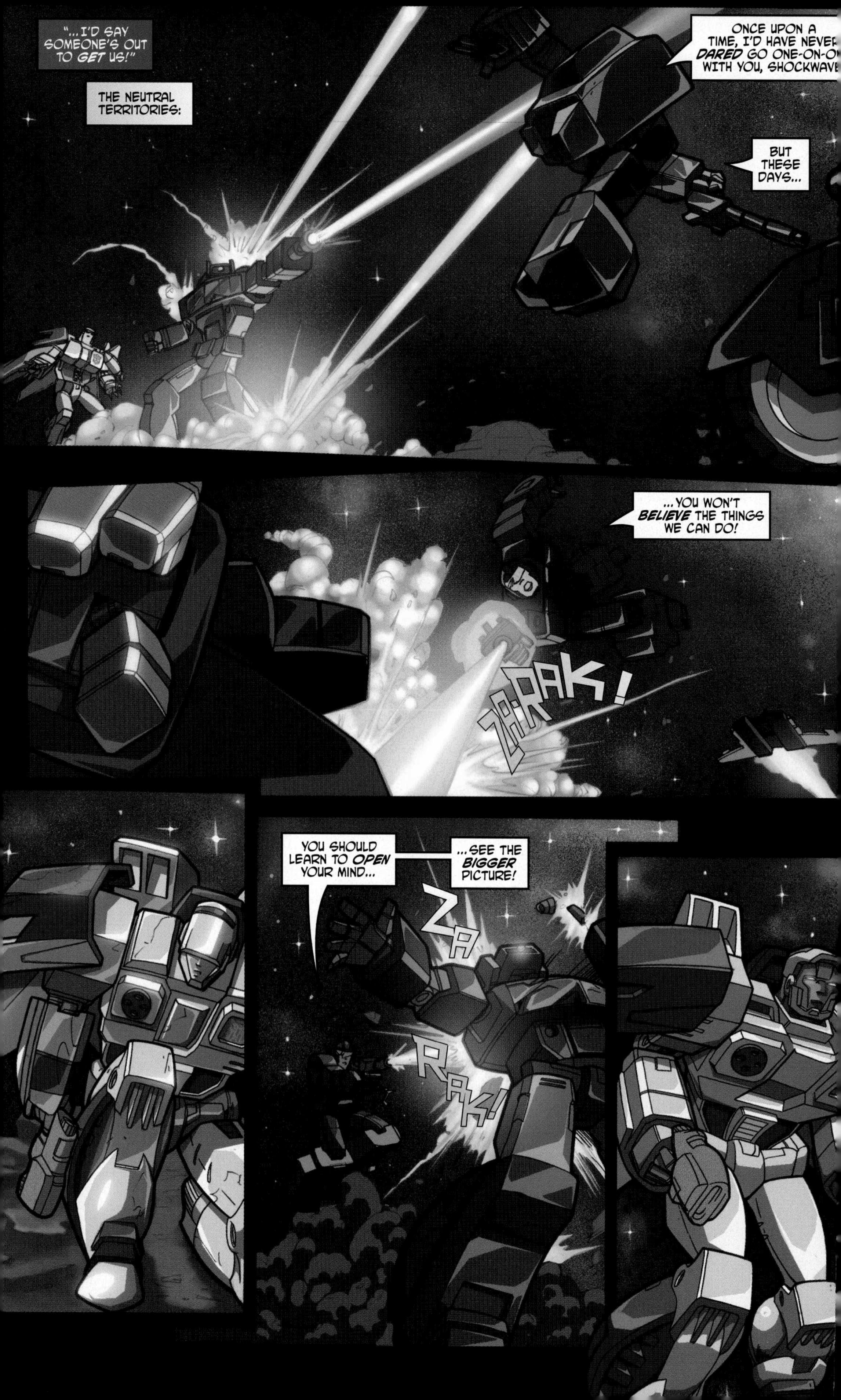
"...I'D SAY SOMEONE'S OUT TO GET US!"
THE NEUTRAL TERRITORIES:
ONCE UPON A TIME, I'D HAVE NEVER DARED GO ONE-ON-ON WITH YOU, SHOCKWAVE
BUT THESE DAYS...
...YOU WON'T BELIEVE THE THINGS WE CAN DO!
ZA-RAK!
YOU SHOULD LEARN TO OPEN YOUR MIND...
...SEE THE BIGGER PICTURE!
ZA
RAK!

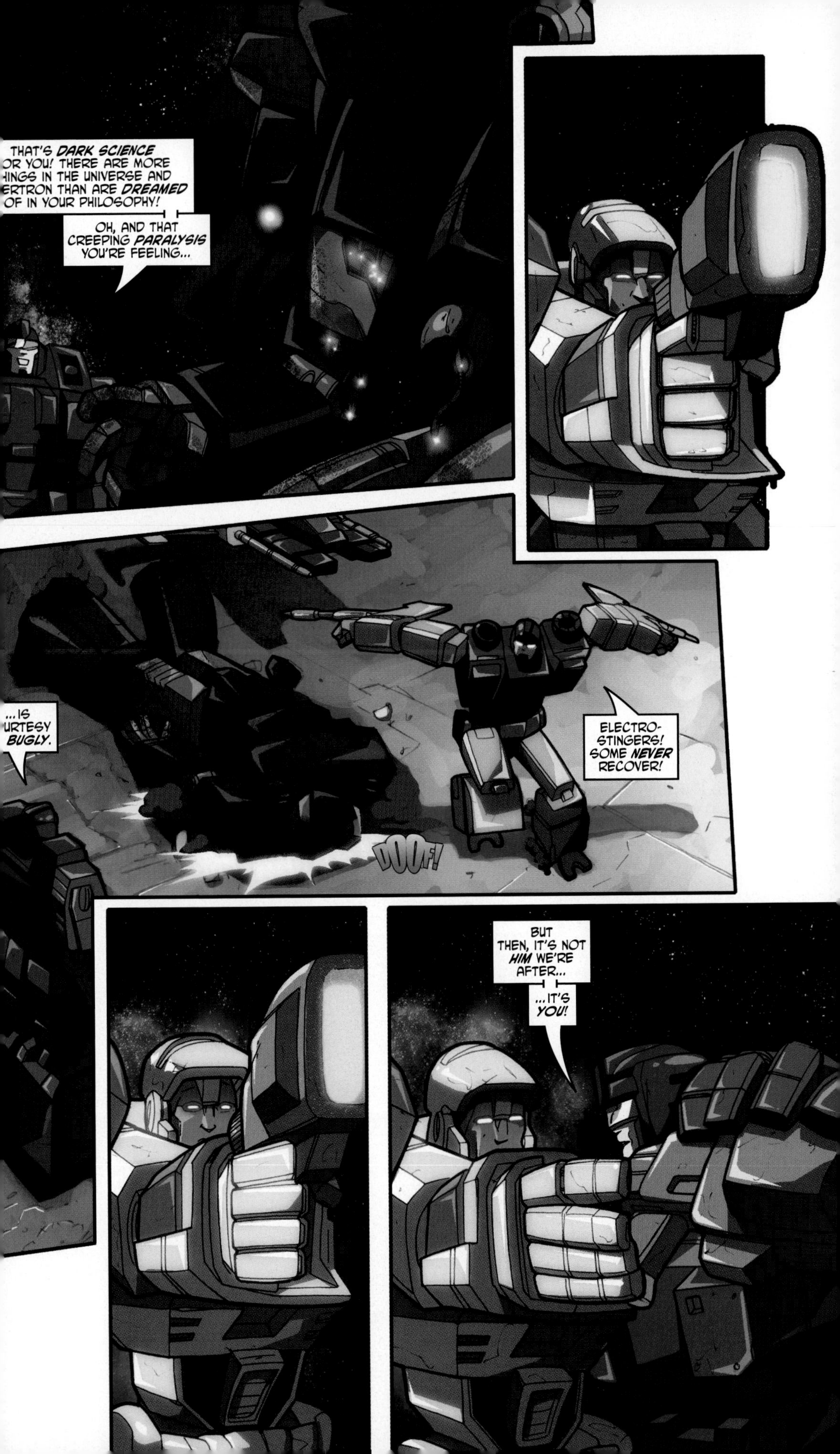
THAT'S DARK SCIENCE
OR YOU! THERE ARE MORE
HINGS IN THE UNIVERSE AND
ERTRON THAN ARE DREAMED
OF IN YOUR PHILOSOPHY!
OH, AND THAT CREEPING PARALYSIS YOU'RE FEELING...
...IS
URTESY
BUGLY.
ELECTRO-STINGERS! SOME NEVER RECOVER!
DOOF!
BUT THEN, IT'S NOT HIM WE'RE AFTER...
...IT'S YOU!

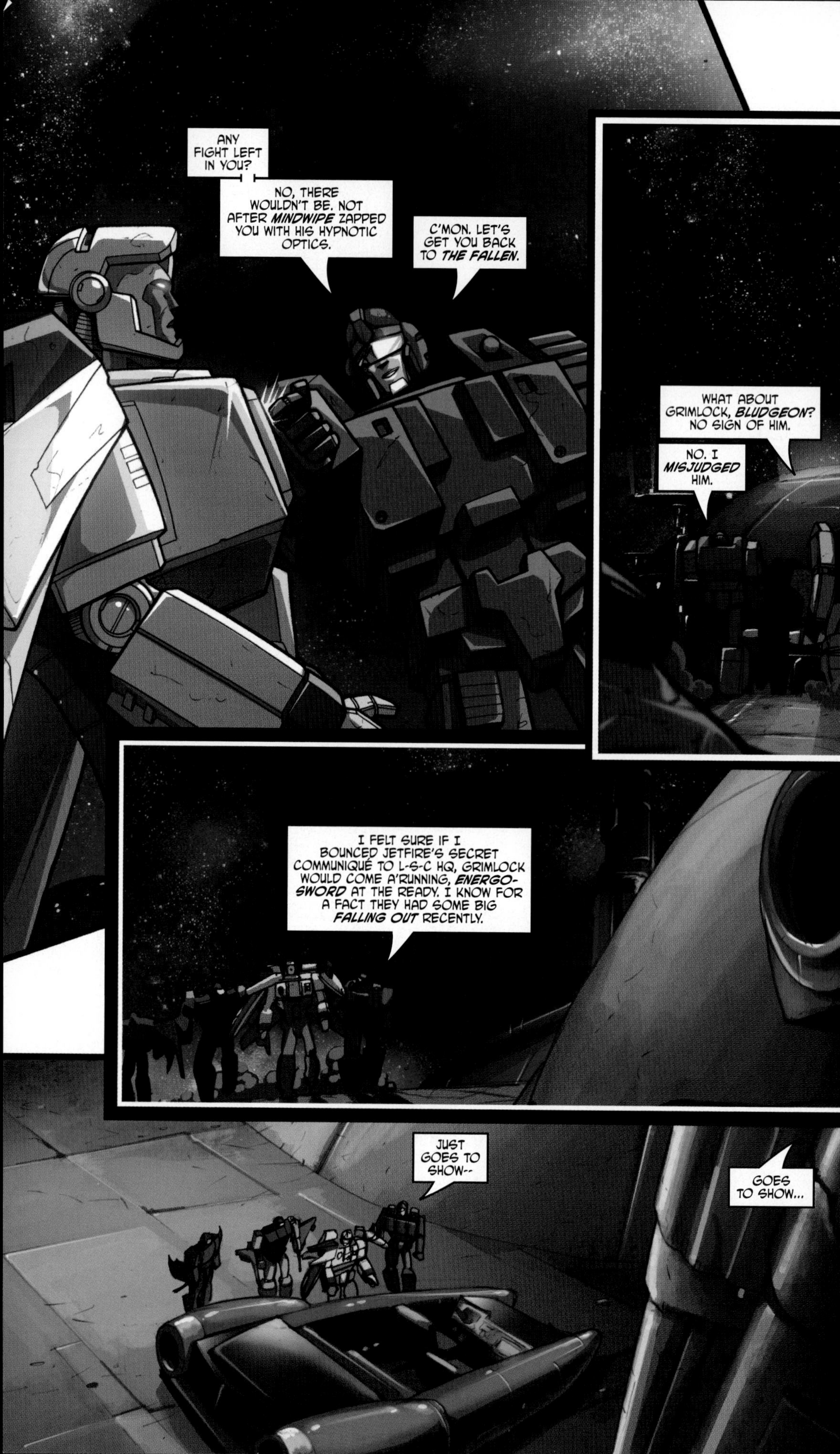
ANY FIGHT LEFT IN YOU?
NO, THERE WOULDN'T BE. NOT AFTER MINDWIPE ZAPPED YOU WITH HIS HYPNOTIC OPTICS.
C'MON. LET'S GET YOU BACK TO THE FALLEN.
WHAT ABOUT GRIMLOCK, BLUDGEON? NO SIGN OF HIM.
NO. I MISJUDGED HIM.
I FELT SURE IF I BOUNCED JETFIRE'S SECRET COMMUNIQUÉ TO L-S-C HQ, GRIMLOCK WOULD COME A'RUNNING, ENERGO-SWORD AT THE READY. I KNOW FOR A FACT THEY HAD SOME BIG FALLING OUT RECENTLY.
JUST GOES TO SHOW--
GOES TO SHOW...

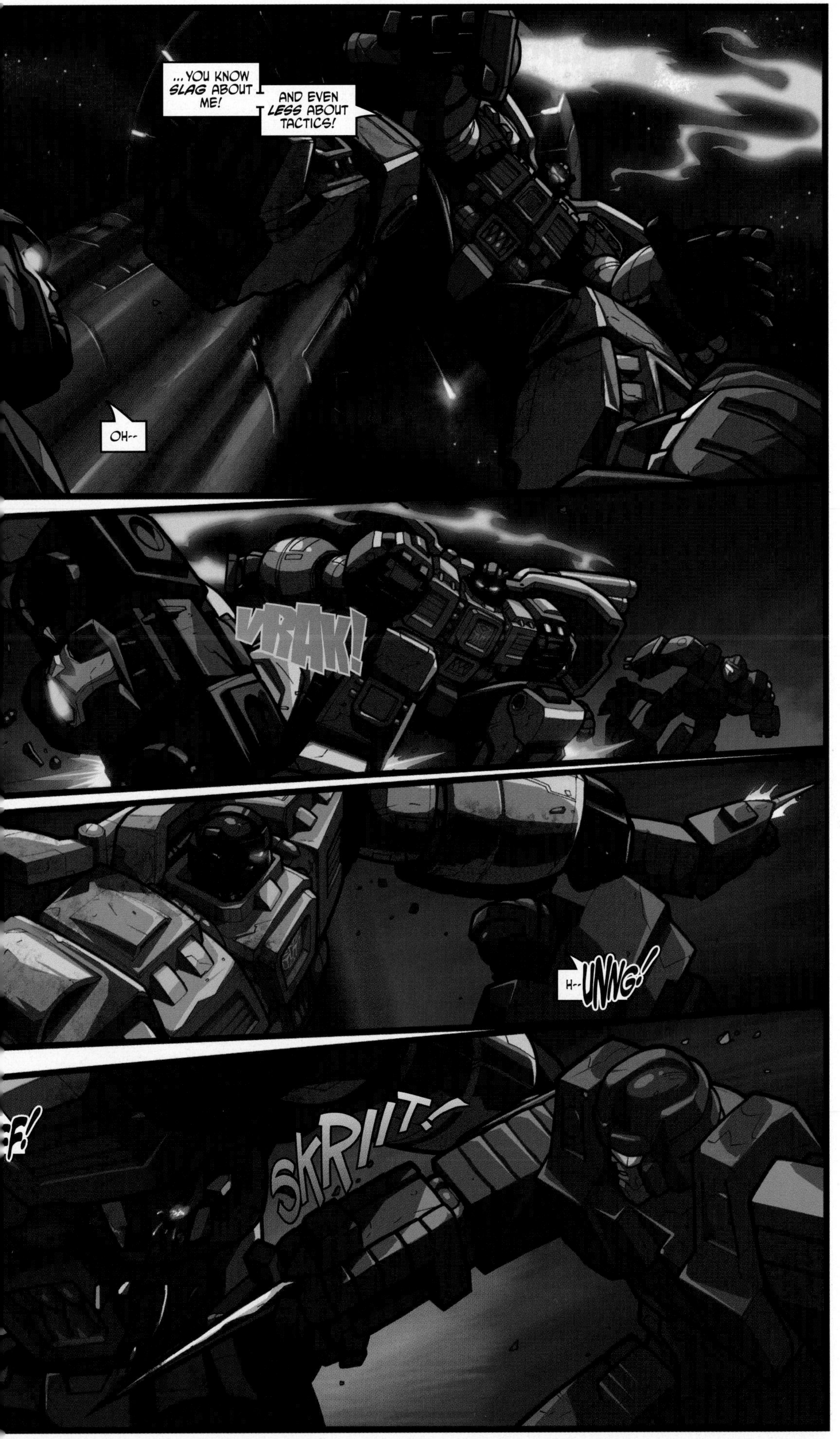

...YOU KNOW SLAG ABOUT ME!
AND EVEN LESS ABOUT TACTICS!
OH--
VRAK!
H--UNNG!
SKRIIT!

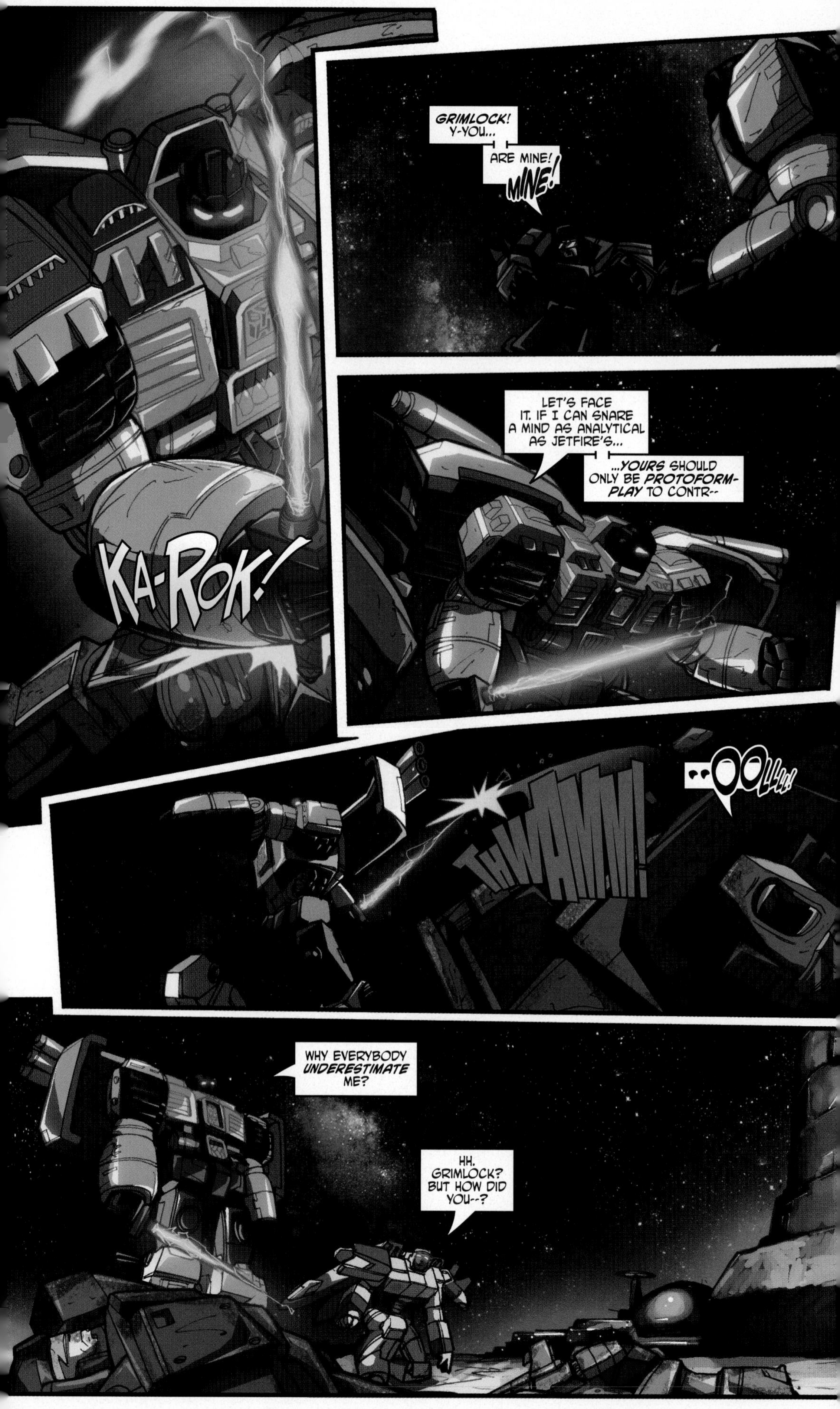
GRIMLOCK! Y-YOU...
ARE MINE! MINE!
KA-ROK!
LET'S FACE IT. IF I CAN SNARE A MIND AS ANALYTICAL AS JETFIRE'S...
...YOURS SHOULD ONLY BE PROTOFORM-PLAY TO CONTR--
THWAMM!
--OOLLL!
WHY EVERYBODY UNDERESTIMATE ME?
HH. GRIMLOCK? BUT HOW DID YOU--?

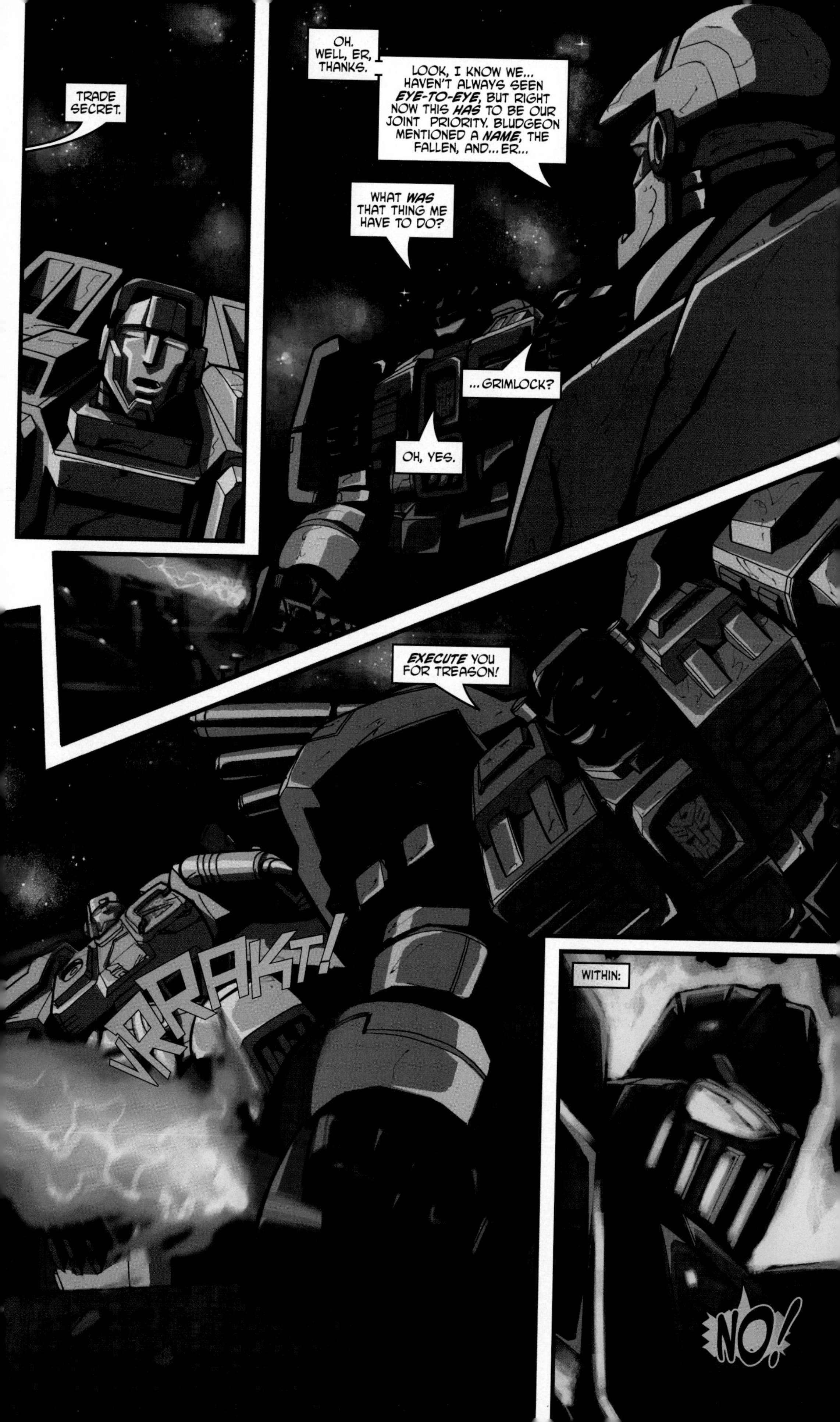
TRADE SECRET.
OH. WELL, ER, THANKS.
LOOK, I KNOW WE... HAVEN'T ALWAYS SEEN EYE-TO-EYE, BUT RIGHT NOW THIS HAS TO BE OUR JOINT PRIORITY. BLUDGEON MENTIONED A NAME, THE FALLEN, AND... ER...
WHAT WAS THAT THING ME HAVE TO DO?
...GRIMLOCK?
OH, YES.
EXECUTE YOU FOR TREASON!
VRRAKT!
WITHIN:
NO!

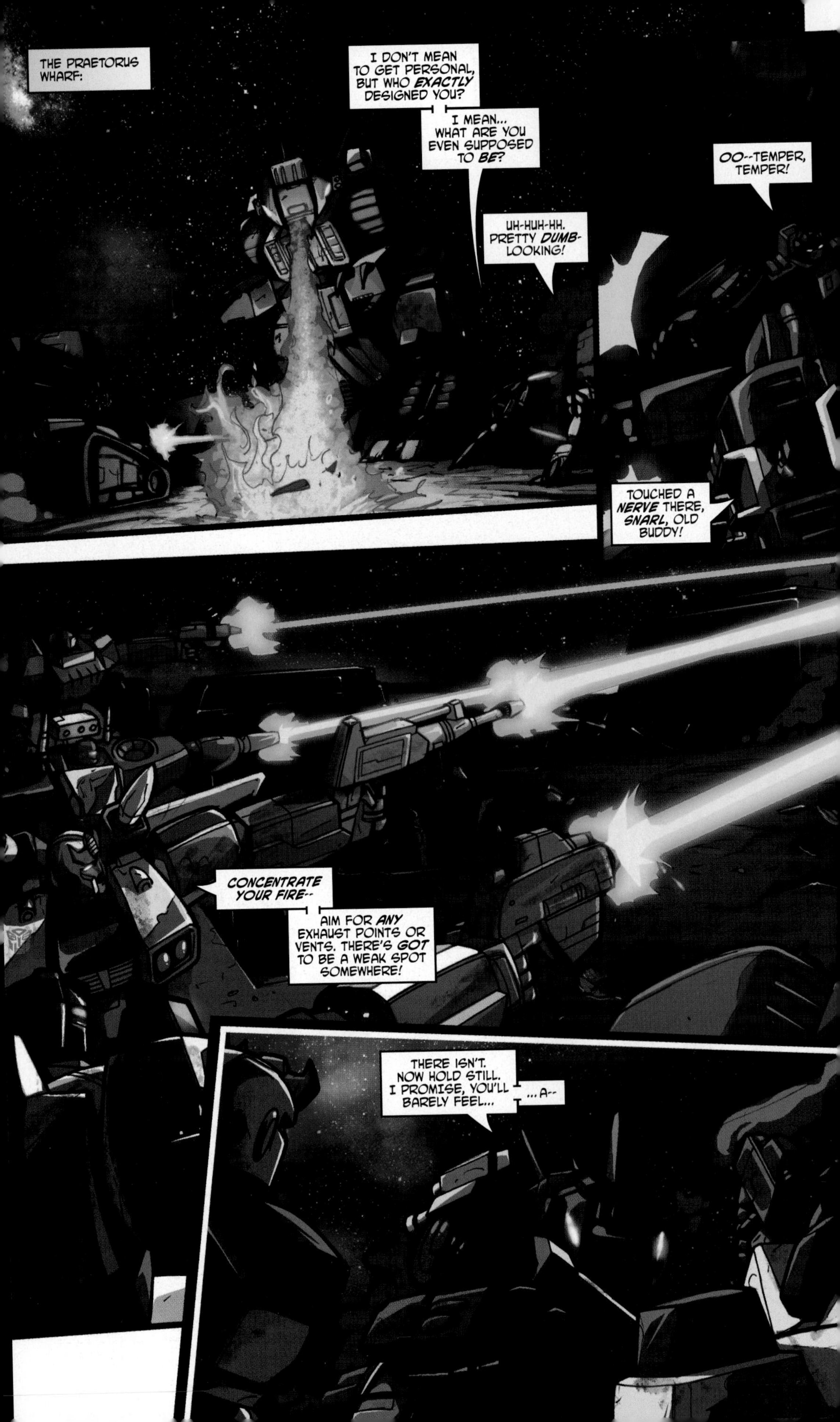
THE PRAETORUS WHARF:
I DON'T MEAN TO GET PERSONAL, BUT WHO EXACTLY DESIGNED YOU?
I MEAN... WHAT ARE YOU EVEN SUPPOSED TO BE?
UH-HUH-HH. PRETTY DUMB-LOOKING!
OO--TEMPER, TEMPER!
TOUCHED A NERVE THERE, SNARL, OLD BUDDY!
CONCENTRATE YOUR FIRE--
AIM FOR ANY EXHAUST POINTS OR VENTS. THERE'S GOT TO BE A WEAK SPOT SOMEWHERE!
THERE ISN'T. NOW HOLD STILL. I PROMISE, YOU'LL BARELY FEEL...
...A--

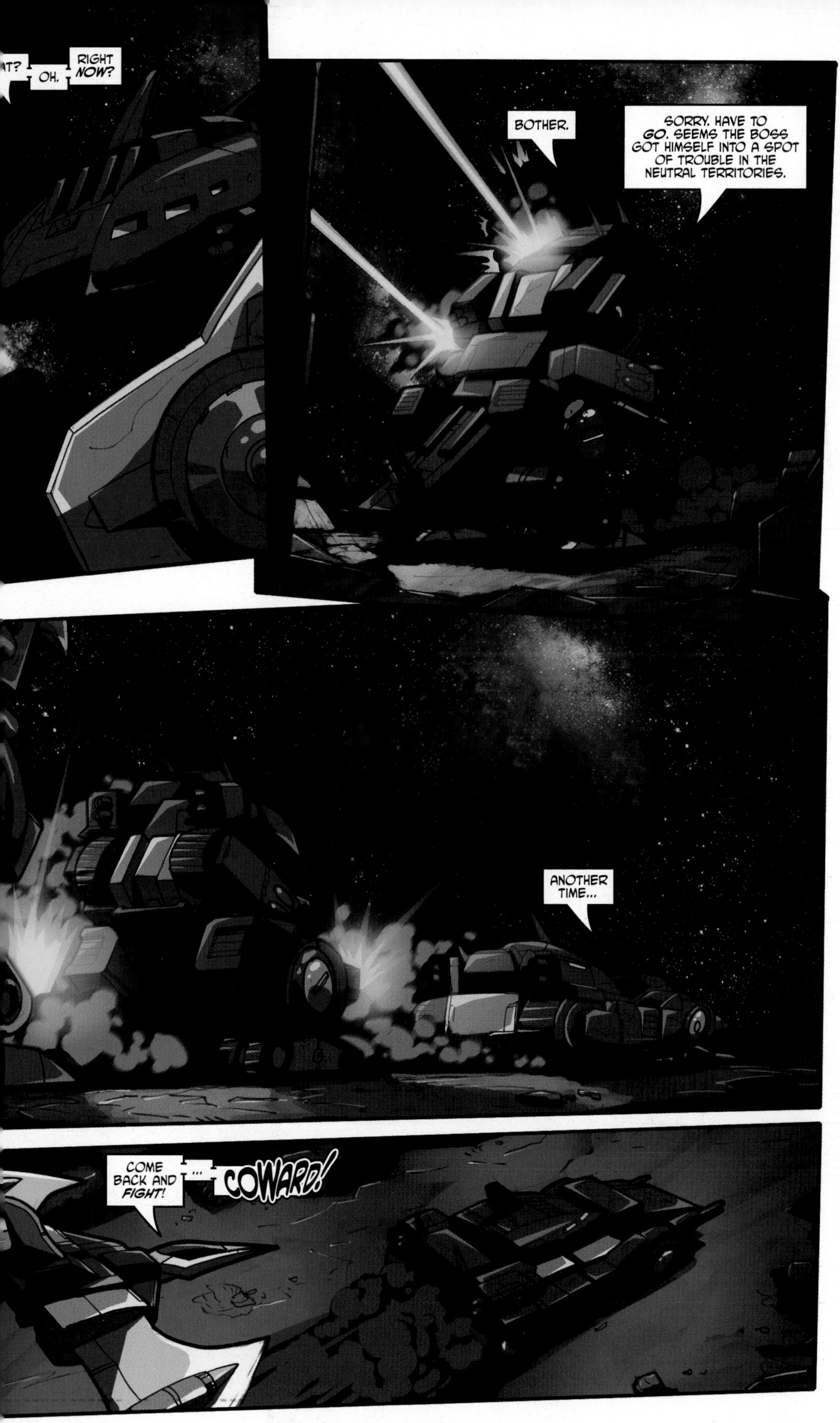
AT?
OH.
RIGHT NOW?
BOTHER.
SORRY. HAVE TO GO. SEEMS THE BOSS GOT HIMSELF INTO A SPOT OF TROUBLE IN THE NEUTRAL TERRITORIES.
ANOTHER TIME...
COME BACK AND FIGHT!
...
COWARD!

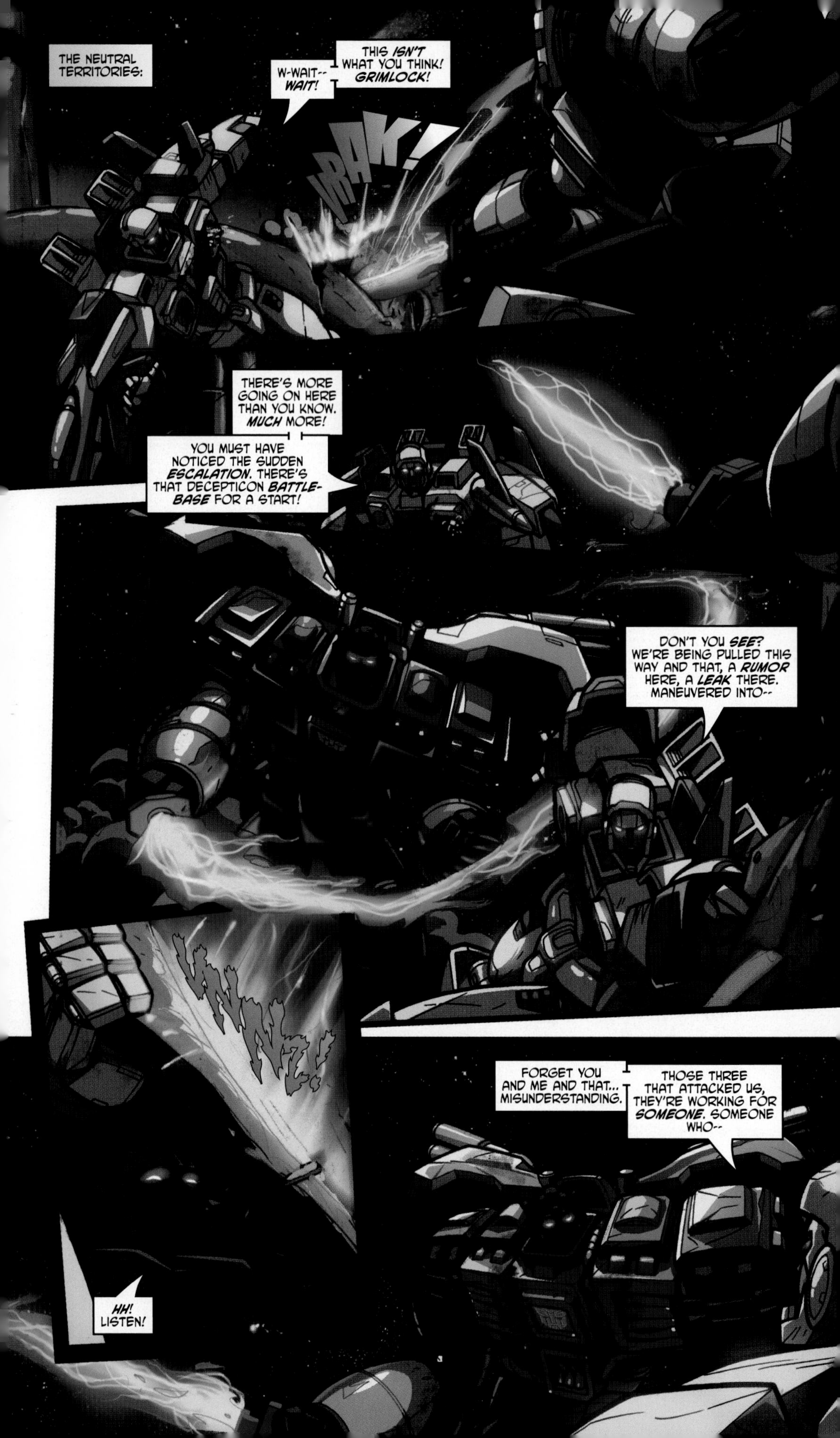
THE NEUTRAL TERRITORIES:
W-WAIT-- WAIT!
THIS ISN'T WHAT YOU THINK! GRIMLOCK!
KRAK!
THERE'S MORE GOING ON HERE THAN YOU KNOW. MUCH MORE!
YOU MUST HAVE NOTICED THE SUDDEN ESCALATION. THERE'S THAT DECEPTICON BATTLE-BASE FOR A START!
DON'T YOU SEE? WE'RE BEING PULLED THIS WAY AND THAT, A RUMOR HERE, A LEAK THERE. MANEUVERED INTO--
UNNH!
HH! LISTEN!
FORGET YOU AND ME AND THAT... MISUNDERSTANDING.
THOSE THREE THAT ATTACKED US, THEY'RE WORKING FOR SOMEONE. SOMEONE WHO--

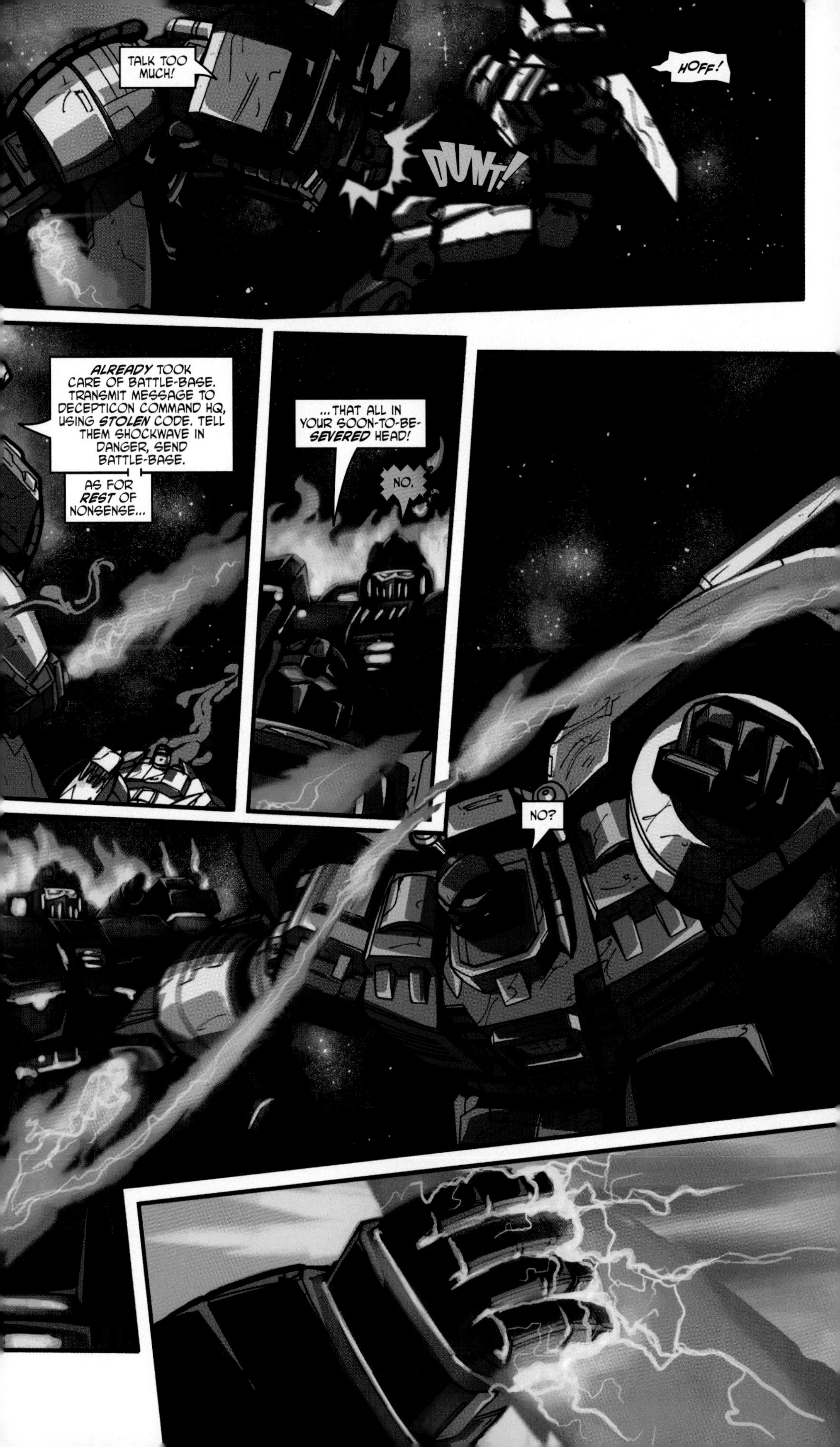
TALK TOO MUCH!
HOFF!
DUNT!
ALREADY TOOK CARE OF BATTLE-BASE. TRANSMIT MESSAGE TO DECEPTICON COMMAND HQ, USING STOLEN CODE. TELL THEM SHOCKWAVE IN DANGER, SEND BATTLE-BASE.
AS FOR REST OF NONSENSE...
...THAT ALL IN YOUR SOON-TO-BE-SEVERED HEAD!
NO.
NO?

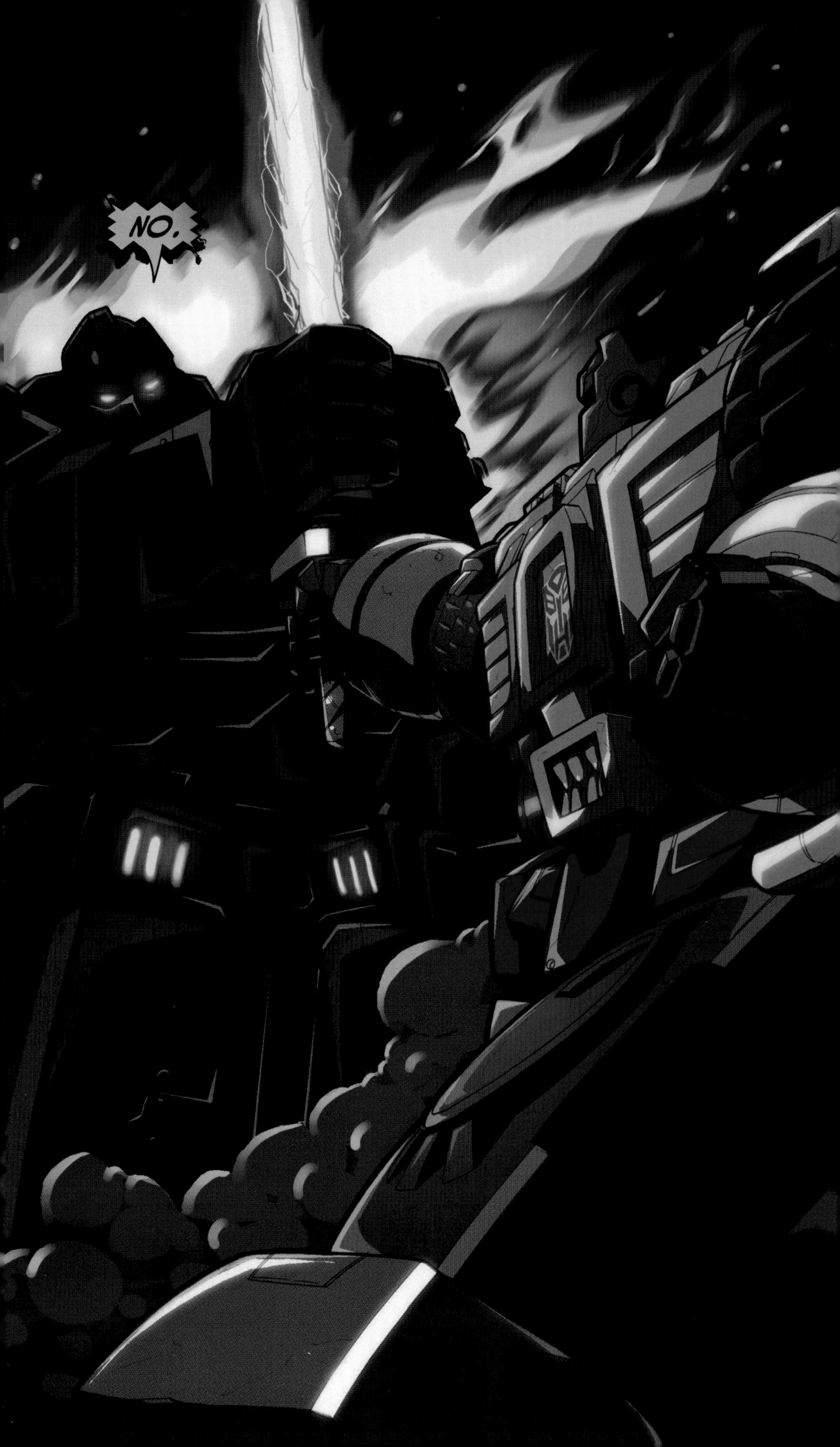
NO.

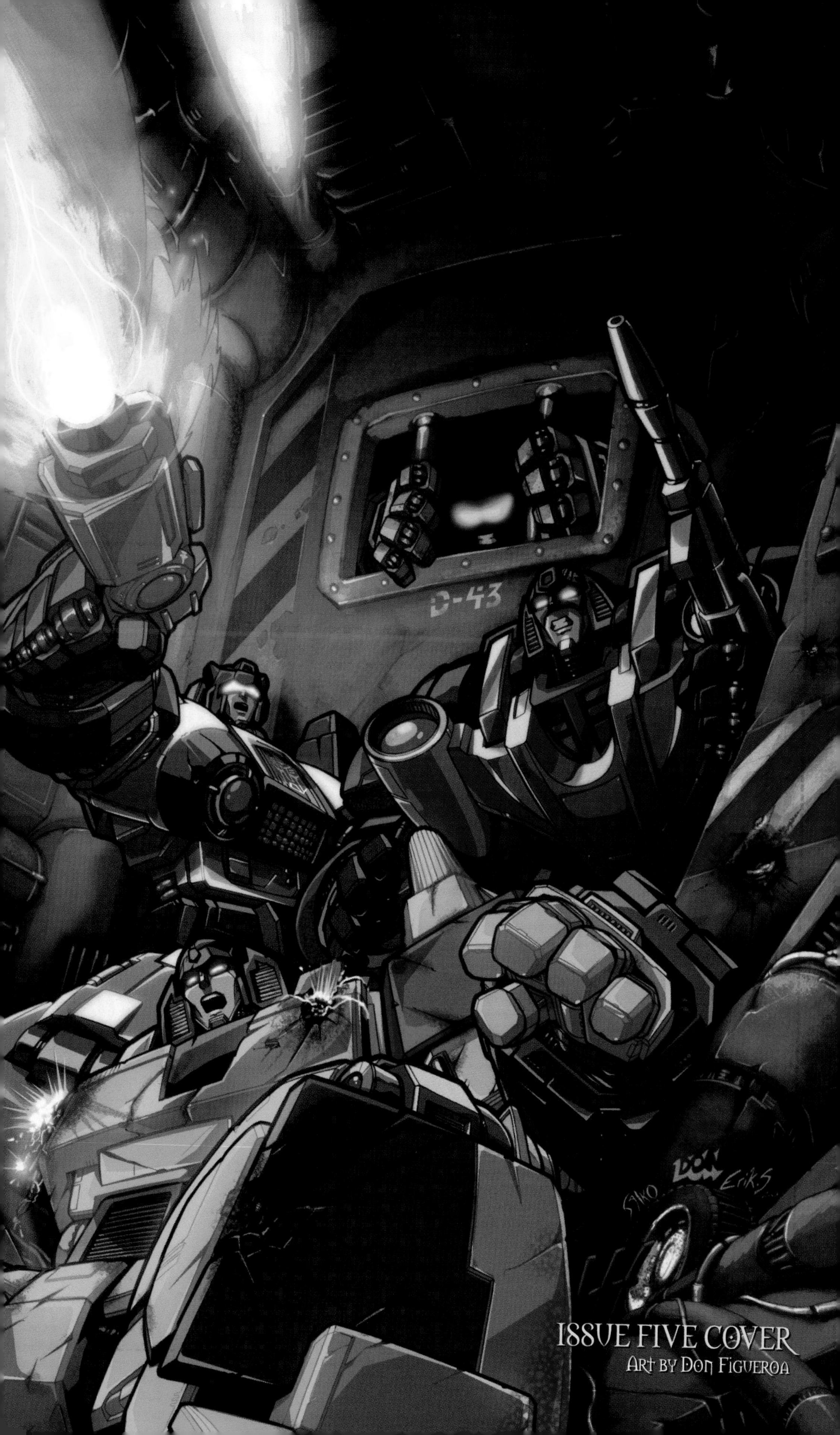
D-43

ISSUE FIVE COVER
Art by Don Figueroa

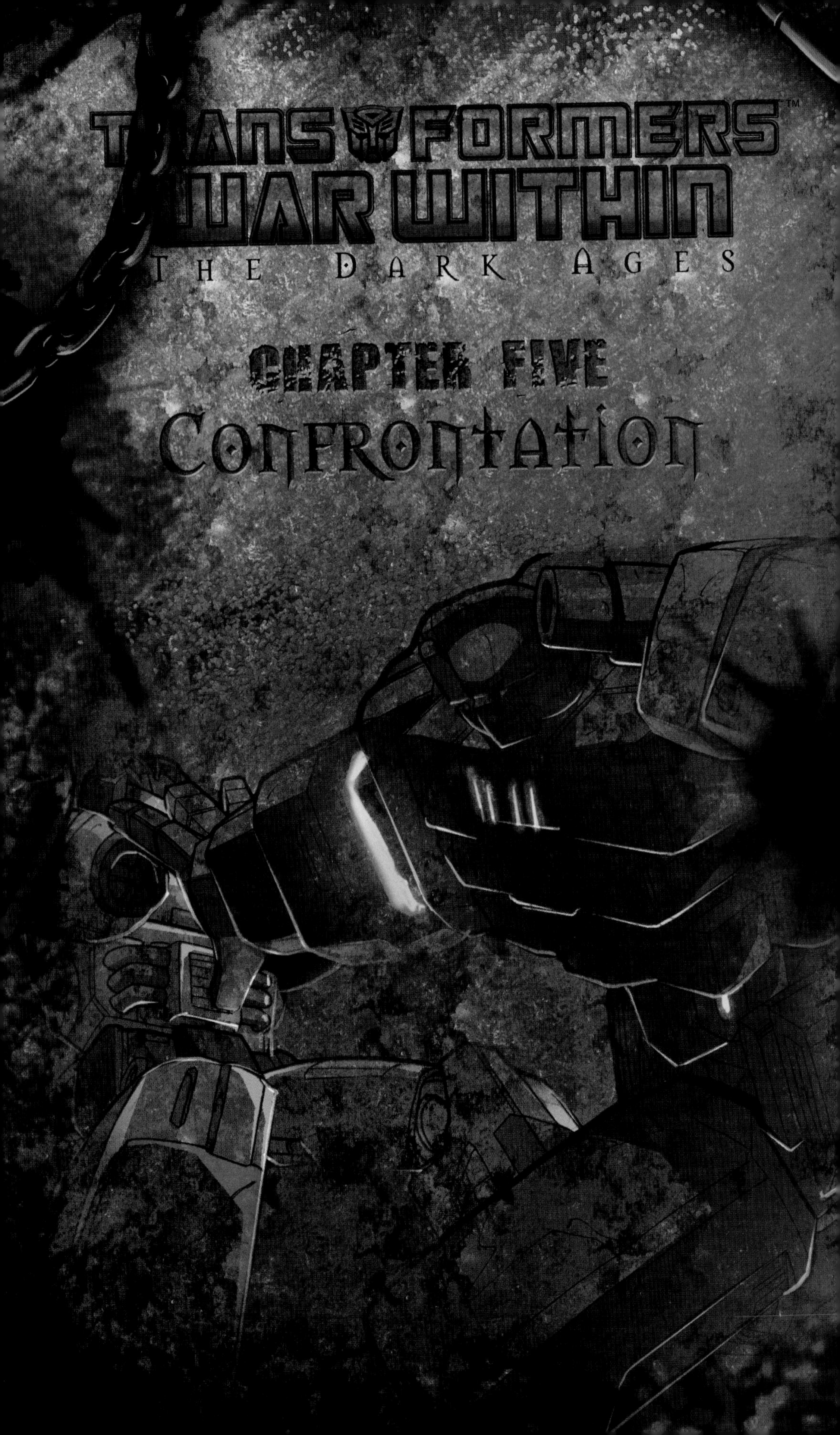
TRANSFORMERS
WAR WITHIN
THE DARK AGES
CHAPTER FIVE
Confrontation

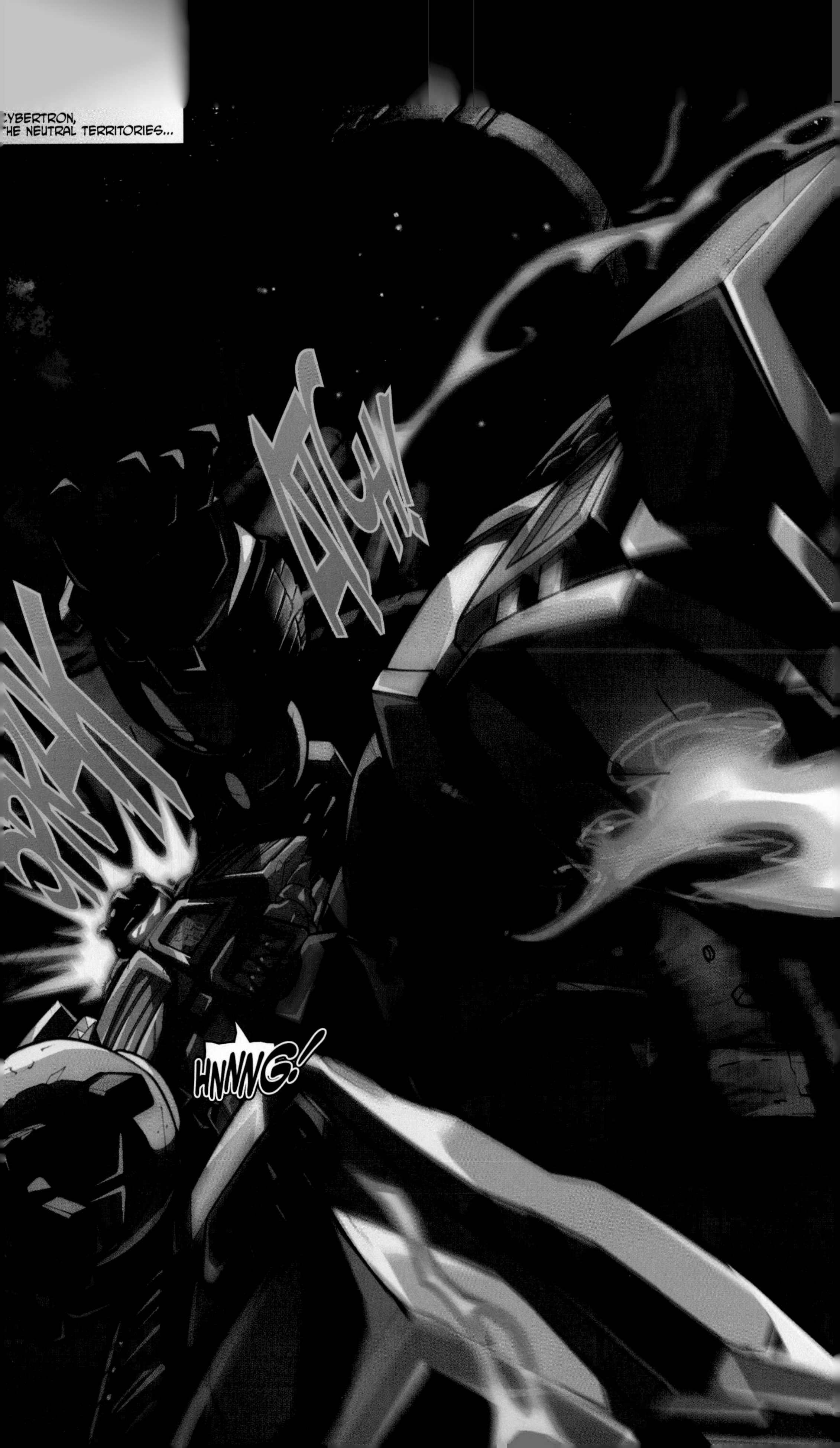
CYBERTRON,
THE NEUTRAL TERRITORIES...
HNNNG!

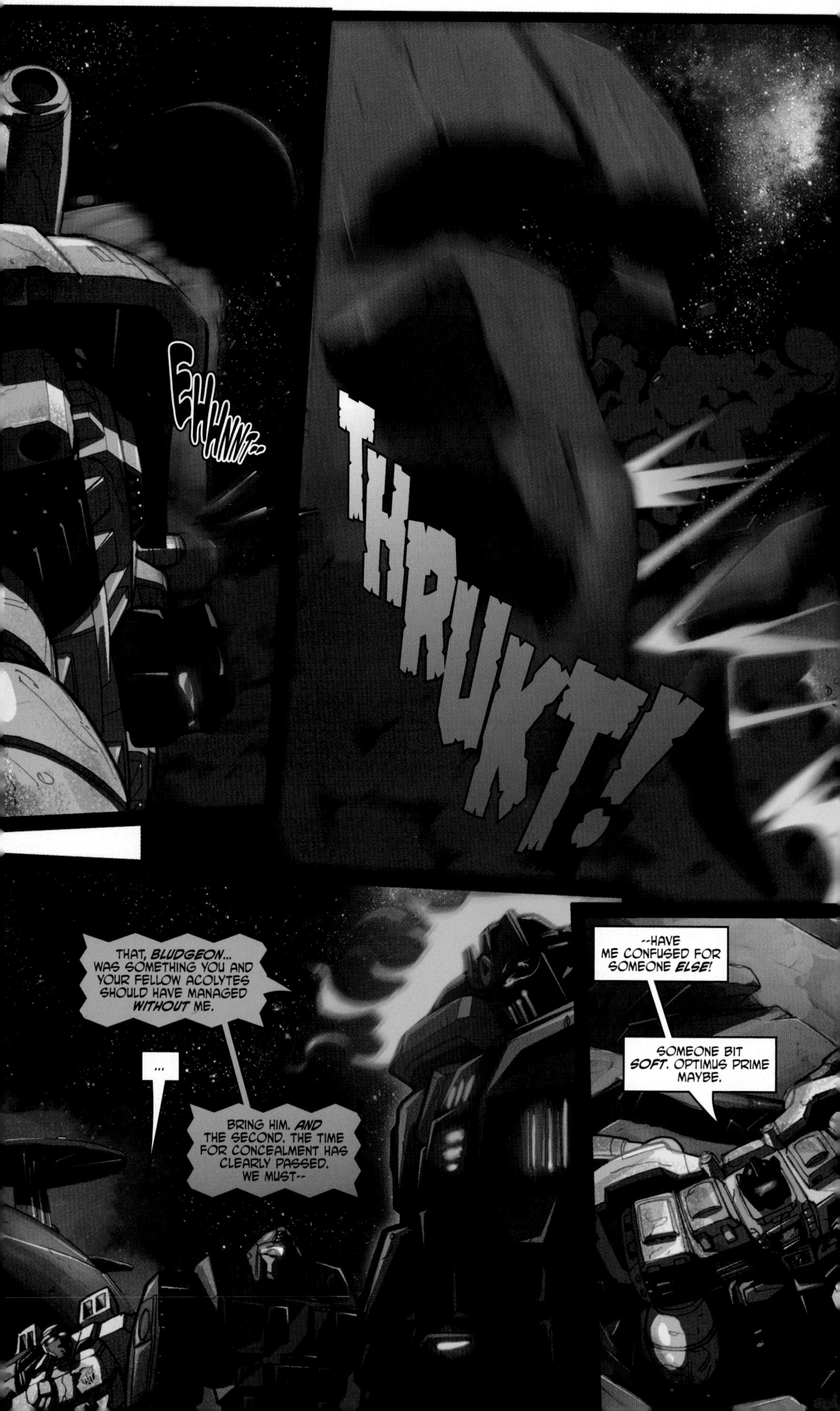
EHHNNT--
THRUKT!
THAT, BLUDGEON... WAS SOMETHING YOU AND YOUR FELLOW ACOLYTES SHOULD HAVE MANAGED WITHOUT ME.
...
BRING HIM. AND THE SECOND. THE TIME FOR CONCEALMENT HAS CLEARLY PASSED. WE MUST--
--HAVE ME CONFUSED FOR SOMEONE ELSE!
SOMEONE BIT SOFT. OPTIMUS PRIME MAYBE.

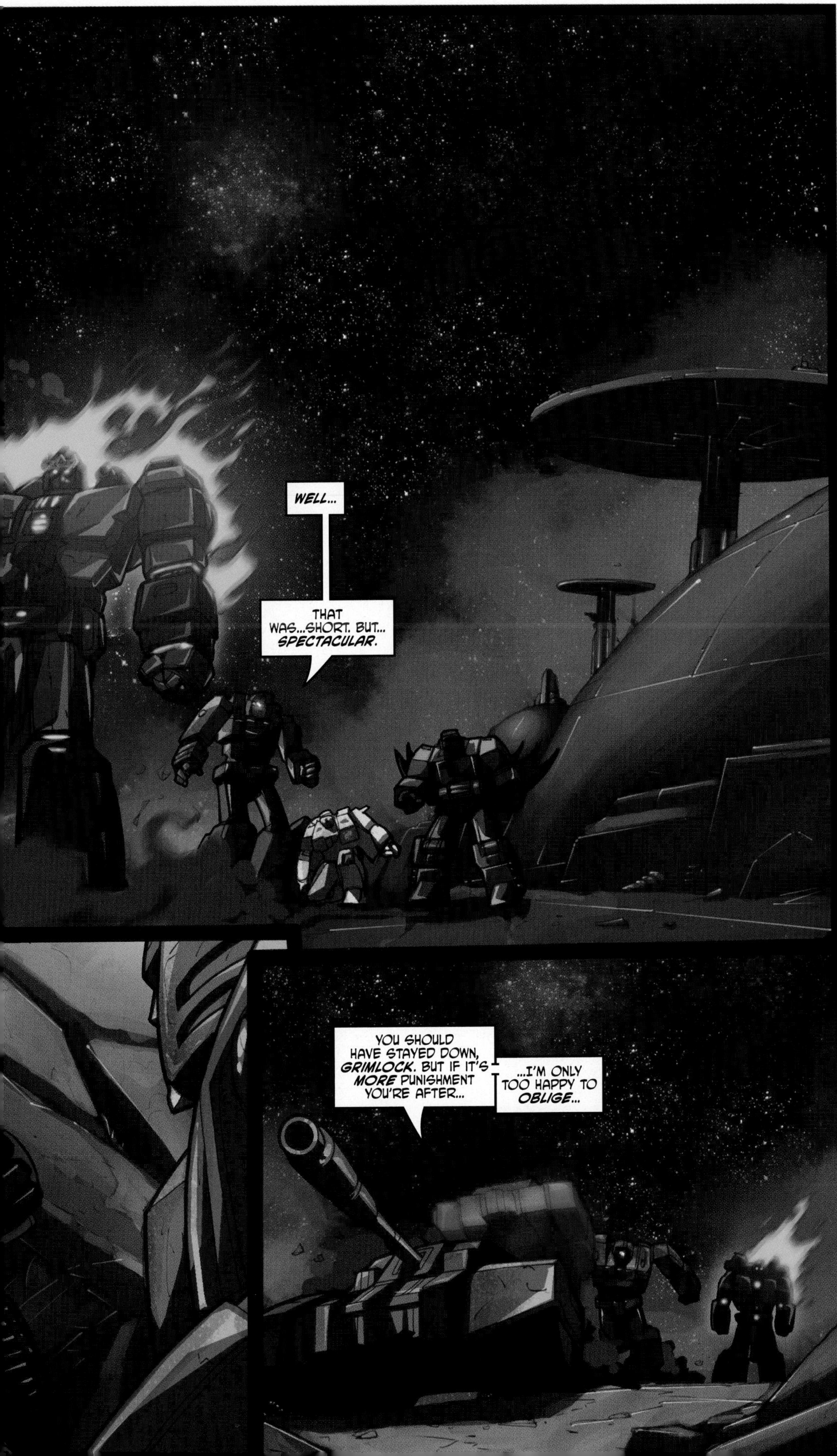
WELL...
THAT WAS...SHORT. BUT... SPECTACULAR.
YOU SHOULD HAVE STAYED DOWN, GRIMLOCK. BUT IF IT'S MORE PUNISHMENT YOU'RE AFTER...
...I'M ONLY TOO HAPPY TO OBLIGE...

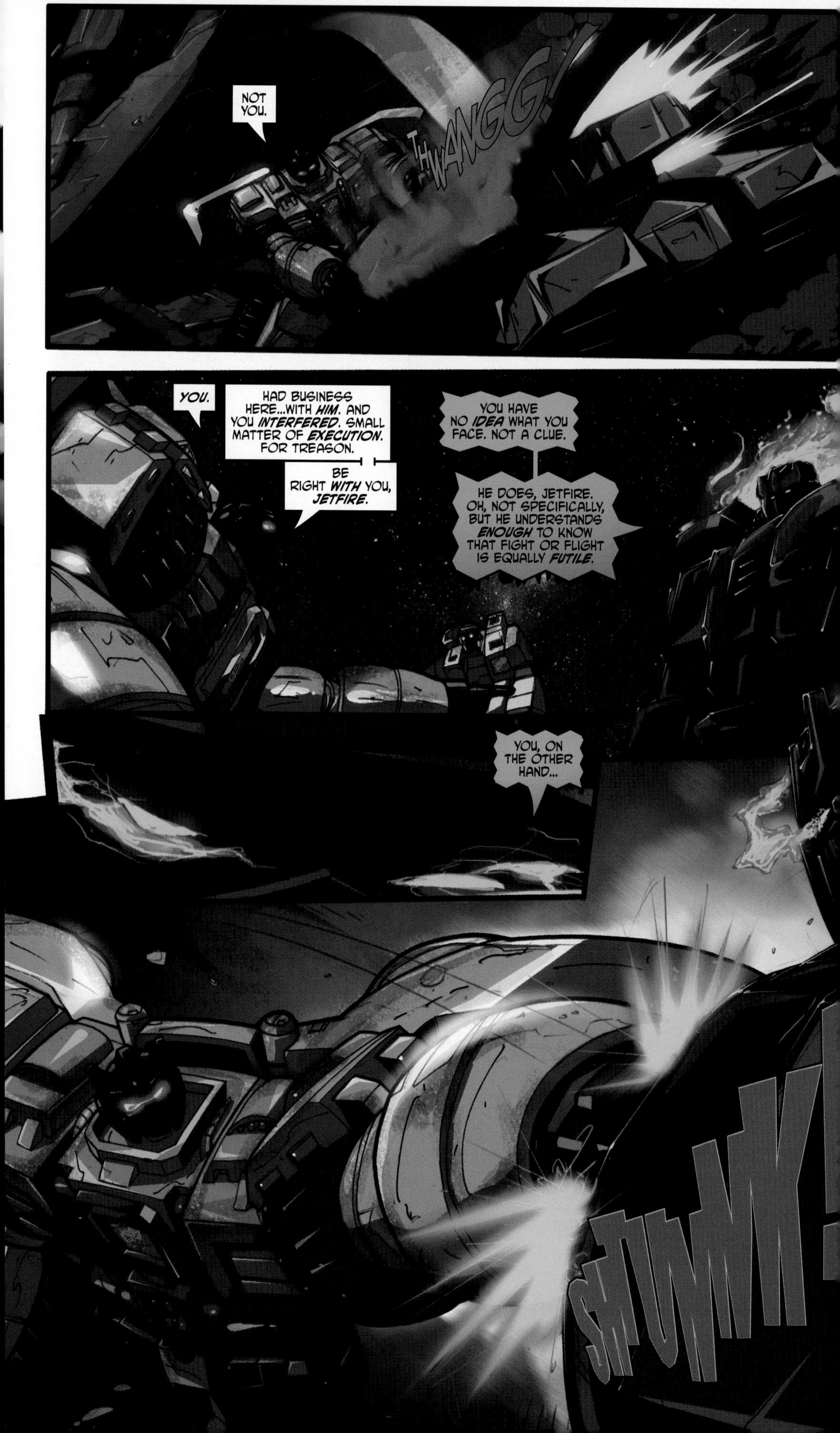
NOT YOU.
THWANGG!
YOU.
HAD BUSINESS HERE...WITH HIM. AND YOU INTERFERED. SMALL MATTER OF EXECUTION. FOR TREASON.
BE RIGHT WITH YOU, JETFIRE.
YOU HAVE NO IDEA WHAT YOU FACE. NOT A CLUE.
HE DOES, JETFIRE. OH, NOT SPECIFICALLY, BUT HE UNDERSTANDS ENOUGH TO KNOW THAT FIGHT OR FLIGHT IS EQUALLY FUTILE.
YOU, ON THE OTHER HAND...
SHUNNK!

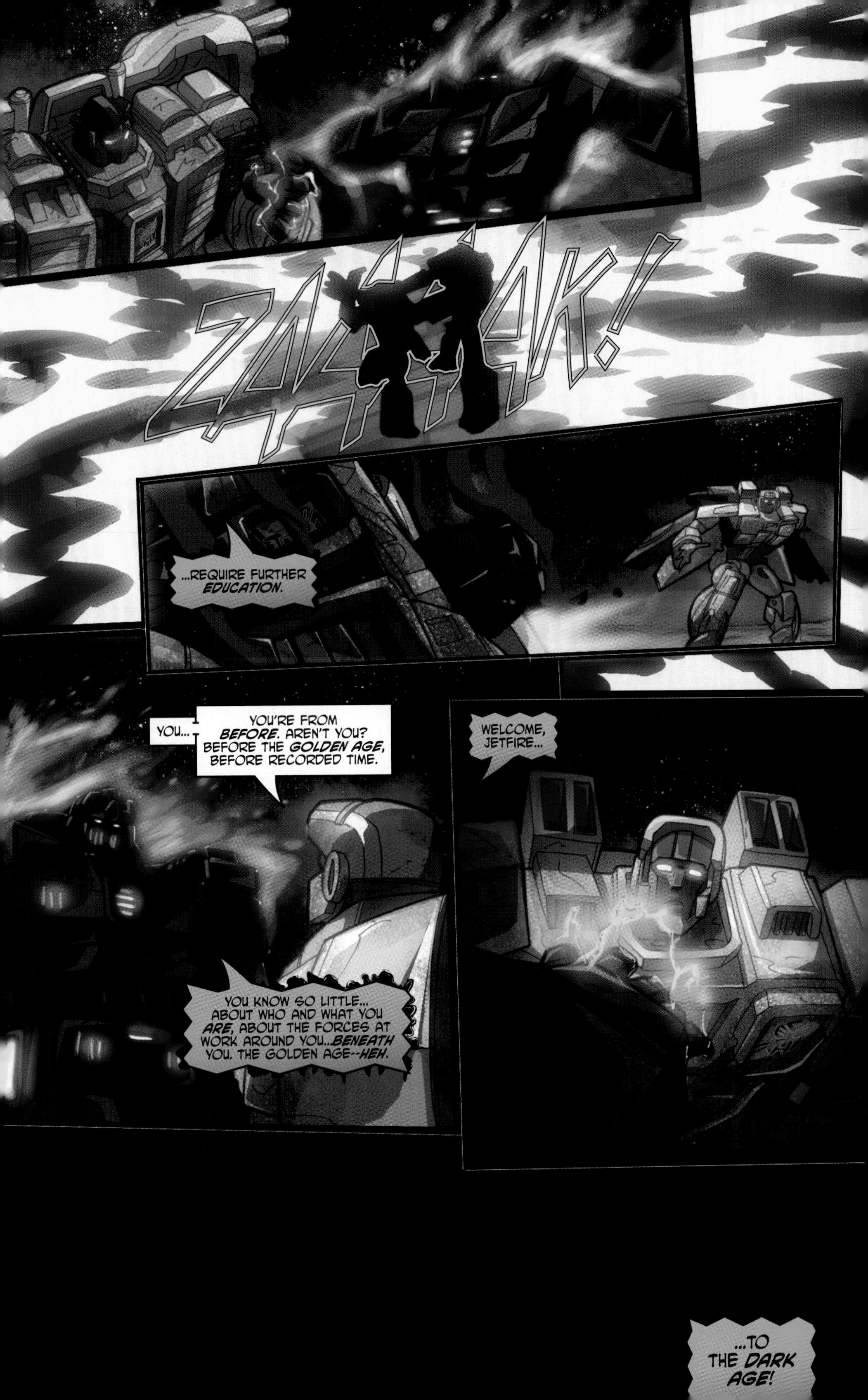
ZAKRAK!
...REQUIRE FURTHER EDUCATION.
YOU...
YOU'RE FROM BEFORE. AREN'T YOU? BEFORE THE GOLDEN AGE, BEFORE RECORDED TIME.
YOU KNOW SO LITTLE... ABOUT WHO AND WHAT YOU ARE, ABOUT THE FORCES AT WORK AROUND YOU...BENEATH YOU. THE GOLDEN AGE--HEH.
WELCOME, JETFIRE...
...TO THE DARK AGE!

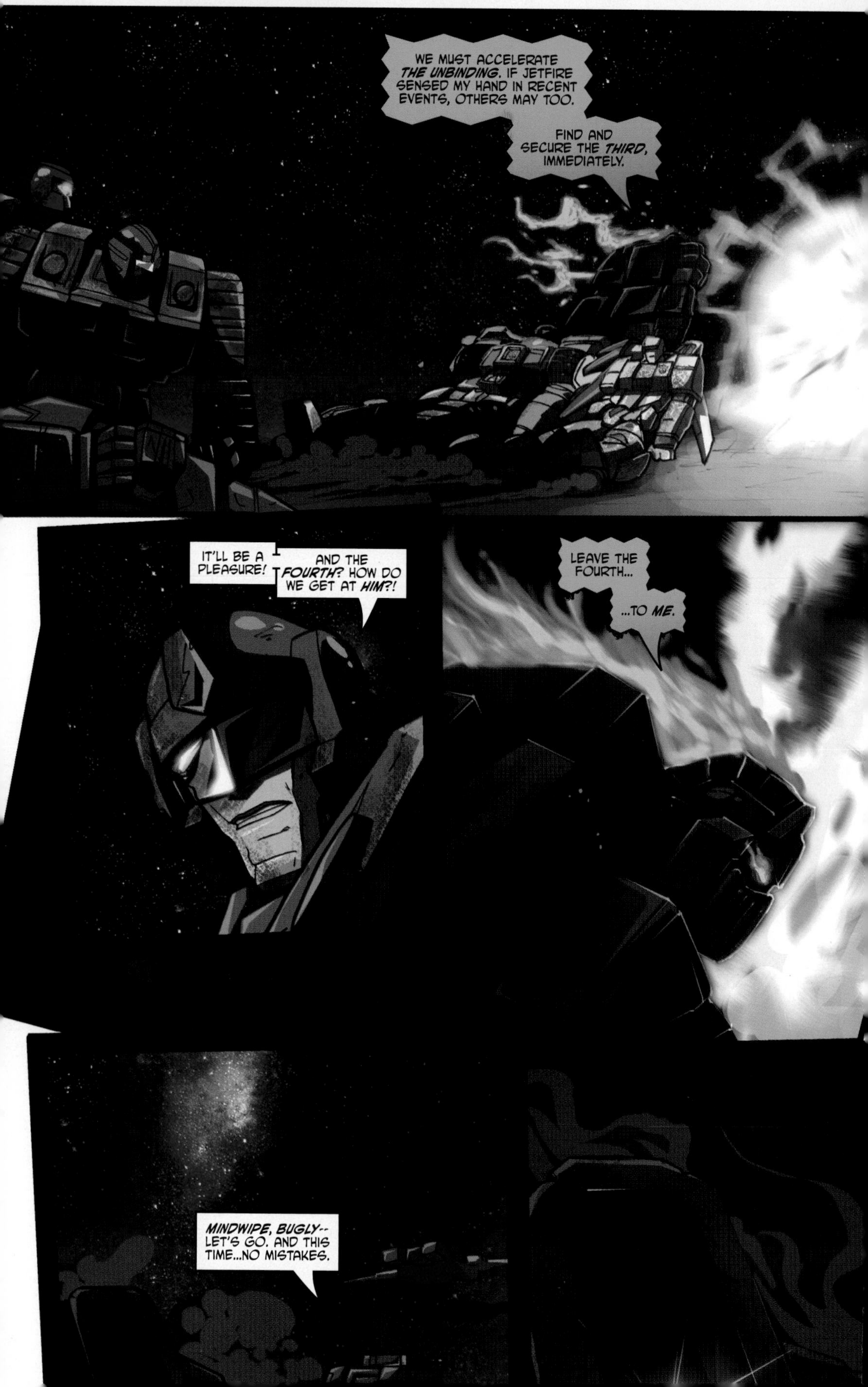
WE MUST ACCELERATE *THE UNBINDING*. IF JETFIRE SENSED MY HAND IN RECENT EVENTS, OTHERS MAY TOO.
FIND AND SECURE THE *THIRD*, IMMEDIATELY.
IT'LL BE A PLEASURE!
AND THE *FOURTH*? HOW DO WE GET AT *HIM*?!
LEAVE THE FOURTH...
...TO *ME*.
MINDWIPE, BUGLY-- LET'S GO. AND THIS TIME...NO MISTAKES.

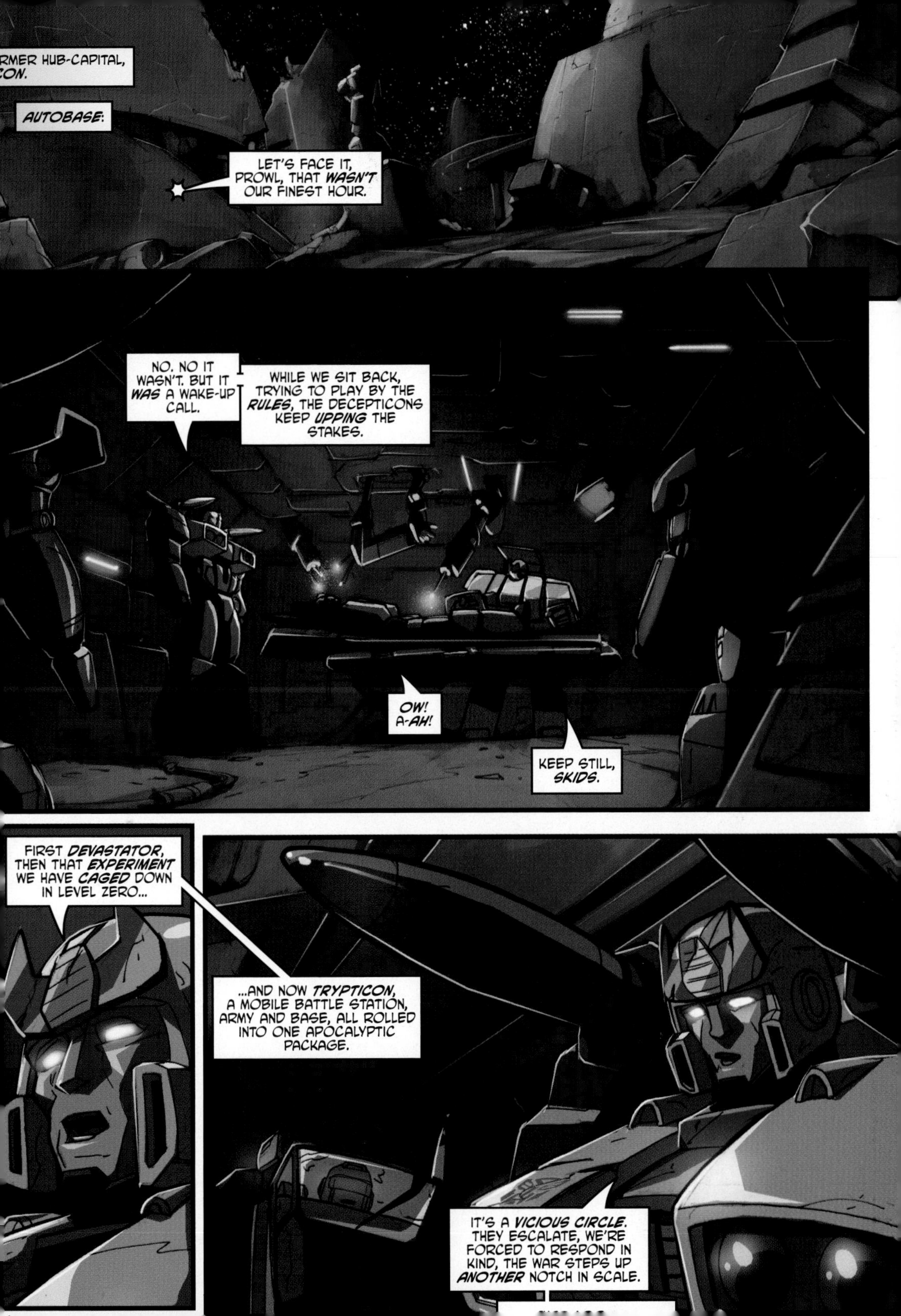
RMER HUB-CAPITAL,
CON.
AUTOBASE:
LET'S FACE IT, PROWL, THAT WASN'T OUR FINEST HOUR.
NO. NO IT WASN'T. BUT IT WAS A WAKE-UP CALL.
WHILE WE SIT BACK, TRYING TO PLAY BY THE RULES, THE DECEPTICONS KEEP UPPING THE STAKES.
OW! A-AH!
KEEP STILL, SKIDS.
FIRST DEVASTATOR, THEN THAT EXPERIMENT WE HAVE CAGED DOWN IN LEVEL ZERO...
...AND NOW TRYPTICON, A MOBILE BATTLE STATION, ARMY AND BASE, ALL ROLLED INTO ONE APOCALYPTIC PACKAGE.
IT'S A VICIOUS CIRCLE. THEY ESCALATE, WE'RE FORCED TO RESPOND IN KIND, THE WAR STEPS UP ANOTHER NOTCH IN SCALE.

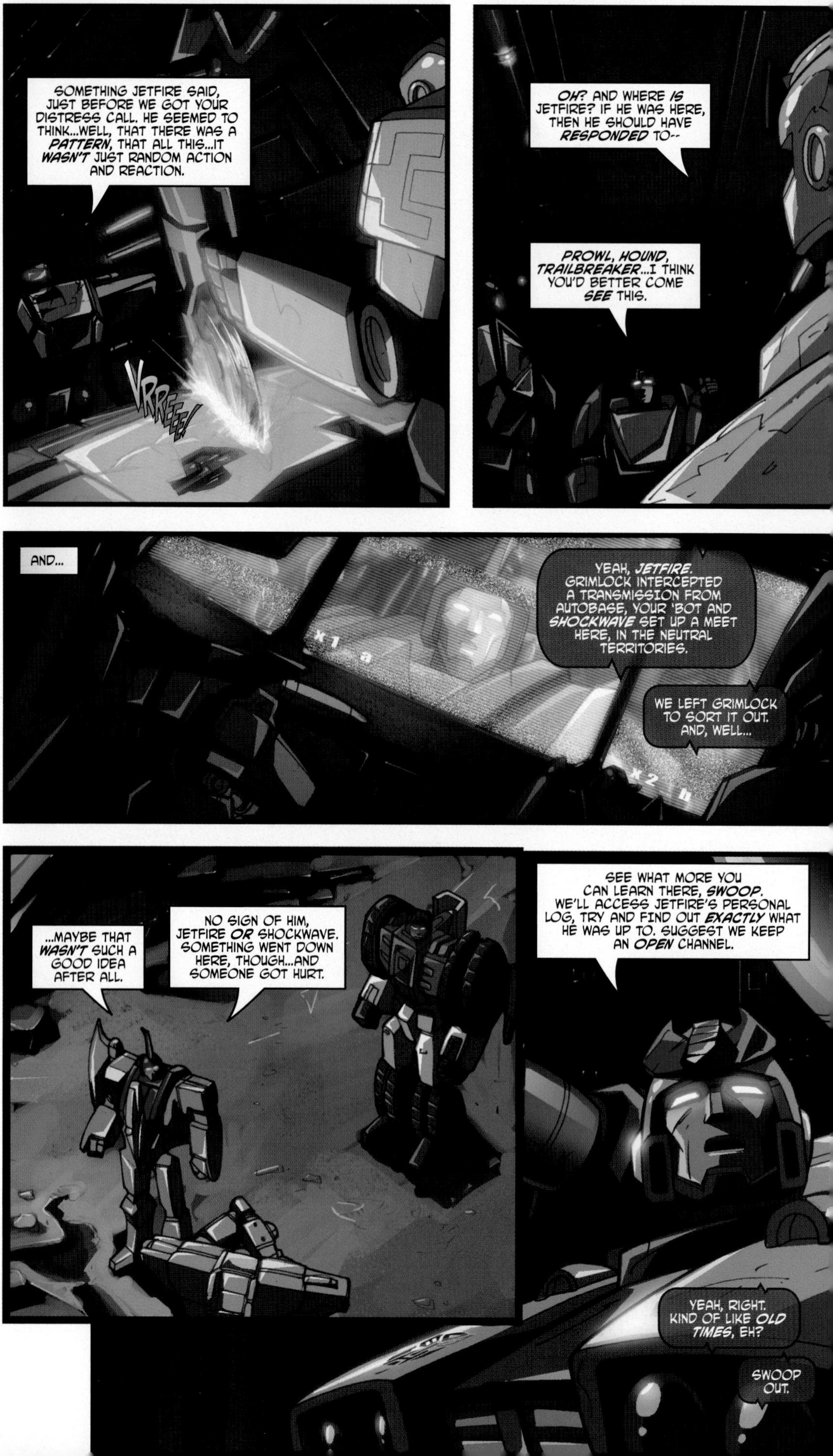
SOMETHING JETFIRE SAID, JUST BEFORE WE GOT YOUR DISTRESS CALL. HE SEEMED TO THINK...WELL, THAT THERE WAS A *PATTERN*, THAT ALL THIS...IT *WASN'T* JUST RANDOM ACTION AND REACTION.
OH? AND WHERE *IS* JETFIRE? IF HE WAS HERE, THEN HE SHOULD HAVE *RESPONDED* TO--
PROWL, HOUND, TRAILBREAKER...I THINK YOU'D BETTER COME *SEE* THIS.
AND...
YEAH, *JETFIRE*. GRIMLOCK INTERCEPTED A TRANSMISSION FROM AUTOBASE, YOUR 'BOT AND *SHOCKWAVE* SET UP A MEET HERE, IN THE NEUTRAL TERRITORIES.
WE LEFT GRIMLOCK TO SORT IT OUT. AND, WELL...
...MAYBE THAT *WASN'T* SUCH A GOOD IDEA AFTER ALL.
NO SIGN OF HIM, JETFIRE *OR* SHOCKWAVE. SOMETHING WENT DOWN HERE, THOUGH...AND SOMEONE GOT HURT.
SEE WHAT MORE YOU CAN LEARN THERE, *SWOOP*. WE'LL ACCESS JETFIRE'S PERSONAL LOG, TRY AND FIND OUT *EXACTLY* WHAT HE WAS UP TO. SUGGEST WE KEEP AN *OPEN* CHANNEL.
YEAH, RIGHT. KIND OF LIKE *OLD TIMES*, EH?
SWOOP OUT.

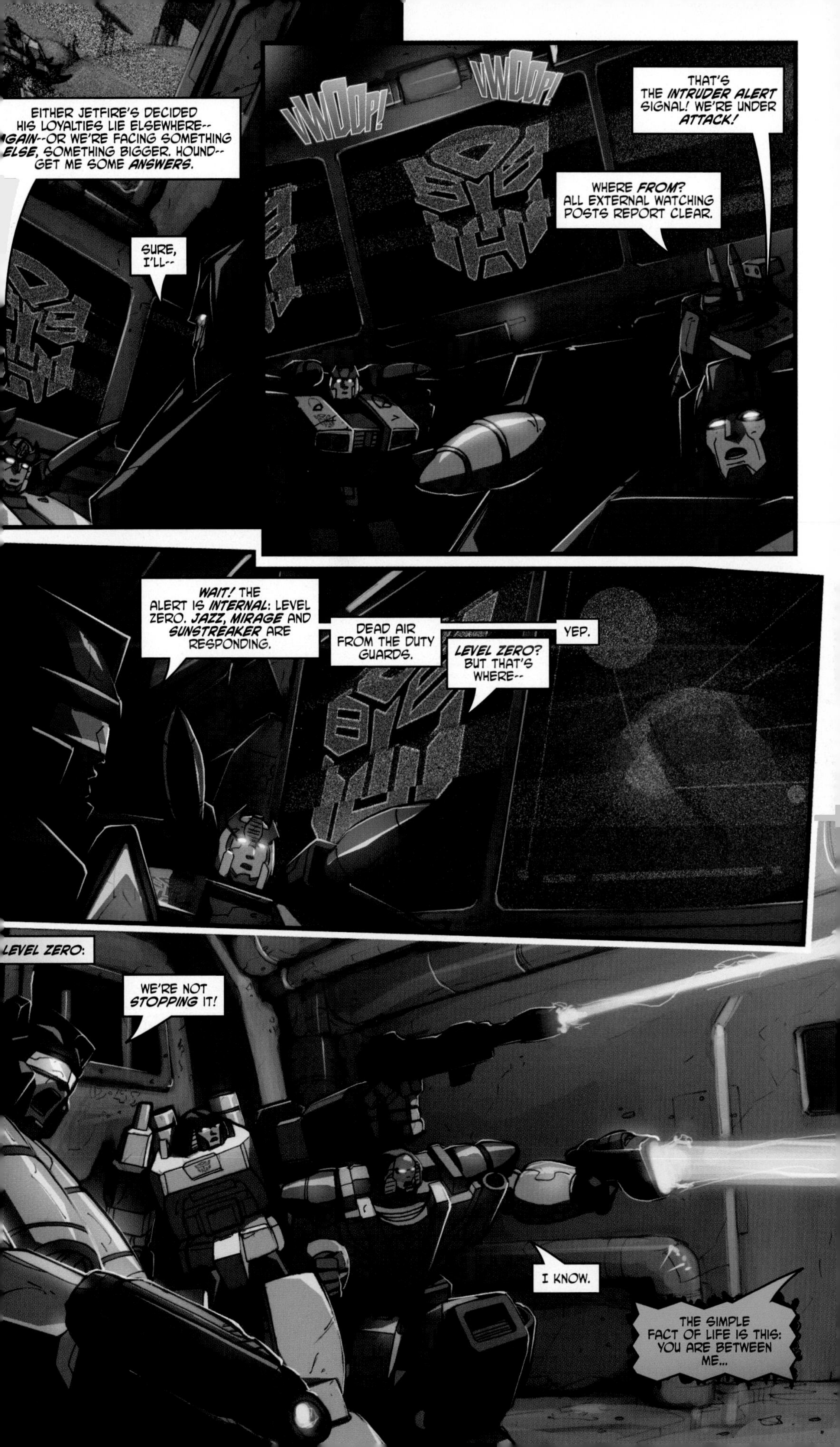

EITHER JETFIRE'S DECIDED HIS LOYALTIES LIE ELSEWHERE--AGAIN--OR WE'RE FACING SOMETHING ELSE, SOMETHING BIGGER. HOUND--GET ME SOME ANSWERS.
SURE, I'LL--
VWOOP!
VWOOP!
THAT'S THE INTRUDER ALERT SIGNAL! WE'RE UNDER ATTACK!
WHERE FROM? ALL EXTERNAL WATCHING POSTS REPORT CLEAR.
WAIT! THE ALERT IS INTERNAL: LEVEL ZERO. JAZZ, MIRAGE AND SUNSTREAKER ARE RESPONDING.
DEAD AIR FROM THE DUTY GUARDS.
YEP.
LEVEL ZERO? BUT THAT'S WHERE--
LEVEL ZERO:
WE'RE NOT STOPPING IT!
I KNOW.
THE SIMPLE FACT OF LIFE IS THIS: YOU ARE BETWEEN ME...

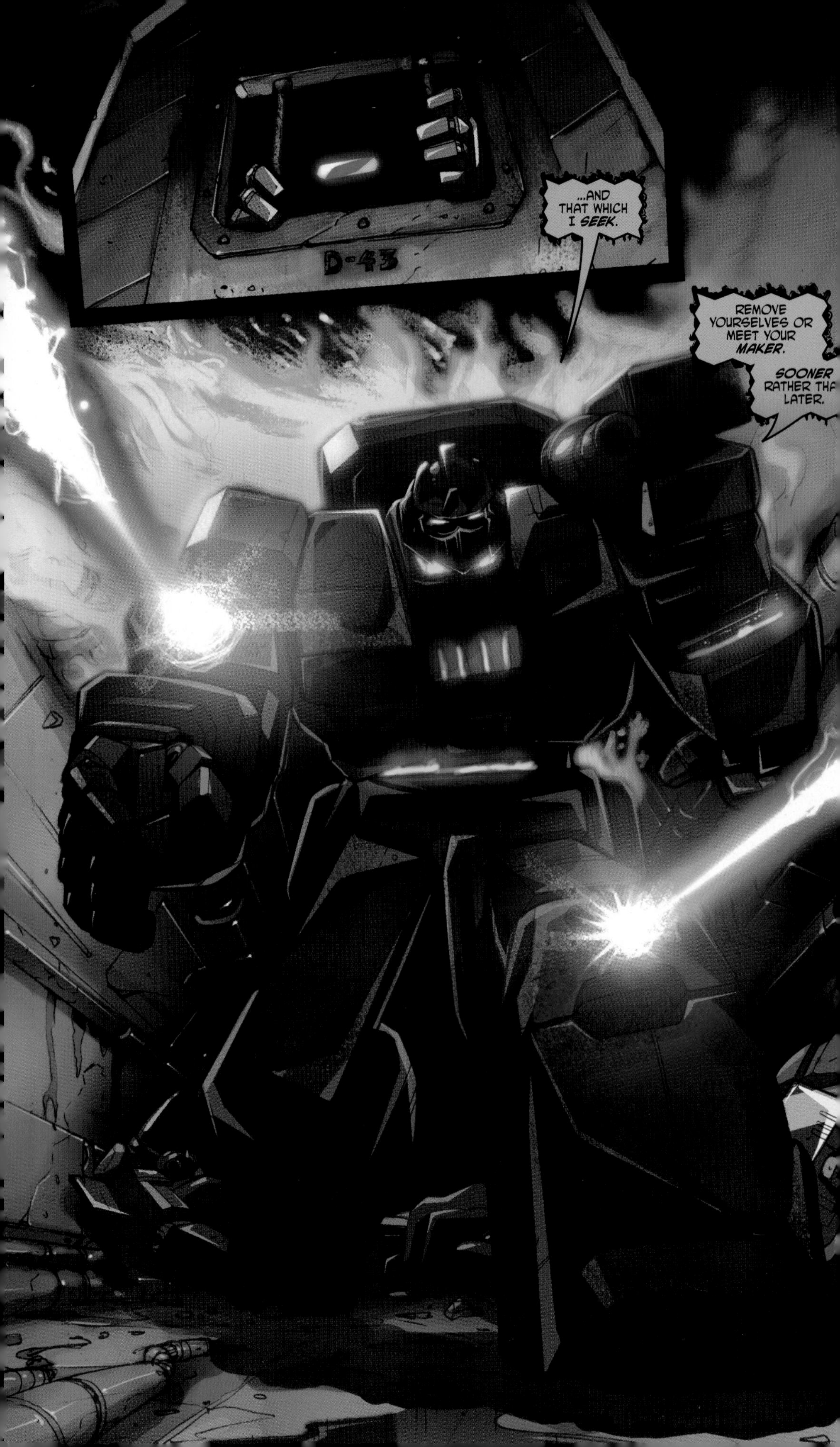

...AND THAT WHICH I SEEK.
REMOVE YOURSELVES OR MEET YOUR MAKER.
SOONER RATHER THA
LATER.
D-43

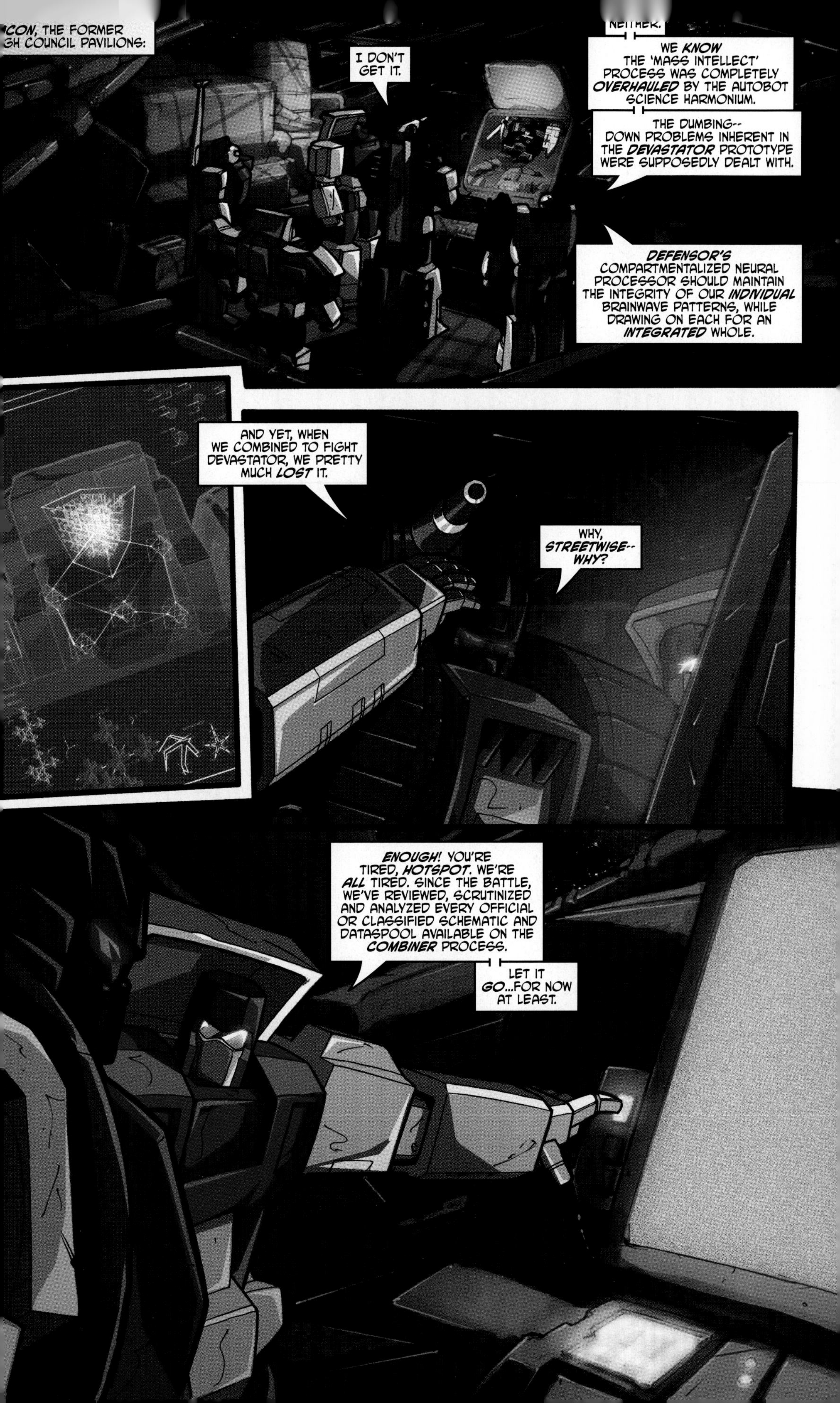

CON, THE FORMER
GH COUNCIL PAVILIONS:
I DON'T GET IT.
NEITHER.
WE KNOW THE 'MASS INTELLECT' PROCESS WAS COMPLETELY OVERHAULED BY THE AUTOBOT SCIENCE HARMONIUM.
THE DUMBING--DOWN PROBLEMS INHERENT IN THE DEVASTATOR PROTOTYPE WERE SUPPOSEDLY DEALT WITH.
DEFENSOR'S COMPARTMENTALIZED NEURAL PROCESSOR SHOULD MAINTAIN THE INTEGRITY OF OUR INDIVIDUAL BRAINWAVE PATTERNS, WHILE DRAWING ON EACH FOR AN INTEGRATED WHOLE.
AND YET, WHEN WE COMBINED TO FIGHT DEVASTATOR, WE PRETTY MUCH LOST IT.
WHY, STREETWISE--WHY?
ENOUGH! YOU'RE TIRED, HOTSPOT. WE'RE ALL TIRED. SINCE THE BATTLE, WE'VE REVIEWED, SCRUTINIZED AND ANALYZED EVERY OFFICIAL OR CLASSIFIED SCHEMATIC AND DATASPOOL AVAILABLE ON THE COMBINER PROCESS.
LET IT GO...FOR NOW AT LEAST.

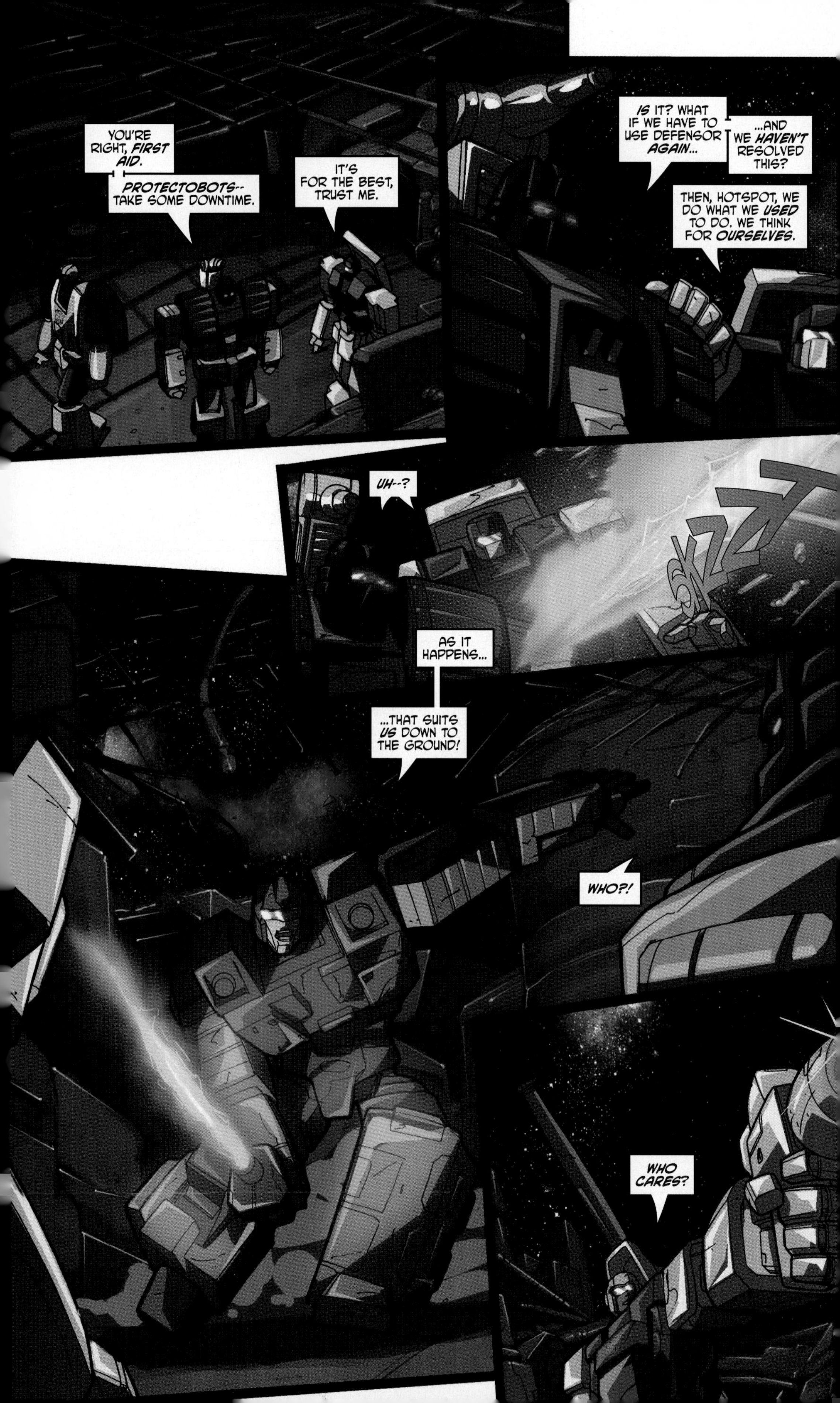
YOU'RE RIGHT, FIRST AID.
PROTECTOBOTS-- TAKE SOME DOWNTIME.
IT'S FOR THE BEST, TRUST ME.
IS IT? WHAT IF WE HAVE TO USE DEFENSOR AGAIN...
...AND WE HAVEN'T RESOLVED THIS?
THEN, HOTSPOT, WE DO WHAT WE USED TO DO. WE THINK FOR OURSELVES.
UH--?
SKZZZT
AS IT HAPPENS...
...THAT SUITS US DOWN TO THE GROUND!
WHO?!
WHO CARES?

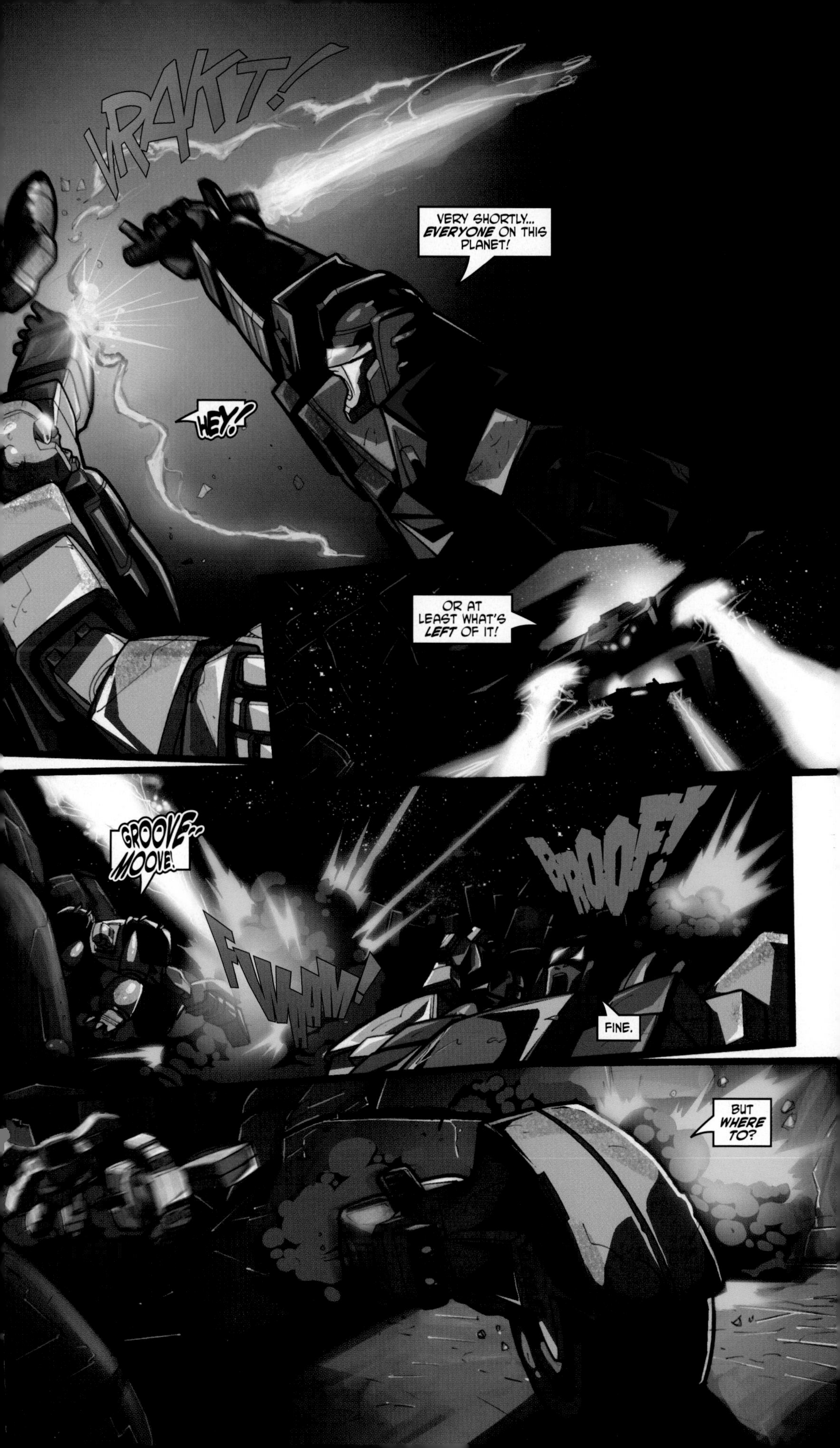
VRAKT!
VERY SHORTLY... EVERYONE ON THIS PLANET!
HEY!
OR AT LEAST WHAT'S LEFT OF IT!
GROOVE-- MOOVE!
FWHAM!
BROOOF!
FINE.
BUT WHERE TO?

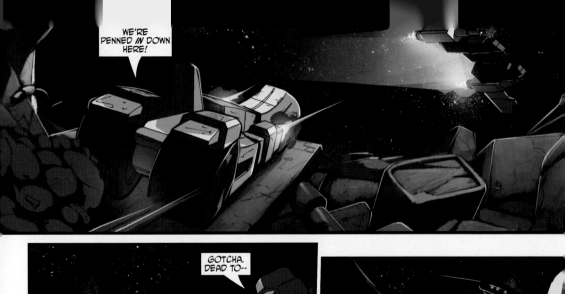

WE'RE PENNED *IN* DOWN HERE!

GOTCHA. DEAD TO--

STREETWISE! LISTEN CAREFULLY.

FORGET BLUDGEON...

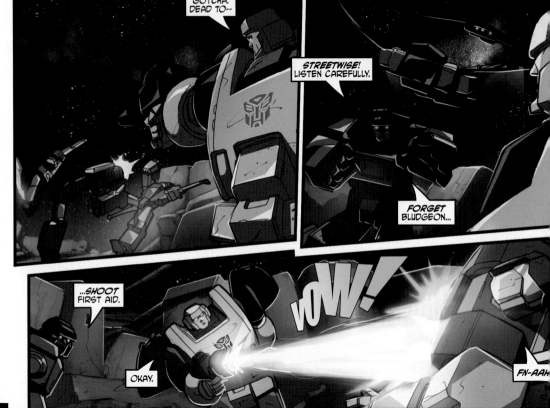

...*SHOOT* FIRST AID.

OKAY.

VOW!

FN-AAH

HOTSPOT--THEY'RE TURNING PROTECTOBOT *AGAINST* PROTECTOBOT!

INITIATE THE *INTERLINK*...IT SHOULD OVERRIDE THEIR CONTROL. WE *NEED* DEFENSOR.

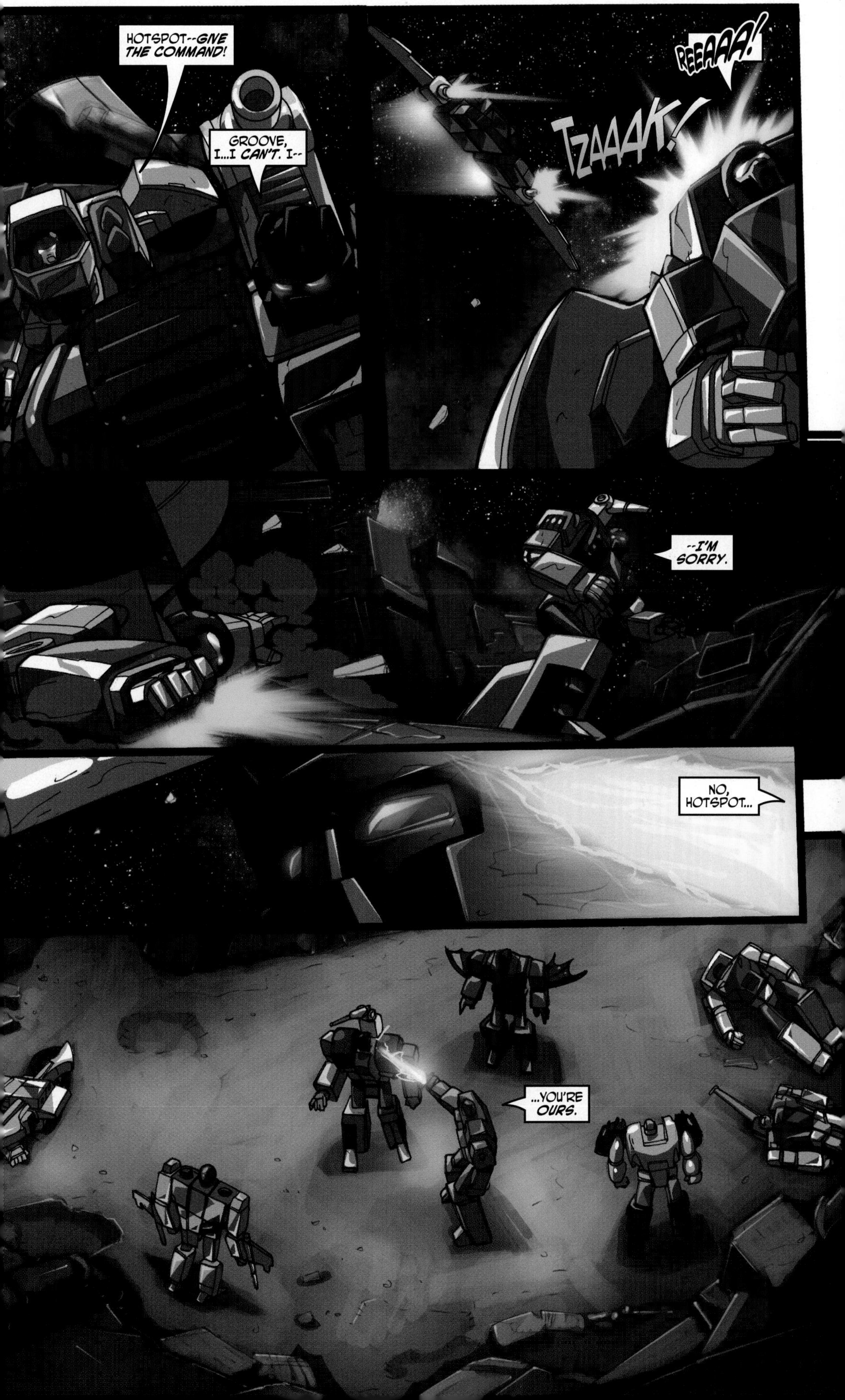
HOTSPOT--GIVE THE COMMAND!
GROOVE, I...I CAN'T. I--
REEEAAA!
TZAAAK!
--I'M SORRY.
NO, HOTSPOT...
...YOU'RE OURS.

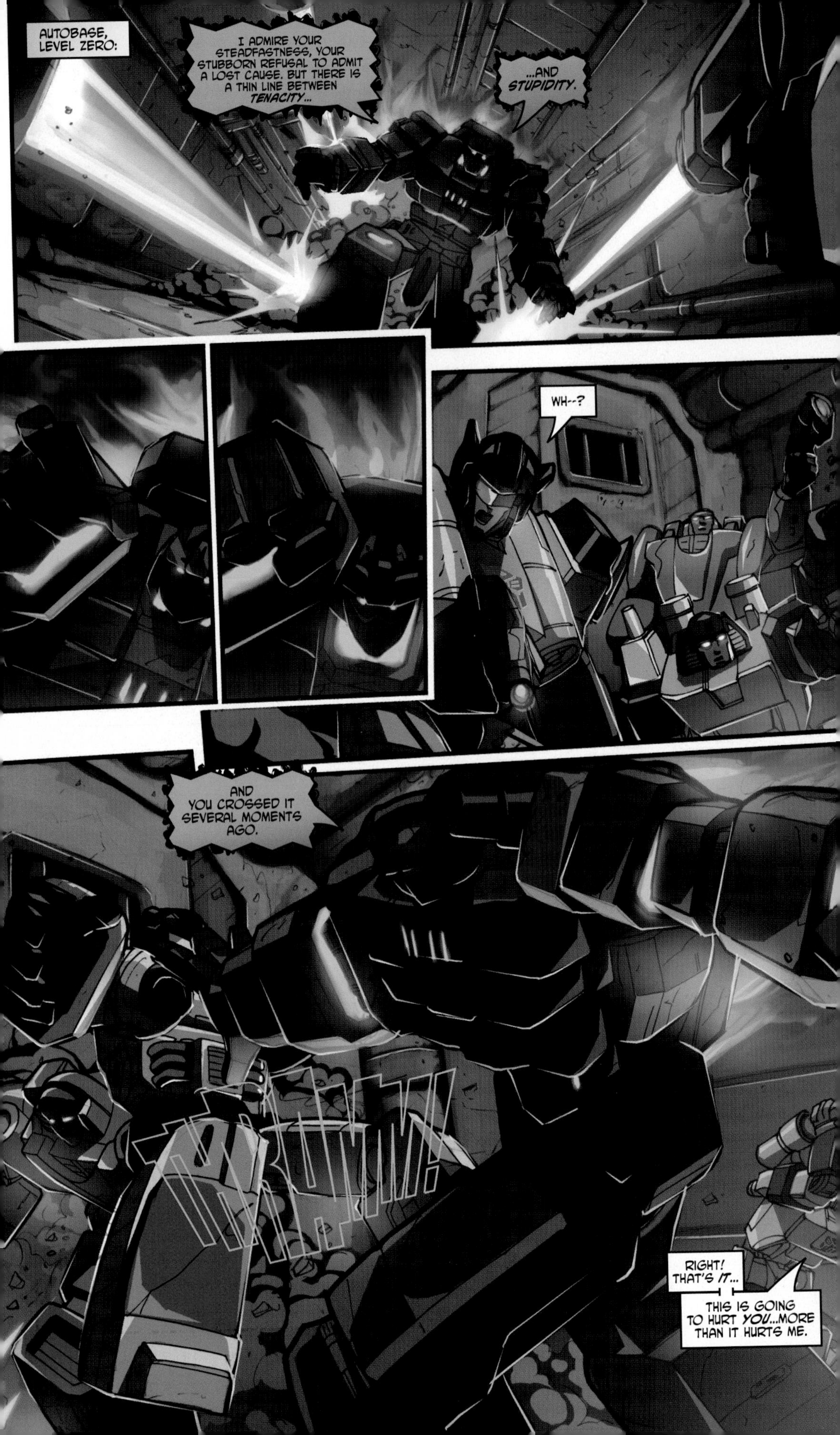
AUTOBASE, LEVEL ZERO:
I ADMIRE YOUR STEADFASTNESS, YOUR STUBBORN REFUSAL TO ADMIT A LOST CAUSE. BUT THERE IS A THIN LINE BETWEEN *TENACITY*...
...AND *STUPIDITY*.
WH--?
AND YOU CROSSED IT SEVERAL MOMENTS AGO.
THRAHMM!
RIGHT! THAT'S *IT*...
THIS IS GOING TO HURT *YOU*...MORE THAN IT HURTS ME.

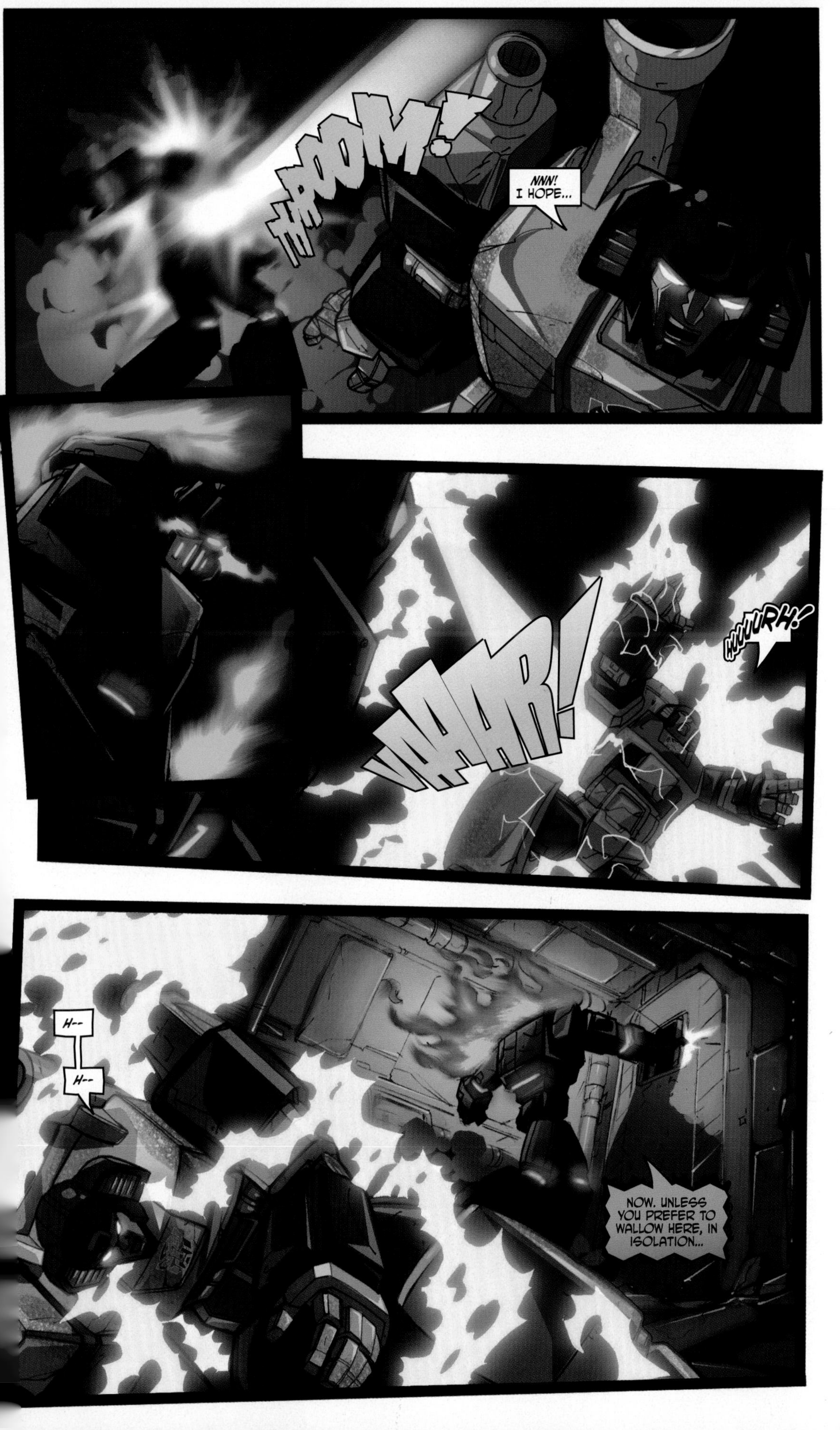
THROOM!
NNN! I HOPE...
VAAR!
HUUUURH!
H--
H--
NOW. UNLESS YOU PREFER TO WALLOW HERE, IN ISOLATION...

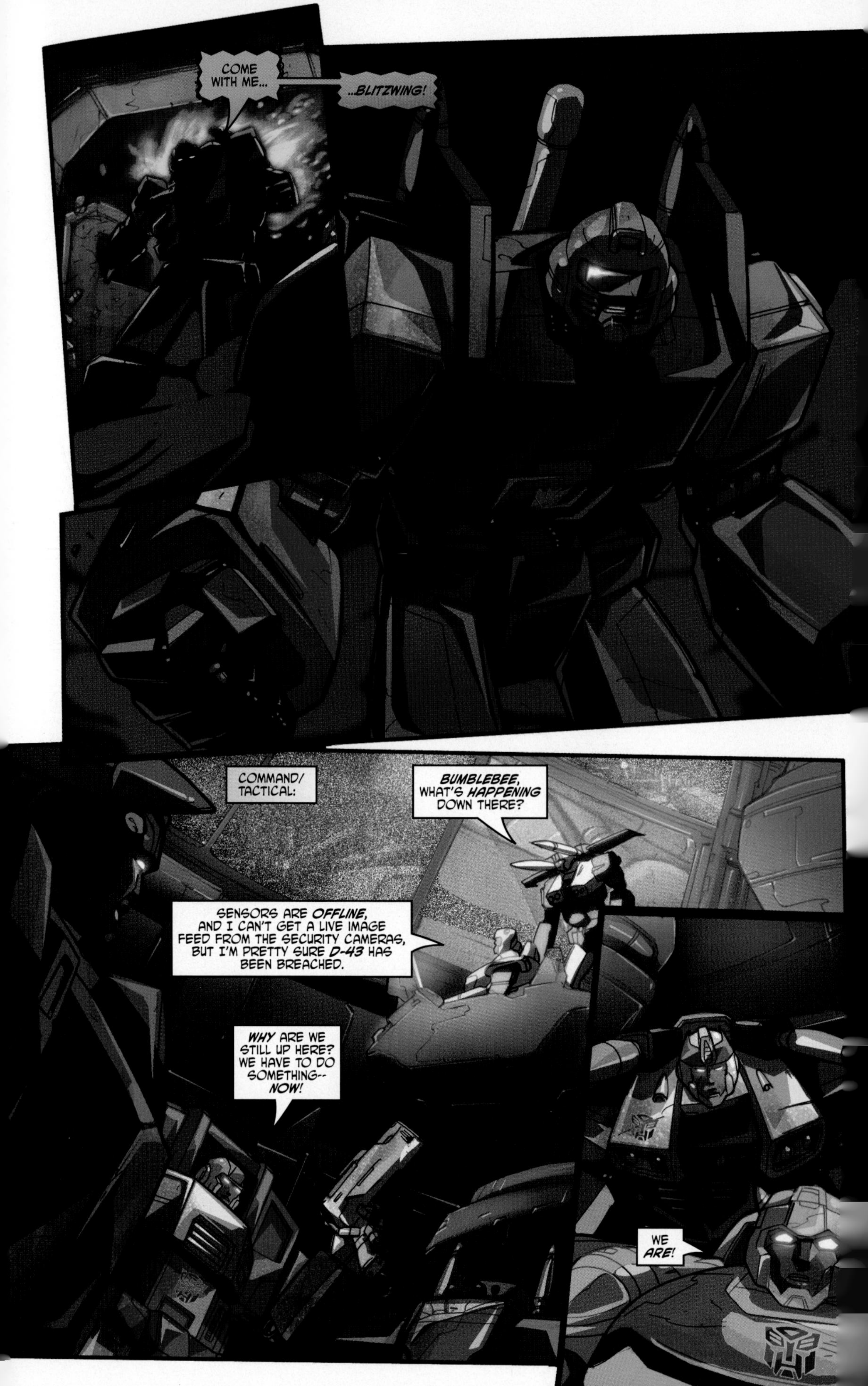
COME WITH ME...
..BLITZWING!
COMMAND/ TACTICAL:
BUMBLEBEE, WHAT'S HAPPENING DOWN THERE?
SENSORS ARE OFFLINE, AND I CAN'T GET A LIVE IMAGE FEED FROM THE SECURITY CAMERAS, BUT I'M PRETTY SURE D-43 HAS BEEN BREACHED.
WHY ARE WE STILL UP HERE? WE HAVE TO DO SOMETHING--NOW!
WE ARE!

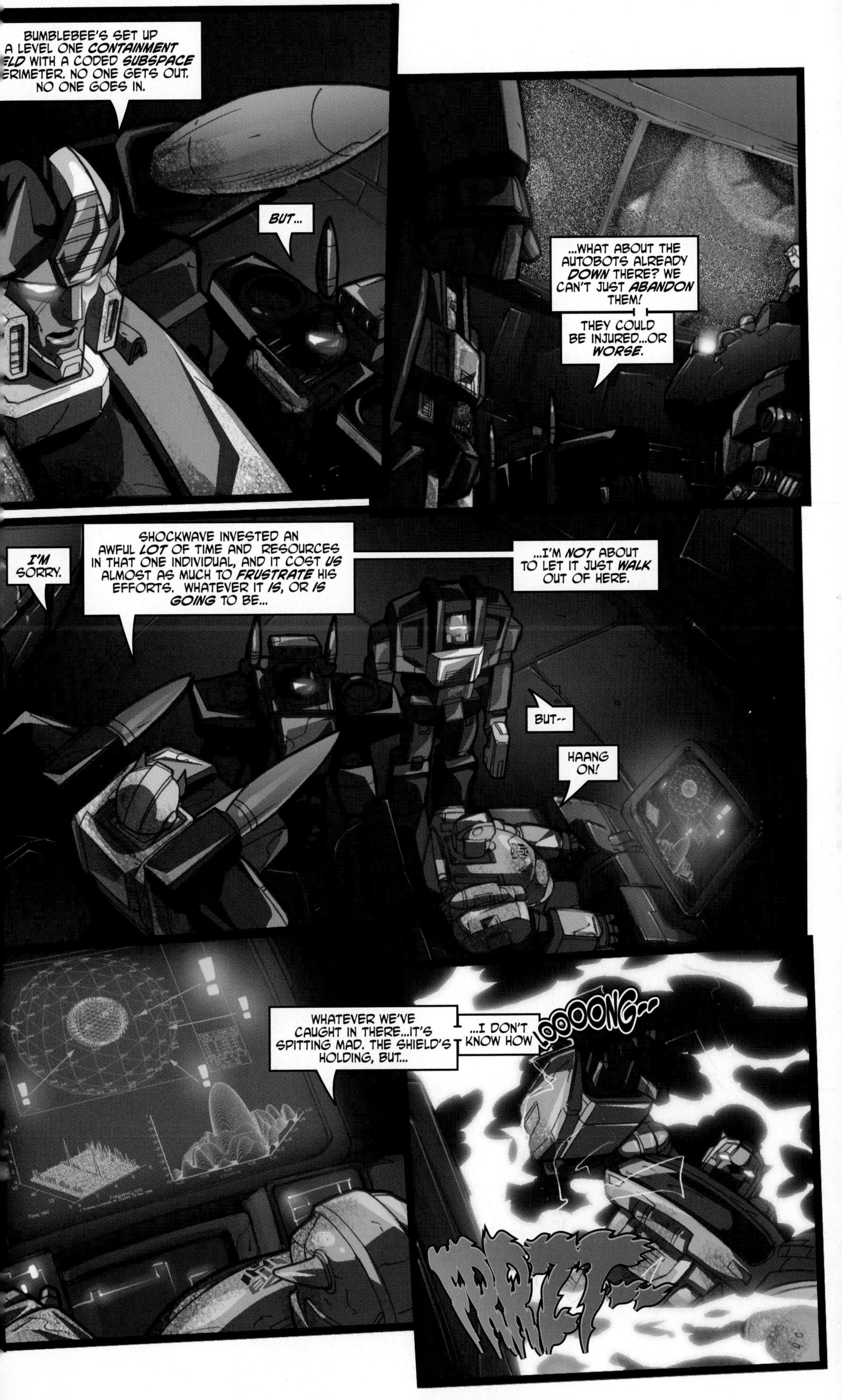

BUMBLEBEE'S SET UP A LEVEL ONE CONTAINMENT ELD WITH A CODED SUBSPACE ERIMETER. NO ONE GETS OUT. NO ONE GOES IN.
BUT...
...WHAT ABOUT THE AUTOBOTS ALREADY DOWN THERE? WE CAN'T JUST ABANDON THEM!
THEY COULD BE INJURED...OR WORSE.
I'M SORRY.
SHOCKWAVE INVESTED AN AWFUL LOT OF TIME AND RESOURCES IN THAT ONE INDIVIDUAL, AND IT COST US ALMOST AS MUCH TO FRUSTRATE HIS EFFORTS. WHATEVER IT IS, OR IS GOING TO BE...
...I'M NOT ABOUT TO LET IT JUST WALK OUT OF HERE.
BUT--
HAANG ON!
WHATEVER WE'VE CAUGHT IN THERE...IT'S SPITTING MAD. THE SHIELD'S HOLDING, BUT...
...I DON'T KNOW HOW
LOOOONG--
MRZZT

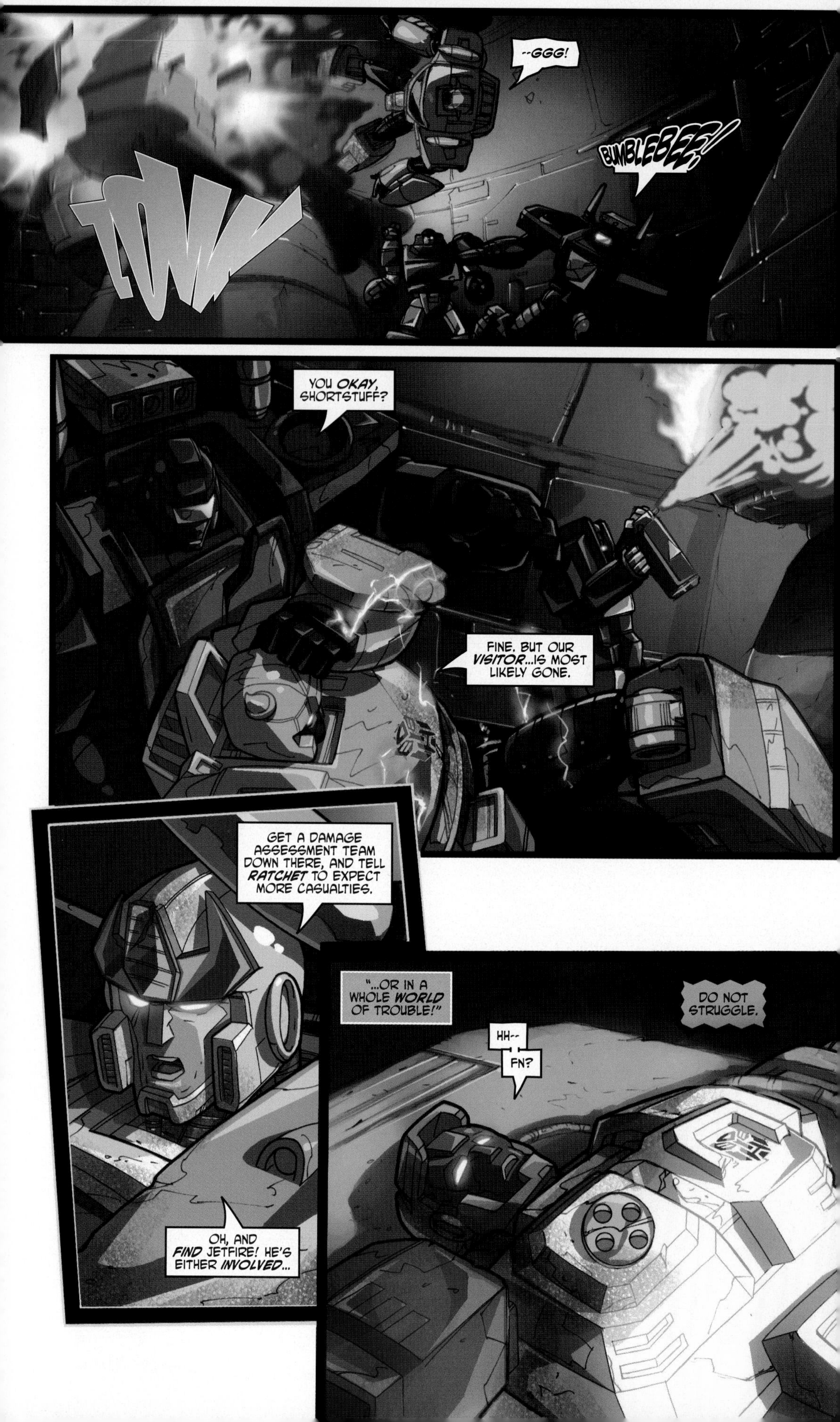
--GGG!
TOWW
BUMBLEBEE!
YOU OKAY, SHORTSTUFF?
FINE. BUT OUR VISITOR...IS MOST LIKELY GONE.
GET A DAMAGE ASSESSMENT TEAM DOWN THERE, AND TELL RATCHET TO EXPECT MORE CASUALTIES.
OH, AND FIND JETFIRE! HE'S EITHER INVOLVED...
"...OR IN A WHOLE WORLD OF TROUBLE!"
DO NOT STRUGGLE.
HH--
FN?

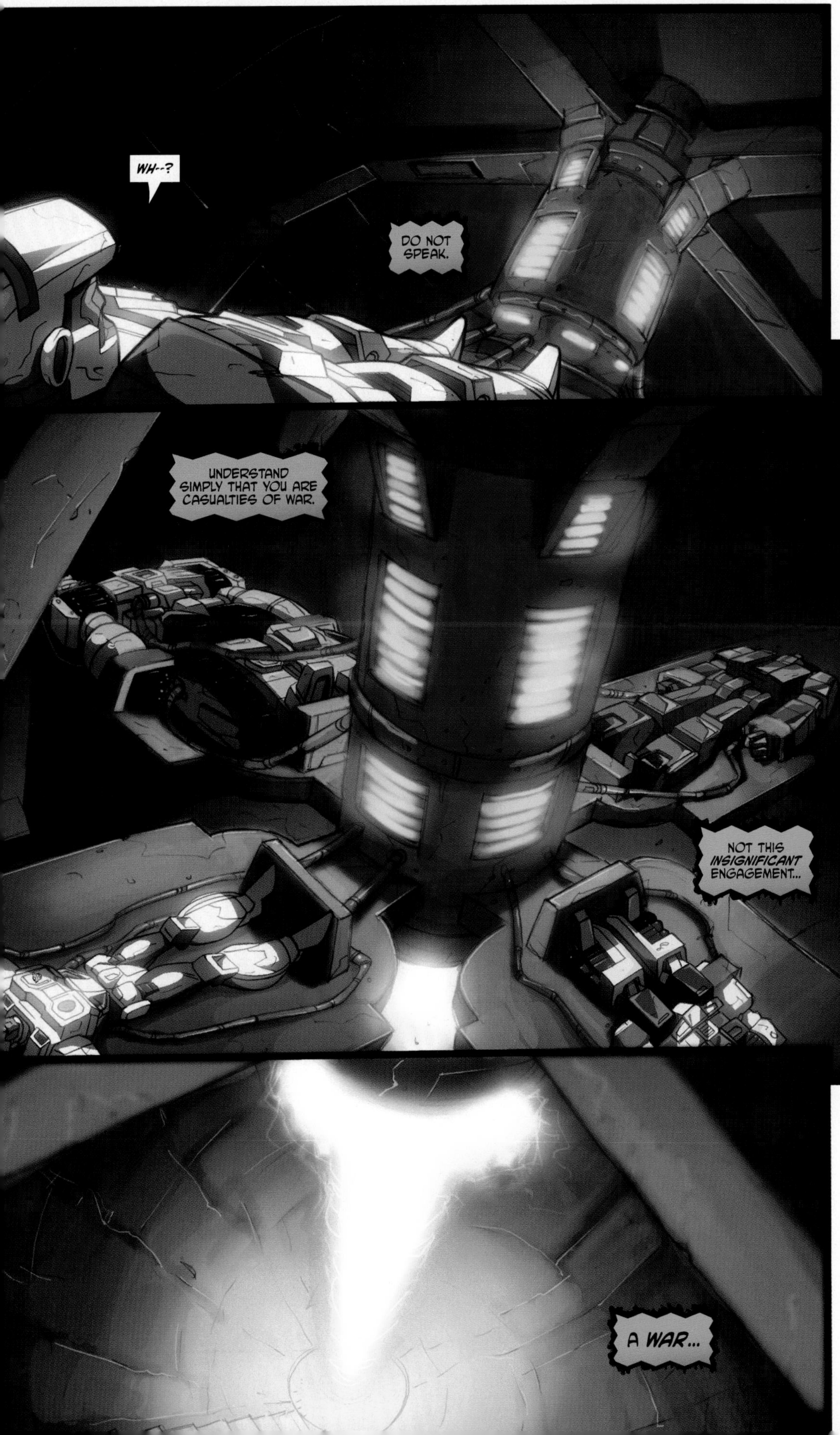
WH--?
DO NOT SPEAK.
UNDERSTAND SIMPLY THAT YOU ARE CASUALTIES OF WAR.
NOT THIS *INSIGNIFICANT* ENGAGEMENT...
A *WAR*...

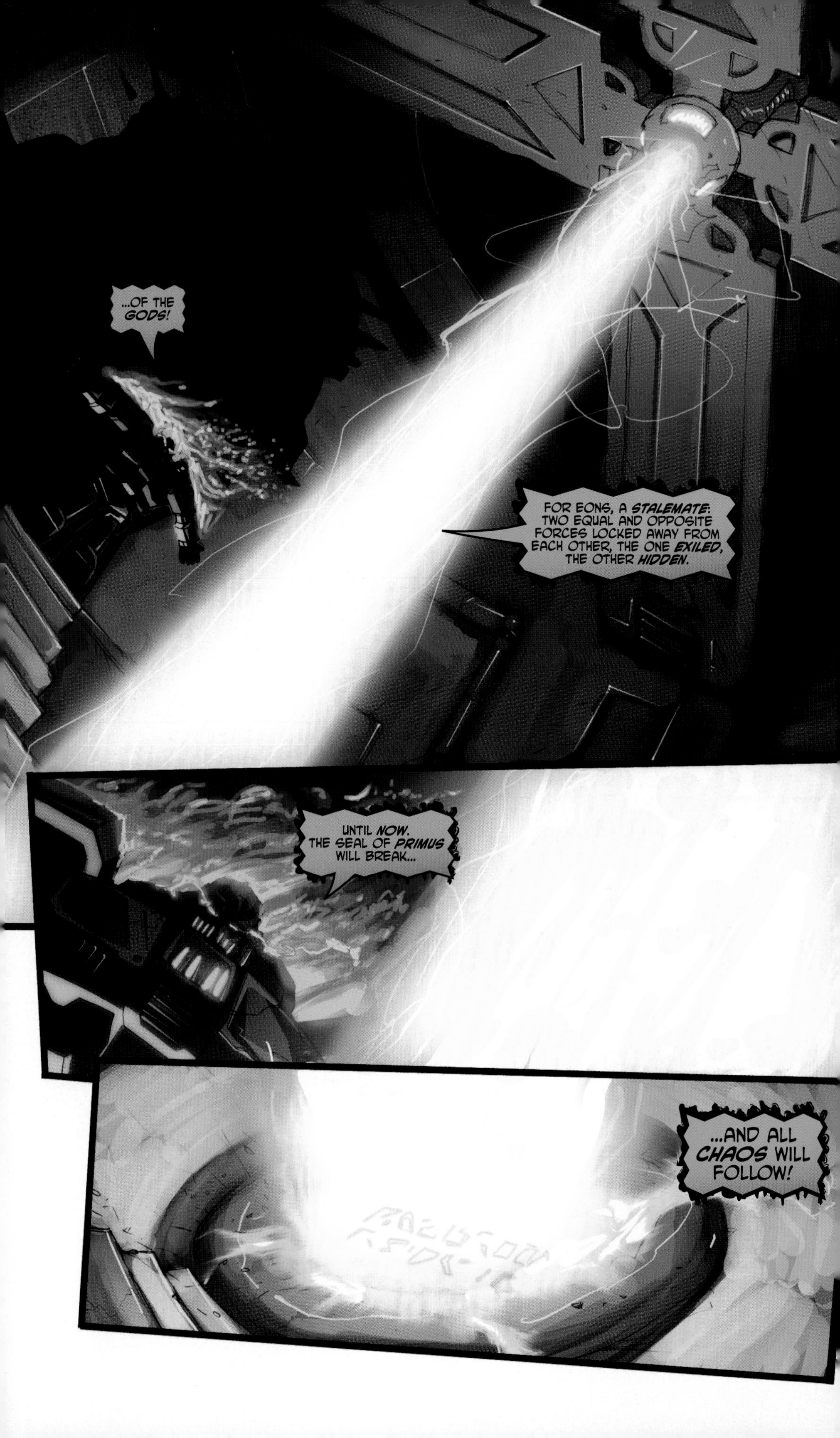
...OF THE GODS!
FOR EONS, A STALEMATE: TWO EQUAL AND OPPOSITE FORCES LOCKED AWAY FROM EACH OTHER, THE ONE EXILED, THE OTHER HIDDEN.
UNTIL NOW. THE SEAL OF PRIMUS WILL BREAK...
...AND ALL CHAOS WILL FOLLOW!

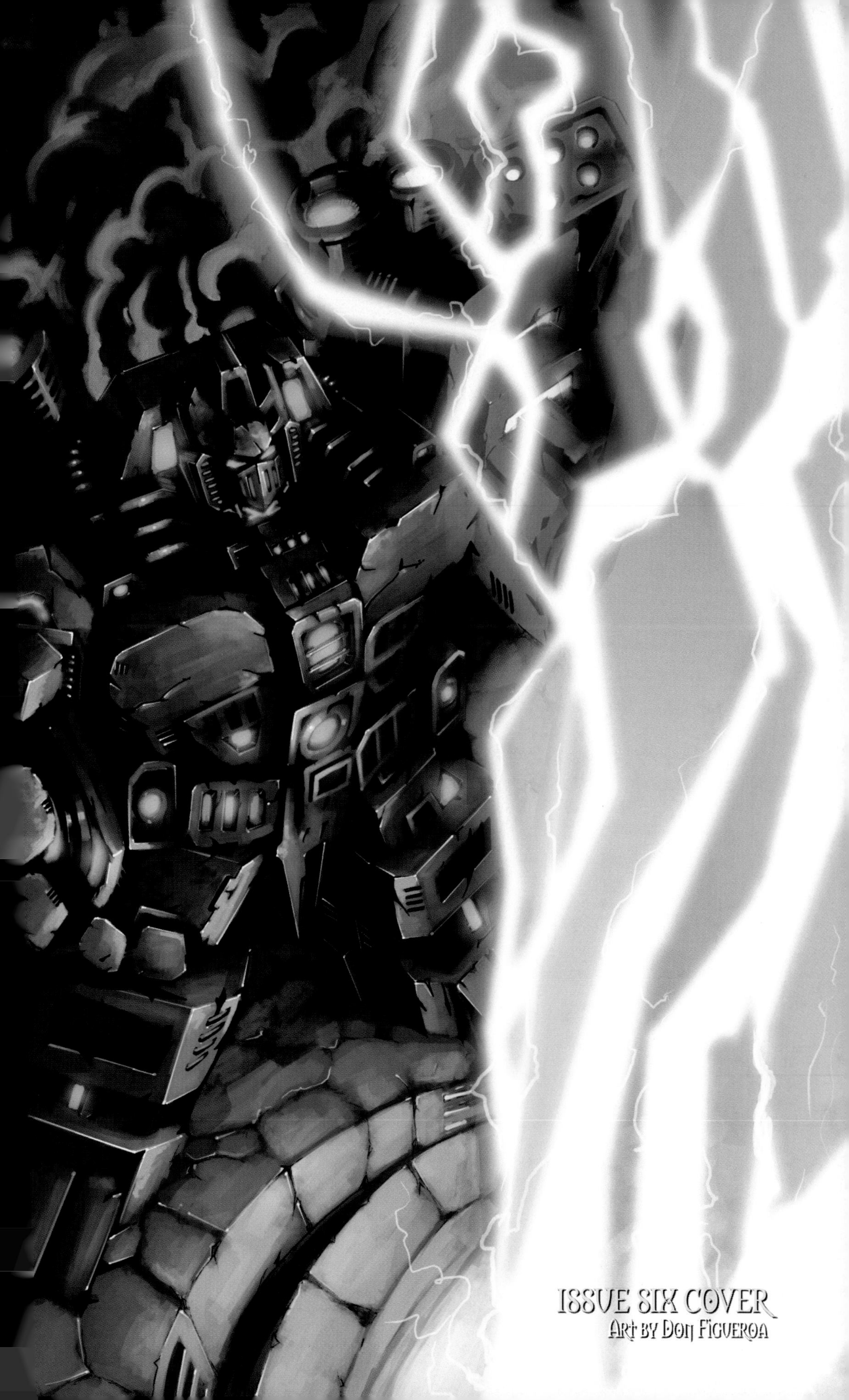

ISSUE SIX COVER
Art by Don Figueroa

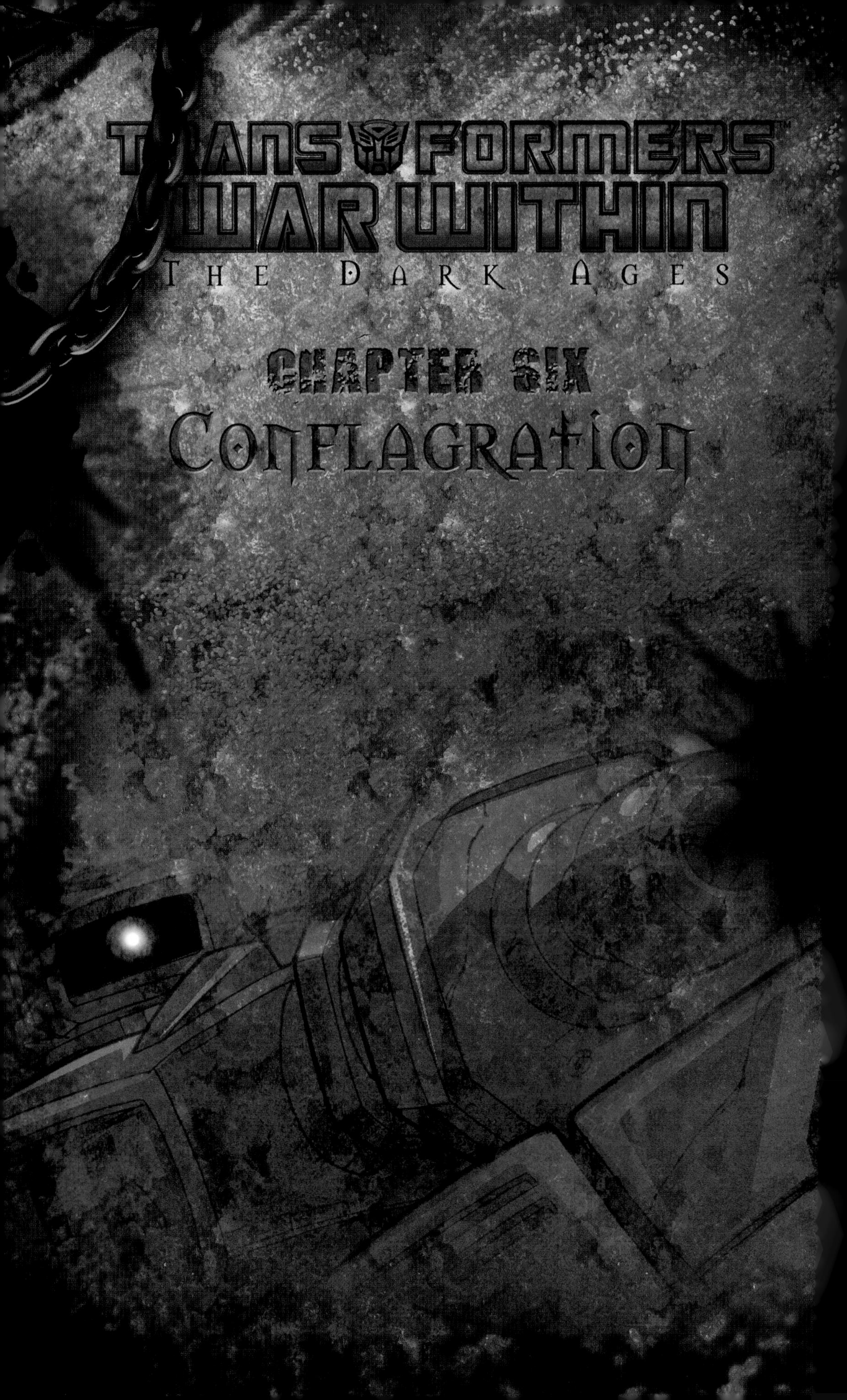
TRANSFORMERS
WAR WITHIN
THE DARK AGES
CHAPTER SIX
Conflagration

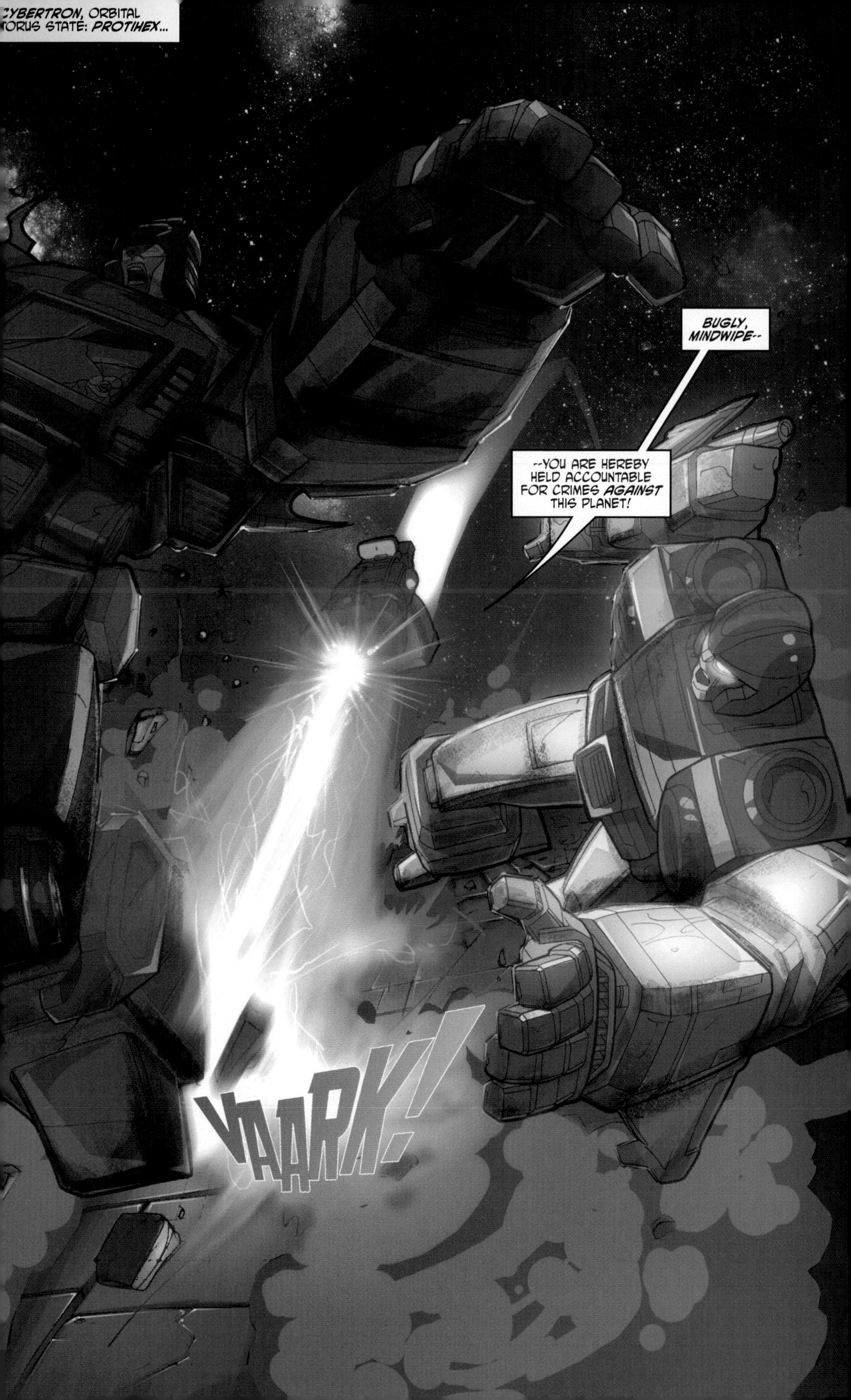
CYBERTRON, ORBITAL TORUS STATE: PROTIHEX...
BUGLY, MINDWIPE--
--YOU ARE HEREBY HELD ACCOUNTABLE FOR CRIMES AGAINST THIS PLANET!
VAARK!

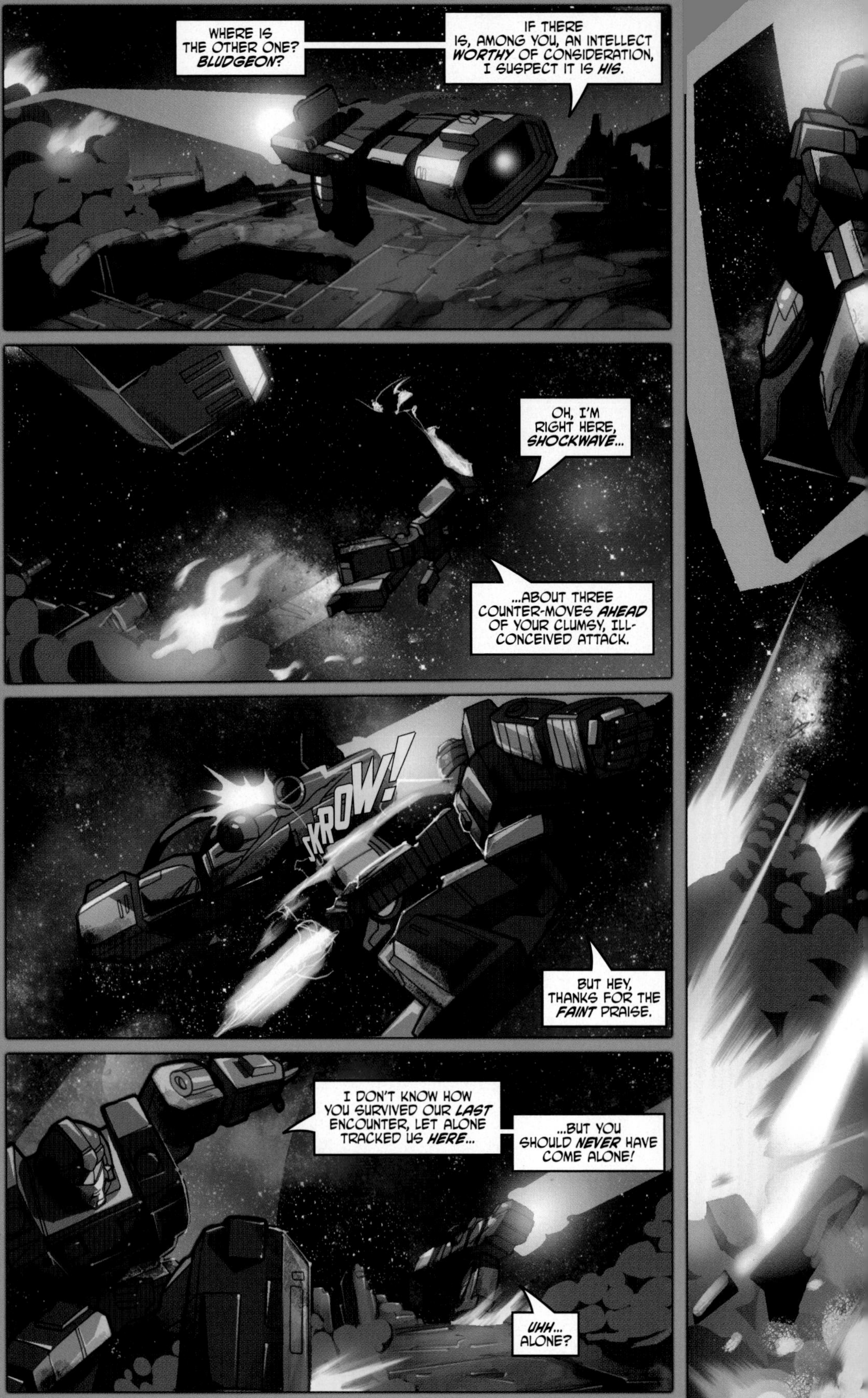

WHERE IS THE OTHER ONE? BLUDGEON?
IF THERE IS, AMONG YOU, AN INTELLECT WORTHY OF CONSIDERATION, I SUSPECT IT IS HIS.
OH, I'M RIGHT HERE, SHOCKWAVE...
...ABOUT THREE COUNTER-MOVES AHEAD OF YOUR CLUMSY, ILL-CONCEIVED ATTACK.
SKROW!
BUT HEY, THANKS FOR THE FAINT PRAISE.
I DON'T KNOW HOW YOU SURVIVED OUR LAST ENCOUNTER, LET ALONE TRACKED US HERE...
...BUT YOU SHOULD NEVER HAVE COME ALONE!
UHH... ALONE?

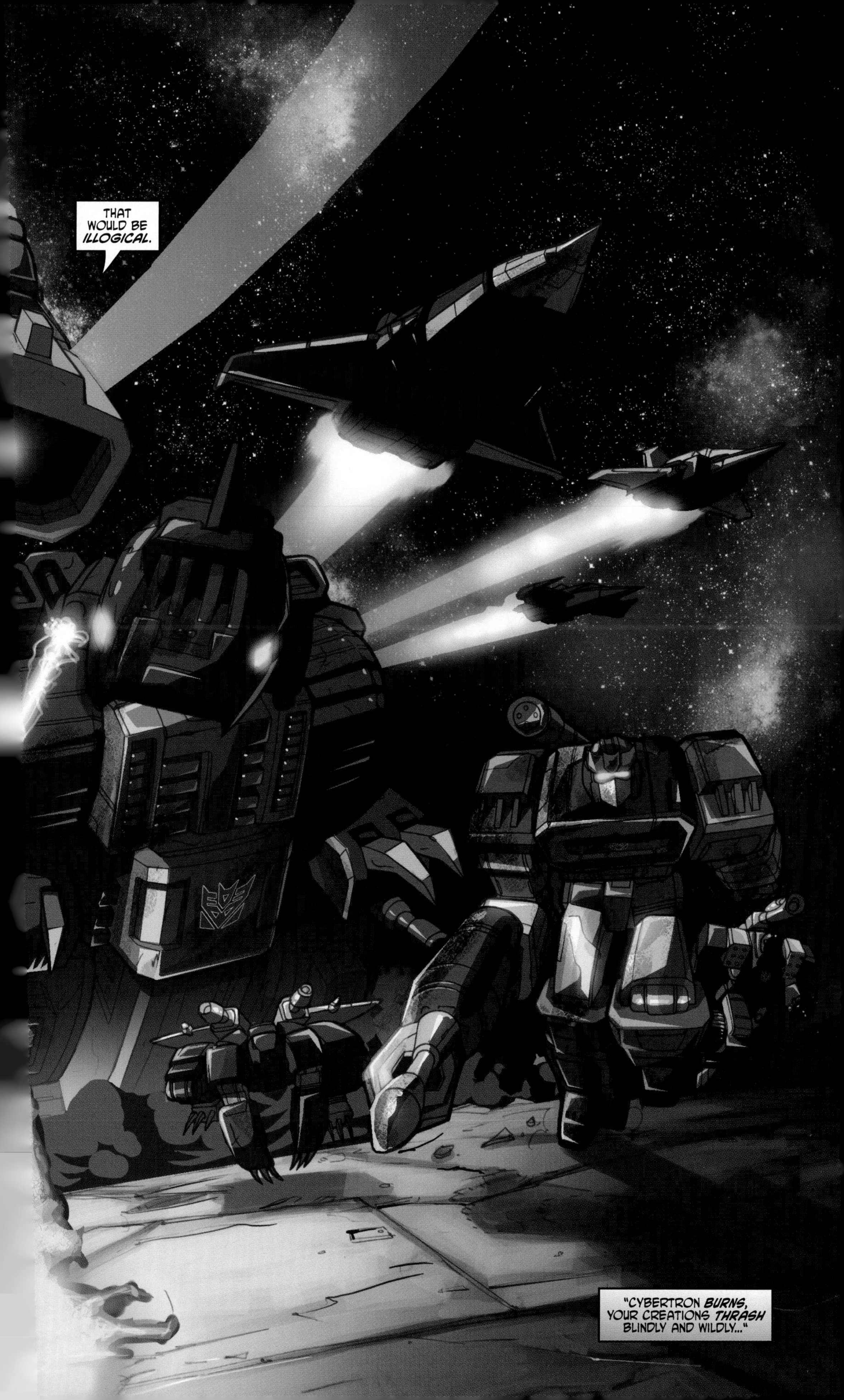
THAT WOULD BE ILLOGICAL.
"CYBERTRON BURNS, YOUR CREATIONS THRASH BLINDLY AND WILDLY..."

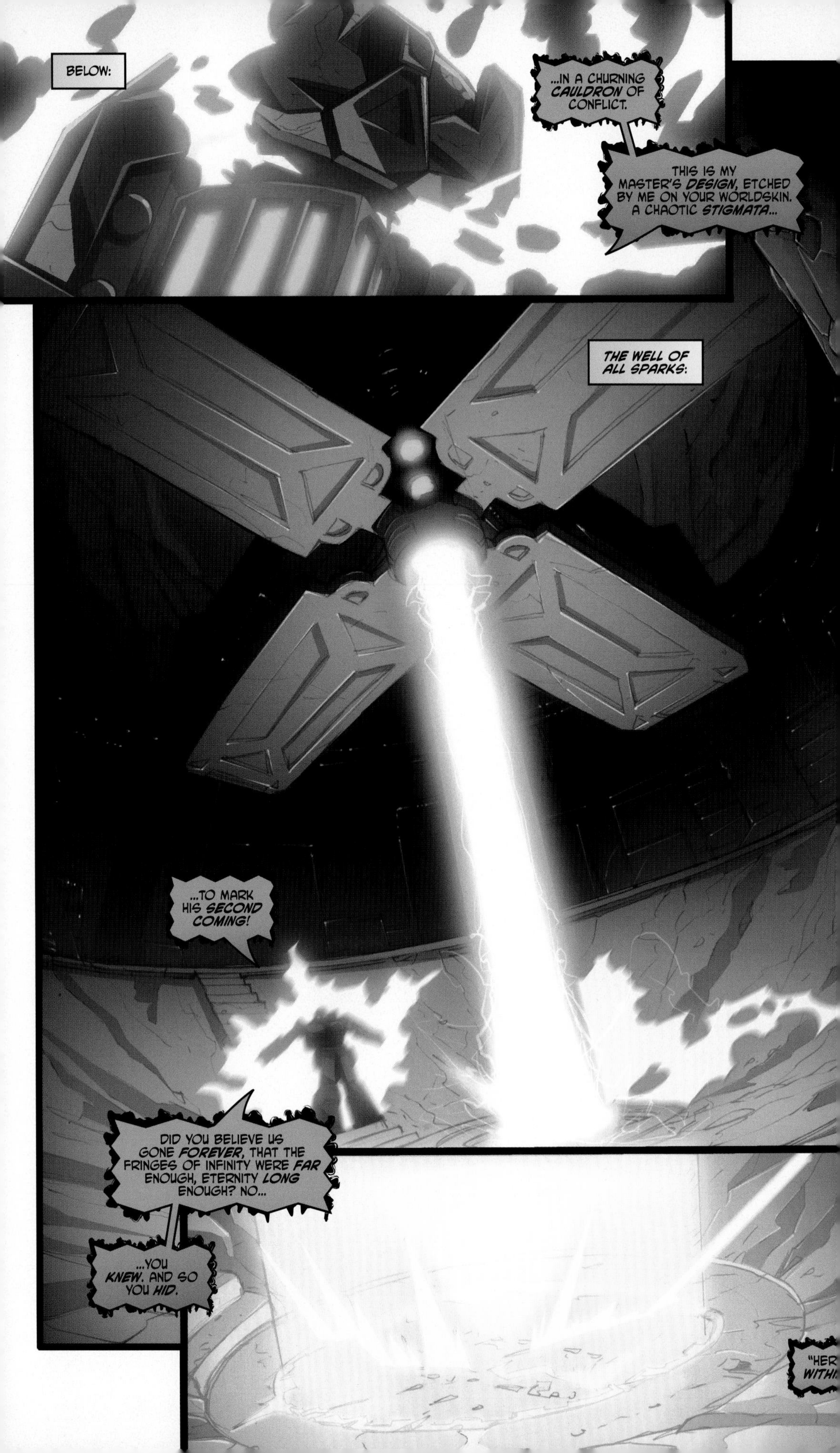

BELOW:
...IN A CHURNING CAULDRON OF CONFLICT.
THIS IS MY MASTER'S DESIGN, ETCHED BY ME ON YOUR WORLDSKIN. A CHAOTIC STIGMATA...
THE WELL OF ALL SPARKS:
...TO MARK HIS SECOND COMING!
DID YOU BELIEVE US GONE FOREVER, THAT THE FRINGES OF INFINITY WERE FAR ENOUGH, ETERNITY LONG ENOUGH? NO...
...YOU KNEW. AND SO YOU HID.

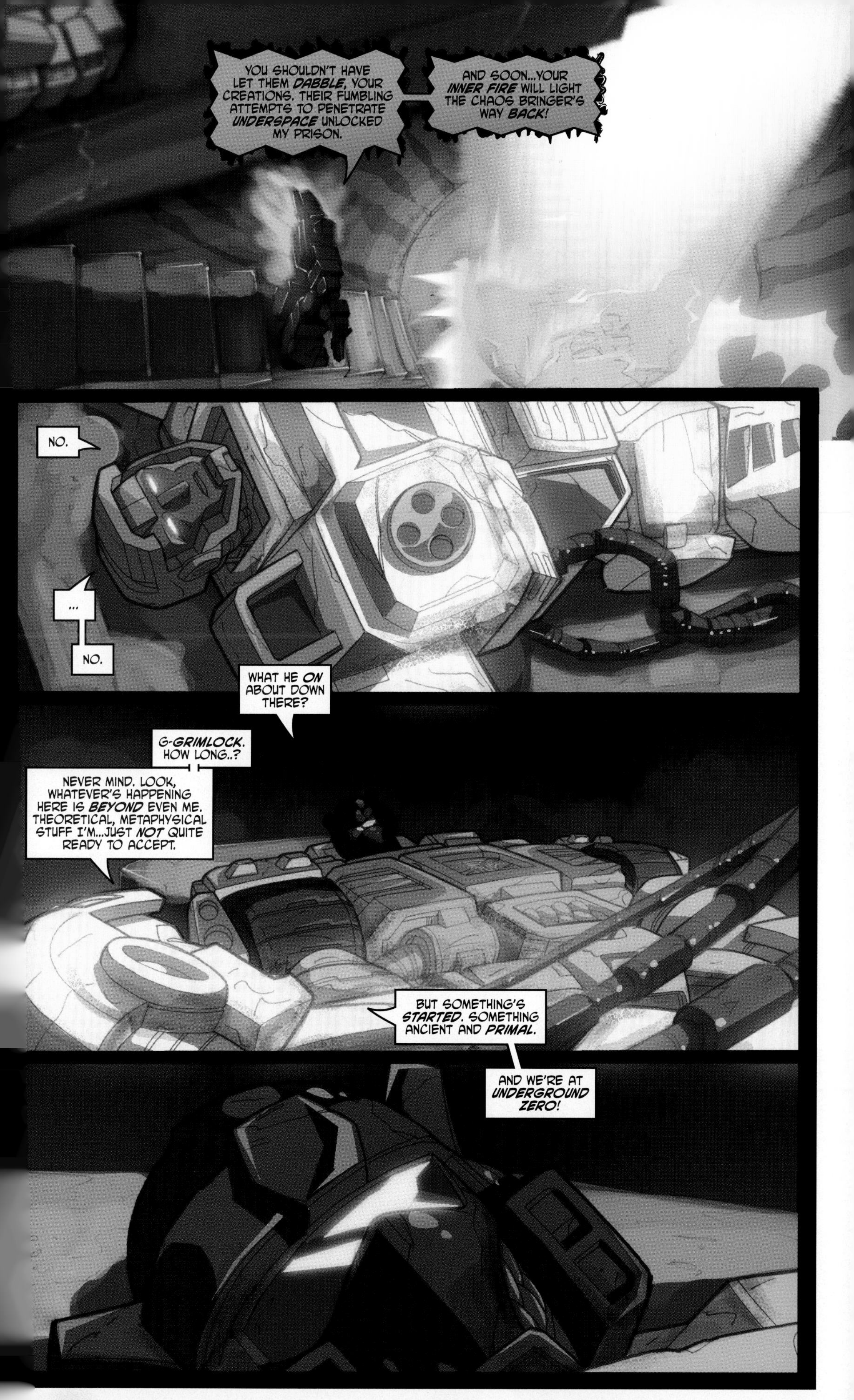
YOU SHOULDN'T HAVE LET THEM DABBLE, YOUR CREATIONS. THEIR FUMBLING ATTEMPTS TO PENETRATE UNDERSPACE UNLOCKED MY PRISON.
AND SOON...YOUR INNER FIRE WILL LIGHT THE CHAOS BRINGER'S WAY BACK!
NO.
...
NO.
WHAT HE ON ABOUT DOWN THERE?
G-GRIMLOCK. HOW LONG..?
NEVER MIND. LOOK, WHATEVER'S HAPPENING HERE IS BEYOND EVEN ME. THEORETICAL, METAPHYSICAL STUFF I'M...JUST NOT QUITE READY TO ACCEPT.
BUT SOMETHING'S STARTED. SOMETHING ANCIENT AND PRIMAL.
AND WE'RE AT UNDERGROUND ZERO!

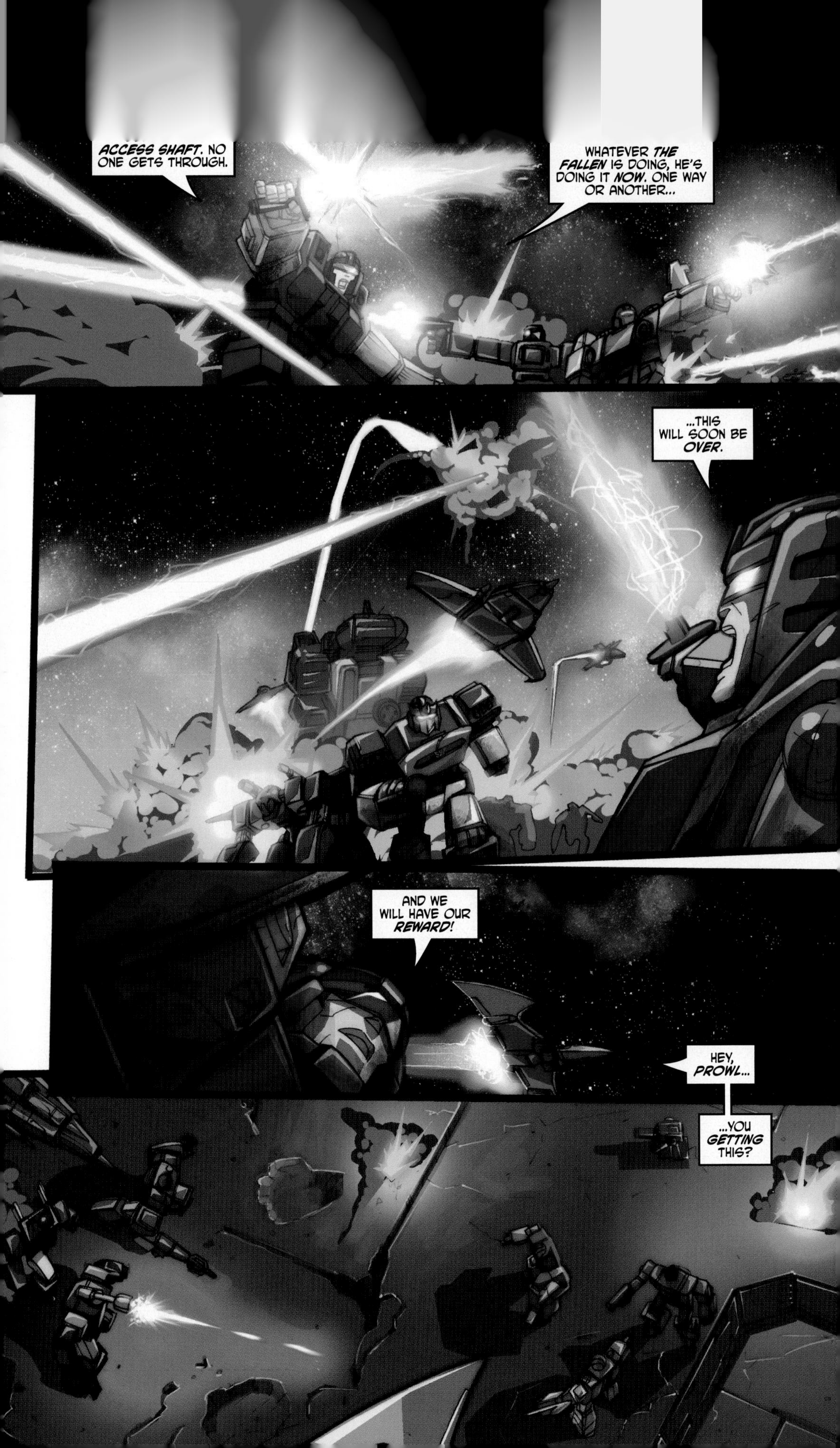
ACCESS SHAFT. NO ONE GETS THROUGH.
WHATEVER THE FALLEN IS DOING, HE'S DOING IT NOW. ONE WAY OR ANOTHER...
...THIS WILL SOON BE OVER.
AND WE WILL HAVE OUR REWARD!
HEY, PROWL...
...YOU GETTING THIS?

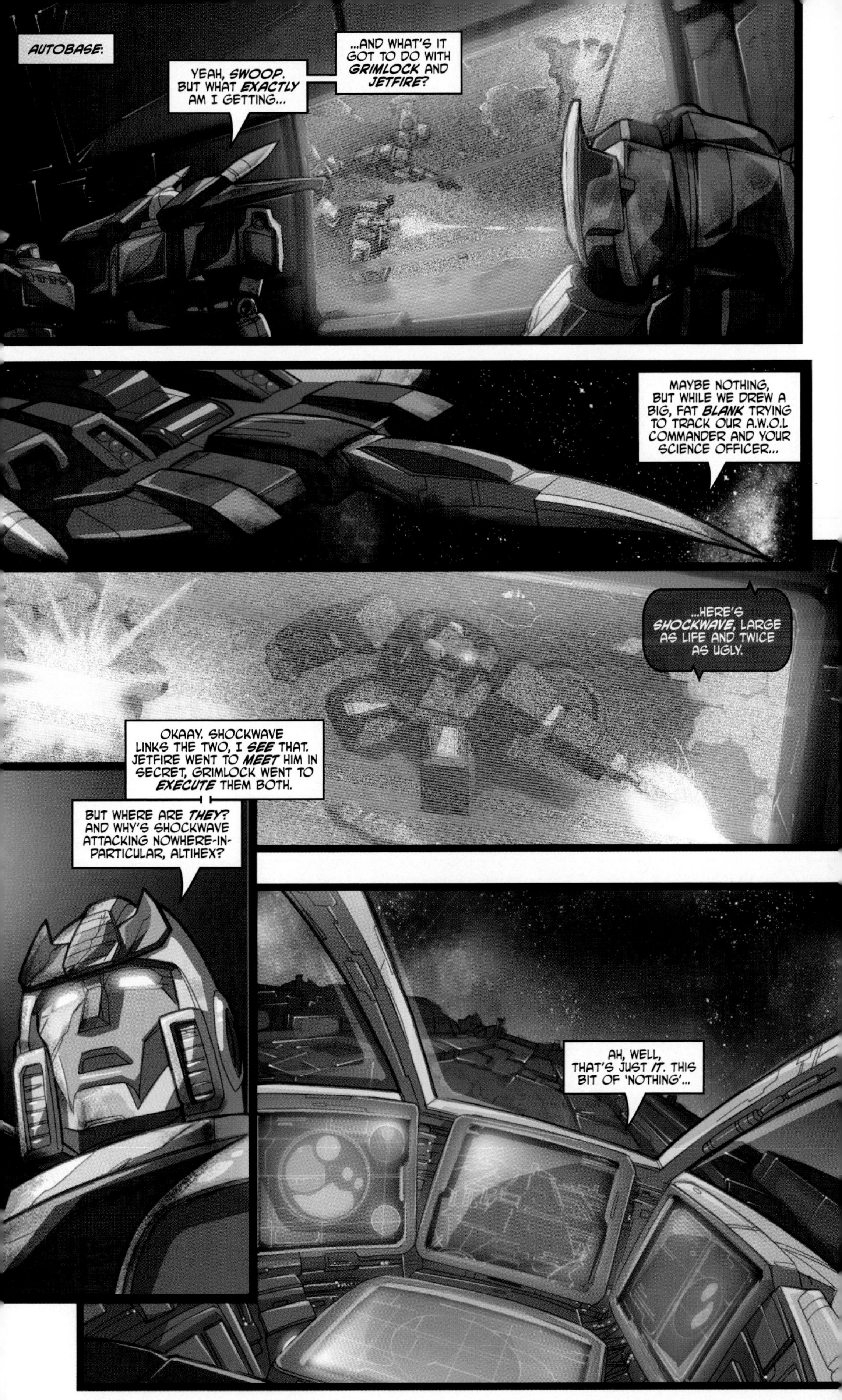
AUTOBASE:
YEAH, SWOOP. BUT WHAT EXACTLY AM I GETTING...
...AND WHAT'S IT GOT TO DO WITH GRIMLOCK AND JETFIRE?
MAYBE NOTHING, BUT WHILE WE DREW A BIG, FAT BLANK TRYING TO TRACK OUR A.W.O.L COMMANDER AND YOUR SCIENCE OFFICER...
...HERE'S SHOCKWAVE, LARGE AS LIFE AND TWICE AS UGLY.
OKAAY. SHOCKWAVE LINKS THE TWO, I SEE THAT. JETFIRE WENT TO MEET HIM IN SECRET, GRIMLOCK WENT TO EXECUTE THEM BOTH.
BUT WHERE ARE THEY? AND WHY'S SHOCKWAVE ATTACKING NOWHERE-IN-PARTICULAR, ALTIHEX?
AH, WELL, THAT'S JUST IT. THIS BIT OF 'NOTHING'...

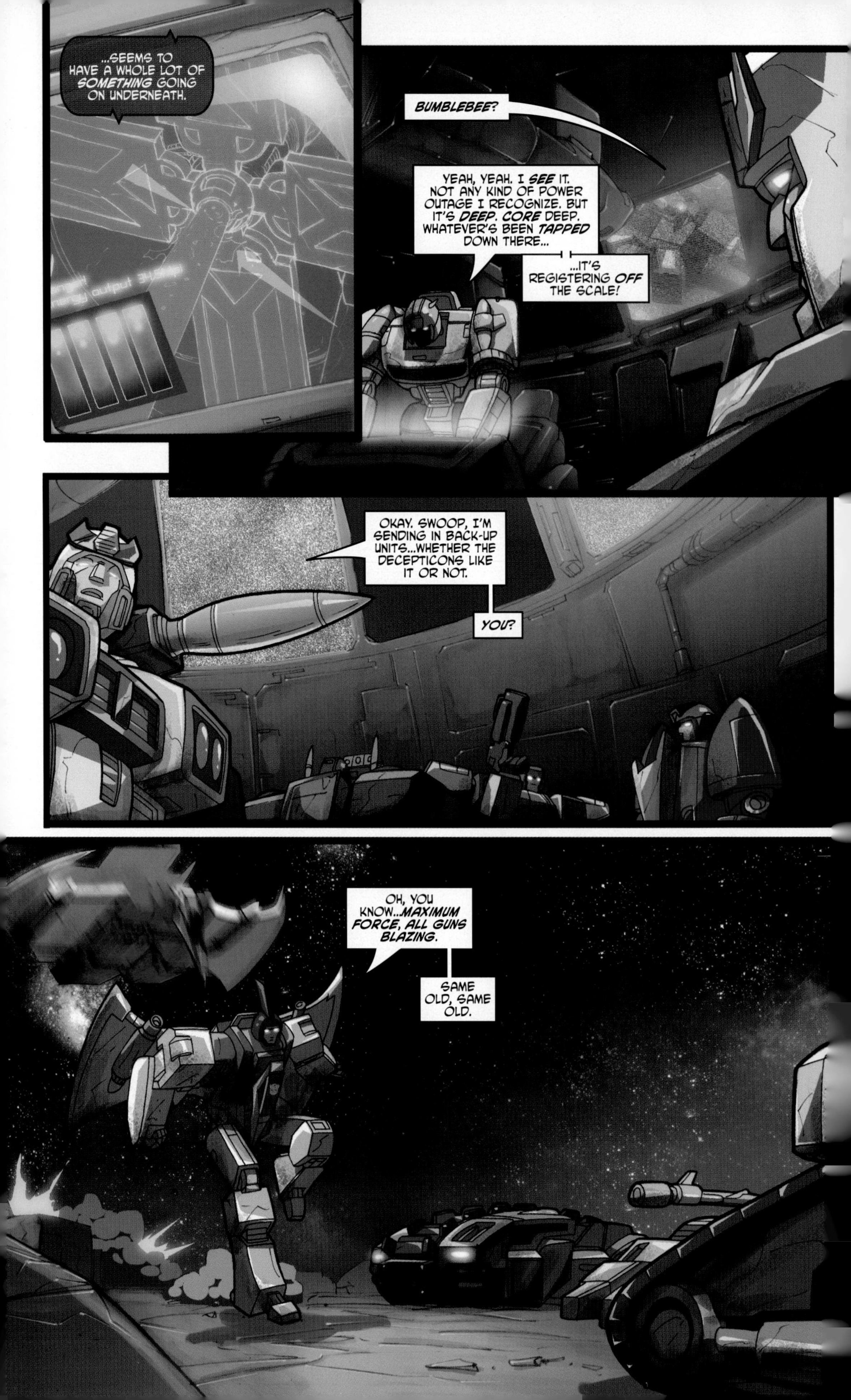
...SEEMS TO HAVE A WHOLE LOT OF SOMETHING GOING ON UNDERNEATH.
BUMBLEBEE?
YEAH, YEAH. I SEE IT. NOT ANY KIND OF POWER OUTAGE I RECOGNIZE. BUT IT'S DEEP. CORE DEEP. WHATEVER'S BEEN TAPPED DOWN THERE...
...IT'S REGISTERING OFF THE SCALE!
OKAY. SWOOP, I'M SENDING IN BACK-UP UNITS...WHETHER THE DECEPTICONS LIKE IT OR NOT.
YOU?
OH, YOU KNOW...MAXIMUM FORCE, ALL GUNS BLAZING.
SAME OLD, SAME OLD.

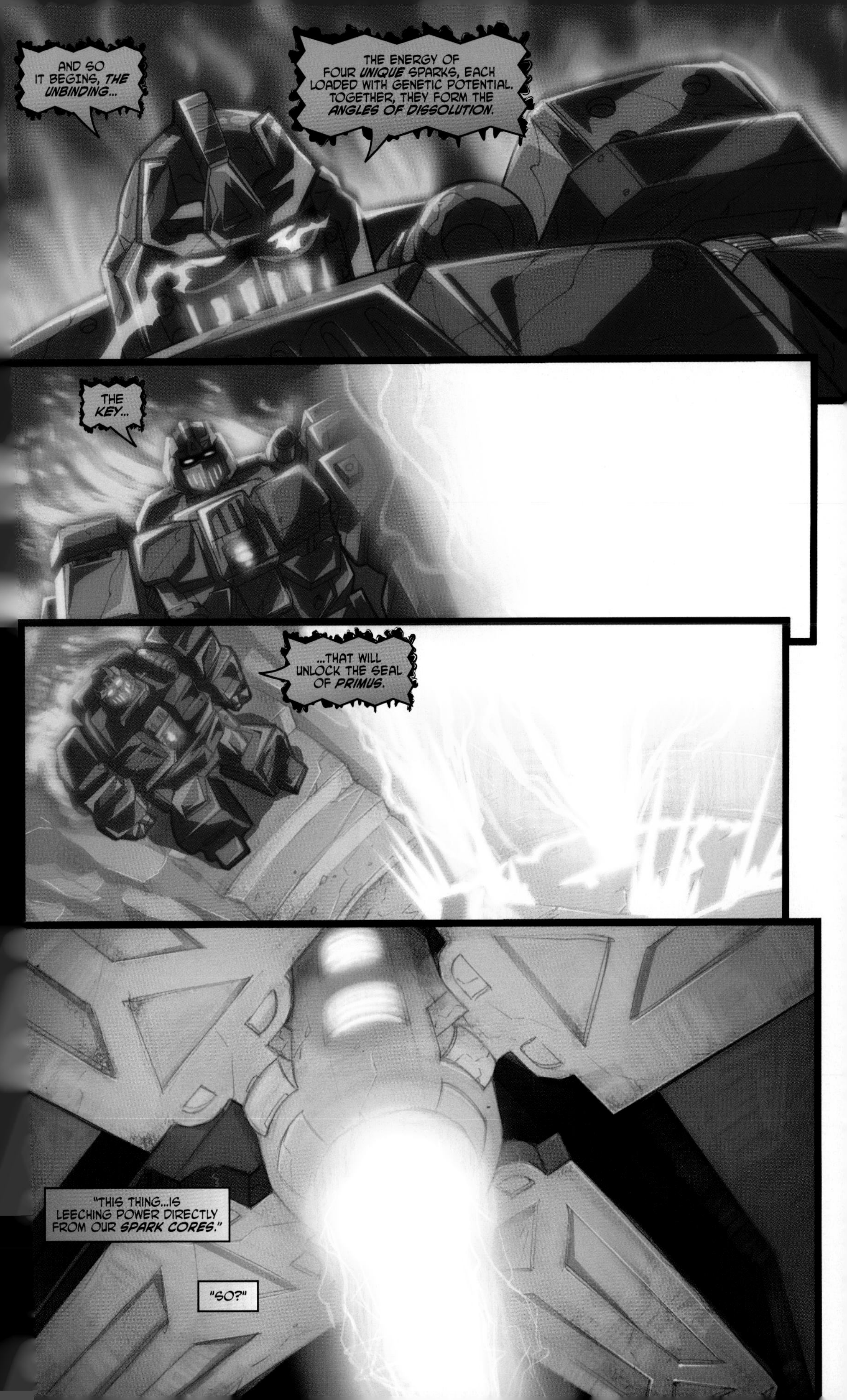
AND SO IT BEGINS, THE UNBINDING...
THE ENERGY OF FOUR UNIQUE SPARKS, EACH LOADED WITH GENETIC POTENTIAL. TOGETHER, THEY FORM THE ANGLES OF DISSOLUTION.
THE KEY...
...THAT WILL UNLOCK THE SEAL OF PRIMUS.
"THIS THING...IS LEECHING POWER DIRECTLY FROM OUR SPARK CORES."
"SO?"

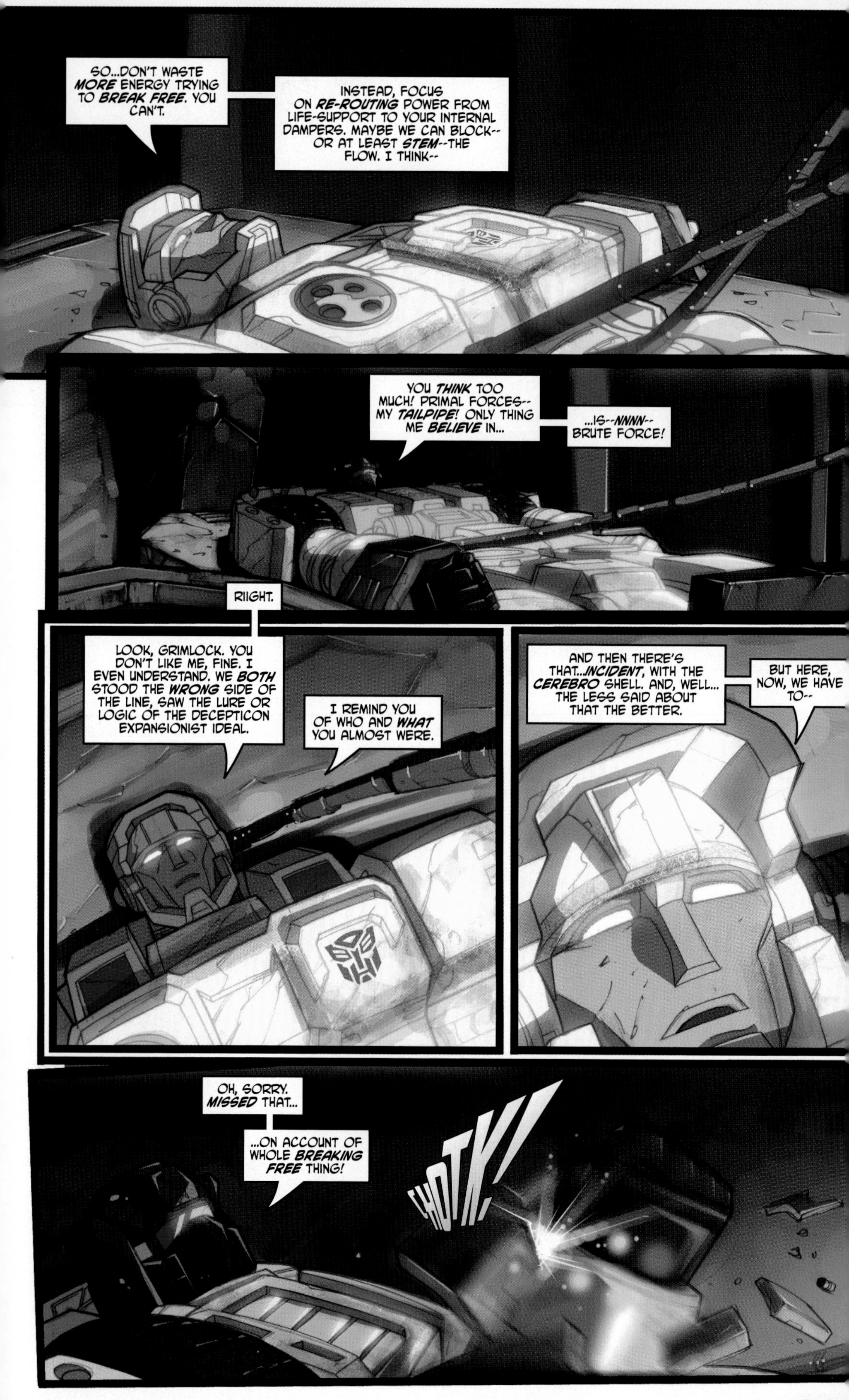
SO...DON'T WASTE MORE ENERGY TRYING TO BREAK FREE. YOU CAN'T.
INSTEAD, FOCUS ON RE-ROUTING POWER FROM LIFE-SUPPORT TO YOUR INTERNAL DAMPERS. MAYBE WE CAN BLOCK-- OR AT LEAST STEM--THE FLOW. I THINK--
YOU THINK TOO MUCH! PRIMAL FORCES-- MY TAILPIPE! ONLY THING ME BELIEVE IN...
...IS--NNNN-- BRUTE FORCE!
RIIGHT.
LOOK, GRIMLOCK. YOU DON'T LIKE ME, FINE. I EVEN UNDERSTAND. WE BOTH STOOD THE WRONG SIDE OF THE LINE, SAW THE LURE OR LOGIC OF THE DECEPTICON EXPANSIONIST IDEAL.
I REMIND YOU OF WHO AND WHAT YOU ALMOST WERE.
AND THEN THERE'S THAT...INCIDENT, WITH THE CEREBRO SHELL. AND, WELL... THE LESS SAID ABOUT THAT THE BETTER.
BUT HERE, NOW, WE HAVE TO--
OH, SORRY. MISSED THAT...
...ON ACCOUNT OF WHOLE BREAKING FREE THING!
CHOTK!

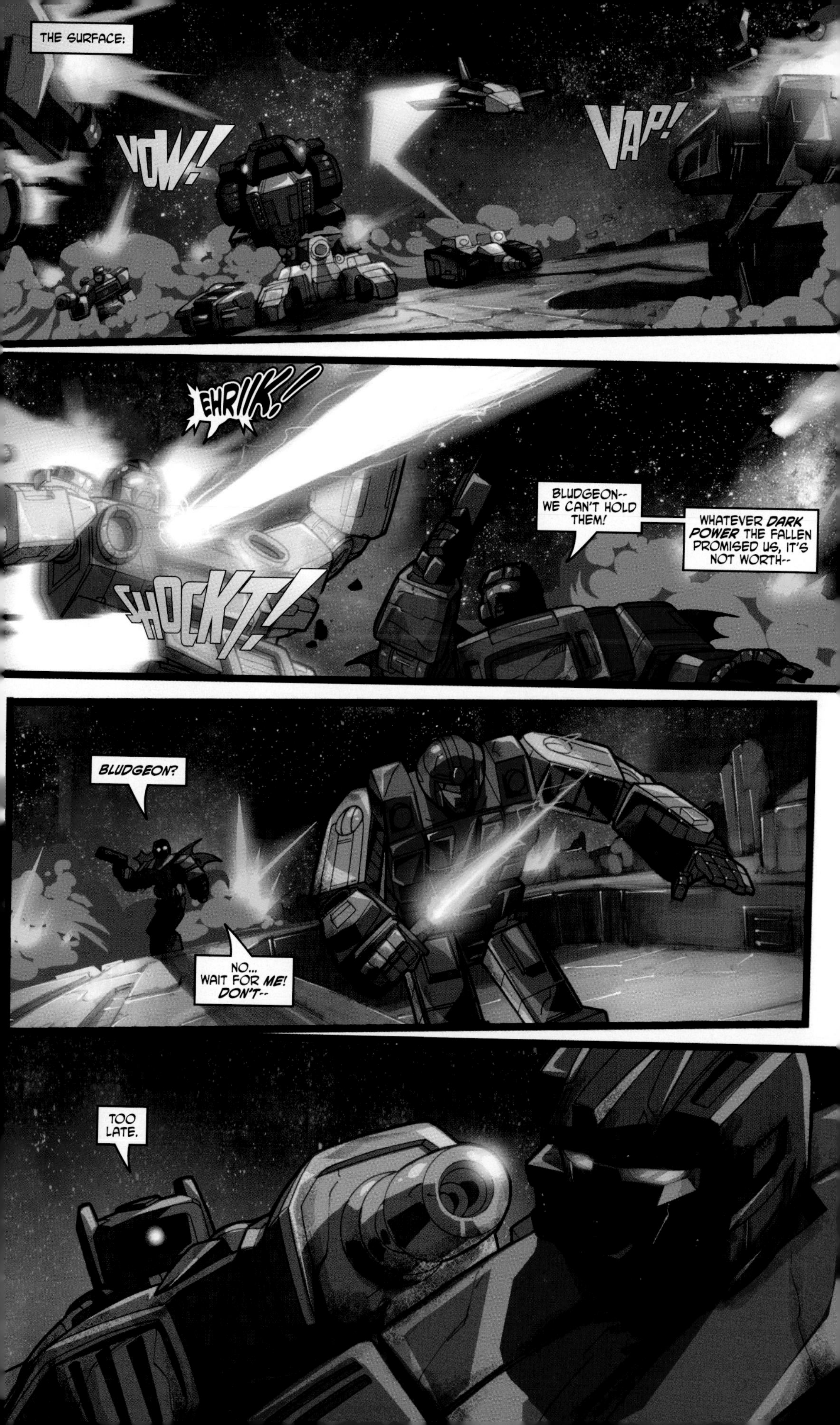
THE SURFACE:
VOW!
VAP!
EHRIIK!
SHOCKT!
BLUDGEON-- WE CAN'T HOLD THEM!
WHATEVER DARK POWER THE FALLEN PROMISED US, IT'S NOT WORTH--
BLUDGEON?
NO... WAIT FOR ME! DON'T--
TOO LATE.

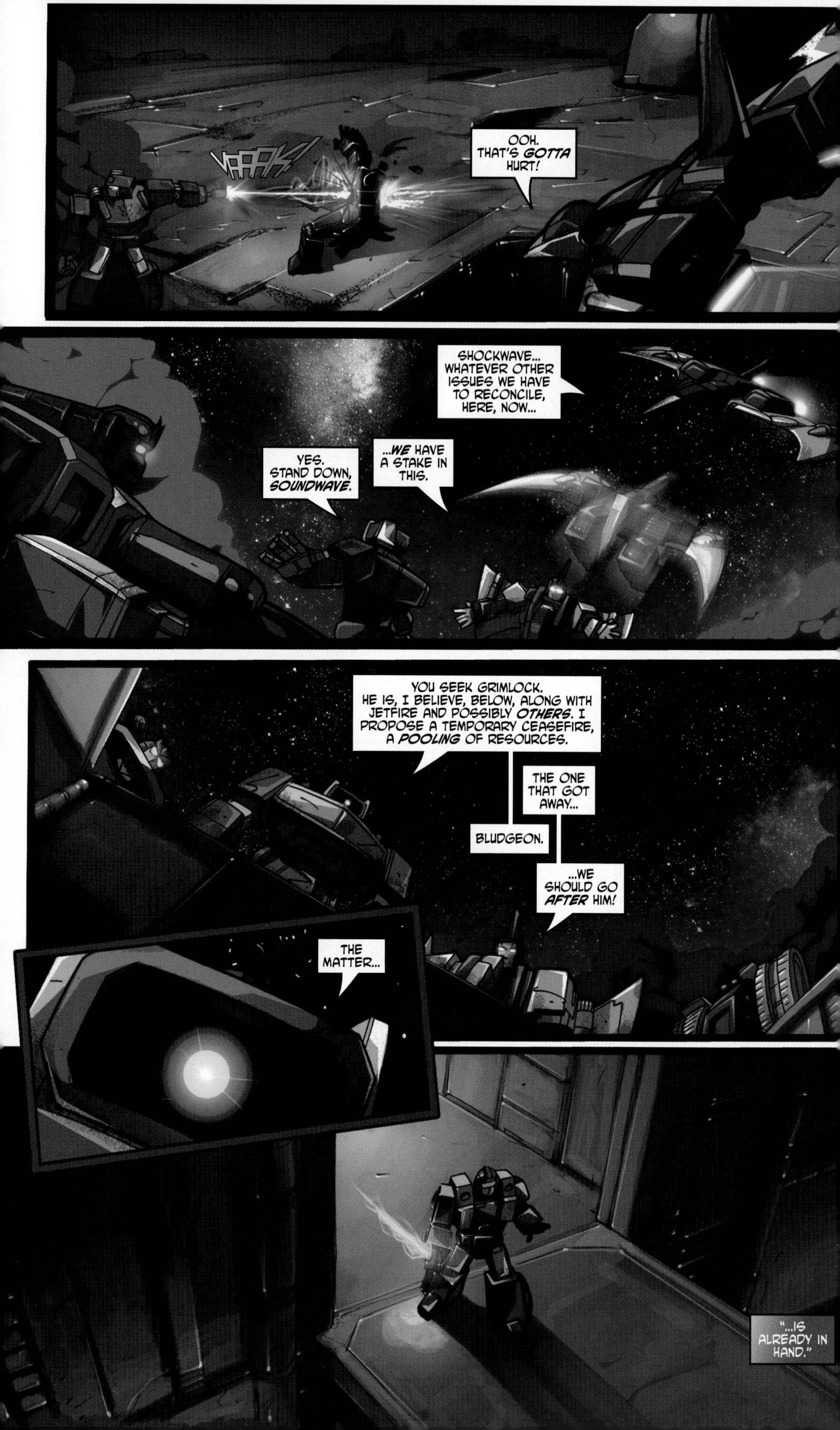
VRRRK!
OOH. THAT'S GOTTA HURT!
SHOCKWAVE... WHATEVER OTHER ISSUES WE HAVE TO RECONCILE, HERE, NOW...
YES. STAND DOWN, SOUNDWAVE.
...WE HAVE A STAKE IN THIS.
YOU SEEK GRIMLOCK. HE IS, I BELIEVE, BELOW, ALONG WITH JETFIRE AND POSSIBLY OTHERS. I PROPOSE A TEMPORARY CEASEFIRE, A POOLING OF RESOURCES.
THE ONE THAT GOT AWAY...
BLUDGEON.
...WE SHOULD GO AFTER HIM!
THE MATTER...
"...IS ALREADY IN HAND."

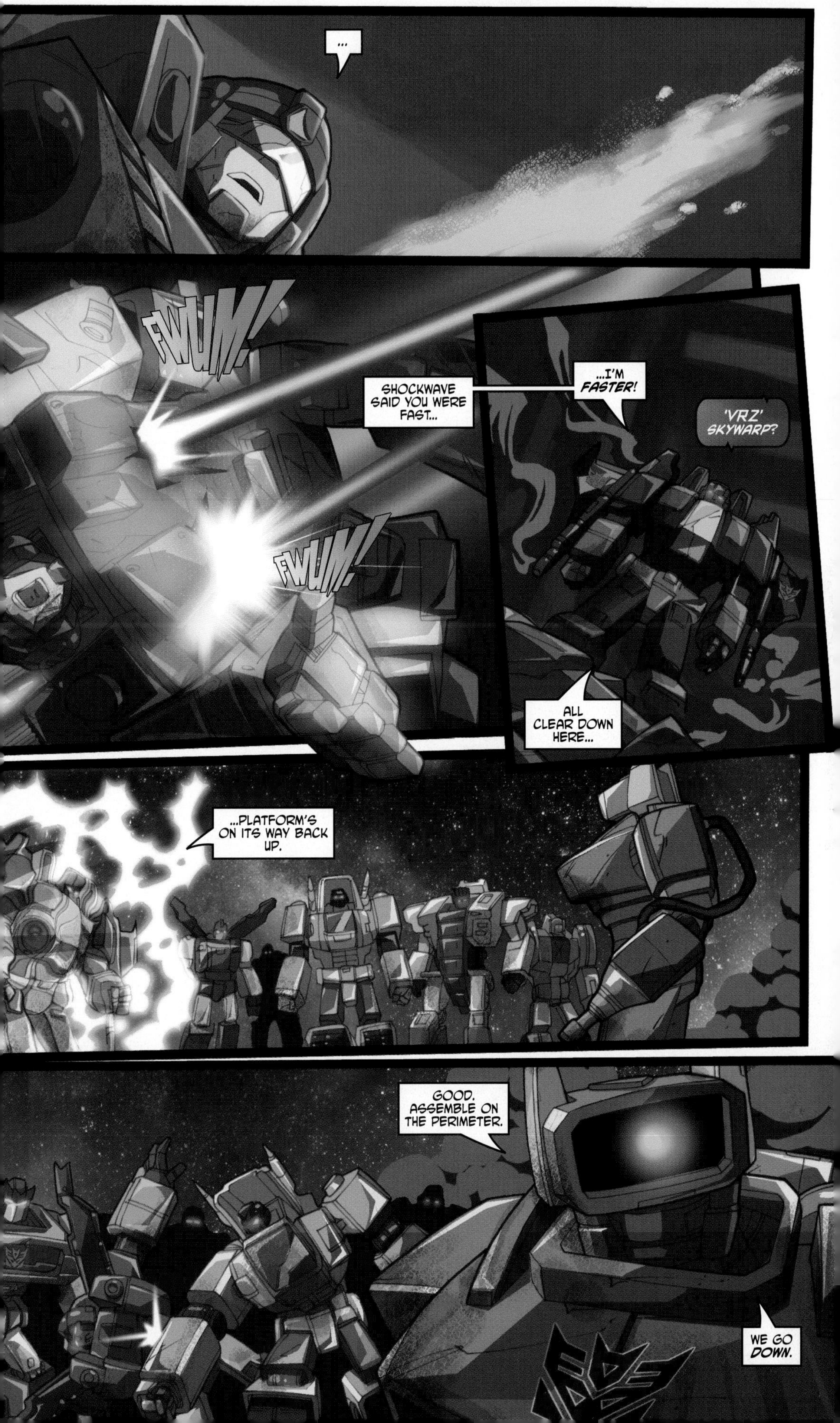
...
FWUM!
SHOCKWAVE SAID YOU WERE FAST...
...I'M FASTER!
FWUM!
'VRZ' SKYWARP?
ALL CLEAR DOWN HERE...
...PLATFORM'S ON ITS WAY BACK UP.
GOOD. ASSEMBLE ON THE PERIMETER.
WE GO DOWN.

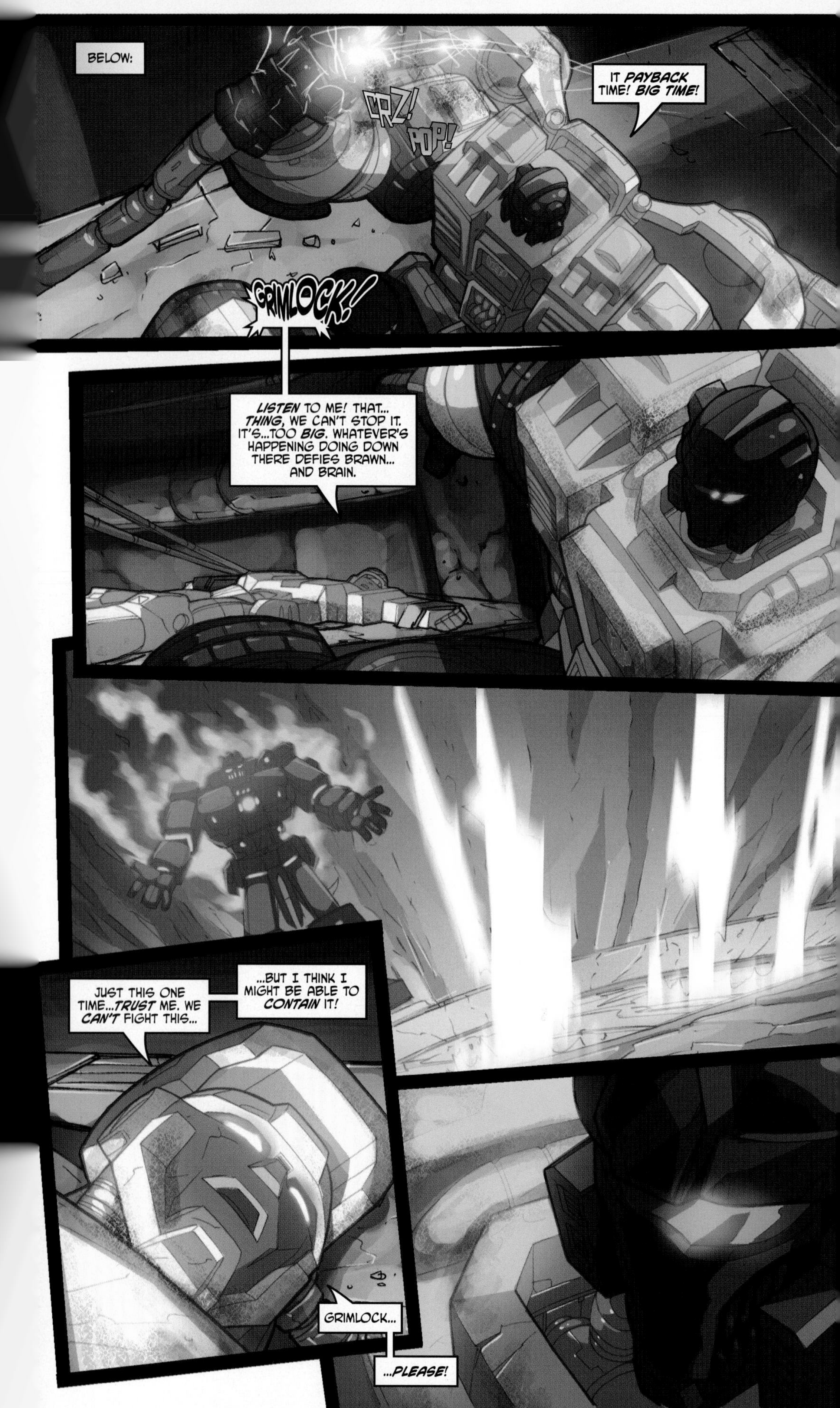
BELOW:
CRZ!
POP!
IT PAYBACK TIME! BIG TIME!
GRIMLOCK!
LISTEN TO ME! THAT... THING, WE CAN'T STOP IT. IT'S...TOO BIG. WHATEVER'S HAPPENING DOING DOWN THERE DEFIES BRAWN... AND BRAIN.
JUST THIS ONE TIME...TRUST ME. WE CAN'T FIGHT THIS...
...BUT I THINK I MIGHT BE ABLE TO CONTAIN IT!
GRIMLOCK...
...PLEASE!

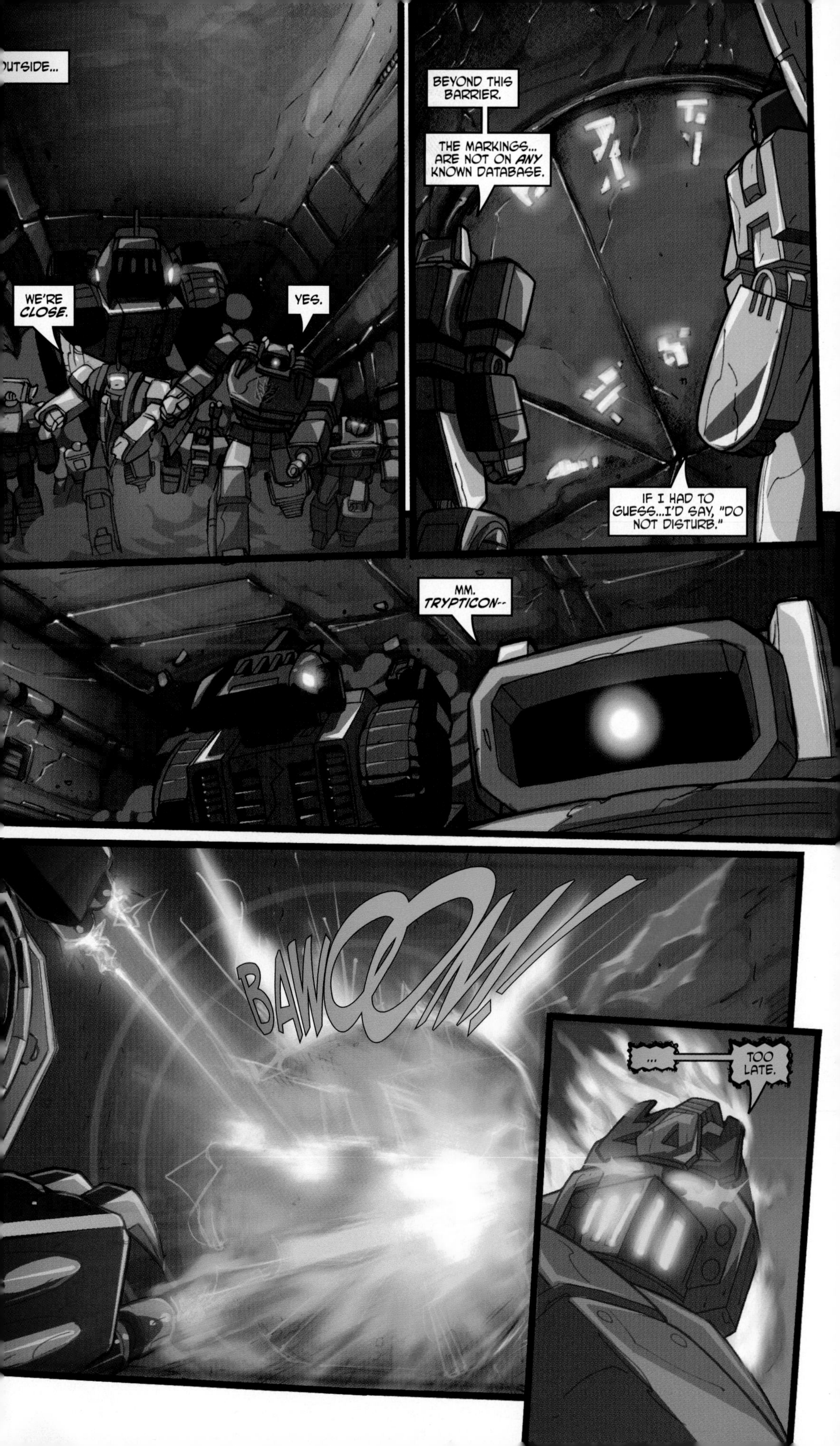
...UTSIDE...
WE'RE CLOSE.
YES.
BEYOND THIS BARRIER.
THE MARKINGS... ARE NOT ON ANY KNOWN DATABASE.
IF I HAD TO GUESS...I'D SAY, "DO NOT DISTURB."
MM. TRYPTICON--
BAWOOM!
...
TOO LATE.

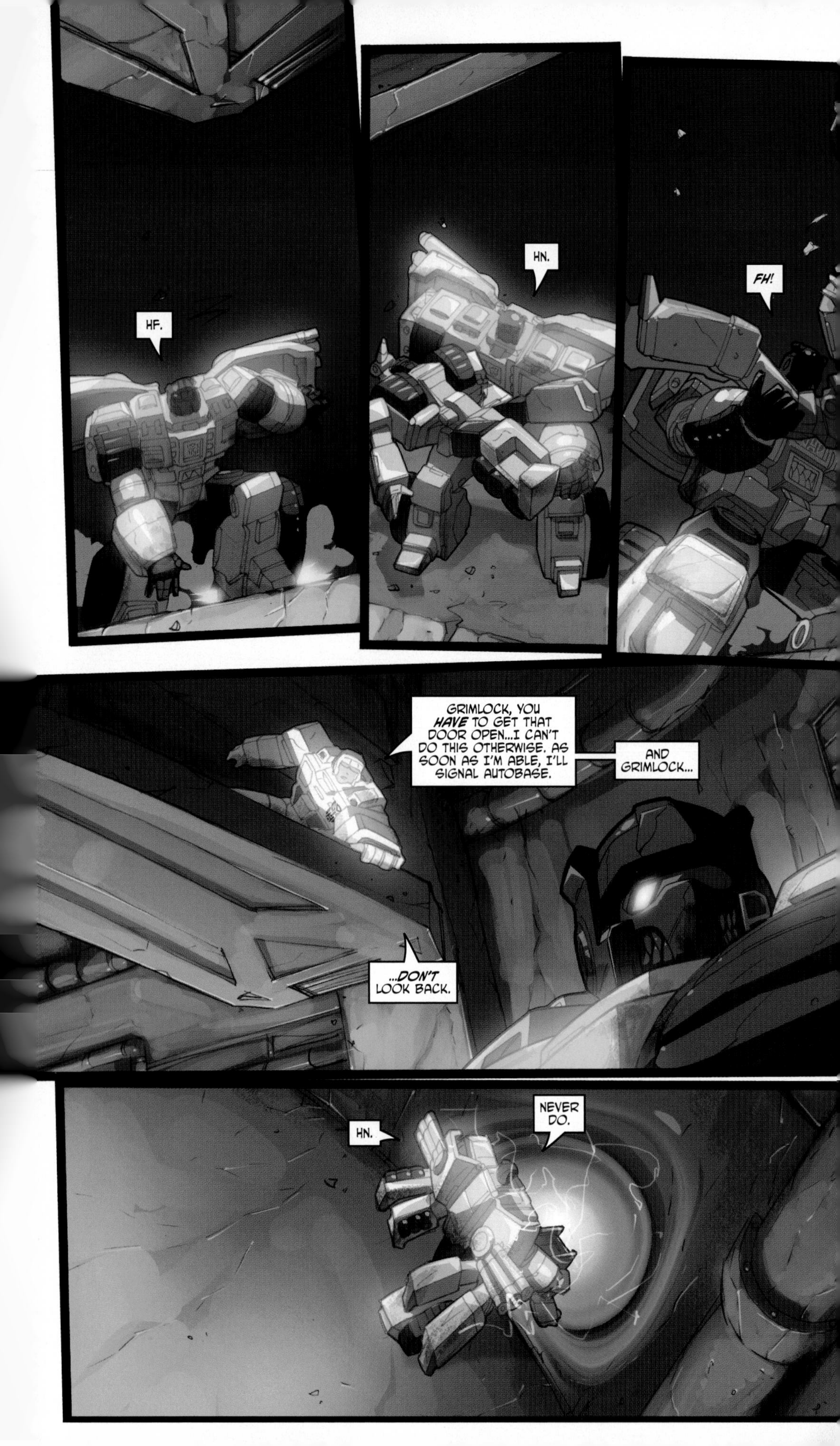
HF.
HN.
FH!
GRIMLOCK, YOU HAVE TO GET THAT DOOR OPEN...I CAN'T DO THIS OTHERWISE. AS SOON AS I'M ABLE, I'LL SIGNAL AUTOBASE.
AND GRIMLOCK...
...DON'T LOOK BACK.
HN.
NEVER DO.

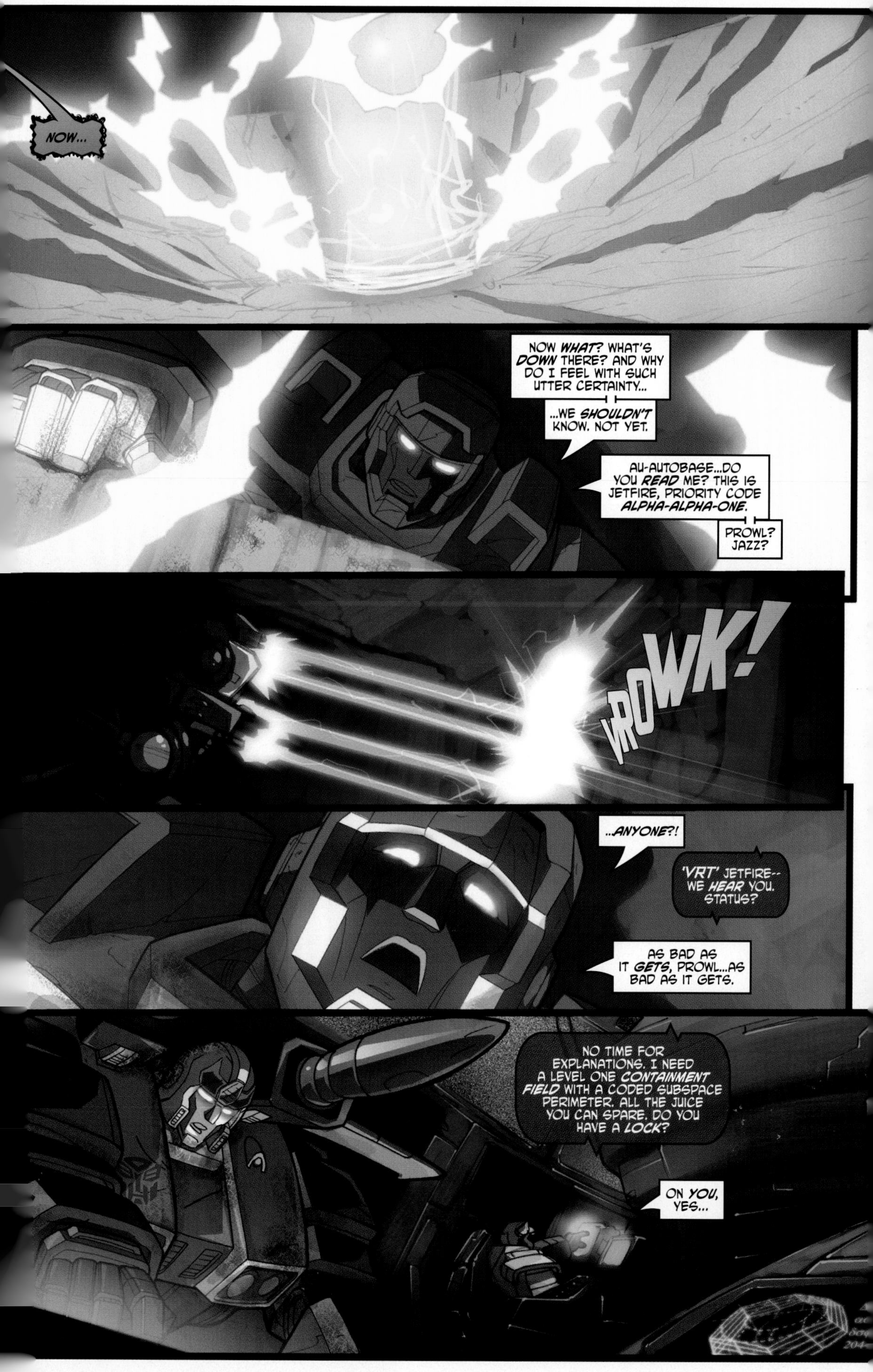
NOW...
NOW WHAT? WHAT'S DOWN THERE? AND WHY DO I FEEL WITH SUCH UTTER CERTAINTY...
...WE SHOULDN'T KNOW. NOT YET.
AU-AUTOBASE...DO YOU READ ME? THIS IS JETFIRE, PRIORITY CODE ALPHA-ALPHA-ONE.
PROWL? JAZZ?
VROWK!
..ANYONE?!
'VRT' JETFIRE-- WE HEAR YOU. STATUS?
AS BAD AS IT GETS, PROWL...AS BAD AS IT GETS.
NO TIME FOR EXPLANATIONS. I NEED A LEVEL ONE CONTAINMENT FIELD WITH A CODED SUBSPACE PERIMETER. ALL THE JUICE YOU CAN SPARE. DO YOU HAVE A LOCK?
ON YOU, YES...

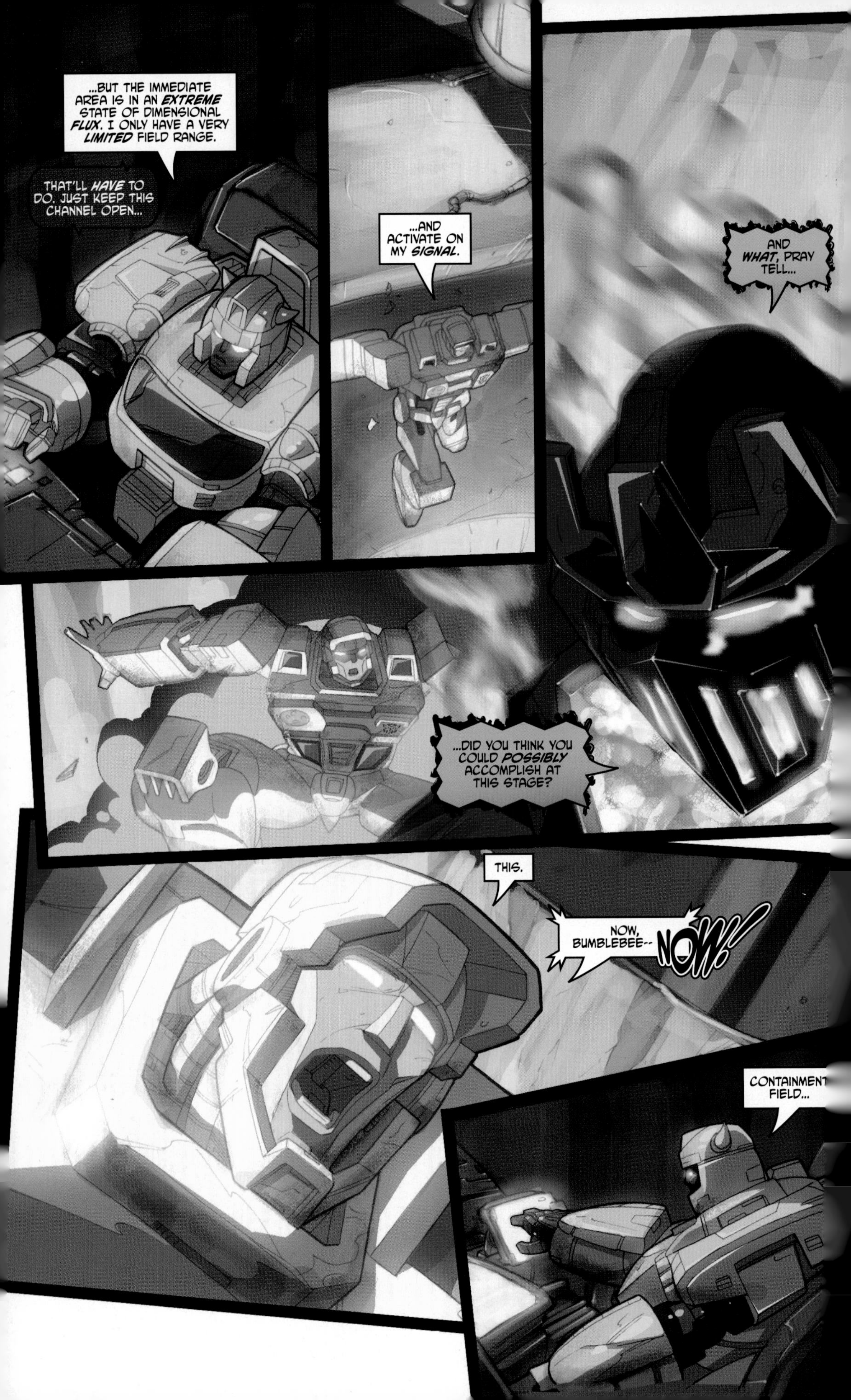

...BUT THE IMMEDIATE AREA IS IN AN EXTREME STATE OF DIMENSIONAL FLUX. I ONLY HAVE A VERY LIMITED FIELD RANGE.
THAT'LL HAVE TO DO. JUST KEEP THIS CHANNEL OPEN...
...AND ACTIVATE ON MY SIGNAL.
AND WHAT, PRAY TELL...
...DID YOU THINK YOU COULD POSSIBLY ACCOMPLISH AT THIS STAGE?
THIS.
NOW, BUMBLEBEE-- NOW!
CONTAINMENT FIELD...

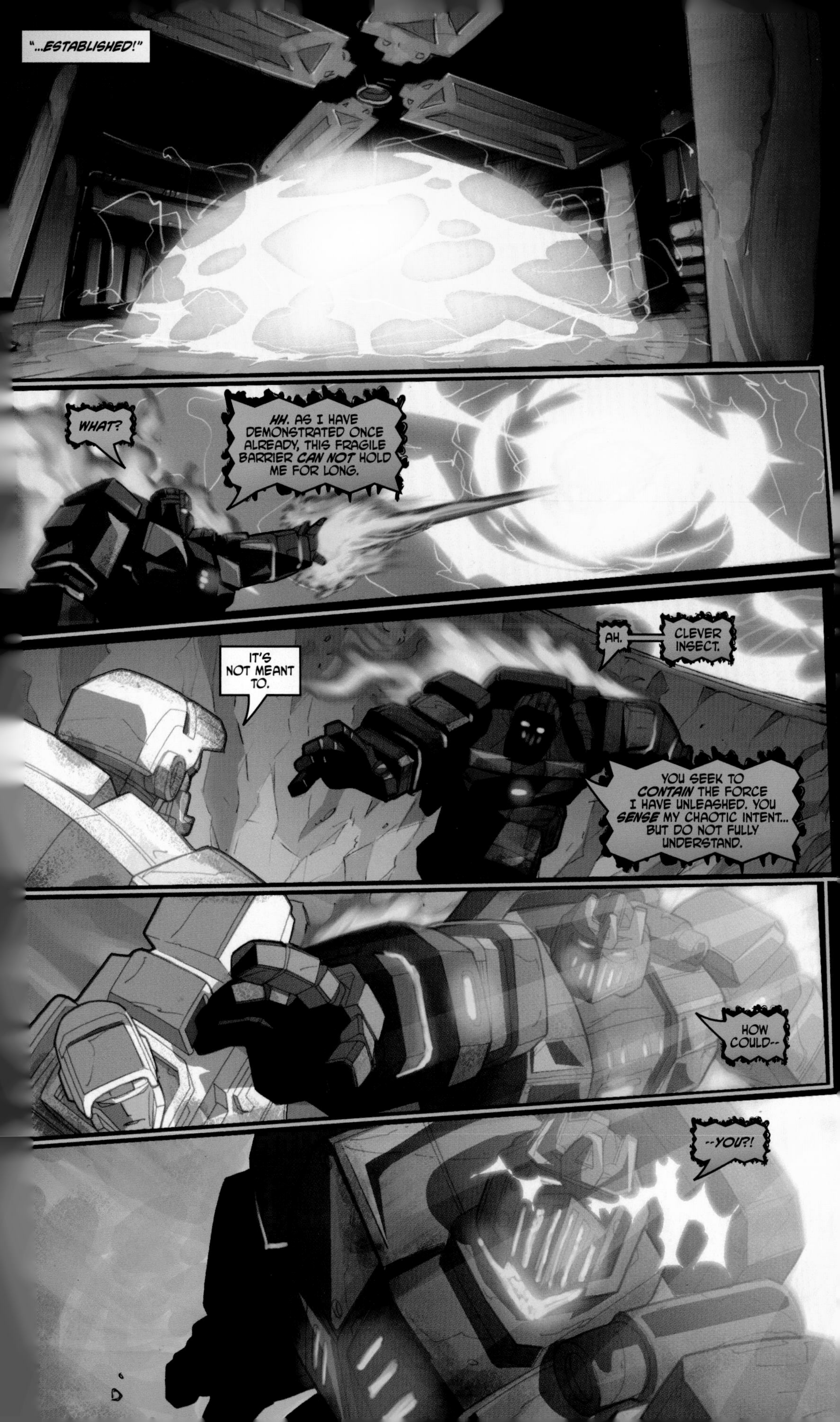
"...ESTABLISHED!"
WHAT?
HH. AS I HAVE DEMONSTRATED ONCE ALREADY, THIS FRAGILE BARRIER CAN NOT HOLD ME FOR LONG.
IT'S NOT MEANT TO.
AH.
CLEVER INSECT.
YOU SEEK TO CONTAIN THE FORCE I HAVE UNLEASHED. YOU SENSE MY CHAOTIC INTENT... BUT DO NOT FULLY UNDERSTAND.
HOW COULD--
--YOU?!

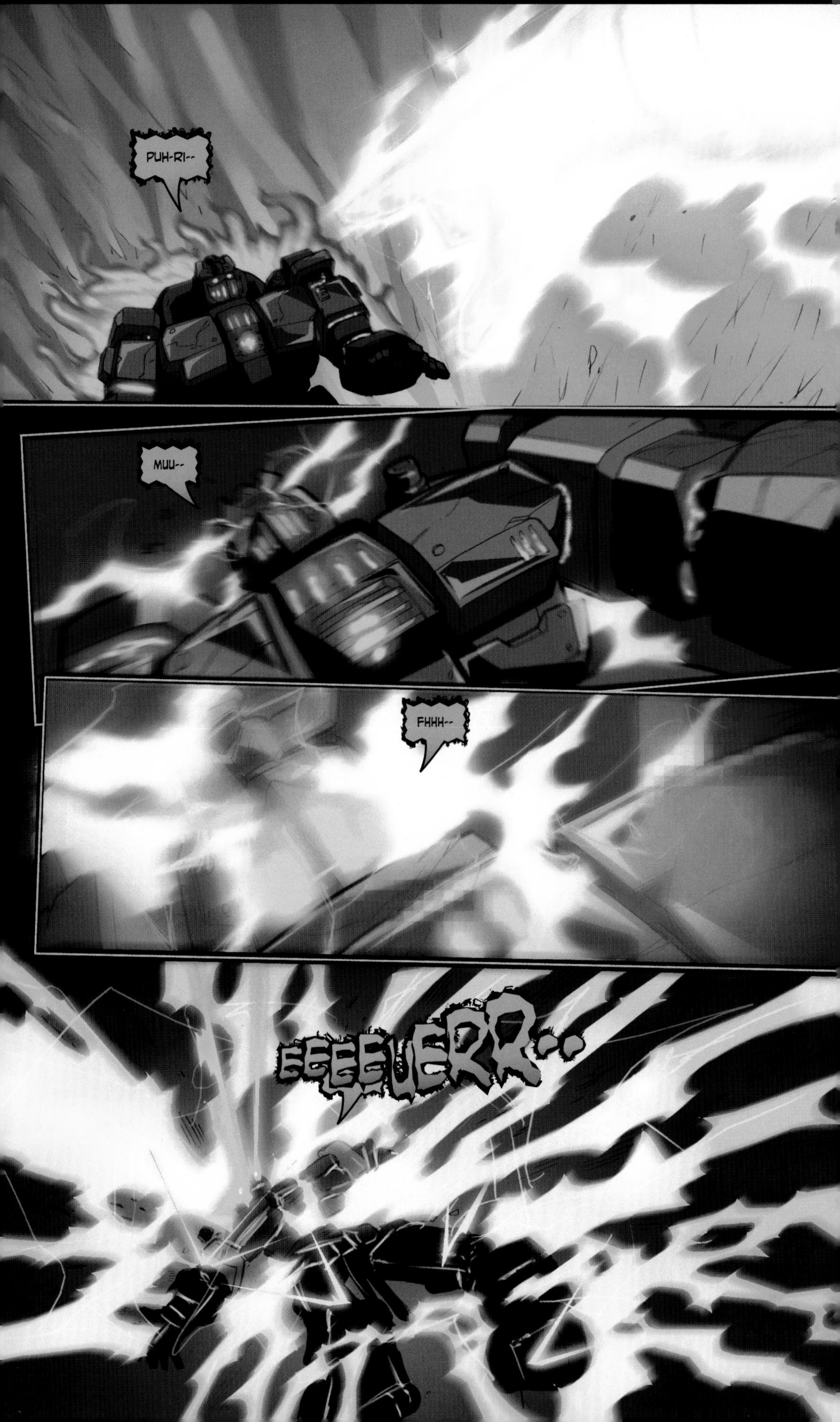
PUH-RI--
MUU--
FHHH--
EEEEUERR--

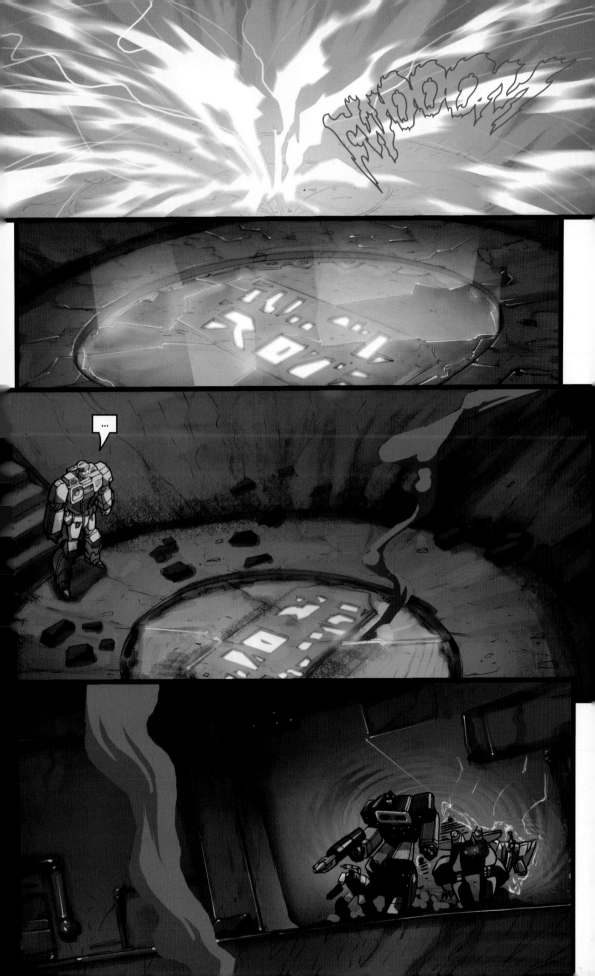

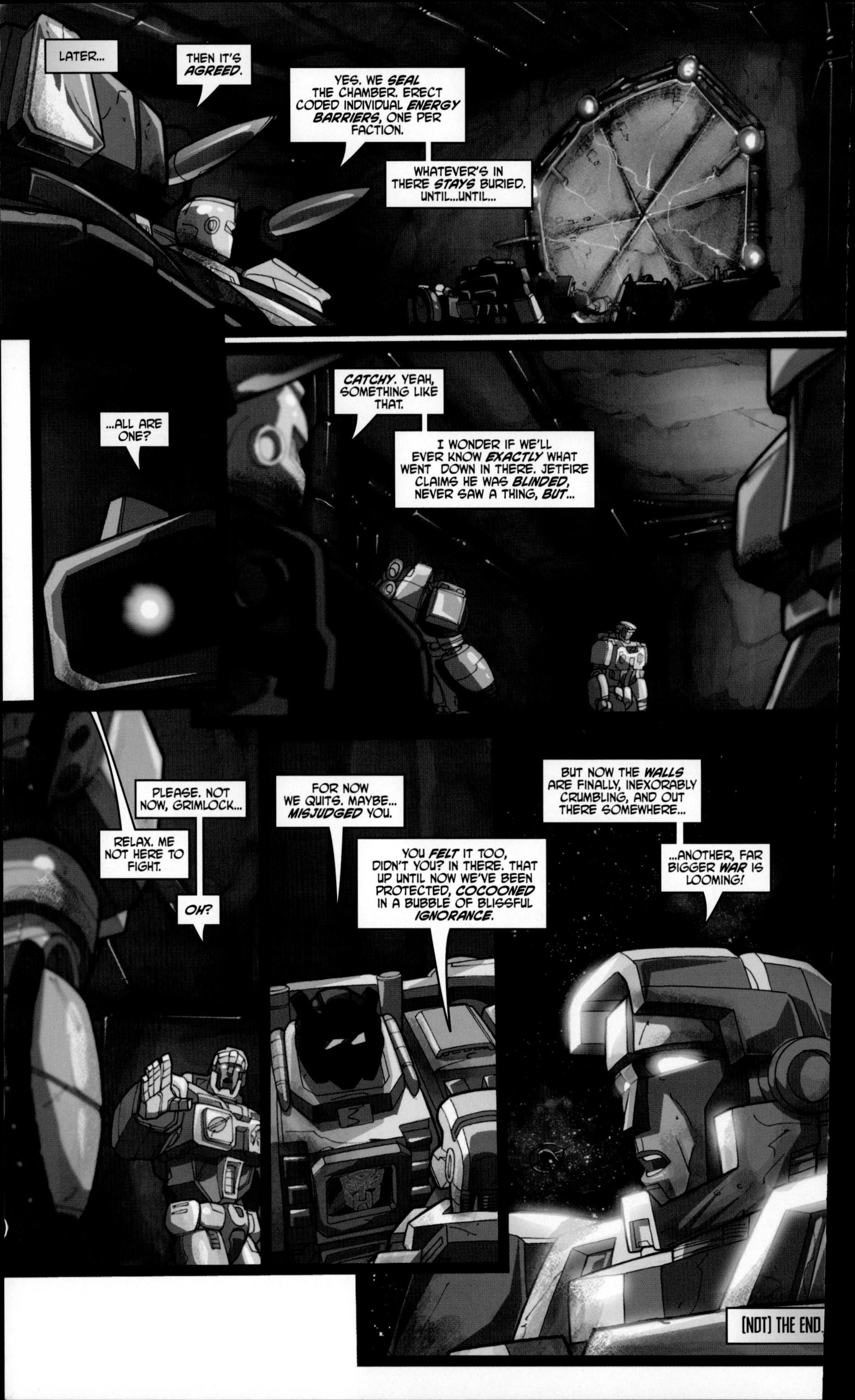
LATER...
THEN IT'S AGREED.
YES. WE SEAL THE CHAMBER. ERECT CODED INDIVIDUAL ENERGY BARRIERS, ONE PER FACTION.
WHATEVER'S IN THERE STAYS BURIED. UNTIL...UNTIL...
...ALL ARE ONE?
CATCHY. YEAH, SOMETHING LIKE THAT.
I WONDER IF WE'LL EVER KNOW EXACTLY WHAT WENT DOWN IN THERE. JETFIRE CLAIMS HE WAS BLINDED, NEVER SAW A THING, BUT...
PLEASE. NOT NOW, GRIMLOCK...
RELAX. ME NOT HERE TO FIGHT.
OH?
FOR NOW WE QUITS. MAYBE... MISJUDGED YOU.
YOU FELT IT TOO, DIDN'T YOU? IN THERE. THAT UP UNTIL NOW WE'VE BEEN PROTECTED, COCOONED IN A BUBBLE OF BLISSFUL IGNORANCE.
BUT NOW THE WALLS ARE FINALLY, INEXORABLY CRUMBLING, AND OUT THERE SOMEWHERE...
...ANOTHER, FAR BIGGER WAR IS LOOMING!
[NOT] THE END.

Extras

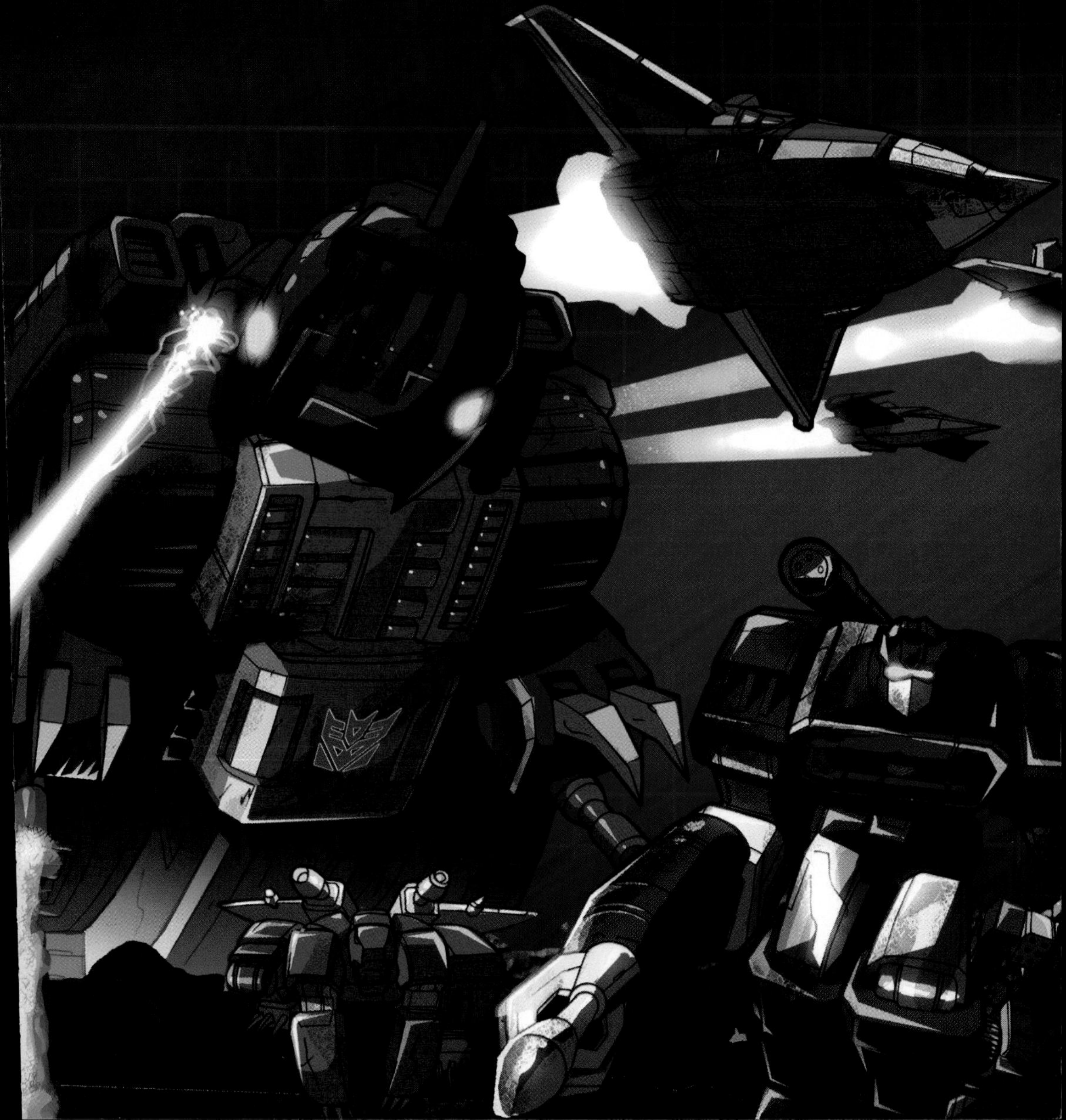

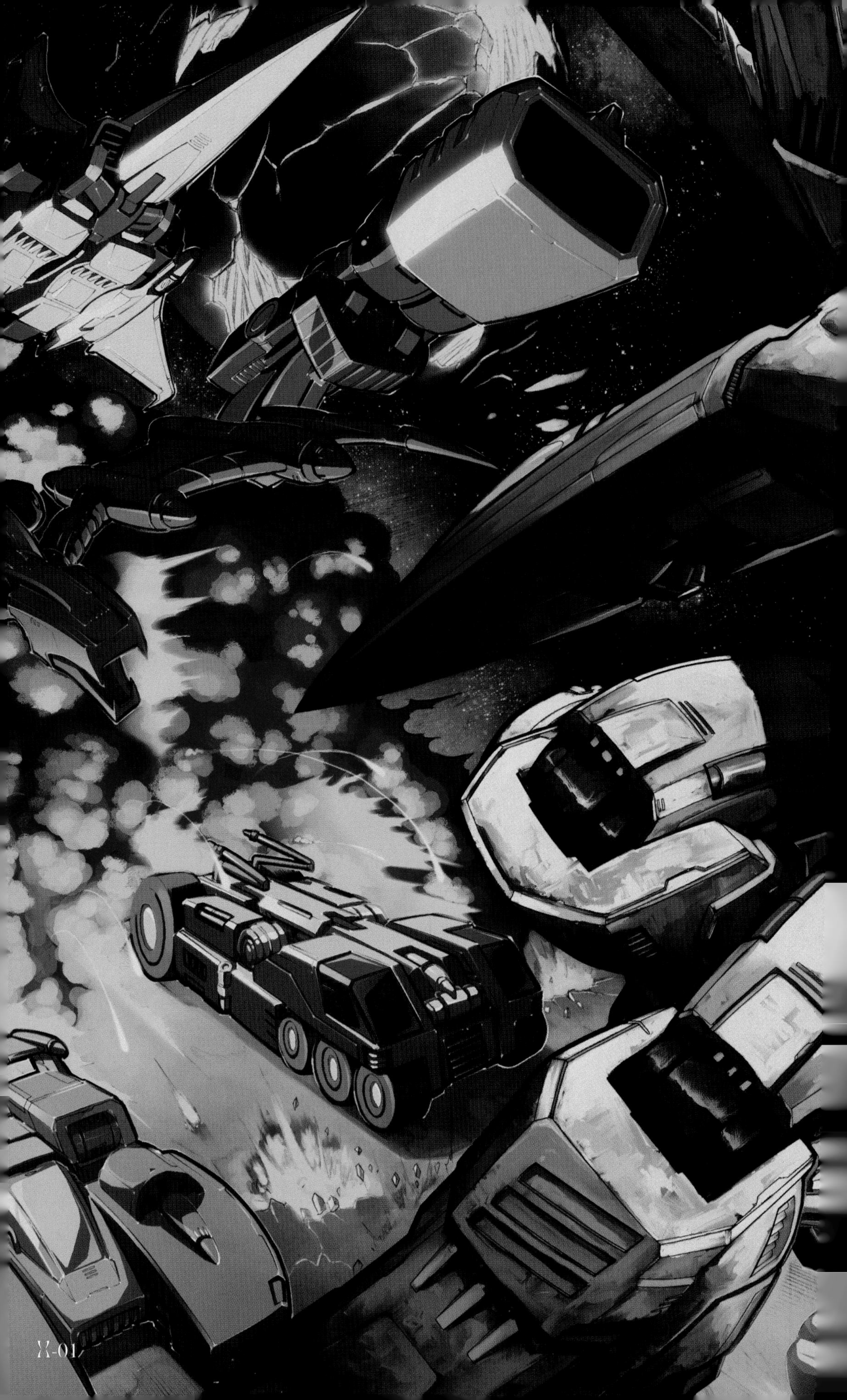
X-01

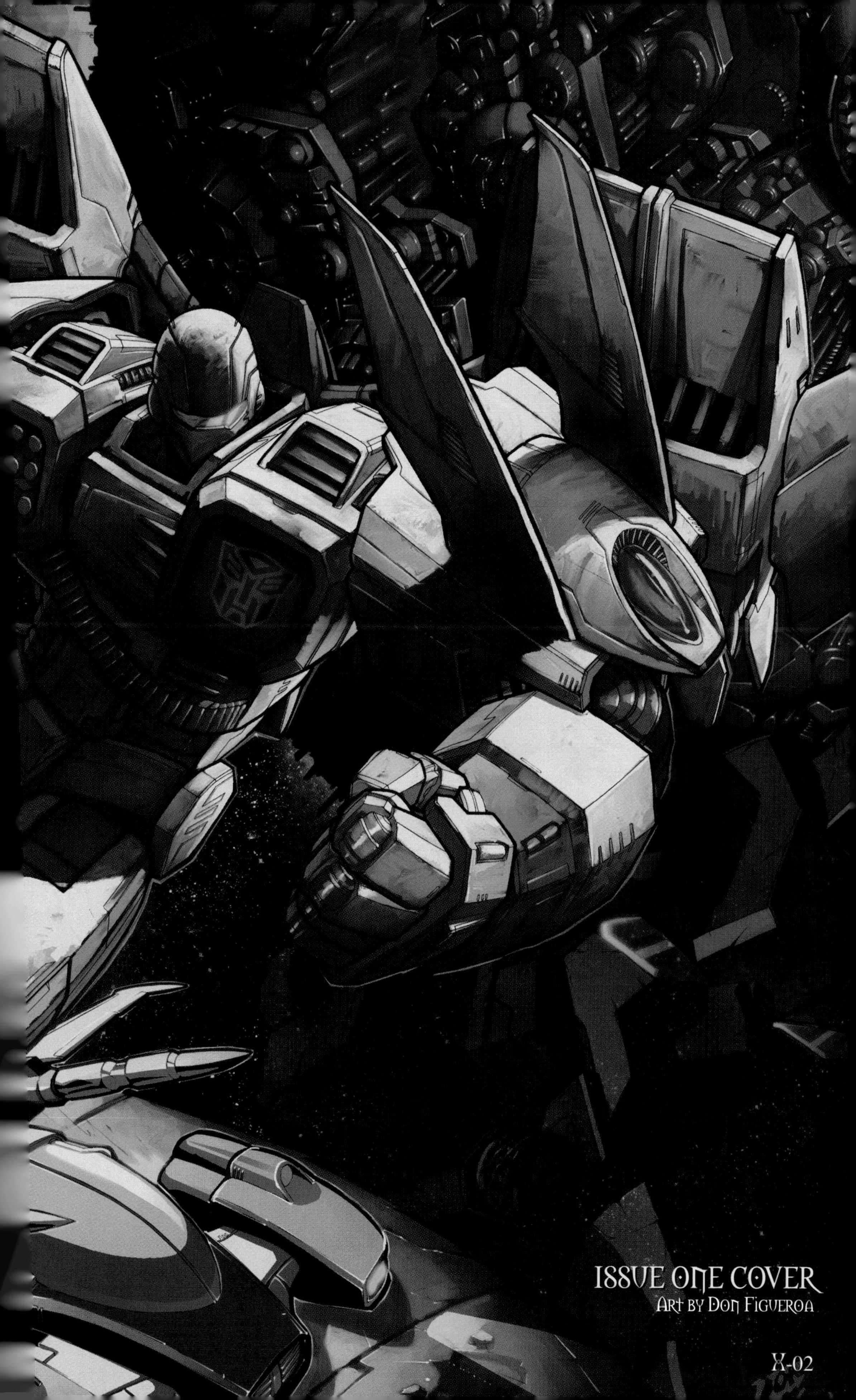

ISSUE ONE COVER
Art by Don Figueroa

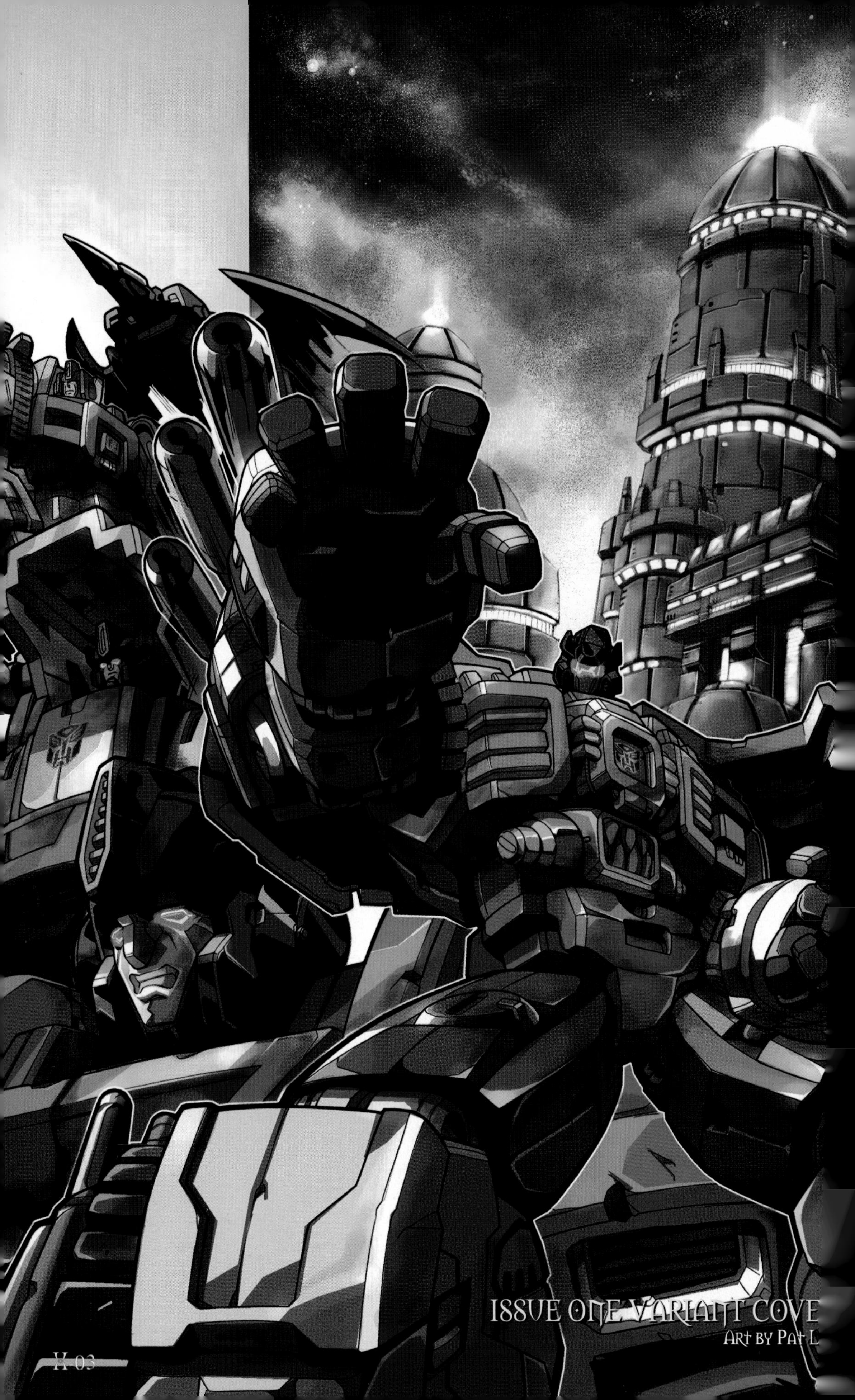

ISSUE ONE VARIANT COVE
ART BY PAT L

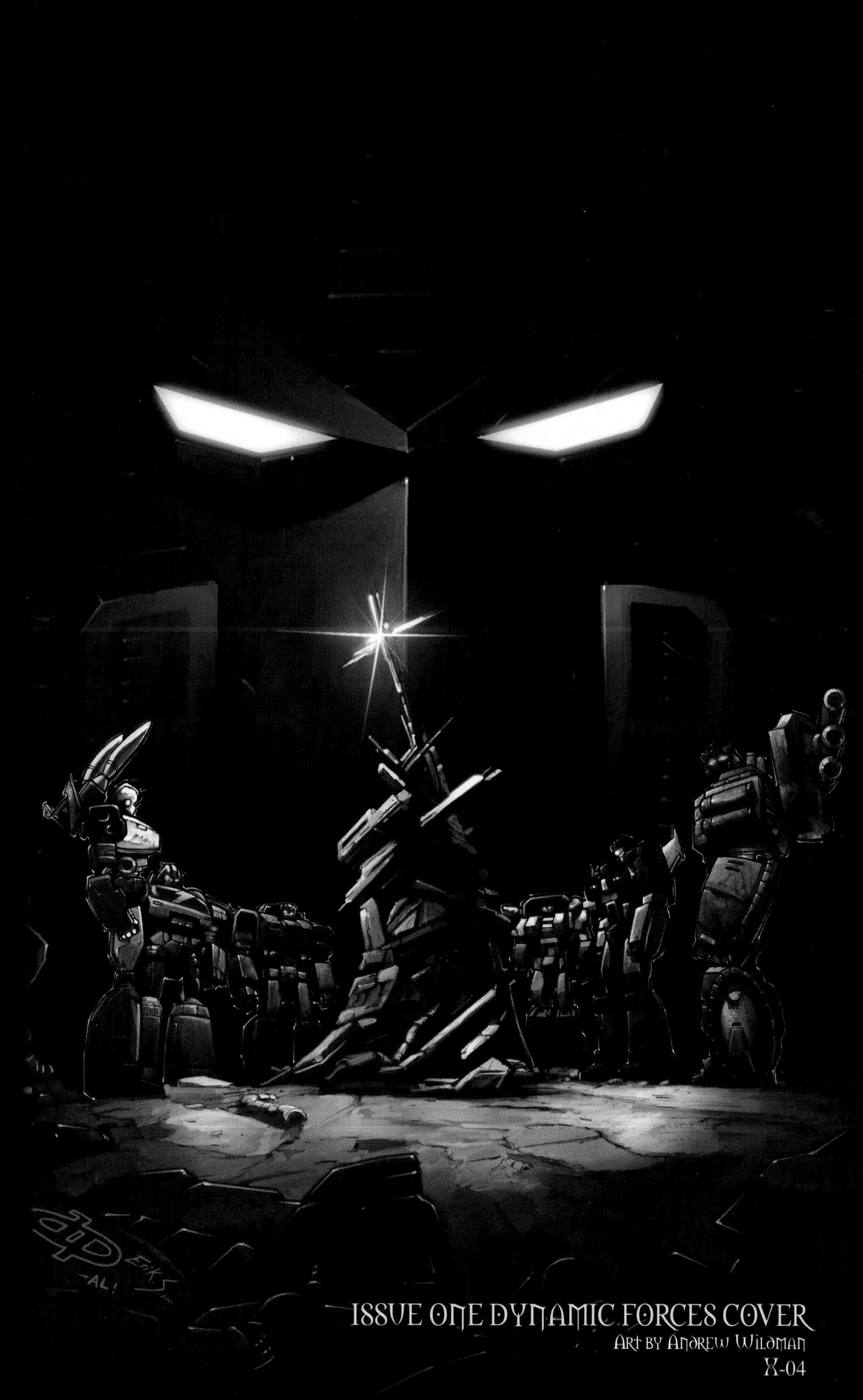

ISSUE ONE DYNAMIC FORCES COVER
Art by Andrew Wildman
X-04

The Dark Ages
ALLEGIANCES

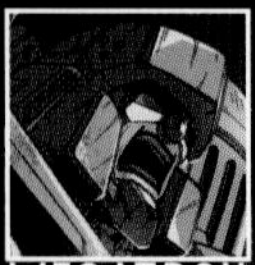
MEGATRON

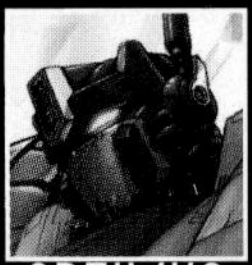
OPTIMUS PRIME

Following the abrupt disappearance (and presumed death) of OPTIMUS PRIME and MEGATRON, the civil war descended into a splintered border conflict between six key factions: the Autobots, the Decepticons, the Ultracons, the Wreckers, the Lightning Strike Coalition and the Predacons. While the Autobots and the former Autobot factions (Wreckers and L-S-C) remained loosely allied, their agendas and methodology/ideology differed markedly.

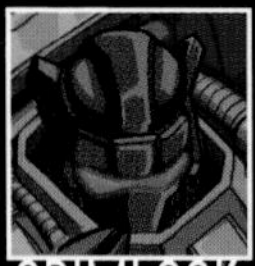
GRIMLOCK

THE LIGHTNING STRIKE COALITION

Frustrated by acting Autobot commander, PROWL, GRIMLOCK formed his own rapid action splinter group. Freed from some of the more rigorous constraints of the Autobot Code, the L-S-C established a heavily defended bunker power base in Uraya and brutally targeted every conceivable weakness in the power structures of the Decepticon and former Decepticon factions.

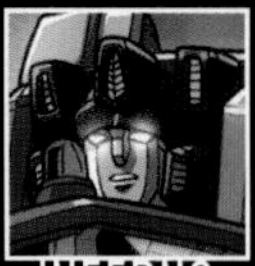
INFERNO

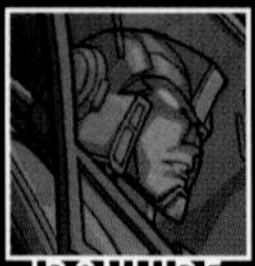
IRONHIDE

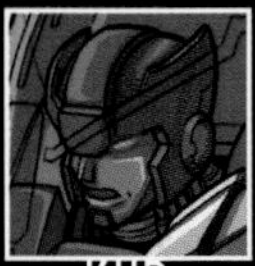
KUP

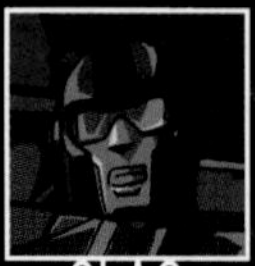
SLAG

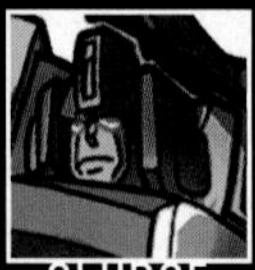
SLUDGE

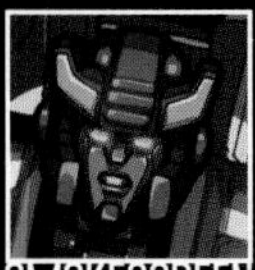
SMOKESCREEN

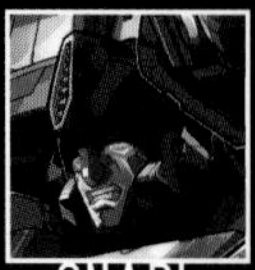
SNARL

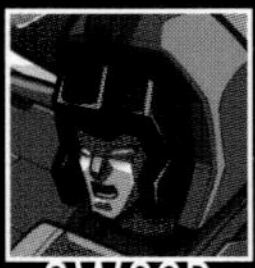
SWOOP

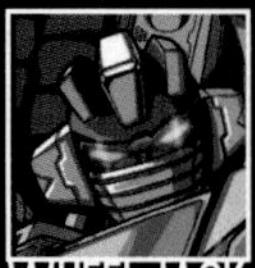
WHEELJACK

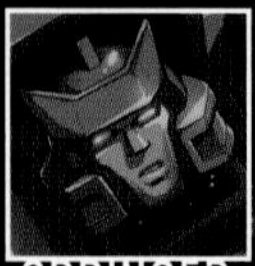
SPRINGER

THE WRECKERS

Already a semi-autonomous unit within the Autobot forces, SPRINGER's elite unit, The Wreckers, felt best suited to a fully independent troubleshooting role in the escalating conflict and established their own mobile command. Their remit expanded to include lightning raids in enemy territory and fast drops into combat zones, enforcing borders wherever they were breached.

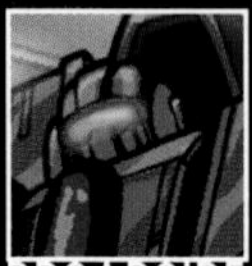
BROADSIDE

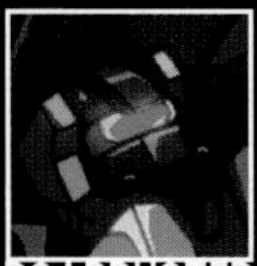
ROADBUSTER

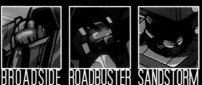

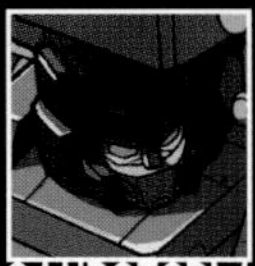
SANDSTORM

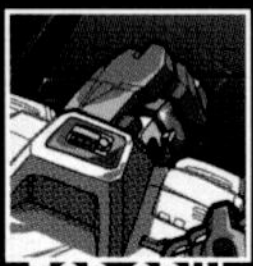
TOP SPIN

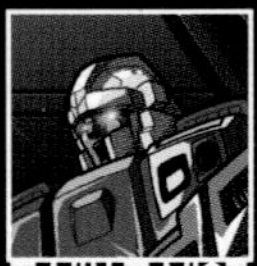
TWIN TWIST

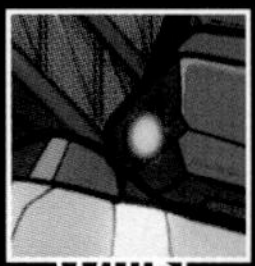
WHIRL

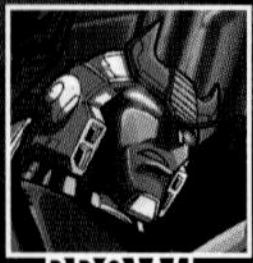
PROWL

THE AUTOBOTS

Already reeling from the loss of OPTIMUS PRIME (and the subsequent decision of ULTRA MAGNUS to forego command), acting commander PROWL stepped up, resulting in a significan part of his forces opting for independent status. Nevertheless, though lacking somewhat in visio and proactive planning, PROWL managed to keep a lid on the escalating tensions.

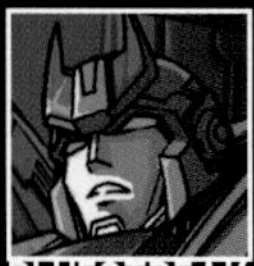
BLUESTREAK

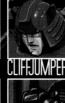

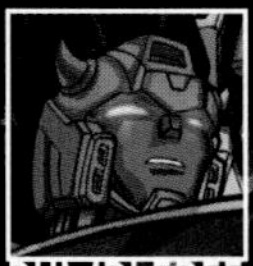
BUMBLEBEE

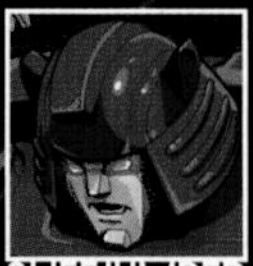
CLIFFJUMPER

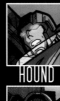

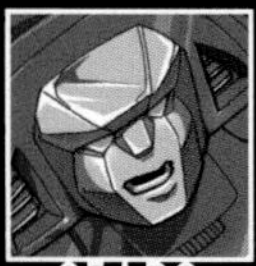
GEARS

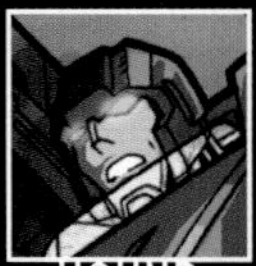
HOUND

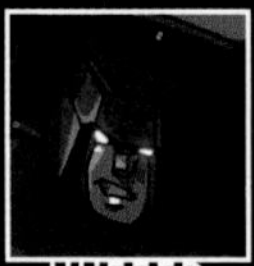
HUFFER

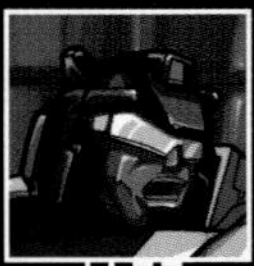
JAZZ

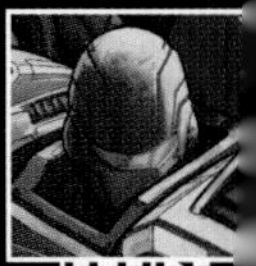
JETFIRE

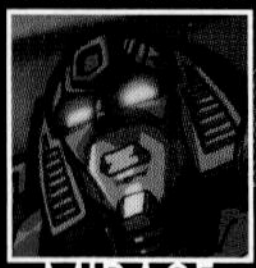
MIRAGE

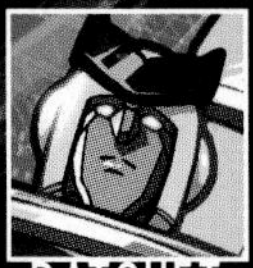
RATCHET

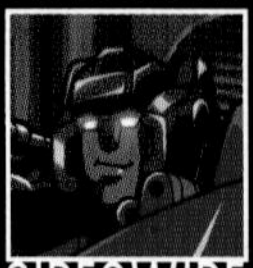
SIDESWIPE

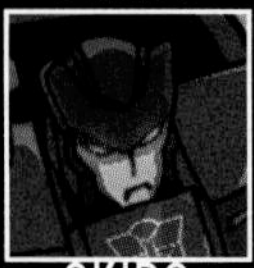
SKIDS

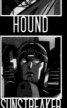

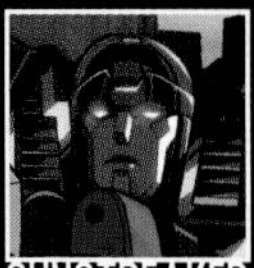
SUNSTREAKER

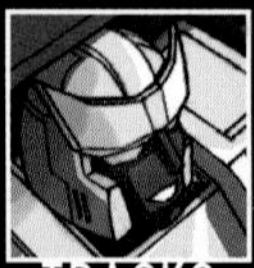
TRACKS

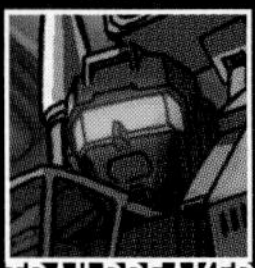
TRAILBREAKER

THE PREDACONS

With MEGATRON gone, STARSCREAM gathered a band of fellow malcontents and borderline psychotics and staged an impromptu coup, attempting to wrest power from acting Decepticon commander SHOCKWAVE. Though he failed, the group subsequently claimed independent status and established a raiding base on Cybertron's Moon Alpha.

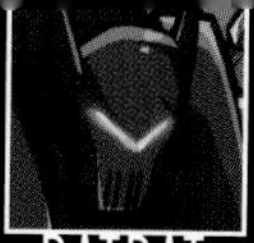

RATBAT

THE ULTRACONS

The schism within the Decepticon ranks widened further when High Auditor RATBAT decided that the war could be managed more efficiently with a smaller, more dedicated unit, gradually widening its power base and controlling key resources. Setting up base in Polyhex's southern expanse, RATBAT'S Ultracons soon made significant territorial advances.

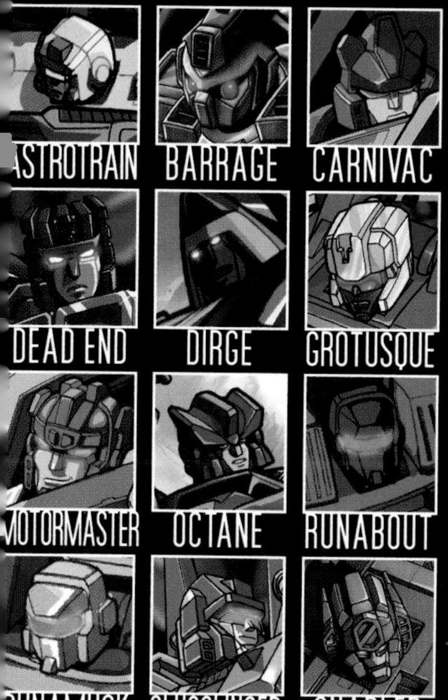

ASTROTRAIN BARRAGE CARNIVAC
DEAD END DIRGE GROTUSQUE
MOTORMASTER OCTANE RUNABOUT
RUNAMUCK SLUGSLINGER SNARLER

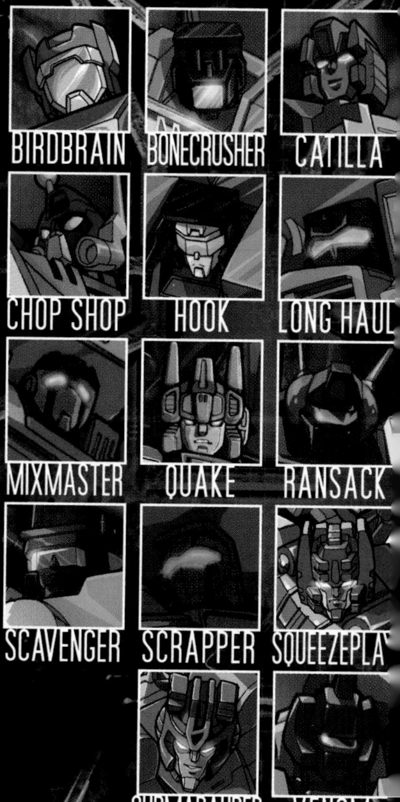

BIRDBRAIN BONECRUSHER CATILLA
CHOP SHOP HOOK LONG HAUL
MIXMASTER QUAKE RANSACK
SCAVENGER SCRAPPER SQUEEZEPLAY
SUBMARAUDER VENOM

THE DECEPTICONS

Barely fazed by the assorted defections and insurrections within his ranks, SHOCKWAVE continued his policy of advancement and consolidation for the betterment and long-term survival of the planet. Patient, logical, constantly analyzing planetary data in terms of threat assessment and long-term strategy, in many ways the stripped-down Decepticons were an even greater threat.

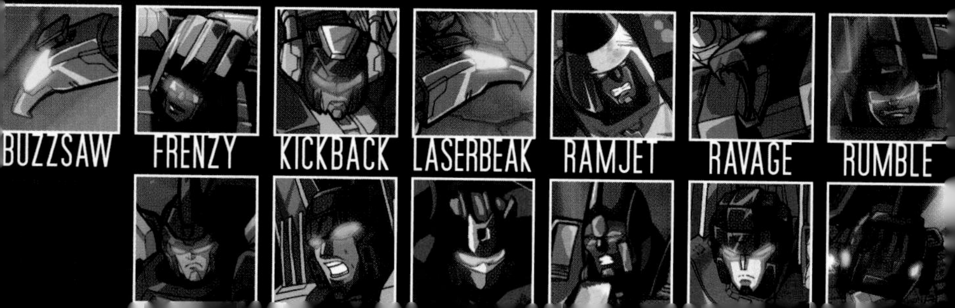

BUZZSAW FRENZY KICKBACK LASERBEAK RAMJET RAVAGE RUMBLE

THE FALLEN

With Simon Furman and Pat Lee

Interview by **Matt Hansen**

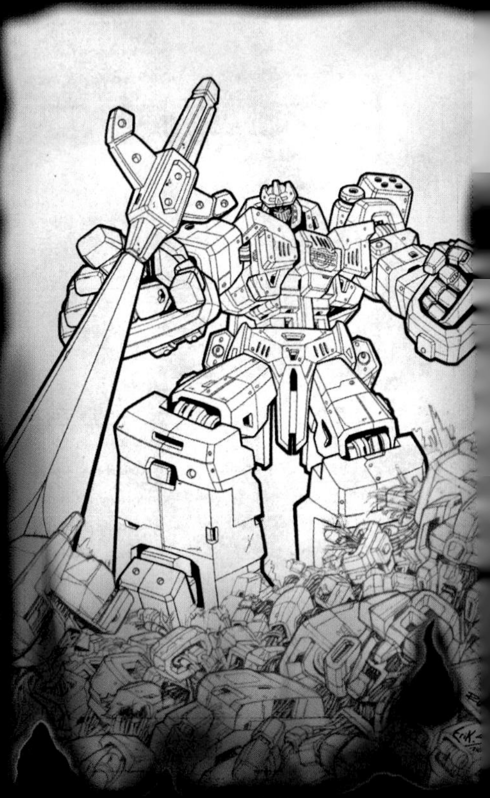

Transformers: War Within: The Dark Ages featured a character that had many fans saying "who's that?" He appears as a mystical, dark robot that has powers and a look unlike other Transformers. The Fallen was part of Simon Furman's reconstructing of life on Cybertron before the fateful voyage to Earth. To help understand The Fallen, Dreamwave spoke with the two men behind him: writer Furman, and penciler Pat Lee.

Dreamwave: Let's begin with Simon. Did you conceptualize the idea of The Fallen before you actually finished the storyline? How crucial was he to the original idea of the second Volume?

Simon Furman: The Fallen was there right from the start. He was really the crux of the entire series, and the concept that he was one of the original thirteen Transformers, the "Judas" of the bunch, was something that had been percolating in my mind for a while. The idea of Cybertron as a spacecraft, roaming the galaxy at some distant point in TF pre-history, had been introduced in the first War Within and my intention was always to expand on that. Featuring at least one of the original "crew" seemed a good bet, especially as he had been "turned to the dark side" and, we assume, betrayed the others. The Fallen was the perfect agitator for my Dark Ages brew of fear and suspicion. I wanted a real "cauldron" feel to a post-Optimus/Megatron Cybertron, a world on the brink of total anarchy and chaos, and thematically, the Fallen played right into that

DW: What did you think of the idea whe[n] you first saw it, Pat?

Pat Lee: I thought it was great from the sta[rt]. The concept, the appearance that Simon wanted, everything, it sounded really excit[ing] for both of us. I was pretty hyped up to d[o] this too as it was my first original Transfor[mer] design, and I knew that it had to be differ[ent] from any other Transformer.

DW: How much information did you pro[vide] Pat with initially, Simon?

SF: Pat and I exchanged a number of em[ails] on the look and feel of the Fallen and I tu[rned] that into a full description. One of the thin[gs I] wanted most of the Fallen, visually, was th

looked the part. He had to somehow look "older" than other Transformers, and again, playing into that Dark Ages feel, I went all out in my original description of the character to make him almost medieval.

PL: Yeah, since we knew that this was something involving the history of The Transformers, we needed to create a sort of "ancient" look. That's where the feeling of his armor, his visor, the distinct "knight-like" look comes from. We really had to make The Fallen stand out from the rest, as he is an obscure character, and the visual was key.

DW: How many revision and versions were there to the initial sketches?

SF: Pat's first sketches (for the incentive cover) were a little too clean for my liking and he was happy to dirty and darken him up. I loved the internal furnace effect that Pat worked in and the colorists picked up on. The perpetual flame effect came later, once Andrew Wildman got to draw the character in the actual first issue.

DW: It must have been challenging to come up with a new "old" character, and to figure out the transformation, all that sort of thing.

PL: It was actually really interesting to come up with the transformation. Like I said, I really wanted to make him a standout villain, and this meant putting a lot of thought into his robot form, and making sure the transformation into a Tank worked well.

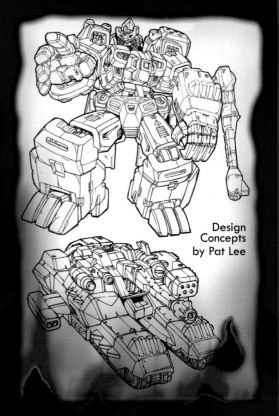

Design Concepts by Pat Lee

DW: What was the initial reaction of other people at Dreamwave?

PL: It was a great one. Everyone really thought the idea and the opportunity to create a new character was incredible. There was a lot of positive energy about it.

SF: Agreed. Everyone at Dreamwave was very receptive to creating a new character for The Dark Ages, excited even. It felt like we were making a real mark on the TF backstory. I'm sure James McDonough had a few nervous flutters, in case I introduced some vast twist that was going to compromise his G1 plans, but we were also working with Hasbro on a whole larger framework, into which everything had to fit.

DW: Is this the last we have seen of the Fallen?

SF: The Fallen has become a part of all this larger outline I've created, and everything flowed onwards and upwards throughout the saga. One of these days, maybe, I'll get to go back further into TF pre-history and show the original crew and chart the Fallen's, well, fall from grace.

I was stumped when I came to Jetfire's design at first. I figured I could always just rely on his cartoon or toy form but the appeal of the War Within series is to see what the TFs looked millions of years before. They had to go through all sorts of changes by the time they landed on earth (just think, Primal went through a bunch in not so many years) and so I remembered my Strikefire design from my old Macromaster Fanfic and I just said, why not? Strikefire was meant to be Jetfire in Macromasters anyway.

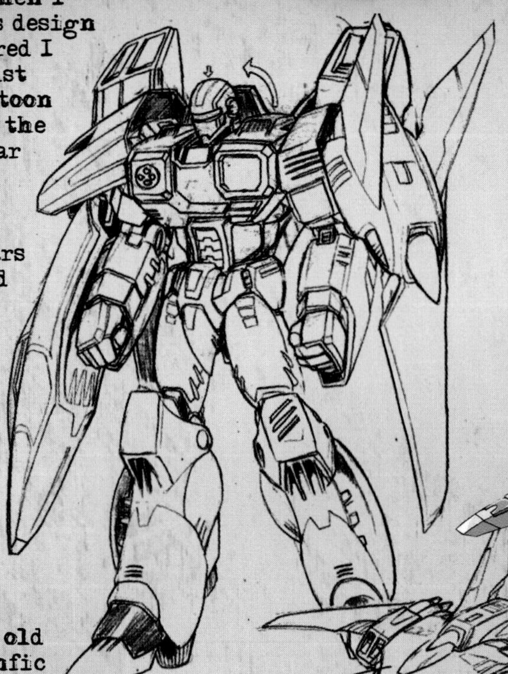

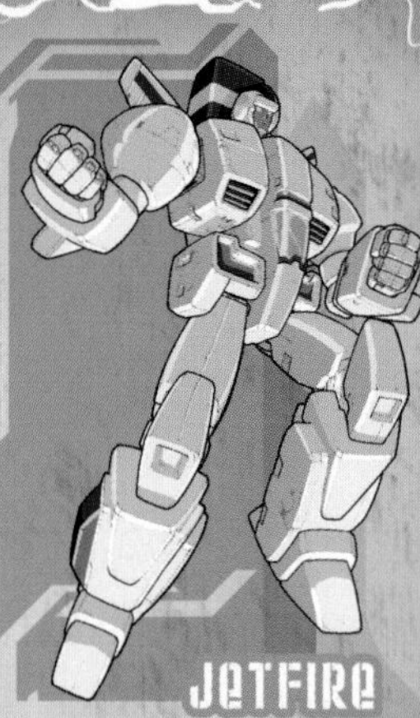
JETFIRE

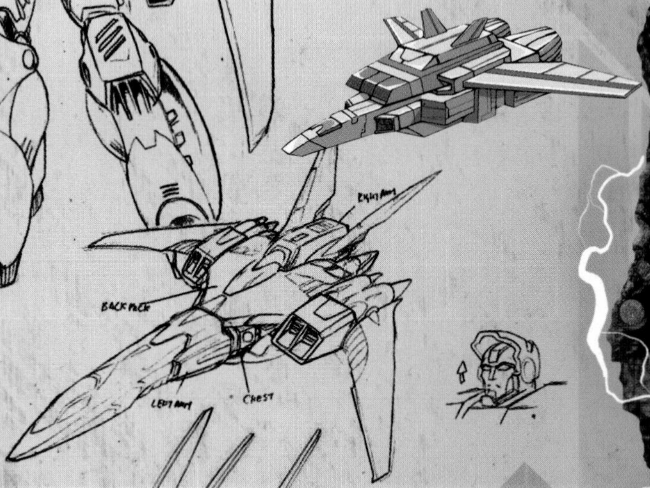
BACK PIECE
LEFT ARM
CHEST

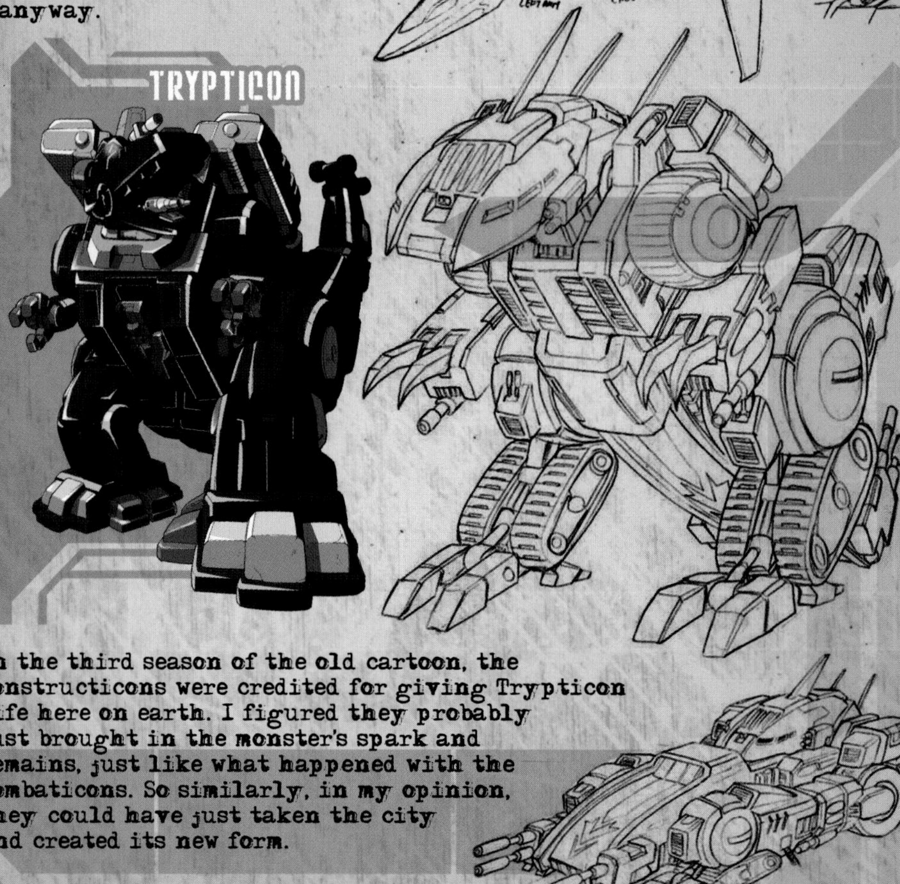
TRYPTICON

In the third season of the old cartoon, the Constructicons were credited for giving Trypticon life here on earth. I figured they probably just brought in the monster's spark and remains, just like what happened with the Combaticons. So similarly, in my opinion, they could have just taken the city and created its new form.

Designs and commentary by Don Figueroa

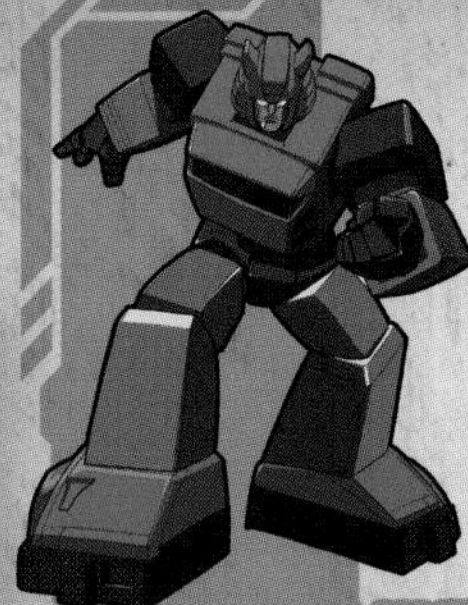

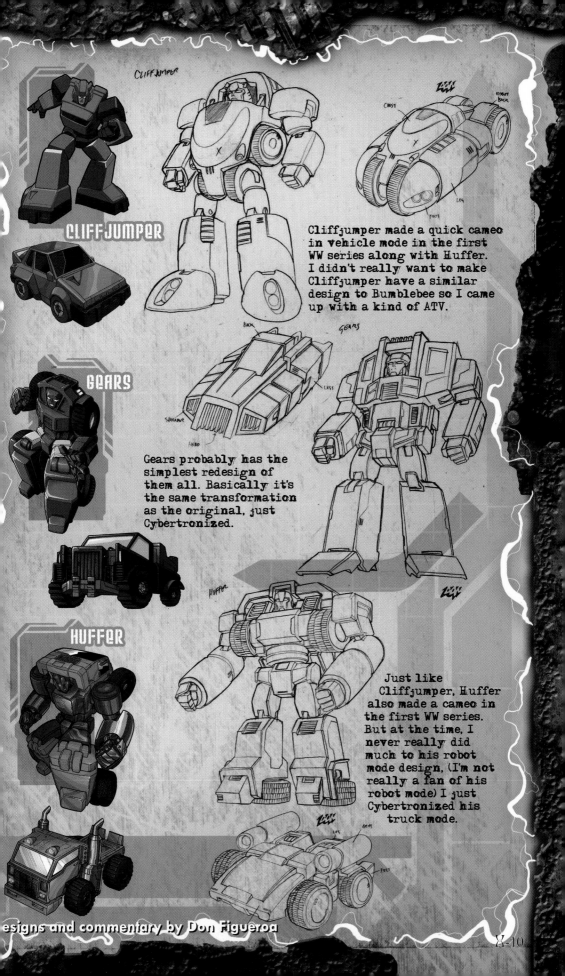

CLIFFJUMPER

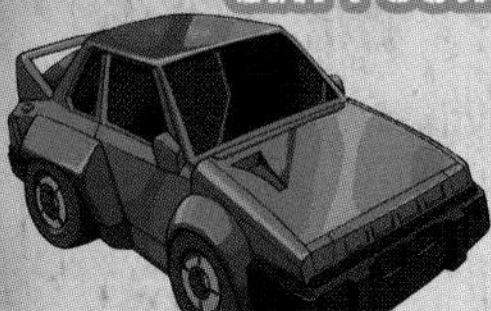

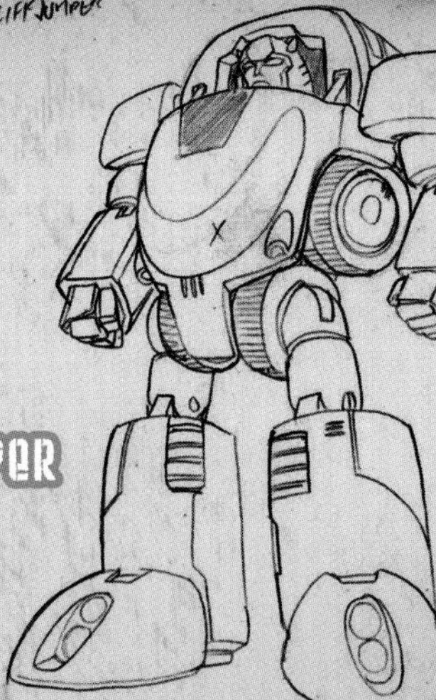
CLIFFJUMPER

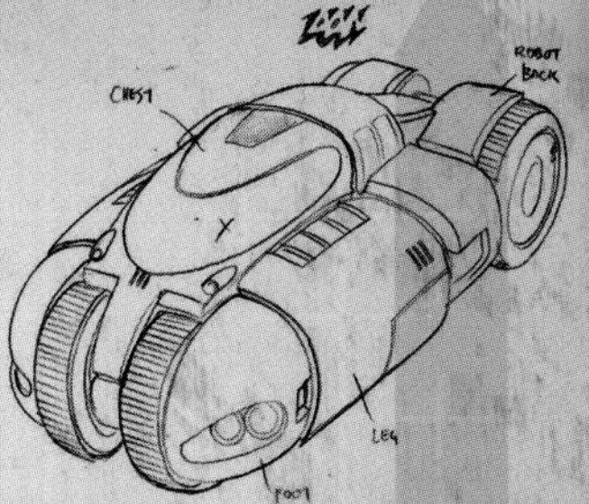
CHEST
ROBOT BACK
LEG
FOOT

Cliffjumper made a quick cameo in vehicle mode in the first WW series along with Huffer. I didn't really want to make Cliffjumper have a similar design to Bumblebee so I came up with a kind of ATV.

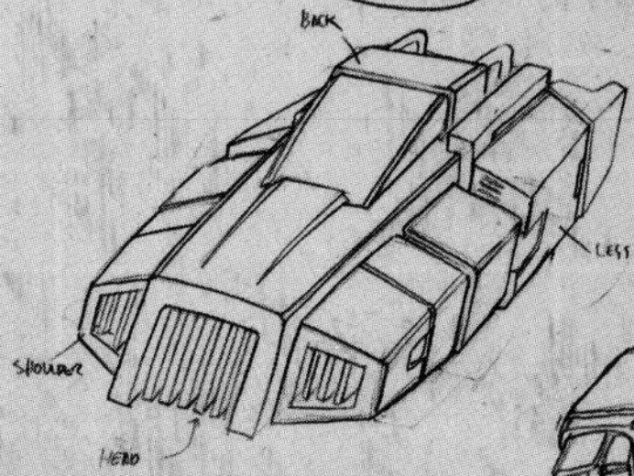
BACK
LEGS
SHOULDER
HEAD

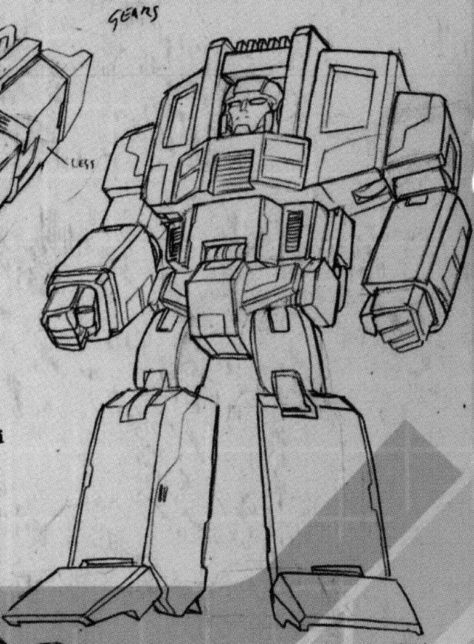
GEARS

GEARS

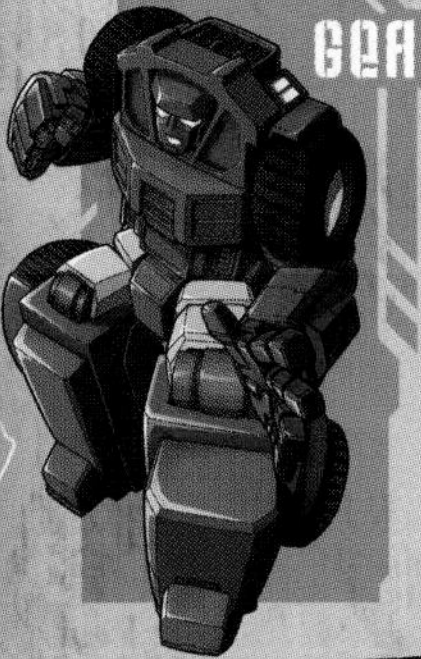

Gears probably has the simplest redesign of them all. Basically it's the same transformation as the original, just Cybertronized.

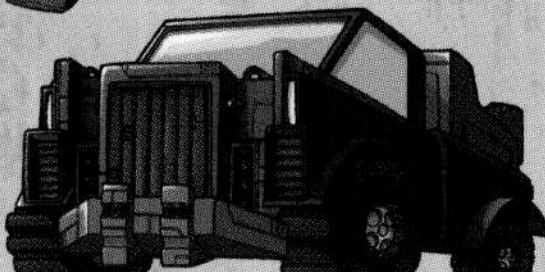

HUFFER

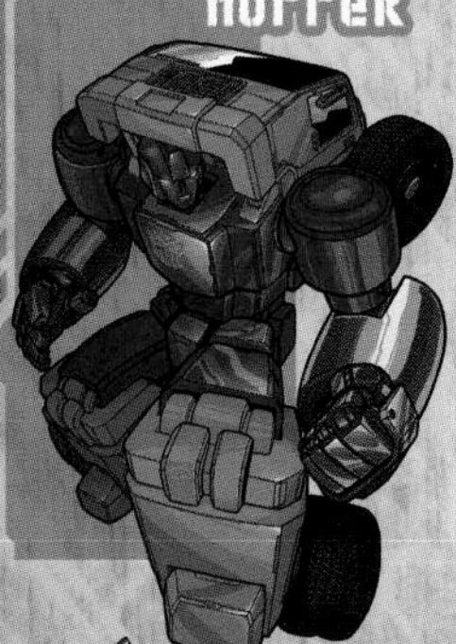

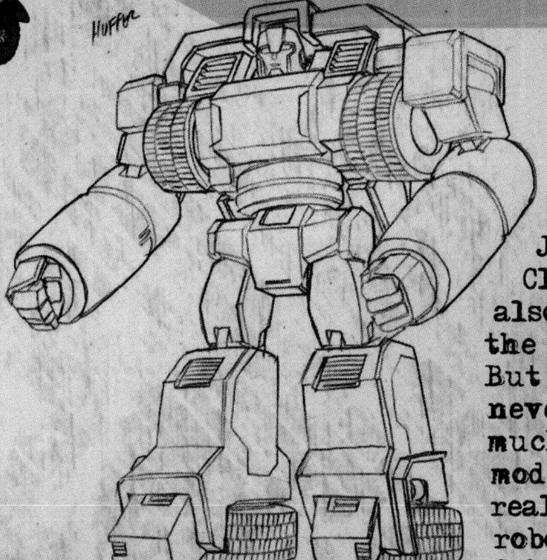
HUFFER

Just like Cliffjumper, Huffer also made a cameo in the first WW series. But at the time, I never really did much to his robot mode design, (I'm not really a fan of his robot mode) I just Cybertronized his truck mode.

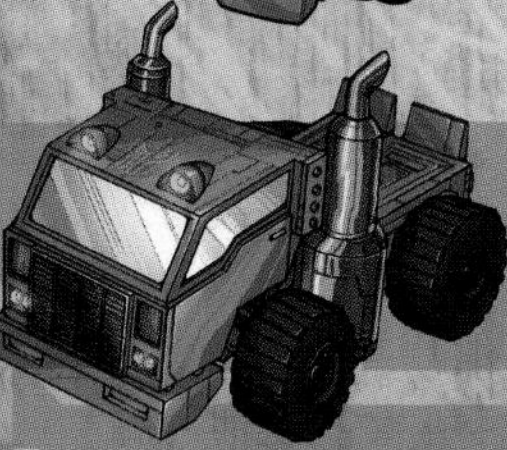

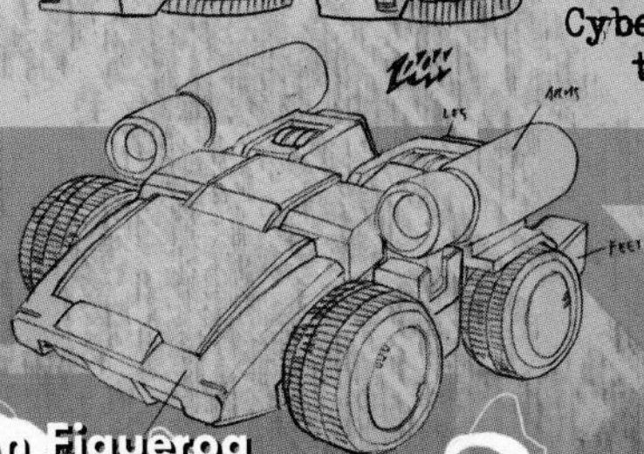
LEG
ARMS
FEET

esigns and commentary by Don Figueroa

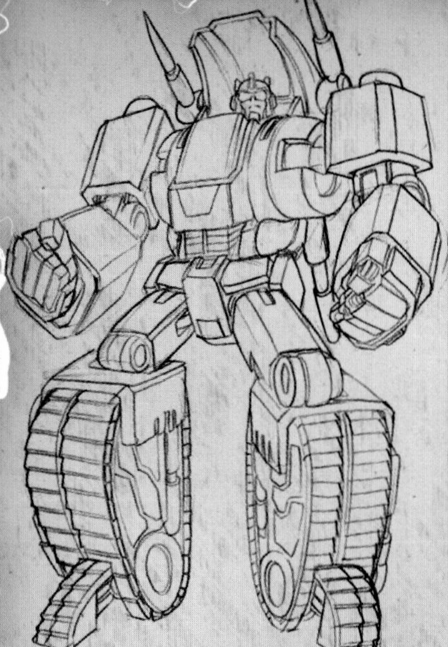

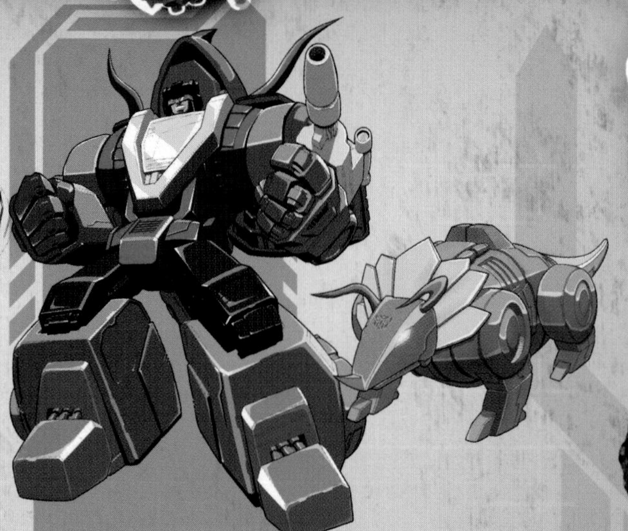

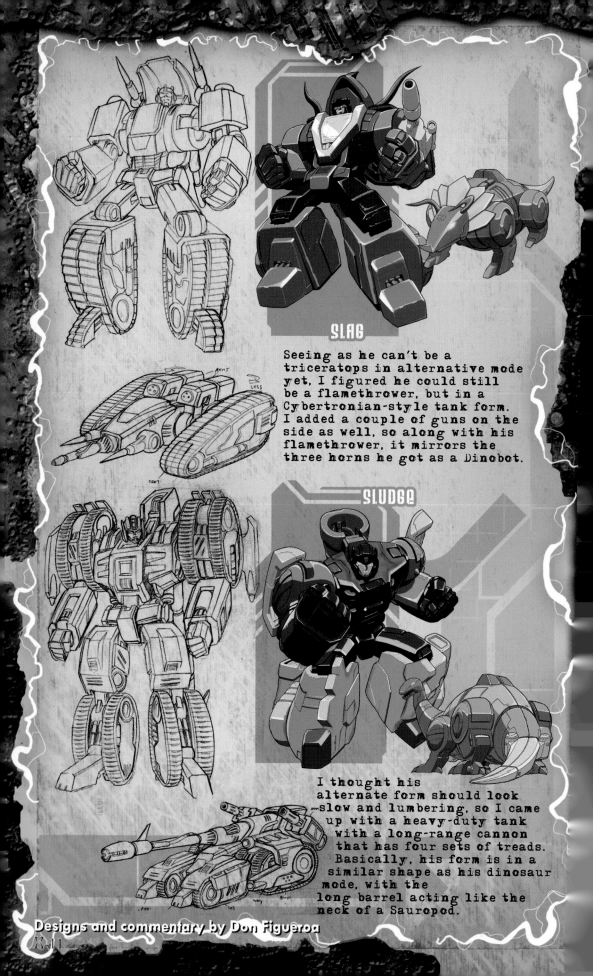

SLAG

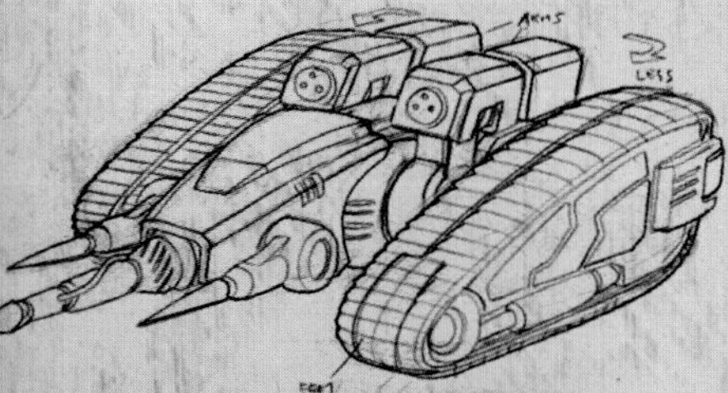

Seeing as he can't be a triceratops in alternative mode yet, I figured he could still be a flamethrower, but in a Cybertronian-style tank form. I added a couple of guns on the side as well, so along with his flamethrower, it mirrors the three horns he got as a Dinobot.

SLUDGE

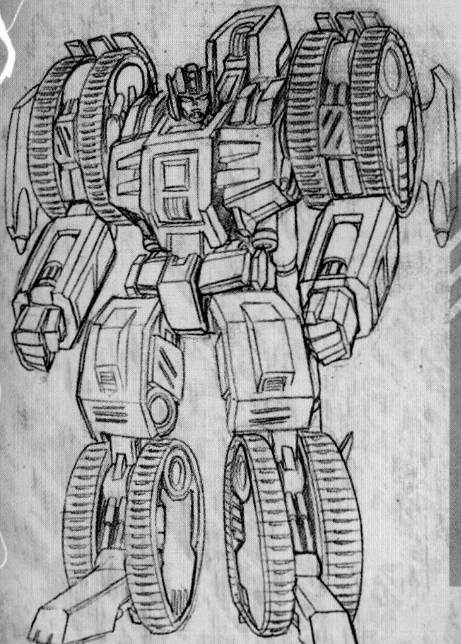

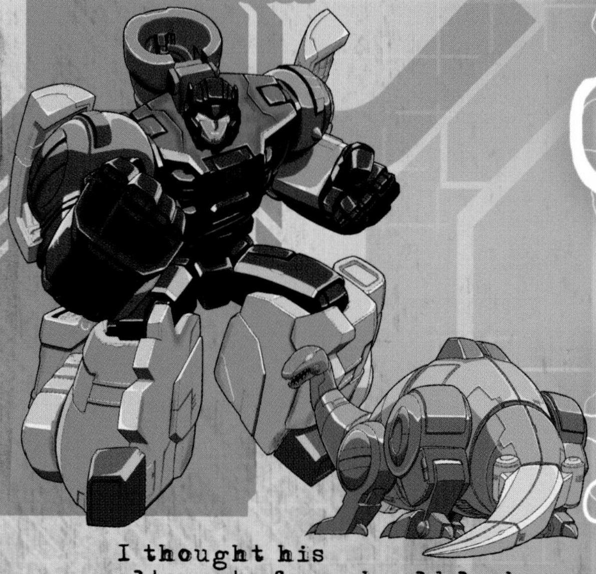

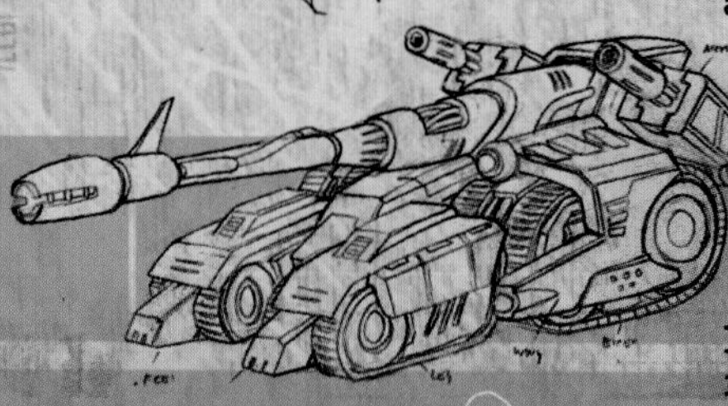

I thought his alternate form should look slow and lumbering, so I came up with a heavy-duty tank with a long-range cannon that has four sets of treads. Basically, his form is in a similar shape as his dinosaur mode, with the long barrel acting like the neck of a Sauropod.

Designs and commentary by Don Figueroa

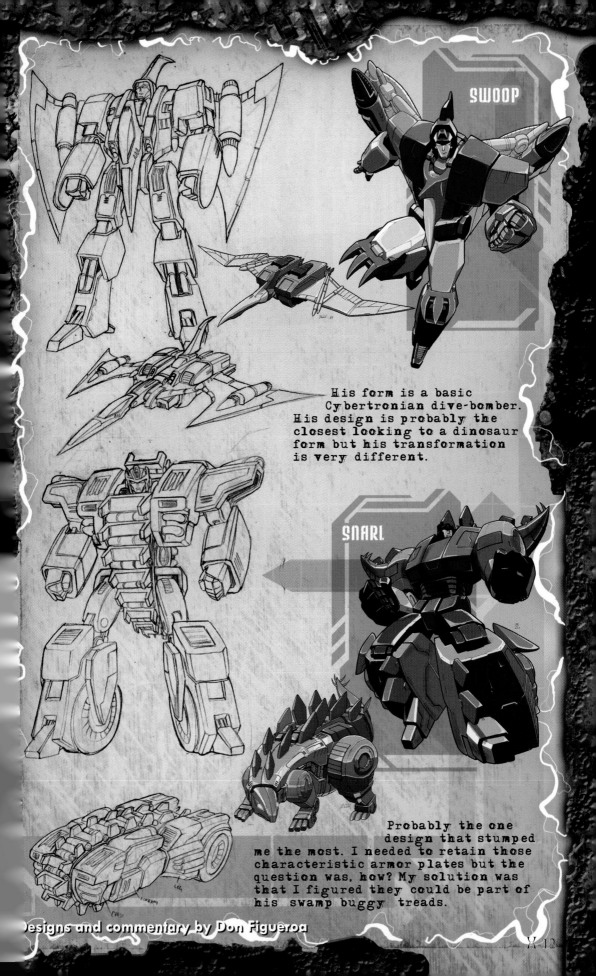

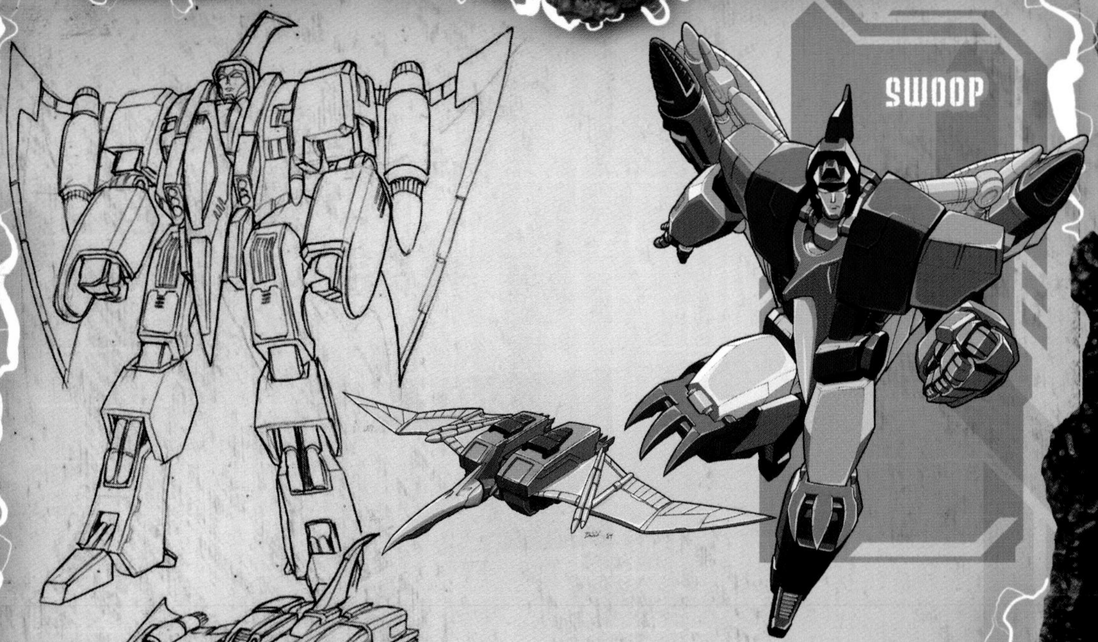
SWOOP

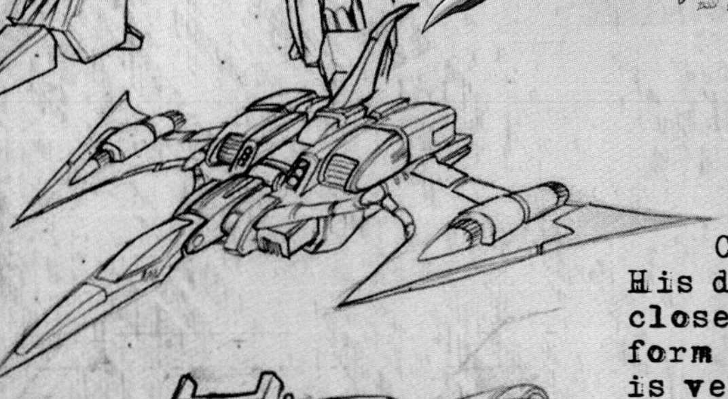

His form is a basic Cybertronian dive-bomber. His design is probably the closest looking to a dinosaur form but his transformation is very different.

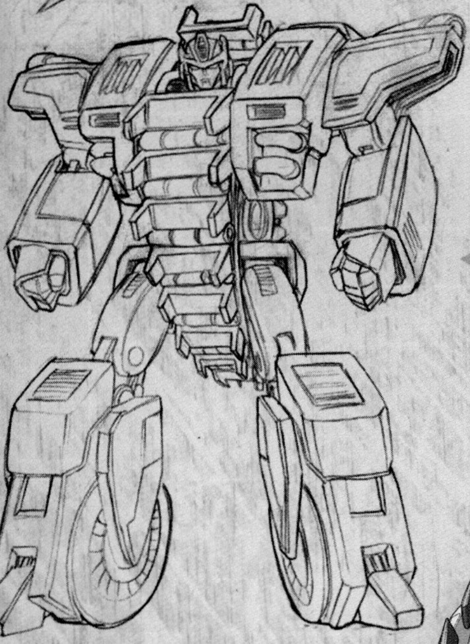

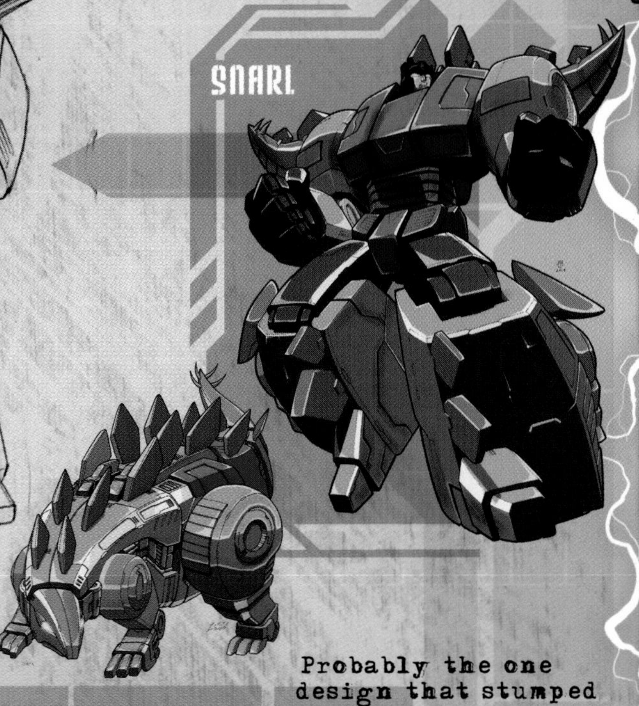
SNARL

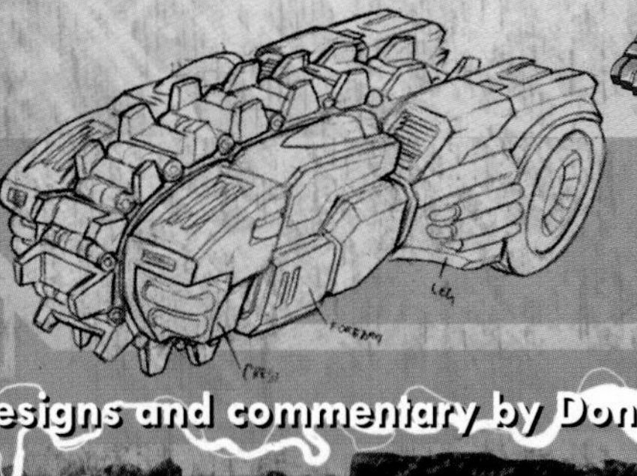

Probably the one design that stumped me the most. I needed to retain those characteristic armor plates but the question was, how? My solution was that I figured they could be part of his swamp buggy treads.

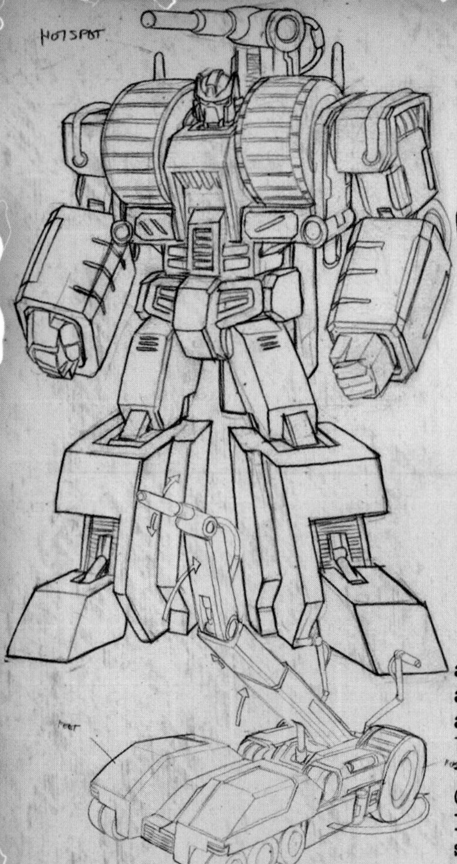
HOTSPOT

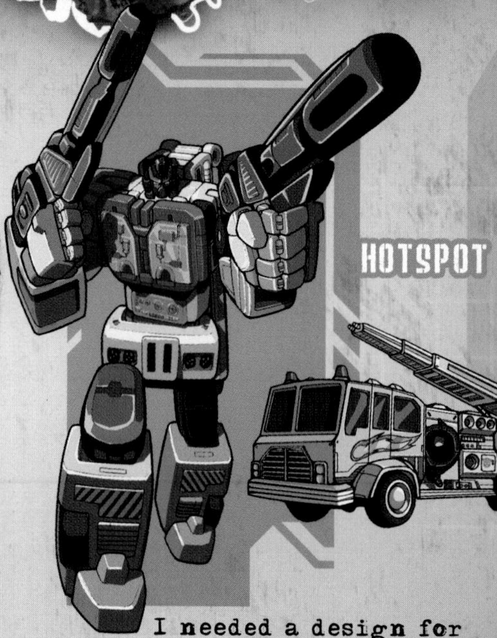
HOTSPOT

I needed a design for Hotspot that still retained a fire truck look as well as the ability to merge into Defensor. I always liked the extendable booms better than ladders so I opted for those. To be honest, I don t think Cybertronians would be scaling ladders anyway -- if Ravage was stuck up an Energon tree, I figure someone would just fly up there.

My first design for Ratbat was as a Cybertron-style, multi-purpose cassette that had a bat-like alternate mode. But after Simon said he was not originally one of Soundwave's cassettes, I came up with a sort of bat-inspired jet glider. Plus, I added a couple of fangs in the intake to retain a beast-like quality to him.

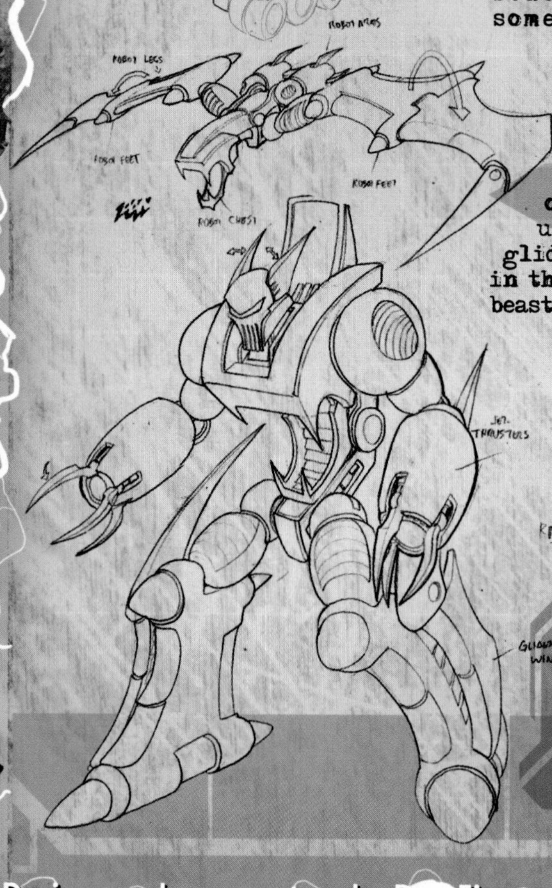

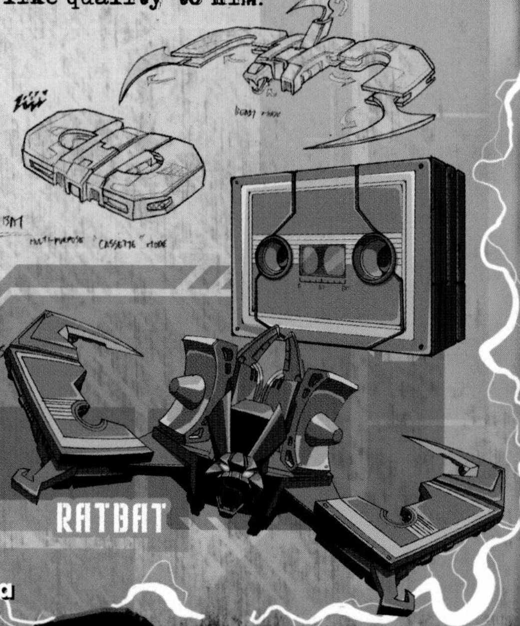
RATBAT

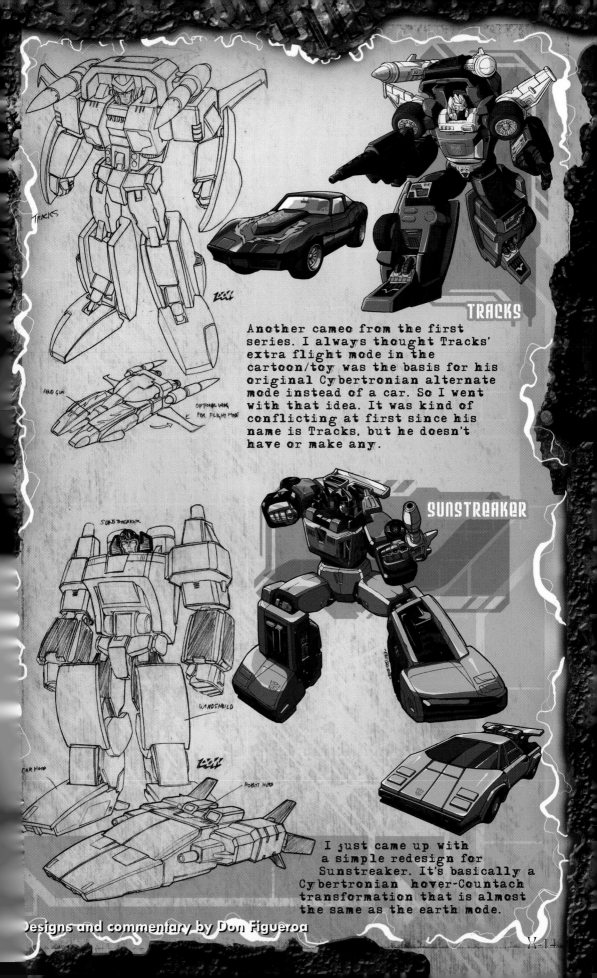

TRACKS

HAND GUN

OPTIONAL WING FOR FLIGHT MODE

TRACKS

Another cameo from the first series. I always thought Tracks' extra flight mode in the cartoon/toy was the basis for his original Cybertronian alternate mode instead of a car. So I went with that idea. It was kind of conflicting at first since his name is Tracks, but he doesn't have or make any.

SUNSTREAKER

SUNSTREAKER

WINDSHIELD

CAR HOOD

ROBOT HEAD

I just came up with a simple redesign for Sunstreaker. It's basically a Cybertronian hover-Countach transformation that is almost the same as the earth mode.

Designs and commentary by Don Figueroa

X-14

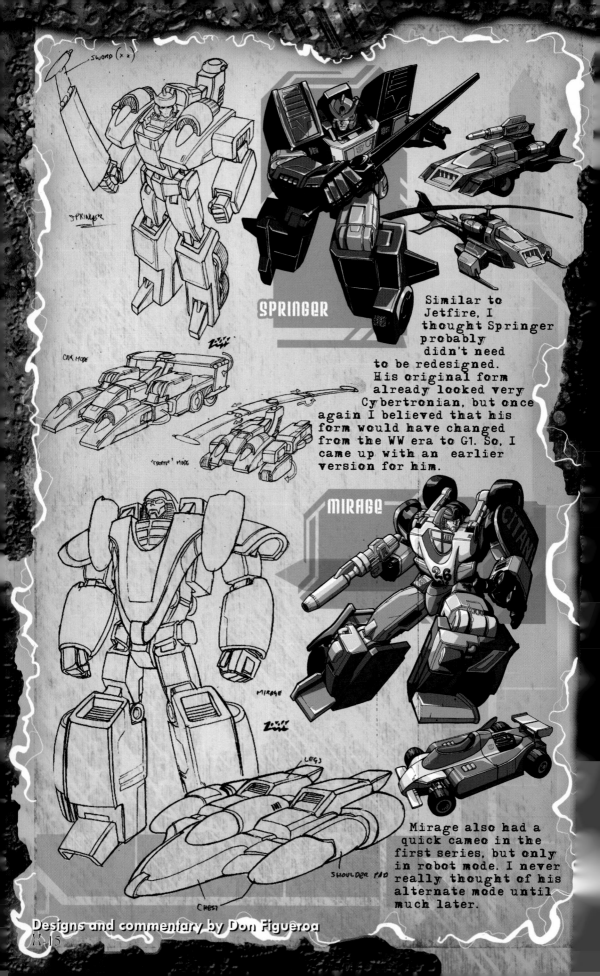

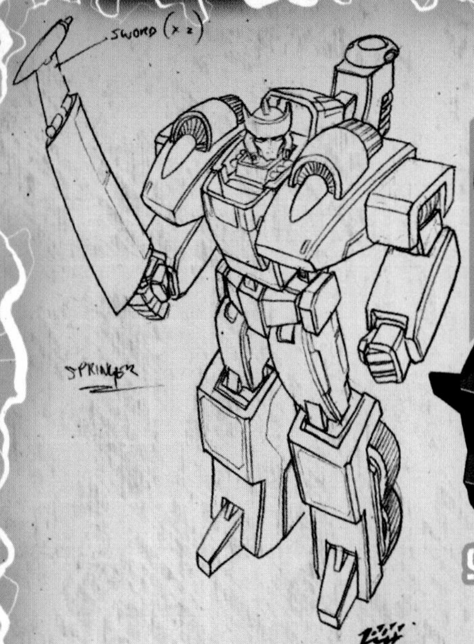
SWORD (X 2)
SPRINGER

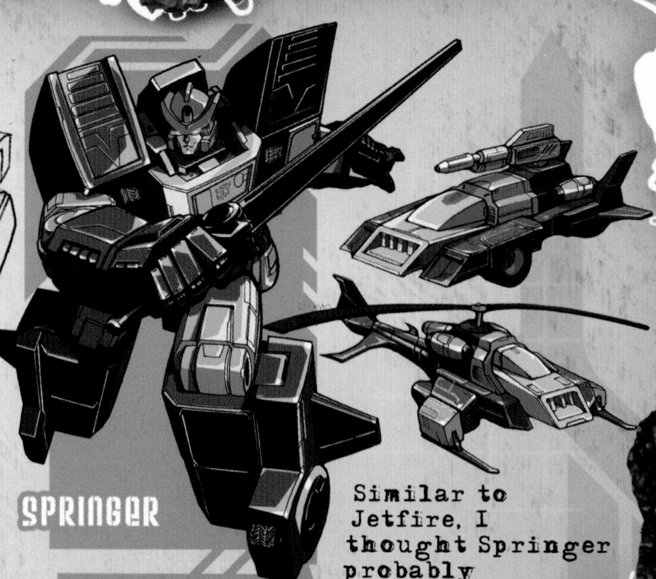

SPRINGER

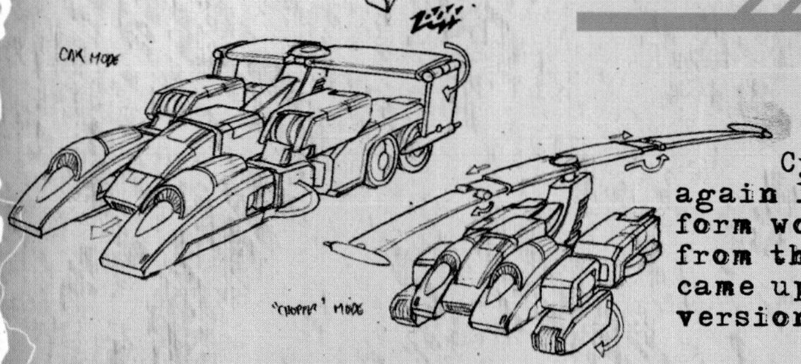
CAR MODE
"CHOPPER" MODE

Similar to Jetfire, I thought Springer probably didn't need to be redesigned. His original form already looked very Cybertronian, but once again I believed that his form would have changed from the WW era to G1. So, I came up with an earlier version for him.

MIRAGE

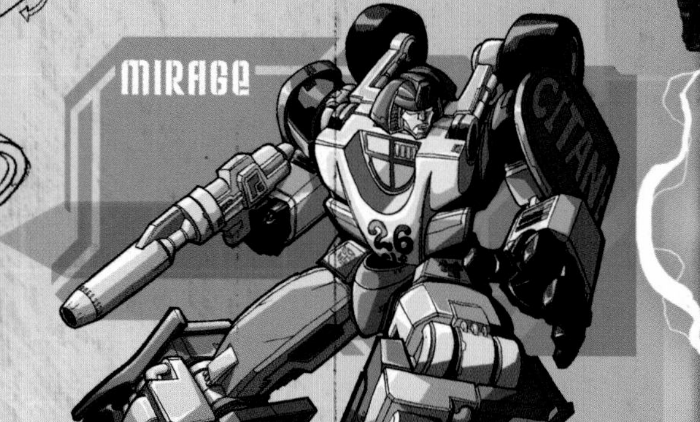

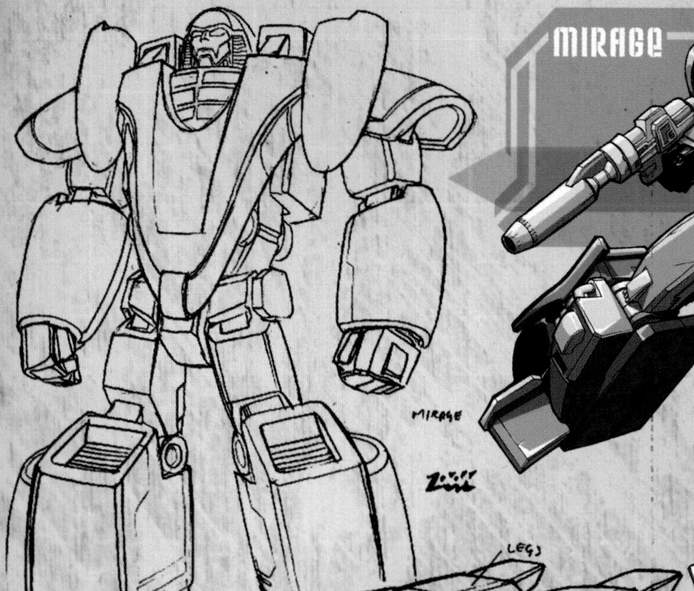
MIRAGE
LEGS
SHOULDER PAD
CHEST

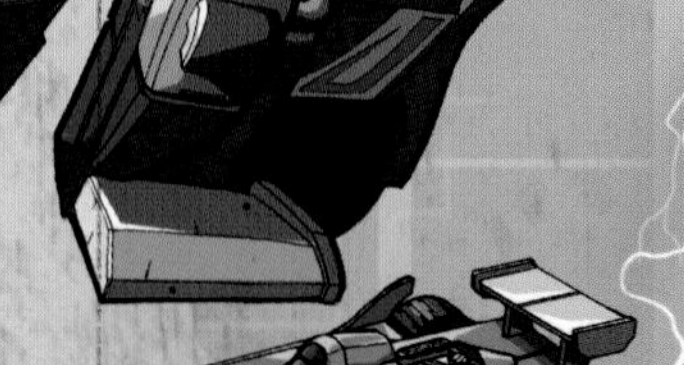

Mirage also had a quick cameo in the first series, but only in robot mode. I never really thought of his alternate mode until much later.

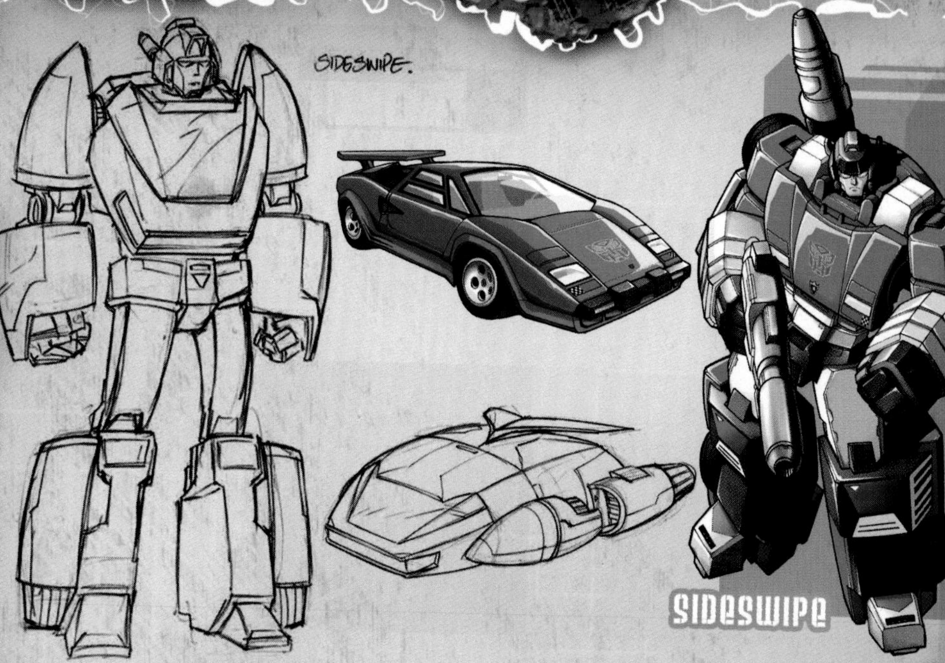
SIDESWIPE.
SIDESWIPE

Having seen what Don had done previously, it occurred to me that certain elements in any design needed to be retained. Body color was always the thing that would make them most recognizable. The other consideration was that it always looked more cool to have flying cars rather than wheels. Other than that there were no restrictions. -ANDREW WILDMAN

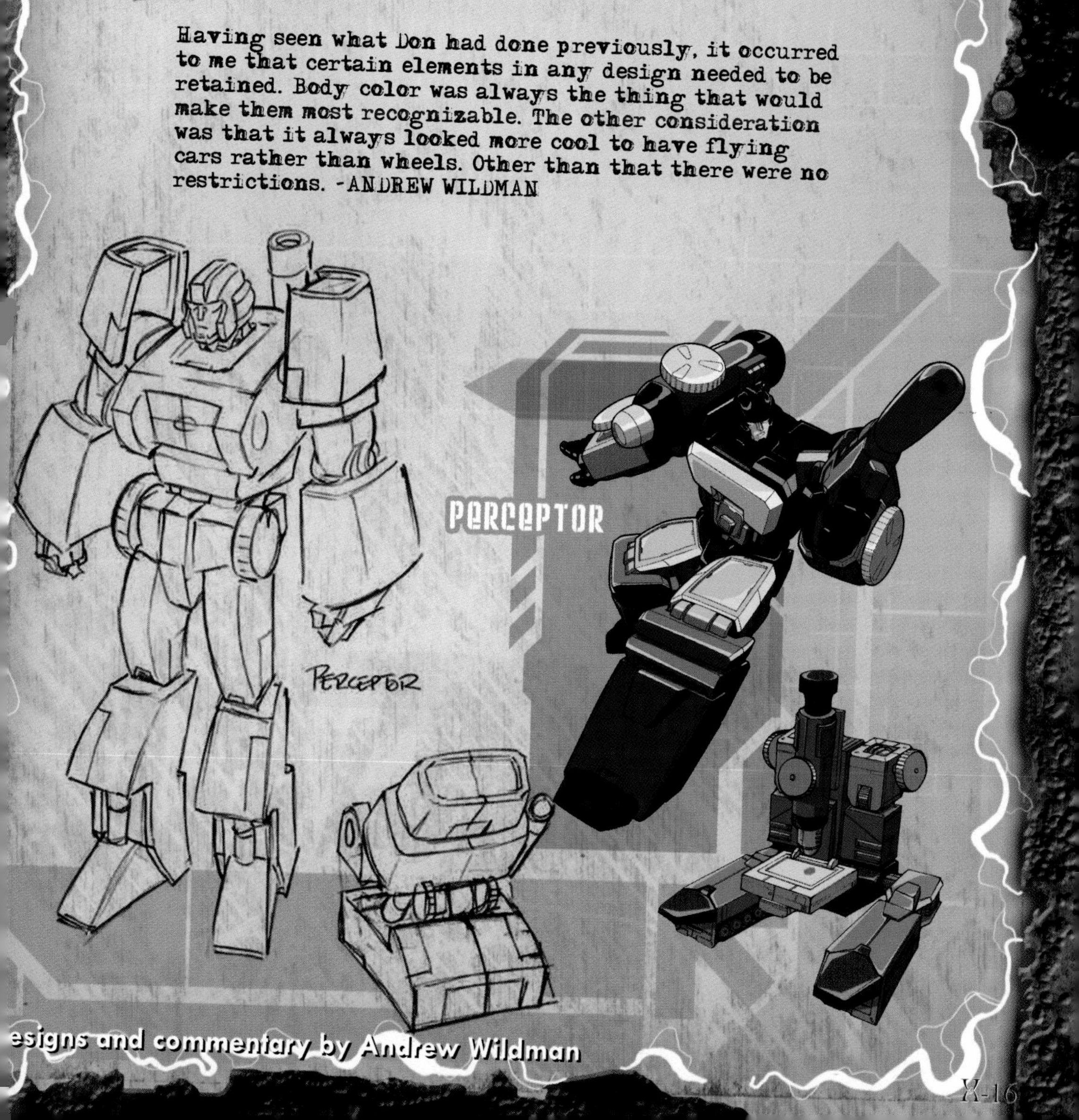
PERCEPTOR
PERCEPTOR

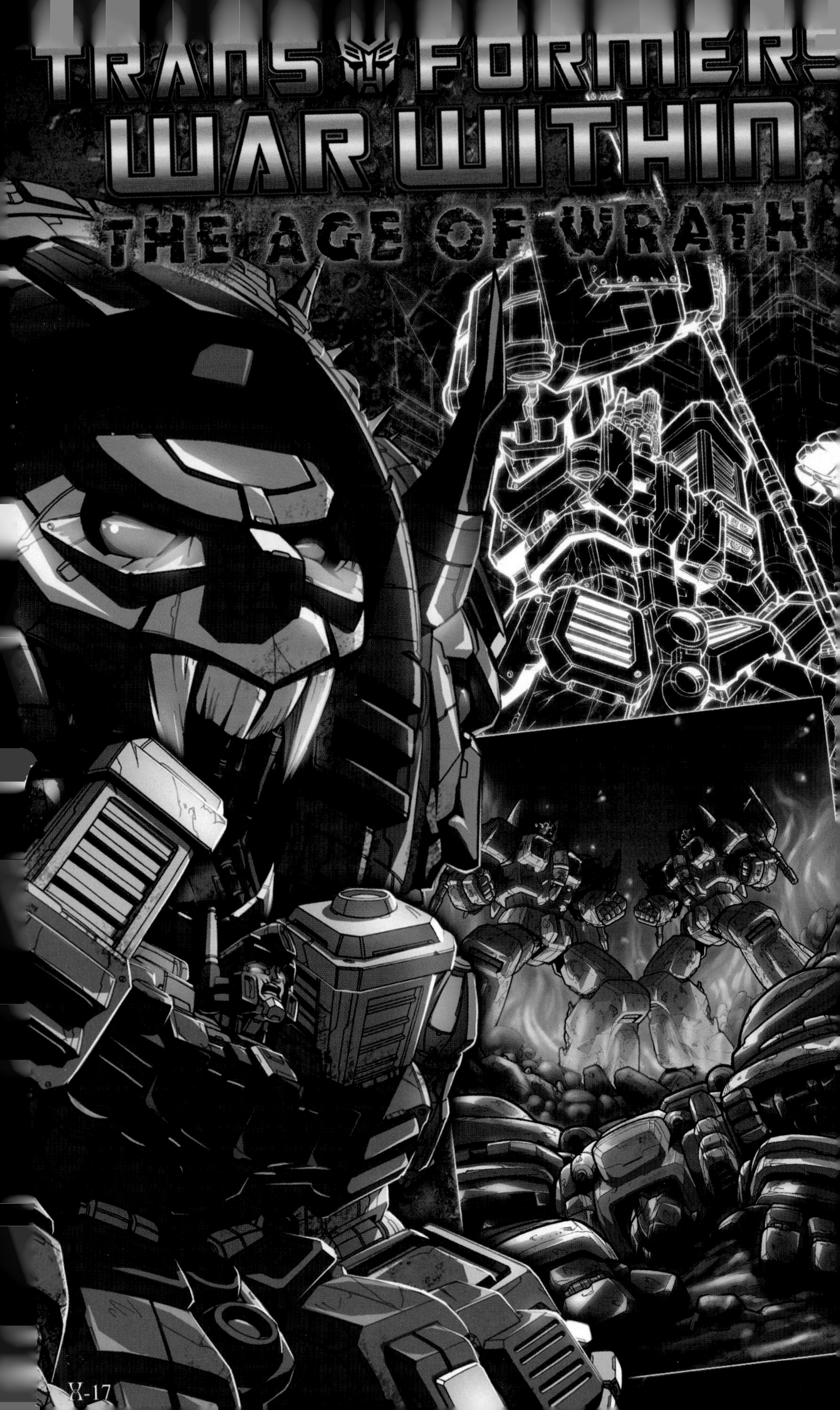
TRANSFORMERS
WAR WITHIN
THE AGE OF WRATH
X-17

On the verge of peace... the unthinkable happens: CYBERTRON is conquered, the AUTOBOTS enslaved, and the planet itself brutally torn asunder. Yep...MEGATRON is back As the third volume of THE WAR WITHIN opens, the worst of the worst returns, more powerful than ever. But is MEGATRON'S victory as cut and dried as it first appears? What is the secret of his massed clone army? And who really is pulling the strings? Witness the chilling dawn...of the AGE OF WRATH!

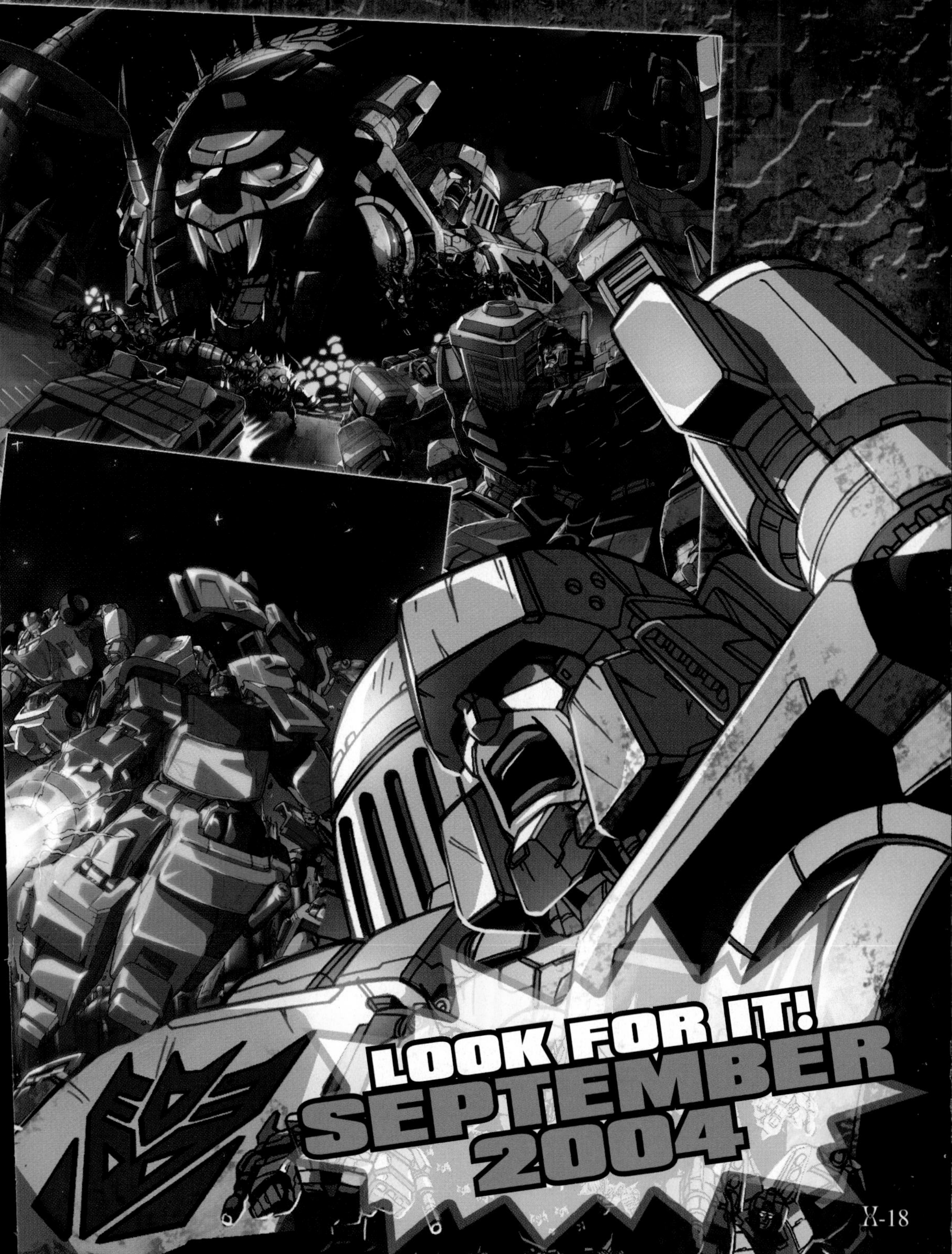
LOOK FOR IT!
SEPTEMBER
2004

Simon FURMAN

English scribe **Simon Furman**'s love for the *TRANSFORMERS* has most definitely stood the test of time. Writing in the 1980s for both the original North American comic series, and the UK series, he quickly became a fan favorite creator. In the 90s Simon returned to the TF universe with the *TRANSFORMERS GENERATION 2* comics, and also wrote the final climatic episode of the hit *TRANSFORMERS: BEAST WARS* animated series.

Beyond the realm of the 'Robots in Disguise', Simon has been writer on a range of comic series including *Robocop, She-Hulk, Alpha Flight*, and is the creator of *Death's Head*. In the animation world he has worked on several prominent series such as *Dan Dare, Roswell Conspiracies, X-Men Evolution* and *Legend of the Dragon*.

Currently Simon writes *Dreamwave*'s ongoing *TRANSFORMERS ENERGON* series, as well as the prequel series *TRANSFORMERS WAR WITHIN*. He also edits and supervises *Titan Books*' line of classic *TRANSFORMERS* reprints and is the author of *Dorling Kindersley*'s comprehensive *TRANSFORMERS THE ULTIMATE GUIDE*.

Andrew WILDMAN

Andrew Wildman is a designer/illustrator with over twenty-five years of experience in the industry. His work has been featured in numerous advertisements and publications, but it is in the field of comic book art that he is best known. Early work included strips in a host of *Marvel UK* titles, including *The Real Ghostbusters, Thundercats, Galaxy Rangers* and *Transformers* (UK). Shortly thereafter, Wildman graduated to the US *Transformers* comic (as of issue #69), handling the art chores throughout the rest of the book's run. Firmly ensconced at Marvel US, Wildman then worked on a number of their titles, including *G.I. Joe, X-Men Adventures, The Hulk, Spider-Man, Venom, Fantastic Four Unplugged* and *Spider-Man 2099*, as well as a brief stint on *Nightman* for Malibu Comics. His other work includes character design and animated movie production for the video games industry, providing storyboards for *Wing Commander* and design/concept work on *The Mummy, Gunlok, Gunfighter, Delta Force, Largo Winch*, and *Dredd vs Death*. More recently, Wildman returned to the comics world with *Transformers War Within: The Dark Ages*, with longtime collaborator **Simon Furman**. Wildman is currently designing characters for the animated TV show *Legend of the Dragon*, plus development work for other upcoming series.